The Voice of Conscience

About the Series

The **Political Theory and Contemporary Philosophy** series stages an ongoing dialogue between contemporary European philosophy and political theory. Following Hannah Arendt's and Leo Strauss's repeated insistence on the qualitative distinction between political *theory* and political *philosophy*, the series showcases the lessons each discipline can draw from the other. One of the most significant outcomes of this dialogue is an innovative integration of 1) the findings of twentieth- and twenty-first-century phenomenology, existentialism, hermeneutics, psychoanalysis, and deconstruction (to name but a few salient currents) and 2) classical as well as modern political concepts, such as sovereignty, polity, justice, constitution, statehood, self-determination, etc.

In many instances, the volumes in the series both re-conceptualize age-old political categories in light of contemporary philosophical theses and find broader applications for the ostensibly non- or apolitical aspects of philosophical inquiry. In all cases, political thought and philosophy are featured as equal partners in an interdisciplinary conversation, the goal of which is to bring about a greater understanding of today's rapidly changing political realities.

The series is edited by Michael Marder, Ikerbasque Research Professor in the Department of Philosophy at the University of the Basque Country, Vitoria-Gasteiz.

Other volumes in the series include:

Deconstructing Zionism by Michael Marder and Santiago Zabala
Heidegger on Hegel's Philosophy of Right by Marcia Sa Cavalcante
Schuback, Michael Marder and Peter Trawny
The Metaphysics of Terror by Rasmus Ugilt
The Negative Revolution by Artemy Magun
The Voice of Conscience by Mika Ojakangas

The Voice of Conscience

A Political Genealogy of Western Ethical Experience

Mika Ojakangas

B L O O M S B U R Y

NEW YORK • LONDON • NEW DELHI • SYDNEY

Bloomsbury Academic
An imprint of Bloomsbury Publishing Plc

1385 Broadway
New York
NY 10018
USA

50 Bedford Square
London
WC1B 3DP
UK

www.bloomsbury.com

First published 2013
Paperback edition first published 2015

© Mika Ojakangas, 2013

Library of Congress Cataloging-in-Publication Data
A catalog record for this book is available from the Library of Congress.

ISBN: HB: 978-1-6235-6678-4
PB: 978-1-4742-1818-4
ePUB: 978-1-6235-6720-0
ePDF: 978-1-6235-6167-3

Typeset by Fakenham Prepress Solutions, Fakenham, Norfolk NR21 8NN
Printed and bound in the United States of America

The wind blows where it wills, and you hear the sound of it, but you do not know whence it comes or whither it goes; so is it with every one who is born of the Spirit
John 3.8

*After God, let us have our conscience [*conscientia*] as our mentor and rule in all things, so that we may know which way the wind is blowing and set our sails accordingly*
John Climacus, Scala Paradisi

Contents

Acknowledgements

First I would like to express my gratitude to the readers of the manuscript of this book, Elisa Heinämäki and Sergei Prozorov, for their valuable comments and discussions. I also want to thank Merja Hintsa for her assistance as I started to grapple with this impossible subject and Tuomas Parsio for his indispensable help with Greek and Latin materials as well as for his comments on my, perhaps extraordinary, reading of Plato. My deepest thank I owe to Soili Petäjäniemi-Brown, not only for having corrected my English in her efficient way, but also for her incredible patience with a writer who apparently could not finish anything.

I also want to thank the wonderful – indeed amazing – personnel of the Department of Social Science and Philosophy at the University of Jyväskylä, where this book was completed. My special thanks in Jyväskylä go to the members of the Plato reading group: Mikko Yrjönsuuri, Miira Tuominen and Arto Laitinen. Without them, I would never had grasped that it is not Nietzsche but Plato that cannot be read without laughing often, richly and hilariously – and that those who have not done so, have not, in a sense, read Plato at all.

To all the above-mentioned people (as well as to Markku Koivusalo and Olli-Pekka Moisio!), I also want to express my gratitude for their friendship, which in this 'heartless' world is the most valuable treasure one can possess, at least if we are to believe Aristotle and Cicero.

I also want to thank the series editor Michael Marder for believing in and advancing this project, as well as the various people at Bloomsbury (particularly Marie-Claire Antoine, Ally-Jane Grossan and Kaitlin Fontana) for their kind and professional help at the final steps of the project.

Academy of Finland and the Network for European Studies (University of Helsinki) provided generous funding for this research, whilst the Helsinki Collegium for Advanced Studies at the University of Helsinki provided an excellent research environment as well as a great opportunity to work with leading scholars from all over the world. Without the support of Academy, Network and Collegium, this book would have never seen the light of day.

The book is dedicated to my wife Elisa with love. I have investigated the history of conscience for years and I am still perplexed about it. She knows it by heart.

1

Introduction

I

'I have followed my conscience,' President George W. Bush announced in his farewell speech to the American people on 15 January 2009.[1] In a famous speech, 'A Politics of Conscience', delivered on 23 June 2007, Barack Obama likewise called for an awakening of the American conscience, concluding with the following declaration: 'So let's rededicate ourselves to a new kind of politics – a politics of conscience.'[2] Yet there is nothing particularly new in this kind of politics, since conscience has always been at the heart of Western politics. Conscience is the 'only sure clue which will eternally guide a man,' as Thomas Jefferson wrote.[3] It has 'a rightful authority over us' by 'the commission of God Almighty', as John Adams put it.[4] In his speech to his SS troops at Poznań on 4 October 1943, even Heinrich Himmler stated that the virtue of SS man did not consist of obedience for the sake of authorities, but for the sake of conscience. Actually, the only authority an SS soldier ought to have is the voice of his conscience:

> It will not always be possible to verify whether the order has been carried out. With us, the verification must not, must never be left to a commissar, as it is in Russia. The only commissar we have must be our own conscience [*das eigene Gewissen*].[5]

This book is a genealogy of this uncanny voice within – and given the privileged place of conscience in Western thought, an investigation into the foundations of Western theologico-political anthropology. My intention is not so much to analyse the true nature of conscience, but rather examine how the Western tradition has understood what it has called conscience. My purpose is to give an account of the entire history of the idea since antiquity, not by trying to include all possible nuances, which would

---

[1] George W. Bush, 'The Farewell Address,' accessed 24 August 2012: http://www.presidentialrhetoric.com/speeches/01.15.09.html
[2] Barack Obama, 'A Politics of Conscience,' accessed 24 August 2012: http://www.ucc.org/news/significant-speeches/a-politics-of-conscience.html
[3] Thomas Jefferson, 'A Letter to George Washington (May 10, 1789).' In *The Works of Thomas Jefferson*, ed. P. L. Ford, vol. 5 (New York: G. P. Putnam's Sons, 1904–5), p. 476.
[4] John Adams, 'On Self-Delusion,' in *The Works of John Adams*, ed. S. F. Adams, vol. 3 (Boston: Little, Brown, and Co., 1851), pp. 434–5.
[5] Heinrich Himmler, 'Rede des Reichsführer-SS bei der SS-Gruppenführertagung in Posen Am 4. Oktober 1943,' accessed 24 August 2012: http://www.nationalsozialismus.de/dokumente/texte/page/4

be virtually impossible, but rather by concentrating on general trends and turning points. In the chapter eight of the book, in addition, I outline a theory concerning the common essence of Western conscience. Methodologically, the study is a combination of intellectual history and genealogy of the present. As an intellectual history, it aims at a historical reconstruction of the concept and the idea of conscience, whilst the genealogical aspect of the study is materialized in its attempt to pin down the roots of the Western politics of conscience and to trace the historical sources of the contemporary ethico-political predicament of global capitalism and neoliberal ideology, whereby politics is reduced to ethics and collective action replaced by the expectations of individual responsibility.

One purpose of this book – inspired by Giorgio Agamben's analysis of Western metaphysics as metaphysics of silence ('sigetics')[6] – is to show that the Western ethico-political tradition does not include such radical reversals and ruptures as has been suggested by philosophers and intellectual historians since the 1960s but is rather characterized by a radical continuity. Despite historical change and amidst differences and disputes, one assumption has always remained the same in Western thought: in moral and political matters, people should rely on the inner voice of conscience instead of external authorities, laws and regulations. In this sense, the ethico-political tradition of the West has always been individualist, rebellious and revolutionary, even when it has been collectivist or conservative, since it has not only tirelessly strived for the *displacement* of external laws, rules and regulations by the disorienting experience of conscience but also wanted to *found* these laws and regulations on this very experience. 'Conscience is the deepest internal solitude [*innerliche Einsamkeit*], from which both limit and the external have wholly disappeared,'[7] as G. W. F. Hegel wrote, but at the same time it is and must be the centre of all political principles and institutions:

> If political principles and institutions are separated from the realm of inwardness [*Innerlichkeit*], from the innermost shrine of conscience [*heiligthum des Gewissens*], from the still sanctuary of religion, they lack any real centre [*wirkliche Mittelpunkt*] and remain abstract and indeterminate.[8]

True, the protagonists of conscience themselves have always complained about the impotence of conscience. For them, conscience has remained powerless because the 'world does not heed the inner witness of its own conscience' as it should but 'only obeys external regulations', as Jan Amos Comenius wrote in *The Labyrinth of the World and the Paradise of the Heart* (1623),[9] summarizing neatly the fundamental tenet of Western thought repeated time and again in the history of the West: the source of

---

6   See Giorgio Agamben, *Language and Death: The Place of Negativity*, trans. K. Pinkus and M. Hardt (Minneapolis: University of Minnesota Press, 2006).

7   G. W. F. Hegel, *Philosophy of Right*, trans. S. W. Dyde (Kitchener: Batoche Books, 2001), §136, addition, p. 115.

8   G. W. F. Hegel, *The Philosophy of History*, trans. J. Sibree (Kitchener: Batoche Books, 2001), p. 52. Translation modified.

9   John Comenius, *The Labyrinth of the World and the Paradise of the Heart*, trans. H. Louthan and A. Sterk (Mahwah, NJ: Paulist Press, 1997), p. 205.

truth and justice resides within, in the innermost realm of conscience, whilst those who rely on traditions, customs, public norms and opinions are evil Pharisees ('it is a mark of an evil man always to seek the rules and to want written laws to dictate what he ought to do').[10] But as the advocates of conscience have been compelled to admit, it is the Pharisees and not conscience who dominate the world. When it comes to ethical and political *thought*, however, the conscience has indeed been victorious and dominating: without the voice of conscience, the Western tradition has assumed, there is no sin, no guilt, no virtue, no obligation, no duty, no force of law, no freedom, no responsibility, no individuality, no humanity, not even consciousness:

> The voice of conscience, which imposes his particular duty on each, is the ray of light on which we come forth from the infinite and are established as individual and particular beings; it draws the limits of our personality; it, therefore, is our true original component [*Urbestandteil*], the ground and stuff of our whole life [*der Grund und der Stoff alles Lebens*].[11]

This central role of the experience of conscience in the Western tradition of ethics also explains Aristotle's relatively minor role in this study. Although Aristotle has beyond doubt provided a bunch of concepts and ideas that have been extremely influential in the Western tradition of ethics and ethical politics, there are certain tendencies in his thought that are at odds with this tradition, including his insistence that virtue is based on *public opinion*. A virtuous man is the one who is commonly considered virtuous (*Nichomachean Ethics* 1140a), whilst the vicious and shameless is the one who 'despises public opinion' (*Rhetoric* 1368b20-5).[12] In the Western tradition of ethico-political thought, it is the *virtuous* man who despises public opinion. For the same reason, although he lived before Aristotle, Socrates features prominently in this work. Like his followers, Socrates despised public opinion, what the many said of him: 'We must not consider at all what the many [*hoi polloi*] will say of us' (*Crito* 48a).[13] The Western man of virtue stands alone against crowds and numbers, closing 'himself off from the whole world'.[14] It is not the opinions of others, not even public norms, but his inner voice that has the ultimate authority over him – though this inner voice, so the man of conscience believes, does not work only for his benefit but rather, and even primarily, for the benefit of the whole world. This is a fundamental dogma of the Western tradition of ethics from Cynics to Stoics, from Christians to Enlightenment philosophers, from German Idealists to Nietzsche, from Heidegger to Derrida. It is true that there also exists in the Western tradition

---

[10] Ibid., p. 204.

[11] Johann Gottlieb Fichte, *The Vocation of Man*, trans. P. Preuss (Indianapolis: Hackett Publishing Company, 1987), p. 108.

[12] In Aristotle translations I have consulted Aristotle, *Aristotle in 23 Volumes*, vols 19, 21 and 22, trans. H. Rackham and J. H. Freese (Cambridge, MA: Harvard University Press, 1944).

[13] In Plato translations I have consulted Plato, *Complete Works*, ed. John M. Cooper (Indianapolis: Hackett Publishing Company, 1997) and *Plato in Twelve Volumes*, vols 1, 3, 5–6 and 9, trans. H. N. Fowler, W. R. M. Lamb and P. Shorey (Cambridge, MA: Harvard University Press, 1925–1969).

[14] Søren Kierkegaard, *The Concept of Anxiety*, ed. H. and E. Hong (Princeton: Princeton University Press, 1980), p. 134.

what Friedrich Nietzsche called a morality of the Englishman: a morality of good manners (David Hume) and of little pleasures (Jeremy Bentham). Yet this morality of *das Man*, to use a Heideggerian term, is an exception in the Western tradition – perhaps a ridiculous exception, if we are to believe Nietzsche. Today, even the heroes of capitalism swear by the inner voice, as did Steve Jobs in his speech at Stanford University in 12 June 2005:

> Your time is limited, so don't waste it living someone else's life. Don't be trapped by dogma – which is living with the results of other people's thinking. Don't let the noise of others' opinions drown your own inner voice.[15]

In this regard, Western tradition is characterized by a profound shamelessness – by a curious *anti-dogmatic dogmatics* – and if we would like to figure out the ethico-psychological reasons for the revolutionary character of this tradition, we should, perhaps, take a clue from this fact.

II

Socrates features prominently in this study particularly because the very origin of this shameless, individualist and rebellious ethics of conscience – at least one of these origins – can be traced back to Plato's Socratic dialogues. Unlike Socrates, the Greeks did not usually see any positive value in the experience of conscience (*synoida emautō*),[16] associating it with pain and unhappiness, even sickness: 'What is it? What sickness [*nosos*] is destroying you?' asks Menelaus in Euripides's *Orestes* (395–6), and Orestes replies: 'My conscience [*synesis*], I am aware [*synoida*] that I have done something terrible.'[17] Yet Socrates transformed this painful experience of conscience opposed to happiness into the condition of ethics and politics, even of happiness itself. In Socrates' estimation, a good citizen was no longer one who led a virtuous

---

[15] Stanford University News, Stanford Report, 14 June 2005, accessed 24 August 2012: http://news.stanford.edu/news/2005/june15/jobs-061505.html

[16] The first and the only surviving document from the Classical period where the Greek word for conscience (*syneidēsis*) is mentioned is Democritus' fragment no. 297 (Diels): 'Some people, ignorant about the decomposition of mortal nature and in the *syneidēsis* of evil-doing in life, endure the time of their lives in confusion and fear because of inventing lies about the time after death.' Cited and translated by Philip Bosman, *Conscience in Philo and Paul* (Tübingen: J. C. B. Mohr 2003), p. 61. It is not until the first century BC that the noun came into more frequent usage. This does not signify, however, that the Greeks did not know the experience of conscience, as is sometimes suggested. In order to express this experience they used other nouns such as *synesis* or verbal compounds such as *synoida emautō* ('I know with myself') from which the noun *syndeidēsis* actually derives. The earliest instance of *synoida emautō* expressing guilty conscience can be found in the *Thesmophoriazusae* (476–7) of Aristophanes: 'I know with myself of many terrible things [*ksynoid' emautē polla dein*].' Aristophanes, *Thesmophoriazusae*, in *Aristophanes with English Translation in Three Volumes*, vol. 3, trans. B. B. Rogers (London: William Heinemann, 1963), pp. 170–1. Translation modified.

[17] In Euripides translations I have consulted Euripides, *The Complete Greek Drama*, ed. W. J. Oates and E. O'Neill, Jr. Vol. 2 (New York: Random House, 1938); Euripides, *Cyclops, Alcestis, Medea*, ed. D. Kovacs (Cambridge, MA: Harvard University Press, 1994); and Euripides, *Children of Heracles, Hippolytus, Andromache, Hecuba*, ed. David Kovacs (Cambridge, MA: Harvard University Press, 1995).

life according to the moral and political standards of the *polis*, but one who had an intimate relationship with the 'sickness' of conscience. According to Socrates, a good citizen ought to be continuously conscious of its possibility and welcome it whenever it occurs, because unlike for the Greeks in general, for Socrates the traumatic experience of conscience was not an experience that had to be overcome at all costs, but *a positive experience constitutive of a virtuous citizen*. Although his conscience, as Socrates confesses in *Hippias Major* (304b–e), is always blaming (*oneidizō*) and disgracing (*elengkhō*) him, he believes that 'it is necessary to bear all that', for 'what is fine is hard' – not in the sense that it is difficult to attain fine things, but in the sense that this *hardness itself* actualized in the humiliating experience of conscience constitutes the condition of possibility of all ethics and ethical politics.

As the *Orestes* passage quoted above already indicates, the intellectual backdrop of the Socratic politics of conscience lies in Greek tragedy, and more precisely in the miserable fate of the tragic hero. To the Greeks, the tragic hero was an object of pity because, having acknowledged (*synoida emautō*) responsibility (*aitios*) for his crime (*hamartia*), he lost all the landmarks of moral and political orientation, finding himself abandoned (*erēmos*), helpless (*aporos*), homeless (*aoikos*) and cityless (*apolis*), in the last resort absolutely nothing (*mēdeis*). As Creon bemoans in *Antigone* (1317–22):

> Ah this responsibility [*aitios*] can never be fastened onto any other mortal so as to remove my own! It was I, yes, I, who killed you, I the wretch. I admit the truth. Lead me away, my servants, lead me from here with all haste, who am no more than a dead man [*mēdeis* = nobody]![18]

Nonetheless, it is precisely in the fate of the tragic hero that Socrates saw a model for the formation of the ethico-political subject. This formation is characterized by three interwoven yet analytically separate moments. First, the subject is shattered by the traumatic experience of conscience and thus, subtracted from his habitual world and his innermost identity, cut out of the social bond and lost in the groundless abyss of being without rules or standards: 'I know with myself' (*synoida emautō*) that I know nothing (*Apology* 21b) whereby all the prevailing truths are disclosed as having no foundation whatsoever. He has become abandoned and forlorn (*erēmos aporos*). The second moment is when the subject recognizes that this loss of orientation, this symbolic death, entails that he is no longer *constituted* by the social relations of community (*Gorgias* 513a) but by the same experience within him that cut him off from the social bond in the first place. In other words, although the experience of conscience is a traumatic experience, it is at the same time a *liberating* experience. It renders the subject a *sovereign individual* – resembling now the condition of the Cyclops in Euripide's *Cyclops* (116–20), as they, too, are 'abandoned' (*erēmoi*) and 'solitaires' (*monades*), but for this reason 'none of them is subject to anyone'. Yet although the Socratic subject has now become sovereign and free, he is still without orientation. He has ceased to 'mechanically' repeat the norms and customs (*nomos*)

---

[18] In Sophocles translations I have consulted Sophocles, *The Plays and Fragments*, ed. R. Jebbs (Cambridge: Cambridge University Press, 1908).

of the *polis*, but at the same time he lacks the means to reorient himself in the world as even his innermost identity has become null and void. At this point, the subject has three options: he can stay in the condition of *erēmos aporos* outside the symbolic order of the *polis*, or return to the *polis*, either by readapting himself to its order or by remaining *erēmos aporos within* the walls of the *polis*. The first option is out of question, for it is tantamount to madness. The second option is possible, but it entails a loss of freedom, as it presupposes that the subject assumes a determinate role in the complex of social relations of the *polis*. It is the last option, which is the third and the final moment in the genesis of the Socratic ethico-political subject, this subject must choose. It is the moment of return to the *polis*, not as a member of community who assimilates himself again to the norms and the standards of the *polis* but as a new and *superior* figure of the citizen whose perspective to the affairs of the *polis* is no longer determined by his identity and social status, as he has none, but by the very *nothing* (*mēdeis*) disclosed at the heart of his identity through the experience of conscience. It is precisely his becoming nothing that warrants Socrates' bold proclamation in *Gorgias* (521d):

> I believe that I'm one of a few Athenians – so as not to say I'm not the only one, but the only one among our contemporaries – to take up the true political craft [*epikherein tē hōs alēthōs politikē tekhnē*] and practice politics [*prattein ta politika*].

In what sense, however, is the abandoned and forlorn subject, like Socrates himself, superior to normal citizens? He is superior, according to the logic of Socratic ethical politics, because a normal citizen takes care of the affairs of the *polis* in his own limited and partial perspective, measuring his action and responsibility according to the given norms and values. The displaced *erēmos aporos*, instead, measures his action according to the measureless measure of the nothing of conscience. This entails that he also takes care (*epimeleomai*) of the affairs of the *polis* (of its justice, piety and so on) (*Apology* 36c) in the same modality, that is to say, in the *modality of unlimited responsibility* (*aitios*). Thus the Socratic ethico-political subject is more like a tragic hero than an ordinary Athenian citizen, as the hero, too, feels the weight of absolute responsibility on his shoulders once he becomes conscious of having committed an evil deed. Unlike in tragedies, however, in Socrates' politics of conscience all the tragic elements are put at the heart of everyday life. In Socratic ethical politics, one is no longer an *erēmos aporos* if one finds oneself responsible for a crime. One has to *make* oneself an abandoned outcast, to commit a sort of symbolic *suicide* ('to live in a state as close to death as possible', as Socrates says of himself in *Phaedo* 67d) by means of continuous self-accusation. In other words, the experience of *synoida emautō* must be purposely provoked so that the condition of *erēmos aporos* becomes 'a predicate for the "I am",' to paraphrase Heidegger again.[19] The method of this provocation is

---

[19] For Heidegger, it is *Dasein*'s quality of being-guilty (*Schuldigsein*) revealed by the silent call of conscience that is a predicate for the 'I am'. Martin Heidegger, *Being and Time*, trans. J. Macquarrie and E. Robinson (Oxford: Basil Blackwell 1962), p. 326. But as we will see, such a disclosure of guilt is possible only because the call first detaches *Dasein* from the social bond and abandons (*überlassen*) it to itself.

called elenchus (*elengkhos*). Its aim is not disclose what virtue means but to incur the traumatic experience of conscience, to reveal that all our conceptions of virtue are worthless and to elicit an absolute disorientation in terms of morality and politics, leaving us 'abandoned and forlorn' (*erēmon kai aporon*) (*Philebus* 16b) – for it is such an abandoned and forlorn subject that is capable of true political craft. It is not the Aristotelian *zōon politikon* but this Socratic subject (*erēmos aporos*) that is the paradigmatic figure of the Western citizen.

III

Since Socrates, and especially since the rise of Christianity, the disorienting experience of conscience has determined the framework of the Western ethical and ethico-political orientation. In this experience, which reveals the 'real littleness of ourselves, worthy of resentment, abhorrence, and execration',[20] the Western tradition has discovered its law and its spirit, its autonomy and its freedom. It has done this quite literally, inasmuch as the Roman authors with Stoic persuasion, such as Cicero and Seneca, interpreted this experience as the foundation of natural law, allegedly expressing the immutable and eternal moral order of the world. Christians, whilst subscribing to the Ciceronian teaching of natural law, have also seen in it the realm of the Holy Spirit and God's dwelling: 'Conscience is a little God sitting in the middle of men's hearts,' as William Perkins put it.[21] True, conscience lost its divine dimension during the Enlightenment, but this actually meant a strengthening of the authority of conscience, because it was freed from the Christian prerequisite according to which conscience requires supernatural aid in order properly to bear witness to natural moral law and to make a man acknowledge that he is always already guilty and thereby inexcusable.[22] Not even the ultimate decline of natural law was able to erode the authority of the voice of conscience. In modernity, it has been this voice alone emanating from the abyssal ground of groundless existence that has uprooted the subject from the solid ground and left him bereft in the Nothing without moral, political or religious coordinates whatsoever, so that he may become a sovereign *erēmos aporos*, 'without direction from another' (*ohne Leitung eines andern*), as Kant famously put it,[23] capable of absolute responsibility:

> I am abandoned [*délaissé*] in the world [Jean-Paul Sartre writes in *Being and Nothingness*] not in the sense that I might remain abandoned and passive in a hostile universe like a board floating on the water, but rather in the sense that I find myself suddenly alone and without help [*seul et sans aide = erēmos aporos*]

---

[20] Adam Smith, *Theory of Moral Sentiments* (Milton Keynes: Filiquarian Publishing, 2009), 3.3, p. 172.

[21] William Perkins, *A Discourse of Conscience*, in *William Perkins: His Pioneer Works on Casuistry*, ed. T. F. Merril (Nieuwkoop: B. De Graaf, 1966), p. 9.

[22] It is not a mere coincidence that Matthias Knutzen, the first renowned atheist in the modern West, named the community of his followers the community of *Gewissener*.

[23] Immanuel Kant, 'An Answer to the Question: What is Enlightenment,' in Immanuel Kant, *Practical Philosophy*, ed. M. J. Gregor (Cambridge: Cambridge University Press, 1996), p. 17.

engaged in a world for which I bear the whole responsibility without being able, whatever I do, to tear myself away from this responsibility for an instance.[24]

Now, although the experience of conscience has enjoyed a privileged place in the Western tradition, this does not mean that the history of conscience would have unfolded as monotonous repetition. Many shifts, displacements and reinterpretations have taken place in the course of its history, especially when it comes to the sources and effects of this experience. Since Cicero, on the one hand, almost everybody has agreed that the voice of conscience, although it emanates from within, is not *my* voice but something that 'drives me without my willing and doing', as the sixteenth-century Anabaptist theologian Hans Denck put it.[25] Being 'distinct from us yet present in our inmost being',[26] it renders us autonomous, as Kant had it, but we are *not* autonomous with regard to it as it is 'an involuntary and irresistible drive [*Trieb*] in our nature'.[27] In other words, the Western voice of conscience has always been an alien voice, the voice of the 'other' within.[28] Similarly, philosophers and theologians alike have considered conscience the condition of possibility of concepts such as duty, obligation and responsibility, even freedom, resoluteness and faith. Yet they have been less unanimous, for instance, as to who or what it is that is speaking in the voice of conscience: is it God, nature, tradition, freedom, pure practical reason, parents, society, a crack in the ontological edifice of the universe, or what? After Luther, and particularly after Kant, moreover, the idea of *good* conscience, so dear to Christians, became increasingly suspect. Since the Church Fathers, Christians had almost unanimously subscribed to Chrysostom's opinion that a good conscience (*syneidos agathon*) is the 'greatest festival' of a man, his glory and his gratification,[29] whereas Martin Heidegger, arguably the most outstanding theorist of conscience in the twentieth century, asserts bluntly that a good conscience is not a conscience phenomenon at all.[30] The reason for this turn is simple. Philosophers came to interpret the phenomenon of good conscience now as a mere absence of a bad conscience, arguing that such absence does not indicate, as it at least sometimes did in the pre-Kantian world of natural law and divine providence, presence of the Good but rather *absence of sincerity*: the one who seeks to be ethical must 'avoid good conscience at all costs', as Jacques Derrida put this modern truth.[31]

[24] Jean-Paul Sartre, *Being and Nothingness*, trans. H. E. Barnes (London: Routledge, 2003), p. 701.
[25] Cited in Steven E. Ozment, *Mysticism and Dissent: Religious Ideology and Social Protest in the Sixteenth Century* (New Haven: Yale University Press, 1973), p. 122.
[26] Immanuel Kant, *The Metaphysics of Morals*, in Immanuel Kant, *Practical Philosophy*, ed. M. J. Gregor (Cambridge: Cambridge University Press, 1996), p. 561.
[27] Immanuel Kant, *Lectures on Ethics*, ed. P. Heath and J. B. Schneewind (Cambridge: Cambridge University Press, 1997), p. 88.
[28] Mladen Dolar has made this point succinctly in his study on the anatomy of Western conscience: 'What all this tradition has in common is that the voice comes from the Other, but this is the Other within. The ethical voice is not the subject's own, it is not for the subject to master or control it, although the subject's autonomy is entirely dependent on it.' Mladen Dolar, *A Voice and Nothing More* (Cambridge, MA: The MIT Press, 2006), p. 102.
[29] John Chrysostom, *Sermones V de Anna* 5.1, in *Patrologia cursus completus: Series Graeca*, ed. J. P. Migne (Paris: 1857–66), vol. 54, p. 669A. *Patrologia Graeca* hereafter *PG*.
[30] Heidegger, *Being and Time*, p. 338.
[31] Jacques Derrida, *Aporias: Dying – Awaiting (on another at) the Limits of Truth*, trans. D. Tutoit (Stanford: Stanford University Press, 1993), p. 19.

Finally, it has recently been disputed whether the voice of conscience does render the subject autonomous – whether by obeying this inner voice the subject becomes 'self-sufficient and independent of other creatures, like unto those self-moving engines, which have their principle of motion within themselves', as a Puritan divine had it in the seventeenth century.[32] Today, the experience of conscience does not inevitably result in autonomy, which is denounced as pretentious and arrogant, indeed a false hypothesis, but rather calls autonomy radically into question. According to Emmanuel Levinas, conscience (*la conscience morale*) *is* this calling into question of autonomy:

> It is the revelation of a resistance to my powers that does not counter them as a greater force, but calls into question the naïve right of my powers, my glorious spontaneity as a living being. Morality begins when freedom, instead of being justified by itself, feels itself to be arbitrary and violent.[33]

In many other respects, however, an astonishing unanimity prevails – and, to be honest, even the above mentioned opposition between the traditional and the Levinasian conscience is superficial, for as we will see the heteronomous experience of conscience is constitutive for freedom and even for certain happiness in Levinas as well. Excluding Spinoza, Hume and some of their followers, virtually all the notable authors in the Western tradition of moral and political thought have either preached the indispensable value of the experience of conscience or constructed theories that presuppose this experience. Although Thomas Hobbes severely criticized the Christian doctrines of conscience, he did and could not abandon conscience in his theory of the state, since he acknowledged that the concepts such as obedience and obligation presuppose it. Even Friedrich Nietzsche, though known as one of the fiercest critics of bad conscience in the history of the West, put the experience of conscience at the heart of his ethics and politics, asserting that the philosophers of the future must 'make every Yea and Nay a matter of conscience [*jedem Ja und Nein ein Gewissen macht*]!'[34] – and that they must do so because conscience liberates a man from the morality of custom, rendering him an 'autonomous supramoral individual [*das autonome übersittliche Individuum*]'.[35] As to whether such obedience to the voice of conscience is indispensable to ethics and politics, I have no position on. What I want to do in this book is to give a genealogical account of the history of conscience since antiquity and to show that conscience is not a simple solution to the ethico-political crisis of today. In the next chapter, in any case, we will see that it can also be harnessed for very pernicious purposes.

---

[32] Samuel Ward, *Balme from Gilead to Recouer Conscience* (London: Roger Jackson, 1616), p. 21.
[33] Emmanuel Levinas, *Totality and Infinity: An Essay on Exteriority*, trans. A. Lingis (Pittsburgh: Duquesne University Press, 1969), p. 84.
[34] Friedrich Nietzsche, *The Anti-Christ*, trans. H. L. Mencken (Tucson: See Sharp Press, 1999), §50, p. 72.
[35] Friedrich Nietzsche, *On the Genealogy of Morals*, trans. D. Smith (Oxford: Oxford University Press, 1996), 2.2, p. 41.

2

National Socialism and the Inner Truth

I

More than three decades before becoming Pope Benedictus XVI, the spiritual head of the Roman Catholic Church, Cardinal Joseph Ratzinger gave a lecture to the Reinhold Schneider-Gesellschaft called 'Conscience in Its Age' (*Das Gewissen unserer Zeit*).[1] At the beginning of this lecture, he cites the following passage attributed to Adolf Hitler:

> I am freeing man from the restraints of an intelligence that has taken charge; from the dirty and degrading self-mortification of a chimera called conscience and morality, and from the demands of a freedom and personal independence which only a very few can bear.[2]

On account of this quotation, Ratzinger states that the destruction of conscience is a precondition for totalitarian obedience and totalitarian domination. He then continues:

> Where conscience prevails there is a barrier against the domination of human orders and human whim, something sacred that must remain inviolable and that in an ultimate sovereignty evades control not only by oneself but by every external agency. Only the absoluteness of conscience is the complete antithesis to tyranny.[3]

Ratzinger may be right. At least he is not alone with his views. A league of Western theologians and philosophers has claimed that the sovereignty of conscience evades, if not self-control, at least the control of every external agency. Moreover, by arguing that conscience constitutes an antithesis to tyranny, he reaches the same conclusion as Hannah Arendt, one of the most renowned analysts of National Socialism: 'Conscience itself no longer functioned under totalitarian conditions of political organization.'[4] Yet there is a certain problem in Ratzinger's analysis. Ratzinger's citation is taken from Hermann Rauschning's *Conversations with Hitler* based on his discussions with Hitler between 1932 and 1934. In this memoir, Rauschning, the National Socialist President

---

[1]   The lecture is translated and reprinted in Joseph Ratzinger, *The Church, Ecumenism, and Politics: New Essays in Ecclesiology*, trans. Michael J. Miller (New York: Crossroads, 1987), pp. 165–79.
[2]   Hermann Rauschning, *Hitler Speaks: A Series of Political Conversations with Adolf Hitler on His Real Aims* (London: Thornton Butterworth, 1939), p. 222. Ratzinger omits the first sentence of the Hitler passage: 'Providence has ordained me that I should be the greatest liberator of humanity.'
[3]   Ratzinger, *The Church, Ecumenism, and Politics*, p. 166.
[4]   Hannah Arendt, *The Promise of Politics* (New York: Schocken Books, 2005), p. 24.

of the Danzig Senate in 1933–4, presents page after page of what are purported to be Hitler's most intimate views and plans for the future, allegedly based on dozens of private conversations. We may wish to ask: why would Hitler have had such conversations with an almost unknown provincial officer? Although *Conversations* is one of the most widely quoted sources of information about Hitler's personality and hidden intentions, its authenticity has recently been called into question. It is claimed that these discussions never took place: the words attributed to Hitler were simply invented or lifted from various sources, including the writings of Ernst Jünger and Friedrich Nietzsche.[5]

As to the sources that are unquestionably authentic, it is hard to find evidence in support of the claim that Hitler would have rejected the idea of conscience. On 1 February 1933, two days after his seizure of power, for instance, the new Reich Chancellor addressed the German nation with the following words: 'We are determined, as leaders of the nation, to fulfil as a national government the task which has been given to us, swearing fidelity only to God, our conscience, and our *Volk*.'[6] Moreover, if the conscience had been, in Hitler's view, a dirty and degrading illusion, would it have been possible for Rudolf Hess to use the following words in a public speech given on 14 August 1934, shortly before the 19 August referendum in which ninety per cent of the voters gave their support to Hitler assuming full power as Führer and Chancellor of Germany?

> Someone may say that it is not good to put all power in one hand, since Adolf Hitler might use his authority arbitrarily and thoughtlessly! To that I can only say: The conscience [*Gewissen*] of a moral personality is a far greater protection against the misuse of an office than is the supervision of parliament or the separation of powers. I know no one who has a stronger conscience, or is more true to his people, than Adolf Hitler … The Führer's highest court [*Instanz*] is his conscience and his responsibility [*Verantwortung*] to his people and to history.[7]

In the case of National Socialism, it is of course always hard to tell sincerity from a sheer lie and real conviction from lip service and propaganda – perhaps the firmest conviction of Nazism was faith *in* lies, lip service and propaganda. Yet we cannot deny the fact that the National Socialists also appealed to conscience. Hitler himself appeals to conscience many times in *Mein Kampf*. He tells us, for instance, that when the creeping gas began to gnaw at his eyes at the front and he feared going permanently blind, it was precisely the voice of conscience that made him maintain his courage:

---

[5] Eberhard Jäckel noted long ago that Rauschning was an unreliable source. See Eberhard Jäckel, *Hitler's Worldview: A Blueprint for Power* (Cambridge, MA: Harvard University Press, 1972), pp. 15–17. A recent biographer, Eckhard Jesse, goes further. According to him, *Conversation* is 'untrustworthy through and through – a product of war propaganda'. Eckhard Jesse, 'Hermann Rauschning – Der fragwürdige Kronzeuge,' *Die braune Elite II: 21 weitere biographische Skizzen*, ed. Ronald Smelser et al. (Darmstadt: Wissenschaftliche Buchgesellschaft, 1993), pp. 201–2.

[6] Max Domarus, *Hitler: Reden und Proklamationen 1932-1945: Band I Triumph. Erster Halbband 1932-1934* (München: Süddeutscher Verlag, 1962/3), p. 192.

[7] Rudolf Hess, 'Die Wahl Adolf Hitlers zum Führer,' in Rudolf Hess, *Reden* (Munich: Zentralverlag der NSDAP, 1938), pp. 59–60.

'The voice of conscience cried out immediately: Poor miserable fellow, will you start howling when there are thousands of others whose lot is a hundred times worse than yours!'[8] Hitler did not reject even bad conscience – that infamous conscience that had become the main target of criticism in Friedrich Nietzsche's revaluation of all values. Nietzsche thought that a bad conscience was a poisonous invention of the Jewish priest, but Hitler accuses the *Jews* of having no bad conscience.[9]

According to the views Hitler presented in public, the National Socialists were by no means lacking conscience. Germany needed National Socialists because they were men of conscience, and because it was only such men that were able to carry out tasks that could, even against majority opinion, save the honour of the German people. As Hitler put it in a speech given to his followers in Munich on 27 April 1923:

> What our people needs is not leaders in Parliament, but those who are determined to carry through what they see to be right before God, before the world, and before their own consciences – and to carry that through, if need be, in the teeth of majorities.[10]

The arguably authentic private conversations – such as Hitler's *Table Talk*, recorded at the initiative of Martin Bormann during the first years of the Second World War – also fail to provide any support for the idea that Hitler would have rejected the conscience, although these conversations clearly reveal his hatred of Christianity. Actually, it is precisely owing to his conscience that Hitler wants to do away with Christianity and its 'lies':

> If anyone thinks it's really essential to build the life of human society on a foundation of [Christian] lies, well, in my estimation, such a society is not worth preserving. If, on the other hand, one believes that [scientific] truth is the indispensable foundation, then conscience bids one intervene in the name of truth, and exterminate the lie.[11]

According to Ratzinger, the absoluteness of conscience is the complete antithesis of tyranny, but even the most tyrannical tyrant appeals to conscience. How is this possible? Is it possible because National Socialism is Catholicism without Christianity, as Martin Bormann once suggested?[12] This would, of course, be an outrageous claim. Or is it possible because of different conceptions of what conscience means? This is not easy to establish inasmuch as Hitler never defined the notion. What we can do is

---

[8] Adolf Hitler, *Mein Kampf*, trans. J. Murphy (London: Hurst and Blackett, 1939), p. 164, accessed 24 August 2012: http://archive.org/details/MeinKampf_483

[9] 'As the leader of the trades union movement, he [the Jew] has no pangs of conscience [*Gewissensbisse*] about putting forward demands which not only go beyond the declared purpose of the movement but could not be carried into effect without ruining the national economic structure.' Ibid., p. 252. Translation modified.

[10] Ernst Boepple, ed., *Adolf Hitlers Reden* (München: Deutscher Volksverlag, 1933), p. 62.

[11] H. R. Trevor-Roper, ed., *Hitler's Table Talk 1941–1944* (New York: Enigma Books, 2008), p. 231.

[12] See Joachim C. Fest, *Das Gesicht des Dritten Reiches: Profile einer totalitären Herrschaft* (München: Piper, 2002), p. 175.

to examine Ratzinger's definition of conscience and compare it with Hitler's usage of the term.

Ratzinger's most comprehensive analysis of conscience can be found in his article entitled 'Conscience and Truth', originally presented as the keynote address for the Tenth Bishops' Workshop of the National Catholic Bioethics Centre that took place in February 1991 in Dallas, Texas. In it Ratzinger criticizes the subjectivist (and in his view liberal) interpretation of conscience, stating that the medieval tradition was right in distinguishing two levels of conscience: subjective *conscientia* and objective *synderesis*. Ratzinger interprets this objective or ontological conscience to mean what the Apostle Paul says in the second part of the letter to the Romans (2.15): a law written in the hearts of men. According to Ratzinger, this 'ontological level' of conscience 'consists in the fact that something like a primal memory of the good and true (both are identical) has been implanted in us'.[13] If this ontological level is not taken into account, the empirical experience of conscience (when 'each person determines his own standards') paves the way for relativism, superficial conviction and social conformity.[14] In other words, the conscience must be attentive to 'unconscious' truth by striving to become aware of it, this truth that is implanted in our very being, in order to become a 'good' conscience – not in the sense that it would no longer be capable of perceiving guilt, but in the very opposite sense, perceiving its guilt as acutely as possible.[15] This is also, according to Ratzinger, what distinguishes the conscience of such 'criminals of conviction' as Hitler and Stalin from the correct conscience: the cause of their moral depravity was not that they lacked conscience or conviction but that their consciences were deaf to the 'internal promptings of truth'.[16]

Now, if Hitler had relied on the 'subjectivist interpretation' of conscience, Ratzinger's critique would hit the mark. Hitler forgot the 'truth'. Yet we remember what Hitler said in the passage quoted above: 'Conscience bids one intervene in the name of truth, and exterminate the lie'. In other words, it is not the voice of conscience that legitimizes intervention. It is truth abiding in conscience that makes intervention legitimate.[17] Of course, this passage does not contain any reference to a 'truth' that would explicitly reside within us as a natural law written in the heart by God. Yet it is not entirely clear that Hitler would not have believed in an inner truth. Among the ranks of the National Socialists, there were many who believed in the inner truth. According to Ratzinger, the possibility of the anamnesis of the origin results from the 'godlike constitution of our being',[18] but if we examine the writings of the leading Nazi ideologues it becomes soon clear that many of them also believed in this godlike constitution. This is, in fact, one of the most *conspicuous* features of their anthropology:

---

[13] Joseph Ratzinger, 'Conscience and Truth,' in Joseph Cardinal Ratzinger, *On Conscience* (San Francisco: Ignatius, 2007), pp. 32–3.

[14] Ibid., pp. 16–21.

[15] Ibid., pp. 13–19. This is also the place where the papacy enters the game: the Pope is the 'advocate of the Christian memory'. Ibid., p. 36.

[16] Ibid., p. 38.

[17] 'I believe in truth. I'm sure that, in the long run, truth must be victorious.' Trevor-Roper, ed., *Hitler's Table Talk*, p. 259.

[18] Ratzinger, 'Conscience and Truth', in *On Conscience*, p, 32.

We seek God nowhere but in ourselves. For us the soul is divine, of which the Jew, on the other hand, knows nothing: The Kingdom of Heaven is within you (Luke 17.22), thus God also, who belongs to the Kingdom of Heaven. We feel our soul is immortal, eternal from the beginning, and therefore we refuse to be told that we are created from nothingness.[19]

Thus wrote Hitler's spiritual mentor Dietrich Eckart (to whom Hitler dedicated *Mein Kampf*) at the end of the 1910s. Analogously, one of the leading Nazi propagandists, Alfred Rosenberg, declared: 'The Nordic spiritual inheritance comprised consciousness not only of the divinity of the human soul, but of its equality with God.'[20] To a Christian this might be tantamount to blasphemy. There is a fundamental difference between being created in the image of God and being God. Yet the issue is perhaps more complicated than it seems. On the one hand, Rosenberg does not claim that the divinity within the human soul is immediately present to consciousness, but emphasizes that it requires 'inner work' for one to become conscious of it.[21] On the other hand, rather than from pagan sources, Rosenberg acquired the idea of human divinity from the Dominican priest Meister Eckhart, who believed that there is a divine spark hidden in every human soul.[22] It is true that Eckhart was accused of heresy by the papal authority, but if we examine the historical background of his idea of the divine spark, it is not clear, objectively speaking, whether it is heretical at all. On the contrary, it is quite evident that Eckhart's spark of the soul (or the 'ground of the soul' as he also called it) is a mere transposition of the Scholastic *synderesis*, defined as the divine remnant of the fall within the soul of man. During the Middle Ages, this idea was by no means heretical. Rather, it was one of the most firmly established truths of the Catholic Church. For the Catholics, it remains a truth – as also illustrated by Ratzinger taking it as the point of departure in his analysis of the ontological conscience to which he, not unlike Eckhart, refers as the ground of man's being and existence.[23]

II

All in all, it seems impossible to reserve the idea of conscience exclusively for good Christian, liberal or democratic purposes by denying the authenticity of the appeals to conscience in the cases where these purposes have been refuted. The inner voice of conscience may help, or even force, one to resist the lure of totalitarianism, but it would be erroneous to believe that totalitarianism is antithetical to conscience as such.

---

[19] Cited in Richard Steigmann-Gall, *The Holy Reich: Nazi Conceptions of Christianity, 1919–1945* (Cambridge: Cambridge University Press, 2003), p. 30.
[20] Alfred Rosenberg, *Der Mythus des 20. Jahrhunderts* (München: Hoheneichen Verlag, 1933), p. 246.
[21] Ibid., pp. 221–2.
[22] Ibid., pp. 216–59.
[23] See Ratzinger, 'Conscience and Truth,' in *On Conscience*, pp. 16, 32.

In addition to the words of Heinrich Himmler at Poznań already cited consider Alfred Rosenberg's following words in his *Myth of the 20th Century*:

> The inner voice [*innere Stimme*] now demands that the myth of blood and the myth of soul, race and ego, *Volk* and personality, blood and honour; that this myth, alone and uncompromisingly, must penetrate, bear and determine all life. It demands that, for the German people, the two million dead heroes must not have died in vain. It demands a world revolution and will tolerate no high values in its vicinity other than its own.[24]

It must be taken into account, moreover, that Rosenberg was by no means the only theoretically minded supporter of the German totalitarian regime who believed that the truth resides in the inner voice of conscience, for we very well know that even the most outstanding theorist of conscience in the twentieth century – Martin Heidegger – was a member of the Nazi Party, the NSDAP (*Nationalsozialistische Deutsche Arbeiterpartei*). Given the influence of Heidegger's philosophy on twentieth-century thought, especially in Europe, his analysis of conscience merits closer investigation.

The call of Heidegger's conscience

Like Ratzinger and the medieval schoolmen, Heidegger differentiates between the ontological and empirical ('ontic') conscience. 'Ontic' conscience is the empirical voice of conscience that murmurs back when I have done something wrong or warns me if I am about to do so. This is not the conscience in which Heidegger is primarily interested. According to him, the empirical experience of conscience is merely a derivative of a more profound ontological 'call of conscience' (*Ruf des Gewissens*). What, then, is this ontological call? Its structure and function is almost diametrically opposite to Sigmund Freud's conception conscience as superego, made famous a few years before Heidegger's analysis of conscience in *Being and Time*.[25] Freud thought that the voice of conscience is the voice of the father and, in broader terms, the voice of the authorities and moral norms of the surrounding society, but Heidegger saw its call as the very instance which *liberates* man or what Heidegger calls *Dasein* from the these authorities and norms. In fact, the call of conscience liberates *Dasein* from everything in the surrounding world. This is not to say that Heidegger would have thought that people are usually free from the authorities, rules and opinions of society. On the contrary, these authorities, rules and opinions determine his conduct almost without an exception, as conformism is, as he claims, the rule rather than exception in human societies. For the most part, to use Heidegger's idiosyncratic language,

---

[24] Rosenberg, *Der Mythus*, p. 699. Unlike the German people, Rosenberg continues, the Jewish race has no inner voice by which to live: it is slavishly dependent on artificial constructions that amount to mere methods of life-management rather than to a true expression of what it means to live as a human being.

[25] It is beyond doubt that Heidegger knew Freud's concept of concience, for even though he does not refer to Freud in *Being and Time*, he refers to H. G. Stoker's *Das Gewissen*, in which there is a lengthy analysis of Freud's reduction of conscience to what he calls superego.

every *Dasein* is a 'fallen' and inauthentic being lost in the world of the so-called 'they' (*das Man*). *Dasein* says what the others say and does what the others do. It obeys the rules of society because this is how others behave. It even breaks the rules of society because other people break them. Whatever it does, it does on account of others, not because it has determined by itself, by virtue of its own potentiality, to engage in such and such action. Therefore, when *Dasein* is lost in *das Man*, its choices are not merely irresponsible, but more profoundly, it does not really choose at all. Everything is always-already chosen for it. All its possibilities in future – its 'potentiality-for-Being' – are already decided: 'The "they" has always kept *Dasein* from taking hold of the possibilities of Being.'[26] Moreover, given that the 'they' is nobody rather than somebody, it remains indefinite who has actually done the choosing. Hence, the only choice that an inauthentic *Dasein* is capable of is to choose what is already chosen by the 'nobody': 'So *Dasein* make no choices.'[27] This is why *Dasein*'s way of being in the world is characterized not by occasional irresponsibility, but irresponsibility that penetrates to the very core of its being.

According to Heidegger, however, this inauthentic and irresponsible way of being is not *Dasein*'s irrevocable fate. *Dasein* can escape it by attuning itself to the call of conscience. But how does this happen? Heidegger explains: *Dasein* must *withdraw* from the possibilities that are 'present-at-hand' for it in the immediate everyday environment of the 'they'. It must first choose *not* to choose any of these possibilities.[28] For Heidegger, this choice – the choice to suspend choosing – is, in fact, the first authentic choice, which makes genuine choosing possible in the first place: 'In choosing to make this choice, *Dasein* makes possible, first and foremost, its authentic potentiality-for-Being.'[29] By choosing to suspend the possibilities disclosed in the immediate everyday environment, *Dasein* chooses itself, its own possibilities. In this choosing, *Dasein* transforms the 'mixture of circumstances and accidents'[30] into a situation of its own. Heidegger calls the existential structure of choosing resoluteness (*Entschlossenheit*). It signifies 'letting oneself be summoned [*Aufruf*] out of one's lostness in the "they".'[31] It is here that conscience (*Gewissen*) enters the play. It is the call of conscience, 'coming from me and yet beyond me,'[32] that 'summons *Dasein*'s Self from its lostness' in the 'they'.[33] In order to become authentic, *Dasein* has to be resolute as regards the call of conscience. This is not to say that *Dasein* now of his own will chooses conscience, for Heidegger insists that conscience cannot be chosen. In point of fact, even the first choice to suspend choosing presupposes something

---

[26] Heidegger, *Being and Time*, p. 312.
[27] Ibid.
[28] Ibid., p. 313.
[29] Ibid.
[30] Ibid., p. 346.
[31] Ibid., p. 345.
[32] 'Indeed the call is precisely something which we ourselves have neither planned nor prepared for nor voluntarily performed, nor have we ever done so. "It" calls, against our expectations and even against our will. On the other hand, the call undoubtedly does not come from someone else who is with me in the world. The call comes from me and yet from beyond me.' Ibid., p. 320.
[33] Ibid., p. 319.

that escapes *Dasein*'s own will. It presupposes something that radically disturbs its everyday existence, a disorienting experience Heidegger calls anxiety (*Angst*). Whatever the source of this anxiety in the everyday world, it is this mood that makes manifest in *Dasein* its being towards its ownmost potentiality-for-Being and thereby enables it resolutely to suspend everyday possibilities at hand.[34] Neither such anxiety nor conscience can be chosen. According to Heidegger, however, *Dasein* can and indeed must choose to *want* to have a conscience.[35] Indeed, it is this wanting-to-have-conscience (*Gewissenhabenwollen*) that liberates *Dasein* from its lostness in the 'they' and it does so precisely because this wanting entails readiness for anxiety.[36]

In what sense, however, such wanting is liberating? It is liberating because the call of conscience, which calls against our expectations and against our will, *says nothing*: 'The call asserts nothing, gives no information about the events of the world, it has nothing to tell.'[37] Anxiety prepares us for the call of conscience, but at the same time the silence of conscience itself is the primordial source of anxiety at the root of all everyday sources – and it is this primordial source that liberates *Dasein*. In the silent 'anxiety of conscience',[38] *Dasein* bypasses the noise of the everyday world, the world of *das Man*:

> In calling the one to whom the appeal is made, it [conscience] does not call him into the public idle talk of the 'they,' but calls him back from this into the reticence of his existent potentiality-for-Being.[39]

In other words, the silent call of conscience relentlessly individualizes *Dasein* down to itself.[40] It detaches *Dasein* from the social bond and abandons (*überlassen*) it to itself. It is in this uncanny (*unheimlich*) silence and solitude, in this anxiety of conscience, that *Dasein* comes face to face with itself and particularly with the fact that it is radically free – free for the freedom of choosing its own potentiality-for-Being and taking hold of itself.[41]

Such freedom, however, is not the only thing the silent call implies. At the same time, it enables *Dasein* to become aware that it is *guilty* – not only on some occasions but always already, permanently and irremediably.[42] The silence of the call of conscience makes *Dasein* understand that its most primordial potentiality-for-Being is that of Being-guilty (*Schuldigsein*). What is this 'Being-guilty'? Heidegger first says what it is not. In his view, the idea of Being-guilty must be dissociated from any law such that 'by failing to comply with it one loads himself with guilt'.[43] Such guilt relates to the inauthentic everyday experience of conscience, either pricking or warning,

---

[34] Ibid., p. 323.
[35] Ibid., p. 334.
[36] Ibid., p. 342.
[37] Ibid., p. 318.
[38] Ibid., p. 342.
[39] Ibid., p. 322.
[40] Ibid., p. 354. 'Conscience, in its basis and its essence, is in each case mine. Ibid., p. 323.
[41] Ibid., p. 232.
[42] Ibid., p. 353.
[43] Ibid., p. 328.

which identifies guilt resulting of the transgression of norms or from the omission of duties: 'The everyday experience of the conscience has no acquaintance with anything like getting summoned to Being-guilty.'[44] The Being-guilty should not be confused with original sin either.[45] Instead, *Dasein's* Being-guilty relates to the fact that the essence of *Dasein* is characterized by its *possibilities*. Insofar as these possibilities are always open to *Dasein* – which is Heidegger's way of saying that *Dasein* is radically free – it so to speak 'lags behind its possibilities'.[46] It is this lag that explains its guilt. *Dasein* is guilty of not being able to actualize its potentialities, not because it cannot actualize them all at once, but simply because *Dasein is* its possibilities ('Being-possible'): '*Dasein* as such is guilty.'[47] Therefore, although authentic *Dasein* is radically free with regard to its own possibilities, it can never be *sovereign* over its being. Yet such a lack of sovereignty does not mean that *Dasein* is not responsible over its being. On the contrary, the 'Being-guilty' of *Dasein* does not mean anything else than that *Dasein* is always already, before any transgression or omission, *responsible* (*verantwortlich*), not only for this or that thing but for its existence as such. By revealing to *Dasein* its profound freedom *and* guilt, the call of conscience reveals to *Dasein* its primordial and irrevocable responsibility.

This is not to say that as an authentic being of freedom and responsibility, *Dasein* would surpass the everyday world of *das Man*. This world is unsurpassable: I am always already one of the 'they', always already 'fallen'. Heidegger repeatedly states that authentic existence is not 'something which floats above falling everydayness',[48] a 'modified way' in which such everydayness is 'seized upon'.[49] The difference between inauthentic and authentic existence is merely that as an authentic self *Dasein* realizes that the world of the 'they', its norms and opinions, concerns *it* as a singular being transforming that world into a 'situation' of its own:

> When the call of conscience summons us to our potentiality-for-Being, it does not hold before us some empty ideal of existence, but calls us forth into the Situation.[50]

When *Dasein* attunes itself authentically to the call of conscience calling it forth into the situation, it apprehends that it has to take a singular *stance* regarding it. The very definition of the situation presupposes such a stance. The situation is not a 'mixture of circumstances and accidents' which we encounter. The situation takes place only when *Dasein* takes a singular stance and, more precisely, when it is resolute and ready for action: 'To hear the call authentically, signifies bringing oneself into a factical action.'[51] Hence the call of conscience is not something that somehow prevents action by paralysing *Dasein* on account of its Being-guilty but, on the contrary, something that

---

44 Ibid., p. 339.
45 Ibid., p. 354, footnote 2.
46 Ibid., p. 330.
47 Ibid., p. 331.
48 Heidegger uses falling (*Verfallen*) to signify *Dasein's* absorption and lostness in the world of the 'they'. Ibid., pp. 219–20.
49 Ibid., p. 224.
50 Ibid., p. 347.
51 Ibid., p. 341.

calls for action – and more specifically, for *responsible* action. Even more, this resolve gives *Dasein* the vision to see that it can extend his conscience beyond the limits of its individuality and become conscience for others as well: 'When *Dasein* is resolute, it can become the "conscience" of others.'[52] When this vision is achieved, *Dasein* is no longer marked by the indifference of *das Man*, but that of responsibility and care (*Sorge*) of itself and others.

Yet something is still missing. Although the call of conscience individualizes and renders *Dasein* responsible, this individual responsibility remains imperfect before *Dasein*'s most primordial potentiality is added in the scheme. This primordial potentiality is death – 'the nullity by which *Dasein*'s Being is dominated primordially through and through'.[53] According to Heidegger, it is death qua nullity understood as the possibility of absolute impossibility that is the ownmost, non-relational (*unbezüglich*) and inalienable possibility of *Dasein* that completely individualizes it. When *Dasein* has caught up the possibility of death into its potentiality-for-Being, its authentic responsible existence can no longer be outstripped by anything.[54] Thus, it is with *Dasein*'s ownmost possibility of death and, more exactly, *Dasein*'s primordial 'limit situation' (*Grenzsituation*) of being-*towards*-death that *Dasein* is no longer in any way capable of evading its primordial Being-guilty and infinite responsibility. It cannot do so because it is absolutely impossible to actualize death, as for *Dasein*, death cannot be anything but a possibility.[55] Whereas in Christian understanding death is the moment of final judgement that includes the possibility of redeeming guilt, for Heidegger it becomes the ultimate confirmation of its permanence. Without the call of conscience, however, *Dasein* would not catch up the possibility of death into its potentiality-for-Being, for it is precisely this call that discloses not only *Dasein*'s Being-guilty but also its inalienable possibility of death, that is to say, pure nullity at the heart of its existence.

* * *

If this reading of Heidegger's 'conscience' is correct, there is nothing much in his depiction of conscience that would necessarily contradict the preceding Western understanding of it. Since its conception with Socrates, Epictetus, Cicero and Philo, the conscience has been a source of anxiety and distress. Likewise, it has always been conceived as an instance that distances a person from the rest and especially from their opinions, opening the way for that person to know truth independent of others. (Ratzinger formulates this ancient idea as follows: 'A man of conscience is one who never acquires tolerance, well-being, success, public standpoint, and approval on the part of prevailing opinion at the expense of truth.')[56] Furthermore, already Jerome in his commentary on the Book of Ezekiel (AD 415) speaks of two consciences: the spark

---

[52] Ibid., p. 344.
[53] Ibid., p. 354.
[54] Ibid., pp. 354–5.
[55] 'The closest closeness which one may have in Being towards death as a possibility, is as far as possible from anything actual.' Ibid., pp. 306–7.
[56] Ratzinger, 'Conscience and Truth,' in *On Conscience*, p. 26.

of conscience (*scintilla conscientiae*) and the conscience (*conscientia*), identifying the former with the ineffable and more precisely with the Pauline spirit that 'intercedes for us with ineffable groanings',[57] whilst the latter refers to the 'everyday' experience of conscience. At least this is how the Scholastics understood this distinction calling the ontological spark of conscience *synderesis* and its phenomenal experience *conscientia*. Even Thomas Aquinas, one of the least mystical of the Scholastics, held that *synderesis* apprehends moral truth immediately without reasoning and discourse (*sine inquisitione et discursu*).[58] To be sure, Heidegger's silent call of conscience does not make *Dasein* apprehend any positive truth, let alone divine good and true, not even when *Dasein* hears it correctly. In fact, it has no direct connection to any positive values. It has no such connection because the call of conscience says nothing. Yet not unlike the Scholastic *synderesis* (which, to be honest, gives no positive criteria for one's choices either),[59] the Heideggerian call of conscience is a fundamental prerequisite for morality. Thus the silence of conscience does not entail, according to Heidegger, ethical nihilism. For Heidegger, nihilism is not something that ensues when no objective good or true exists, but rather when a human being (*Dasein*) merely conforms to the authorities, rules and norms of the surrounding society – be those norms divine, natural, positive, those of public opinion, or whatever – without properly choosing them. Attuning to the silent call of conscience is both an exit from this nihilistic conformism and the condition of possibility for the emergence of authentic responsibility. It is such an exit and emergence because the silent call of conscience, which by disclosing the nothing at the heart of *Dasein* reveals that there are no pre-given criteria for *Dasein*'s choices, makes *Dasein* to understand that it *itself* is responsible for the very definition of moral truth. It is precisely this loss of all criteria, deactivation of all prevailing norms and opinions caused by the nullifying call of ontological conscience that is the condition of every authentic and thus responsible choice. When the call of conscience reveals the *Abgrund* of every choice, at the same time it reveals *Dasein*'s absolute responsibility – not accountability before God, the state, law or other people, but rather before the nothing, that is to say, responsibility for the very existence of gods, states, laws and even for others' responsibility.

What is most essential here, however, is that Heidegger did not see any contradiction between his meta-ethics of conscience and the National Socialist movement. In fact, he saw in the movement the very promise of a new awakening of conscience. He saw it as a possibility for a collective realization of individual responsibility that derives from being attuned to the call of conscience. In an appeal to the German students on the occasion of the plebiscite of 12 November 1933, called by Hitler to

---

[57] Jerome, *Commentariorum in Ezekhielem Prophetam Libri Quatuordecim* 1.1.7, in *Patrologia cursus completus: Series Latina*, ed. J. P. Migne (Paris: 1844–55), vol. 25, p. 22a–b. *Patrologia Latina* hereafter *PL*.

[58] Thomas Aquinas, *Quaestiones disputatae de veritate*, q. 16, a. 1, in S. Thomae de Aquino, *Opera Omnia*, accessed 24 August 2012: http://www.corpusthomisticum.org/iopera.html

[59] *Synderesis* gives no criteria but 'tends [*inclinet*] towards what is good'. Aquinas, *De veritate*, q. 16, a. 1. It is a weight (*pondus*) of the will, as Bonaventure had it.

sanction (*ex post facto*) Germany's withdrawal from the League of Nations, Heidegger proclaims:

> Let your loyalty and your will to follow be daily and hourly strengthened. Let your courage grow without ceasing so that you will be able to make the sacrifices necessary to save the essence of our Volk and to elevate its innermost strength in the State. Let not propositions and 'ideas' be the rules of your Being. The Führer alone is the present and future German reality and its law. Learn to know ever more deeply: from now on every single thing demands decision, and every action responsibility.[60]

Such responsible action presupposes the strength to go alone, not 'out of obstinacy and the desire to dominate, but by virtue of the most profound destiny and the broadest obligation'.[61] It means that one also must remain alone, not in the sense that he thereby isolates himself from the community (*Volksgemeinschaft*), but so that he – as a self-responsible being – knows his place and vocation in that community in order to serve it and to follow its destiny, incarnated in the 'towering will of our Führer'.[62]

I

Hannah Arendt, Heidegger's wholehearted devotee, stated that Heidegger's involvement in the Nazi movement could be explained by his naïvety in political matters. But is there really a contradiction between Heidegger's involvement and his philosophy, particularly if we take into account that he always emphasized the rootedness of philosophy in a concrete historical situation? Perhaps it was Arendt who was somewhat naïve in this case? A certain naïvety may also colour her celebrated analysis concerning the banality of Nazi evil in her book on Adolf Eichmann. There she writes:

> For the sad and very uncomfortable truth of the matter probably was that it was not his fanaticism but his very conscience that prompted him to adopt his uncompromising attitude during the last year of the war.[63]

Based on this observation, Arendt famously concludes that Eichmann's evilness is banal. Why banal? Because, Arendt explains, one could not extract any diabolical or demonic profundity from Eichmann. He was not Iago or Macbeth: 'Except for an extraordinary diligence in looking out for his personal advancement, he had no motives at all.'[64]

---

[60] Martin Heidegger, 'German Students,' in *The Heidegger Controversy: A Critical Reader*, ed. Richard Wolin (Cambridge MA: The MIT Press, 1998), p. 46.
[61] Martin Heidegger, 'The Self-Assertion of the German University,' in *Heidegger Controversy*, 34.
[62] Martin Heidegger, 'National Socialist Education,' in *Heidegger Controversy*, pp. 56, 60.
[63] Hannah Arendt, *Eichmann in Jerusalem: A Report on the Banality of Evil* (New York: Penguin Books, 1994), p. 146.
[64] Ibid., p. 287.

Does this conclusion not contradict Arendt's view that Eichmann's conscience made him a willing executioner? Can the voice of conscience not be a motive? Has the voice of conscience not been *the* motive of action in the Western tradition since the advent of Christianity? Since Socrates even? Moreover, why does Arendt think that fanaticism and conscience are incompatible? Is conscience not the very source of Western fanaticism? Recall for instance Martin Luther. Was Luther not a man of conscience to the core? It was his tormented conscience that forced him to revaluate the Catholic values prevalent at the time. It was his conscience that he famously appealed to when accused of heresy at the Diet of Worms:

> My conscience is captive to the Word of God. I cannot and will not retract anything, since it is neither safe nor right to go against conscience. I cannot do otherwise, here I stand, may God help me, Amen.[65]

Was Luther then not a fanatic? Did he not proclaim Pope as Antichrist? Did he – the man who coined the expression 'freedom of conscience' (*Gewissenfreiheit*) – not say that the Anabaptists deserved death? Did he not, in his late years, passionately hate Judaism and the Jewish people, writing a number of anti-Semitic tracts, in one of which he declared that the Jews are liars and bloodhounds whose synagogues, schools and houses have to be torn down and burned, prompting the reader to 'cover with dirt whatever will not burn, so that no man will ever again see a stone or cinder of them'?[66] Certainly, Luther was a fanatic – a 'godly barbarian', as Thomas Mann once said of him.[67]

Actually, it was Luther's conscientious fanaticism that made him a hero for the Nazis as well. During the celebrations of the 450th anniversary of Luther's birth in 1933, the Nazi leaders time and again praised Luther as a German hero whose uncompromised spirit was bearing fruit right then, at the moment when National Socialism was becoming, according to them, the leading worldview. Goebbels, for instance, argued that it was precisely with Luther that the revolution of German blood and feeling against elements alien to the *Volk* was begun, whereas Erich Koch, *Gauleiter* of East Prussia, proclaimed that it was only then that they could enter into Luther's spirit – and so on and so forth.[68] In fact, Hitler himself had hailed Luther as a *völkish* hero in *Mein Kampf*, equalled only by Richard Wagner and Frederick the Great.[69] Surely Luther's fidelity to conscience was not the only reason for this eulogy. He was also celebrated because he 'germanized' Christianity, although this had not necessarily been his intention. And, as we saw above, he was praised because he was a fierce anti-Semite, especially late in his life. Moreover, his attack on reason, which

---

[65] Martin Luther, 'The Speech of Dr. Martin Luther before the Emperor Charles and Princes at Worms,' in *Luther's Works in 55 Volumes*, general ed. Helmut T. Lehmann (St Louis, MN: Concordia Publishing House, Fortress Press, 1957–86), vol. 32, pp. 112–13. *Luther's Works* hereafter *LW*.

[66] Martin Luther, *On the Jews and their Lies*, in *LW*, vol. 47, p. 269.

[67] Thomas Mann, *Reden und Aufsätze* (Frankfurt: Fischer, 1965), vol. 1, p. 62.

[68] See Steigmann-Gall, *The Holy Reich*, pp. 134–40.

[69] Hitler, *Mein Kampf*, 1.8, p. 171.

Luther had once called the 'devil's whore', sparked the excitement of many Nazis. As the president of the Nazi Party court Walter Buch said:

> Luther's eloquent words, 'the intellect is the Devil's whore', confirm my belief that the human spirit of the greatest magnitude is too small to alter the laws of life [*Lebensgesetze*]. And the highest law of life is struggle.[70]

Of course, for Luther, the highest law of life was not struggle. It was not a law at all. The highest 'law' of life was the opposite of law: God's grace. Nevertheless, it was not for nothing that the Nazis praised Luther and his adherence to conscience. By conscience, at least by the Lutheran conscience, one could dispense with reason. Conscience was a matter of faith and all that you needed was faith. Echoing Victor Hugo's famous words ('woe to him who believes in nothing'), Hitler declared at the Party Rally of Honour in Nuremberg in 1936: 'Woe to him who does not believe!'[71]

Hannah Arendt and the nihilism of judgement

As a student of Heidegger, it is not a surprise that Hannah Arendt wrote quite extensively about conscience. It occupied a central place in her dissertation on Augustine, written in the end of 1920s. Here Arendt depicted the Augustinian conscience as something that puts man *coram Deo*, into the presence of God. Conscience is the voice of divine law and opposed to the world insofar as it directs humankind beyond the world and away from worldly habits and habituation:

> Conscience directs man beyond this world and away from habituation. As the voice of the Creator, conscience makes man's dependence on God clear to him. What the law commands, conscience addresses to the one who has already succumbed to the world in habit. The voice of the law summons him against what habit previously entangled him in.[72]

In the 1960s Arendt took up the same theme, but now in order to elaborate a concept of conscience of her own. Although Arendt still thought that conscience is opposed to habit and habituation, being an element which radically disturbs the established order of things, conscience is no longer a voice of divine law, but a side-effect of thinking process.[73] Thinking itself, for Arendt, is a silent intercourse with oneself and thus a

---

[70] Cited in Steigmann-Gall, *The Holy Reich*, p. 55.
[71] 'The one who does not believe has no soul. He is empty. He has no ideals. He has nothing to live for. He has no sunshine, no light, no joy in life. He is a poor, poor man. What is wealth? What are possessions? What does it all mean? Problems come despite them, only faith is left. Woe to him who does not believe!'as Robert Ley explained Hitler's words in 'Schicksal – ich glaube!' Robert Ley, *Wir alle helfen dem Führer* (München: Zentralverlag der NSDAP, 1939), p. 112.
[72] Hannah Arendt, *Love and Saint Augustine*, ed. J. V. Scott and J. C. Stark (Chicago: University of Chicago Press, 1996), p. 84.
[73] Hannah Arendt, *The Life of the Mind*, vol. 1 (New York: Harvest Book, 1978), p. 5.

dual process implying a divided subject or two-in-one,[74] whereas conscience is 'a kind of knowledge actualized in every thinking process'.[75]

The most probable reason why Arendt returned to the theme of conscience in the 1960's pertains to the atrocities of the Second World War and, more broadly speaking, to the question of evil these atrocities had made extremely acute. This subject remains also at the heart of Arendt's last major work, *The Life of the Mind*. At the beginning of the book, Arendt asks:

> Could the activity of thinking as such, the habit of examining whatever happens to come to pass or to attract attention, regardless of results and specific content, could this activity be among the conditions that make men abstain from evil-doing or even actually 'condition' them against it?[76]

The first volume of the book is an extensive attempt to answer this question. The conclusion is not unambiguous:

> The manifestation of the wind of thought is not knowledge; it is the ability to tell right from wrong, beautiful from ugly. And this, at the rare moments when the stakes are on the table, may indeed prevent catastrophes, at least for the self.[77]

In other words, thinking-conscience, which indeed names the ability to tell right from wrong, may prevent personal catastrophes ('evil-doing'), and it may do so because conscience is either a negative afterthought roused by one's bad deeds or the anticipation of such afterthoughts.[78] Thus, conscience concerns the self alone, preventing it at least from such wrongdoing which the self conceives as the cause of negative afterthoughts, disturbing the peace of the soul. On the other hand, Arendt states here that conscience may prevent catastrophes at the rare moments when the stakes are on the table. What does this mean? It pertains to Arendt's insight that the thinking-conscience remains a marginal affair in society except in 'boundary situations',[79] that is, 'in times of crises, when, so to speak, we find ourselves with our back against the wall'.[80] Arendt attributes the term 'boundary' or 'limit situation' (*Grenzsituation*) to Karl Jaspers, who, as she claims, coined it. For Jaspers, limit situations were existential situations, such as death, suffering, conflict, chance and guilt.[81] According to him, moreover, all human existence necessarily involves facing these situations and man becomes truly conscious of himself as man by facing them.[82] In Arendt's view, it is particularly in such limit situations that conscience becomes operative. For Arendt, however, limit situations are more than mere psychological conditions. They also

[74] Hannah Arendt, *Responsibility and Judgement* (New York: Harvest Book, 1978), p. 184.
[75] Arendt, *The Life of the Mind*, vol. 1, p. 5.
[76] Ibid.
[77] Ibid., vol. 1, p. 193.
[78] Ibid., vol. 1, p. 189.
[79] Ibid., vol. 1, p. 192.
[80] Arendt, *Responsibility and Judgement*, p. 122.
[81] Karl Jaspers, *The Way to Wisdom*, trans. R. Manheim (New Haven: Yale University Press, 2003), p. 20.
[82] Karl Jaspers, *Man in the Modern Age*, trans. C. Paul (London: Routledge & Kegan Paul, 1933), p. 72.

denote emergencies: 'The thinking ego and its experience, conscience,' remains a 'marginal affair for society at large except in emergencies.'[83] Emergency is not a psychological but a juridico-political notion and it refers to what Carl Schmitt in his *Political Theology* famously calls the state of exception (*Ausnahmezustand*), based on the sovereign decision which, normatively speaking, 'emanates from nothingness [*aus einem Nichts*].'[84] It is in such emergencies that conscience leaves the margins of society and enters at its heart and, as Arendt writes, conscience is itself a kind of 'emergency measure'.[85] Hence, not unlike the Schmittian sovereign decision which, emanating from the normative nothingness, decides on the emergency measures during the state of exception,[86] the Arendtian conscience bestows life with a measure during the times of crisis when all laws and customs are held in abeyance, preventing and eventually defining evil because the law is not capable of doing it, either because it is suspended or it does not exist at all.

Now, given the fact that on 28 February Hitler proclaimed the Degree for the Protection of the People and the State, which suspended the articles of the Weimar Constitution concerning personal liberties,[87] it would have been consistent if Arendt had seen the Third Reich as a blatant manifestation of the state of exception in which the conscience becomes operative. Instead of that, however, the National Socialist Germany represented for Arendt a collapse of morality 'into a mere set of mores'.[88] In other words, the Third Reich was not one of those rare moments when the stakes are on the table, but rather a normal situation in which people lead their lives without thinking and, hence, without actualizing their consciences. In this respect, the National Socialist Germany was not radically different from other modern societies, as Arendt insists that morality is collapsed into a mere set of empty mores in modernity as a whole – particularly because the individuals of modern mass societies are normalized by innumerable rules imposed by the anonymous machinery of aggressive administration.[89] Modern man is not a man of thought and conscience but an utterly thoughtless being repeating trivial truths:

> Thoughtlessness – the heedless recklessness or hopeless confusion or complacent repetition of 'truths' which have become trivial and empty – seems to me among the outstanding characteristics of our time.[90]

---

[83] Arendt, *Responsibility and Judgement*, p. 188.
[84] Carl Schmitt, *Political Theology*, trans. G. Schwab (Cambridge, MA: The MIT Press, 1985), pp. 31–2.
[85] Arendt, *Responsibility and Judgement*, p. 104.
[86] As a detail, we may note that already Jean Bodin considered the power to judge according to one's conscience to be a mark of sovereignty, parallel to the power 'all judges have where there is no express law or custom'. Jean Bodin, *On Sovereignty: Four Chapters from the Six Books of the Commonwealth*, ed. J. H. Franklin (Cambridge: Cambridge University Press, 1992), p. 86.
[87] 'From a juridical standpoint the entire Third Reich can be considered a state of exception that lasted twelve years.' Giorgio Agamben, *State of Exception*, trans. K. Attell (Chicago: Chicago University Press, 2005), p. 2.
[88] Arendt, *Responsibility and Judgement*, p. 54.
[89] Hannah Arendt, *The Human Condition* (Chicago: The University of Chicago Press, 1958), p. 41.
[90] Ibid., p. 5.

Thus, Nazi Germany is not an exception, but rather a paradigm of modern society which almost by definition lacks both thinking and conscience.

This is not the whole truth, however. Arendt also asserts that the modern world is defined by the *loss* of rules and standards: 'The loss of standards defines the modern world in its facticity and cannot be reversed by any sort of return to the good old days or by some arbitrary promulgation of new standards and values.'[91] In other words, modernity is an epoch of conformity and that of emergency at the same time. Is there a contradiction in Arendt's conception of modernity? Perhaps not. Arendt might have thought that the anonymous administration of the modern mass society imposes rules and standards although *metaphysically speaking* such rules and standards are already impossible. God is dead, at least the 'traditional thought of God',[92] and thus all the rules and standards are necessarily arbitrary and, consequently, all the attempts to present them as something more than that are absolutely illegitimate. If this holds true, modernity, Nazi period including, is indeed an epoch of the state of exception in which the 'centre cannot hold',[93] but meaningless administration draws a veil over this truth by inventing rules and standards that have no grounds whatsoever. This would also make comprehensible why Arendt never says that conscience enters the centre stage in modernity, despite the loss of standards. The loss of standards arouses thinking process which then renders conscience operative, but in modern mass society the loss of standards has remained unnoticed because of complacent repetition of trivial and empty 'truths'.

Hence, in order to render the conscience operative again, we must disclose the emptiness of these 'truths' and unveil the truth that God is dead and that the loss of standards defines the modern world in its facticity. According to Arendt, we are *obliged* to do so, because such a disclosure alone makes us capable of telling right from wrong in the first place. It is not a 'law given from the outside, be it the law of God or the laws of men'[94] that endows us with a capacity to judge. On the contrary, it is the absence of such laws and, ultimately, the absence of all standards that makes us morally and politically mature beings:

> This destruction [of standards] has a liberating effect on another human faculty, the faculty of judgement, which one may call, with some justification, the most political of man's mental abilities. It is the faculty to judge particulars without subsuming them under those general rules which can be taught and learned until they grow into habits that can be replaced by other habits and rules.[95]

According to Arendt, we commonly call a situation without standards nihilism.[96] In this sense, nihilism is, for Arendt, the condition of possibility of all ethics and politics. But Arendt does not call it nihilism. In her view, nihilism is not a situation in which

[91] Arendt, *The Promise of Politics*, p. 104.
[92] Arendt, *The Life of the Mind*, vol. 1, p. 11.
[93] Arendt, *Responsibility and Judgement*, p. 188.
[94] Ibid., p. 68.
[95] Ibid., pp. 188–9.
[96] Ibid., p. 177.

the standards have collapsed, but on the contrary, it is – as it was for Heidegger – a situation in which people conform to standards. Nihilism is conformism and habituation, whereas an authentic ethico-political decision emanates from the very absence of customs, opinions, laws and standards, from the 'two-in-one of the soundless dialogue' actualizing a 'difference within our identity',[97] – a difference called conscience.

* * *

It is of course possible that Rauschning did hear Hitler saying that conscience is a dirty illusion and a 'Jewish invention'.[98] It is also possible that Rauschning is speaking the truth in his report on Hermann Goering's statement concerning the absence of conscience in him: 'I have no conscience. My conscience is called Adolf Hitler.'[99] And we certainly know that many Nazis bitterly attacked such (Christian) ideas as sin, guilt and repentance related to conscience: 'We German Faitlers are of the opinion that the Christian sin, guilt, and repentance feelings are not religious feelings of our German nature', as Professor of Philosophy at the University of Leipzig and leader of the *Nationalkirche* Ernst Bergmann wrote in 1934.[100] Similarly, in Jerusalem, when Eichmann stood accused of crimes committed during the war, he declared that he could be hanged in public as a warning example for all anti-Semites, but he refused to repent what he had done: 'Repentance is for little children.'[101] Moreover, there were, without doubt, matters that were in conflict with the Western tradition of the ethics of conscience in the National Socialist Germany, including a drastic reduction of the private sphere and an overwhelming ritualization of public life.[102] In addition, the Nazi cult of the Will and Nazi virtues such as discipline and honour, perhaps even fidelity and comradeship, were undermining the foundations of the ethics of conscience. At least Sebastian Haffner, whilst reflecting his experiences in the work camp organized for students by the National Socialist regime, came to the conclusion that it was precisely fidelity and comradeship that relieved 'men of responsibility for their actions, before themselves, before God, before their consciences'.[103] In this sense Heidegger, the twentieth-century theorist of conscience, was perfectly right in claiming that the work camp is a vehicle for a 'complete transformation of German *Dasein*',[104] although it did not pave the way for the awakening of conscience and responsibility as Heidegger had hoped but deprived young men and women of all personal freedom and responsibility, and moulded them, at least according to Haffner, 'into an unthinking, indifferent, irresponsible mass'.[105]

---

[97] Arendt, *The Life of the Mind*, vol. 1, p. 193.
[98] Conscience as a Jewish invention, see Rauschning, *Hitler Speaks*, p. 220.
[99] Ibid., p. 84.
[100] Cited in Karla Poewe, *New Religions and the Nazis* (Abingdon: Routledge, 2006), p. 73.
[101] Cited in Arendt, *Eichmann in Jerusalem*, p. 24.
[102] On the ritualization of life in Nazi Germany, see Ernst Cassirer, *The Myth of the State* (New Haven: Yale University Press, 1946), p. 284.
[103] Sebastian Haffner, *Defying Hitler*, trans. O. Pretzel (New York: Picador, 2002), p. 286.
[104] Martin Heidegger, 'The Call to the Labor Service,' in *The Heidegger Controversy*, p. 54.
[105] Haffner, *Defying Hitler*, p. 287.

3

Conscience in Moral and Political Theology

Let us leave politics aside, at least for a whilst, and examine more closely the history of the idea and the concept of conscience itself, first by focusing on this idea and concept in Christian theology. In this respect, one thing is pretty much clear: Christians have always been enthusiastic about conscience. The Apostle Paul (2 Cor. 1.12) boasted of the testimony of his conscience (*syneidēsis*), and since Paul few Christians have ceased to do so – if not about their own conscience then at least about conscience in general. Conscience is the true 'pedagogue of the soul' (Origen);[1] it is 'our interior and unerring tribunal' (Nazianzen);[2] it is an 'incorruptible judge' and a teacher who does not deceive (Chrysostom);[3] it corrects reason where reason goes wrong (Jerome);[4] it draws us into the presence of God with 'a miraculous rapidity' (Augustine);[5] it is our 'guardian angel' (John Climacus),[6] and the 'law of our mind' (John of Damascus).[7] In the conscience 'everything is written with the pen of truth' (Bernard of Clairvaux),[8] for it is the angelic part of the soul (Thomas Aquinas),[9] the peak of the mind (*apex mentis*) (Bonaventure)[10] and the divine remnant of Adam's fall which 'comes immediately from God' (Jean Gerson).[11] After the Reformation, the eulogy of conscience became perhaps even more vociferous: conscience (*conscientia*) is 'superior to all human judgements', for it is a 'middle place [*media*] between God and man' (John Calvin);[12]

[1] Origen, *Commentary on the Epistle to the Romans: Books 1–5* 2.9.3, trans. T. P. Scheck (Washington: The Catholic University of America Press, 2001), p. 133.
[2] Gregory Nazianzen, *Select Orations* 16.5, in *Nicene and Post-Nicene Fathers*, ed. Philip Schaff (Peabody, MA: Hendrickson Publishers, 1995), series 2, vol. 7, p. 512. *Nicene and Post-Nicene Fathers* series 2 hereafter *NPNF2*.
[3] John Chrysostom, *Homiliarum in Genesim continuatio* 64.2, in *PL*, vol. 54, p. 550B.
[4] Jerome, *In Ezekh.* 1.1.7, in *PL*, vol. 25, p. 22A–B.
[5] Augustine, *The City of God* 20.14, in *Nicene and Post-Nicene Fathers*, ed. Philip Schaff (Peabody, MA: Hendrickson Publishers, 1995), series 1, vol. 2, p. 434. Translation modified. *Nicene and Post-Nicene Fathers* series 1 hereafter *NPNF1*.
[6] John Climacus, *The Ladder of Divine Ascent* 26, trans. C. Luibheid and N. Russell (New York: Paulist Press, 1982), p. 260.
[7] John of Damascus, *Exposition of the Orthodox Faith* 4.22, in *NPNF2*, vol. 9, p. 95.
[8] Bernard of Clairvaux, *On Conversion*, in Bernard of Clairvaux, *Selected Writings*, trans. G. R. Evans (New York: Paulist Press, 1987), p. 69.
[9] Aquinas, *De veritate*, q. 16, a. 1, co.
[10] Bonaventure, *The Soul's Journey into God* 1.6, in Bonaventure, *The Soul's Journey into God – The Tree of Life – The Life of St. Francis*, trans. E. Cousins (New Jersey: Paulist Press, 1978), p. 62.
[11] Jean Gerson, *On Mystical Theology* 1.14, in Jean Gerson, *Early Works*, trans. B. P. McGuire (New York: Paulist Press 1988), p. 279.
[12] John Calvin, *Institutes of the Christian Religion*, trans. H. Beveridge (Grand Rapids: Eerdmans Publishing Company, 1989), 4.10.3–5, pp. 415–16.

it is the 'highest judge that is or can be under God' (William Perkins);[13] it is eternal and 'always and internally directed to God' (Johann Arndt);[14] it is a 'little god in us' to do God's office (Richard Sibbes);[15] it 'is the highest sovereignty under Heaven' and 'God's most immediate deputy' (Robert Sanderson);[16] it is the 'aboriginal Vicar of Christ' (Cardinal J. H. Newman),[17] and 'the living and present message of the coming kingdom of God' (Karl Barth);[18] it is 'man's most secret core and sanctuary', where he is 'alone with God whose voice echoes in his depths' (*Gaudium et spes* 16), and so forth. We could continue this list as long as we like, but the point is already made: imagining Christianity without conscience is in effect impossible.

Church fathers between the law and the spirit

I

Although the conscience was seldom treated systematically in the writings of the Church Fathers, the Western understanding of it became, at least to a certain extent, established already at this point in late antiquity. How did they conceive it? For the Fathers, it should be noted first, the conscience (*syneidēsis/syneidos/conscientia*) did not always refer exclusively to moral conscience, but also to what we today call consciousness.[19] In both cases, however, the Fathers viewed the conscience as the most intimate and deepest part of the soul: 'To man anything more inward than conscience is not found', as Augustine wrote.[20] It is deeper than any sea, even an abyss (*abyssus humanae conscientiae*), absolutely hidden and impenetrable to others.[21] Yet even in its impenetrableness, it is wide open to God, who sees the depths of conscience. Conscience brings man into God's presence, laying him naked (*nuda*) before Him.[22] It

---

13 Perkins, *A Discourse of Conscience*, p. 32.

14 Johann Arndt, *True Christianity*, trans. P. Erb (New York: Paulist Press, 1978), p. 53.

15 Richard Sibbes, *Bowels Opened* (London: G. M. for George Edwards, 1639), p. 154.

16 Robert Sanderson, *Ad clerum*, in *XXXVI Sermons viz XVI ad aulam, VI ad clerum, VI ad magistratum, VIII ad populum*, ed. Isaac Walton (London: Tooke, Passenger & Sawbridge, 1686), p. 71.

17 John Henry Newman, 'A Letter Addressed to His Grace the Duke of Norfolk on Occasion of Mr. Gladstone's Recent Expostulation, Dec. 27, 1874,' in John Henry Newman, *Conscience, Consensus and the Development of Doctrine: Revolutionary Texts by John Henry Cardinal Newman*, ed. J. Gaffney (New York: Doubleday, 1992), p. 449.

18 Karl Barth, *Ethics*, trans. G. Bromiley (New York: The Seabury Press, 1981), p. 487.

19 The English 'consciousness' is a relatively late concept. It is Locke's neologism by means of which he wanted to make a difference between moral and non-moral conscience. Christian Wolff introduced this difference in German language by coining the term *Bewusstsein*. There have also been some attempts to coin a word for 'consciousness' in French as well. In his commentary on Locke's *Essay Concerning Human Understanding*, written in French, Leibniz tentatively translates Locke's 'consciousness' as *consciosité*.

20 Augustine, *Expositions on the Book of Psalms* 46.3, in *NPNF1*, vol. 8, p. 156.

21 Augustine, *Confessions* 10.2.2, in *NPNF1*, vol. 1, p. 320; see also Augustine, *Book of Psalms* 7.9, 11.3 and 77.17, in *NPNF1*, vol, 8, pp. 22, 41 and 365.

22 Ambrose, *Concerning Repentance* 2.11.103, in *NPNF2*, vol. 10, p. 358; see also Augustine, *Confessions* 10.2.2, in *NPNF1*, vol. 1, p. 320 and Augustine, *Lectures or Tractates on the Gospel according to St John* 1.7, in *NPNF1*, vol. 7, p. 9.

is in the nakedness of conscience that the Lord operates and addresses, punishes, loves and crowns a man.[23] In this nakedness the true value of man is revealed inasmuch as it is not his wealth or fame but the state of his conscience – whether pure or defiled by sin – that bears witness to it.[24] In this respect, recurrent points of biblical reference were 1 Timothy 1.5: 'the aim of our charge is love that issues from a pure heart and a good conscience [*ek ... syneidēseōs agathēs*] and sincere faith' and Titus 1.15: 'to the pure all things are pure, but to the corrupt [*memiammenois*] and unbelieving nothing is pure; their very minds [*nous*] and consciences [*syneidēsis*] are corrupted [*miainō*].'[25] God accepts pure conscience, but a conscience polluted by sin brings on a divine judgement. Therefore, it was essential that the conscience of a Christian always be pure: 'Let us cleanse our conscience, which is open to the eyes of God' (*purgemus igitur conscientiam, quae oculis Dei pervia est*), as Lactantius exhorts.[26] The clean conscience is the 'greatest festival' that a Christian could possibly experience, his glory and his gratification,[27] whilst the experience of defiled conscience is the most terrifying one, so terrifying that Origen and Ambrose made the fires of Hell to stand for the nightmares of the troubled conscience.[28] Time and again the Fathers returned to Paul's words (2 Cor. 1.12): 'For our boast is this, the testimony of our conscience [*to martyrion tēs syneidēseos hemōn*].'

Yet the absence of the sense of sin did not inevitably entail a pure conscience. John Climacus writes: 'We must carefully consider whether our conscience has ceased to accuse us, not as a result of purity, but because it is immersed in evil.'[29] It was not the absence of the sense of sin that testified to the acceptance of God, but the absence of sin from the abyss of conscience. Hence, the conscience was not a mere consciousness, not even that of sin. Rather, it was a notebook in which our sins are recorded for God to read and to judge at the end of the day. For Ambrose, Origen and Augustine,[30] this is the meaning of Revelation 20.12: 'And the dead were judged by what was written in the books, by what they had done.' It is not our actual consciousness of sin that saves or destroys us but the quality of the book of conscience or heart in which our sins are written as if on wax tablets:

> When we think either good or evil things, certain marks and signs are left behind in our heart as if on wax tablets, both for the good thoughts and for the bad. These marks, which now lie hidden in the breast, are said to be revealed on that day

---

[23] Augustine, *Book of Psalms* 45.27, in *NPNF1*, vol. 8, p. 154.

[24] Ambrose, *On the Duties of the Clergy* 1.12.44, in *NPNF2*, vol. 10, p. 8.

[25] In Bible translations I have consulted the Revised Standard Version.

[26] Lactantius, *The Divine Institutes* 6.24, in *Ante-Nicene Fathers*, ed. Philip Schaff (Peabody, MA: Hendrickson Publishers, 1994), vol. 7, p. 192. *Ante-Nicene Fathers* hereafter *ANF*.

[27] Chrysostom, *De Anna* 5.1, in *PL*, vol. 54, p. 669A.

[28] Origen, *De Principiis* 2.10.4, in *ANF*, vol. 4, p. 295; Ambrose, *On the Duties* 1.12.45, in *NPNF2*, vol. 10, p. 8.

[29] Climacus, *Ladder of Divine Ascent* 5, p. 130. Translation modified.

[30] See Ambrose, *Enarrationes in XII Psalmos Davidicos* 1.52, in *PL*, vol. 14, p. 994; see also Augustine, *City of God* 20.14, in *NPNF1*, vol. 2, p. 434.

[Judgement Day] by none other than him who alone is able to know the secrets of men.[31]

Thus it was not sufficient that a Christian had no sense of sin. On the contrary, it was necessary that he first acknowledged that essentially he is a sinner, that he accepted his sinfulness and, finally, sincerely repented. Before this procedure, he could not even hope to have a pure conscience. Quite often, to be sure, the Fathers maintained that the conscience is at work even in the utterly wicked, which is evident for instance in the fact that no one acts unjustly without inventing plausible excuses. Indeed, one of the most common arguments among the Fathers was that the wicked *must* suffer from bad conscience and thus be the unhappiest, even if they seem to be happy, enjoying wealth and good reputation.[32] In his commentary on the Sermon of the Mount, Augustine writes: 'There is no soul, however wicked, which can yet reason in any way, in whose conscience God does not speak.'[33] Yet the rule was that the pure conscience was not something one possessed as a matter of course where the sense of sin was absent, but something that must be earned through the acknowledgement and confession of sin ensued by sincere repentance. We should not glorify our conscience too eagerly, Augustine argues, since it easily paves the way to self-glorification, whereas a truly pure conscience glorifies God alone.[34] A good conscience may well prove to be a sign of pride, which is a grievous sin in itself.[35]

As to the metaphors associated with conscience, the Fathers described it as a guardian and a guide as well as a witness and a judge. As to its functions, it was said that it accuses and blames, reprehends and protests, condemns and disturbs, oppresses and torments, gnaws and pricks. It teaches and warns, it counsels and exhorts, being a sort of guardian angel who saves us from sin: 'Conscience [*syneidēsis*] reaches our innermost heart [*khardia kryptōs*] and keeps us from evil.'[36] It discerns good from evil and shows what is or is not to be done. It also gives joy, encourages, enlightens and heals.[37] Sometimes these descriptions were given in passing, sometimes with an intention to describe the entire phenomenon. One of the earliest comprehensive descriptions of conscience can be found in John Chrysostom's *De Lazaro* (4.4). According to Chrysostom, God has set in the mind of everyone a judge called conscience (*syneidos*). This judge is the most vigilant one in the world of humans – absolutely impartial, incorruptible and tireless:

> There is no judge, no judge at all among men as sleepless as our conscience. External judges are corrupted by money, influenced by flattery, and induced by fear to give false judgements; and many other factors spoil their upright decision.

---

[31] Origen, *Romans* 2.11.10, p. 134. See also Origen, *De Principiis* 2.10.4, in *ANF*, vol. 4, p. 295.
[32] Augustine, for instance, returns to this theme continuously in his sermons and elsewhere. See *Expositions on the Book of Psalms* 72 for a good illustration.
[33] Augustine, *Our Lord's Sermon on the Mount* 2.9.32, in *NPNF1*, vol. 6, p. 44.
[34] Augustine, *Book of Psalms* 149.7, in *NPNF1*, vol. 8, p. 679.
[35] See Gregory the Great, *Moralium Libri sive expositio in librum B. Job* 9.25.37, in *PL*, vol. 75, p. 878D.
[36] Anonymous, *Quaestiones in N.T.* 26, in *PG*, vol. 28, p. 717D. *Quaestiones* is included in *PG* among the works of Athanasius.
[37] See Philippe Delhaye, *The Christian Conscience* (New York: Desclee Company, 1968), pp. 90–2.

But the court of conscience [*syneidotos dikastērion*] cannot yield to any of these influences. Whether you give bribes, or flatter, or threaten, or do anything else, this court will bring forth a just judgement against your sinful intentions. He who commits sin himself condemns himself even if no one else accuses him. He does this not once only, or twice, but often, and continues through his whole life. Even if a long time passes, the conscience never forgets what has happened, but even during the commission of the sin, and before and after it is committed, the conscience stands against us as a vehement accuser.[38]

The primary task of this judge is to compel us to recognize and condemn our sins. In this assignment, Chrysostom continues, the conscience is not only sleepless but more loving than the most loving father. A father who has rebuked his child once or twice or even ten times, when he sees the child remaining uncorrected, gives up and disinherits him and cuts him off from the family, whilst conscience will not desist until one's last breath: 'In the house, in the streets, at table, in the marketplace, on the road, often even in our very dreams it sets before us the images and appearances of our sins.'[39] Our sins must be continuously exposed to ourselves, because such exposure is the condition that enables us to make ourselves better which is necessary because God will hereafter demand from us an account of our transgressions. Hence, in the last resort, the true function of conscience is to rescue us from the judgement to come. As Chrysostom summarizes:

So in order not to be chastised hereafter, in order not to undergo punishment hereafter, let each of us enter into his own conscience, unfold the storey of his life, examine all his transgressions accurately, condemn his soul which has committed such acts, correct his intentions [*logismos*], afflict and straiten his thoughts. Let him seek penalty for his sins by self-condemnation [*katagnōsis*], by complete repentance [*metanoia*], by tears, by confession, by fasting and almsgiving, by self-control and charity, so that in every way we may become able to put aside all our sins in this life and to depart to the next life with full confidence.[40]

For Chrysostom, confession and repentance in particular are paramount. Through the accusing conscience God wishes us to repent and to confess our sins to him, not only because he can thus deliver the punishment appropriate to our sins but also in order to forgive us. Confession treats the wound of conscience and relieves our pain, not once and for all, but regarding the wounds existing at a time, for the conscience never ceases to operate – and although it does not operate without interruption (this shows the wisdom of God, because if it did, we would 'expire from discouragement'), its operation is continual: 'Continual, so that we may not lapse into carelessness.'[41]

[38] John Chrysostom, *On Wealth and Poverty*, trans. C. Roth (Crestwood: St Vladimir's Seminary Press, 1984), p. 88.
[39] Ibid., p. 96.
[40] Ibid., p. 89.
[41] Ibid., p. 90.

II

Ethico-politically, the most influential and far-reaching point of reference in the patristic discourse of conscience was the following famous passage in the Romans (2.14–15) where Paul proclaims that even though Gentiles have no *nomos*, they are not ignorant of the law because it is written on their heart conscience bearing witness to it:

> When Gentiles who have not the law do by nature [*physis*] what the law requires, they are a law to themselves [*heautois eisin nomos*], even though they do not have the law. They show that what the law requires is written on their hearts, whilst their conscience also bears witness [*symmartyrousēs autōn tēs syneidēseōs*] and their conflicting thoughts accuse or perhaps excuse them.

Virtually all the Fathers believed in the existence of this everlasting and immutable law of nature given by God. It is not written but innate, made manifest within man as if it was flowing from natural spring, as Ambrose writes.[42] It is, says Cyril of Alexandria, the foundation of the Mosaic Law, which is merely its written manifestation.[43] Even iniquity does not erase it, according to Augustine.[44] It is one of the two ways to knowledge of God, the other being the starry heavens, as Chrysostom asserts – more than a thousand years before Kant.[45] Tertullian words it as follows:

> Before the Law of Moses, written in stone-tables, I contend that there was a law unwritten, which was understood naturally, and by the fathers was habitually kept. For whence was Noah 'found righteous,' if in his case the righteousness of a natural law [*naturalis legis justitia*] had not preceded? Whence was Abraham accounted 'a friend of God,' if not on the ground of equity and righteousness, in the observance of a natural law?[46]

At times this eternal and immutable law was established in reason and in mind, in which case the point of reference was usually Paul's words in the Romans 7.23 where it is said that the law of sin at work in his members wages war against the law of his mind (*tō nomō tou noos mou*). At other times it was written in the heart, but frequently also in conscience: 'Our conscience is the law of our mind' (*syneidēsis nomos tou noos hēmon*), as John of Damascus wrote.[47] Chrysostom had it as follows:

> All men have always had the natural law [*nomos physikos*] that dictated from within what is good and what is evil for when God created man, he placed in him this incorruptible judge: the judgement of conscience. The Jews received in

---

[42] Ambrose, *Epistolae Secunda Classis* 73, in *PL*, vol. 16, p. 1251.
[43] Cyril of Alexandria, *Contra Julianum* 3, in *PG*, vol. 76, p. 665AB.
[44] Augustine, *Confessions* 2.4.9, in *NPNF1*, vol. 1, p. 57.
[45] Chrysostom, *De Anna* 1.3, in *PG*, vol. 54, p. 636; see also Chrysostom, *Homilies on the Statutes* 12.4-9, in *NPNF1*, vol. 9, pp. 419–21.
[46] Tertullian, *An Answer to the Jews* 2, in *ANF*, vol. 3, p. 152. Translation modified.
[47] John of Damascus, *Exposition of the Orthodox Faith* 4.22, in *NPNF2*, vol. 9, p. 95.

addition the precious gift of the written law, but the whole human race had its essential in the law of conscience [*ton apo tou syneidotos nomon*].[48]

Furthermore, because everyone has this law in his breast and because he has a conscience by means of which this inner rule executes itself, he does not need external rules and regulations in order to lead his life well. By virtue of conscience, man is self-taught (*autodidaktos*) in moral matters, as Chrysostom continues,[49] which means, ultimately, that he is radically self-sufficient and free. After citing Romans 2.14, Chrysostom writes:

> For the conscience [*syneidos*] and reason [*logismos*] do suffice in the Law's stead. By this he [Paul] showed, first, that God made man self-sufficient [*autarkes*], so as to be able to choose virtue and to avoid vice. And be not surprised that he proves this point, not once or twice, but several times.[50]

II a

At present, there is no unanimity among the scholars as to whether the Pauline law of the heart echoes the Roman teaching of natural law. To the Fathers, however, this connection was usually self-evident. According to Lactantius, for instance, it is this law Cicero speaks about in his *Republic*. In his view, in fact, no one has described this divine law – the Pauline law of the heart – better than this pagan philosopher. Lactantius quotes Cicero at length:

> There is indeed a true law, right reason [*recta ratio*], agreeing with nature, diffused among all, unchanging, everlasting, which calls to duty by commanding, deters from wrong by forbidding; which, however, neither commands nor forbids the good in vain, nor affects the wicked by commanding or forbidding. It is not allowable to alter the provisions of this law, nor is it permitted us to modify it, nor can it be entirely abrogated. Nor, truly, can we be released from this law, either by the senate or by the people; nor is another person to be sought to explain or interpret it. Nor will there be one law at Rome and another at Athens; one law at the present time, and another hereafter: but the same law, everlasting and unchangeable, will bind all nations at all times; and there will be one common master and ruler of all, even God, the framer, arbitrator, and proposer of this law; and he who shall not obey this will flee from himself, and, despising the nature of man, will suffer the greatest punishments through this very thing, even though he shall have escaped the other punishments which are supposed to exist.[51]

Yet it is not only the Christian doctrine of natural law but also the Christian idea of conscience that owes much to the Roman authors, particularly to Cicero and Seneca,

---

[48] John Chrysostom, *Expositio in Psalmos* 147.3, in *PG*, vol. 55, p. 482C.

[49] John Chrysostom, *Homilies on the Statutes* 12.9, in *NPNF1*, vol. 9, p. 421.

[50] John Chrysostom, *Homilies on the Epistle of St Paul the Apostle to the Romans* 5, in *NPNF1*, vol. 11, p. 365. See also Ambrose, *Epistolae Prima Classis* 37, in *PL*, vol. 16, p. 1088C.

[51] Lactantius, *Divine Institutes* 6.8, in *ANF*, vol. 7, pp. 170–1. This passage from Cicero's *Republic* has survived thanks to Lactantius' quotation.

in whose writings the term 'conscience' (*conscientia*) appears more often than in the corpuses of any other non-Christian author in antiquity (seventy-seven times in Cicero, forty-nine times in the younger Seneca). In *Pro Cluentio*, for instance, Cicero asserts that the conscience (*conscientia*) is received from immortal gods, is implanted in the mind, is inalienable, and the best counsellor of all (*optimorum consiliorum*).[52] In *Ad Atticum*, he exhorts that every man is bound to follow the path of right conscience (*recta conscientia*),[53] and in *De legibus* he maintains that the torments of conscience (*angore conscientiae*) bear witness to natural law (*lex*) and natural justice (*ius*).[54] Analogously, Seneca holds that wrong-doers cannot escape punishment, because nature itself punishes them by the whip of conscience (*mala facinora conscientia flagellari*), whilst the fear of this same punishment is additional proof for the existence of natural law.[55]

Although *conscientia* was a significant notion to the Latin authors with Stoic persuasion, there is no evidence that either *syneidēsis* or *syneidos* would have been important notions for the Greek Stoics.[56] In Diogenes Laertius, we find Chrysippus' phrase in which he mentions *syneidēsis*.[57] Although the meaning of the term in the phrase is obscure, it undoubtedly excludes moral conscience. It can be found in Epictetus' fragment (97 Schweighaüser) as well, but this fragment is not considered authentic.[58] On the other hand, in his discourse on the true Cynic, Epictetus uses the Attic form (*syneidos*) of *syneidēsis* as follows:

> To the kings and tyrants of this world, their bodyguards and their arms give power
> to censure people and punish wrong-doers, even though evil themselves, but
> to Cynic, not arms or bodyguards, but his conscience [*syneidos*] gives him this
> authority [*exousia*].[59]

As to the metaphor of the heart (*kardia*), however, we must turn to Hebrew and Greek Stoic sources, as neither Cicero nor Seneca holds that natural law is written on the hearts of

---

[52] Marcus Tullius Cicero, *Pro Cluentio*, in *Cicero, the Speeches*, trans. H. G. Hodge (Cambridge, MA: Harvard University Press, 1927), 58.159, p. 396.

[53] Marcus Tullius Cicero, *Ad Atticum*, in *Cicero's Letters to Atticus in Three Volumes*, vol. 3, trans. E. O. Winstedt (Cambridge, MA: Harvard University Press, 1918), 13.20, p. 142.

[54] Marcus Tullius Cicero, *De legibus*, in *De re publica, De legibus*, trans. C. W. Keyes (Cambridge, MA: Harvard University Press, 1928), 1.35–40, pp. 334–40.

[55] Seneca, *Ad Lucilium*, *Epistula* 97 ('On the Degeneracy of the Age'), in Seneca, *Epistulae Morales with an English Translation in Three Volumes*, vol. 3, trans. R. M. Gummere (London: William Heinemann, 1962), pp. 12–15, 109–17. On Cicero's and Seneca's uses of *conscientia*, see G. Molenaar, 'Seneca's Use of the Term Conscientia,' *Mnemosyne* 22:2 (1969): 170–80.

[56] See Don. E. Marietta, 'Conscience in Greek Stoicism,' *Numen: International Review for the History of Religions* 17:3 (1970): 176–87.

[57] Diogenes Laertius, *Lives of Eminent Philosophers in Two Volumes*, vol. 2, trans. R. D. Hicks (London: William Heinemann, 1925), 7.85, p. 192.

[58] 'When we were children our parents handed us over to a nursery-slave [*paidagōgos*] who should watch over us everywhere lest harm befall us. But when we are grown up, God hands us over to the *syndeidēsis* implanted in us, to protect us. Let us not in any way despise its protection, for should we do so we shall be both ill-pleasing to God and have our own *syneidos* as an enemy.' Quoted and translated by C. A. Pierce, *Conscience in the New Testament* (London: SCM Press, 1955), p. 51.

[59] Epictetus, *The Discourses in Two Volumes*, vol. 2, trans. W. A. Oldfather (London: William Heinemann, 1928), 3.22.94–6, pp. 162–5. Translation modified.

men. Instead, the Greek Stoic doctrine of *hēgemonikon*, the governing part of the soul and a fragment of cosmic fire, resonates with the theme inasmuch as *hēgemonikon* is located in the heart. Many Christians, including Origen, indeed referred to the Stoic *hēgemonikon* as conscience. But Paul never uses the technical term *hēgemonikon* and it is most arguable that the theme of the heart in the Pauline letters rather echoes the vernacular use of the heart in the Greek (*phrēn, kardia*) and Latin (*cor*) languages, designating the seat of moral and religious feelings, than the Greek Stoic philosophical thinking. Moreover, the theme of the heart (*lēb*) is very common in the Hebrew Bible. The heart bears witness to good and evil, it condemns and exonerates: 'Your heart knows that many times you have yourself cursed others', as it is stated in Ecclesiastes (7.22). (In the Vulgate, Jerome translates 'heart' in this passage as *conscientia*: '*scit enim tua conscientia quia et tu crebro maledixisti aliis*'.) Likewise, Jeremiah (17.1) declares that sin is 'engraved on the tablet of their hearts' and Job (27.6) answers to his accusers 'My heart does not reproach me for any of my days.' Even the idea that the law is written on the heart and, more precisely, that it is possible to write the law on the heart can be found in many places, for instance Proverbs (2.1–15 and 3.1–3) and Ezekiel (11.19). In Jeremiah (31.33), we can similarly read: 'I will put my law within them, and I will write it on their hearts.' Yet there is no evidence in the Hebrew Bible that the law written on the heart would be written by nature. This implies that the Pauline expression, after all, owes mostly to Hellenistic culture.

III

Although the Fathers believed in the existence of natural law, this does not entail that they would have agreed with the Roman authors of Stoic persuasion in all aspects of this doctrine. The Roman natural law derived from nature itself, but the Fathers conceived it to be a creation of an omnipotent God beyond nature. As Origen wrote:

> This law has been inscribed by the one who created man in the beginning on the governing part of man's heart [*in principali cordis*] so that at the proper time, when the pages of that mind will have matured, or rather, as the Scripture has designated it, when the tablets of the fleshly heart should begin to be diffused in the inner workings of the conscience and to fill the mind with reason.[60]

The second difference concerned the status of natural law without faith and grace. The natural law is implanted in man's conscience, but it functions properly only if illuminated by the Holy Spirit through baptism and faith. Even if the conscience is a reliable guide, as Origen maintains, it is not much of a help without Spirit and faith. There exists what the Apostle Paul had called a spiritual law (Rom. 7.14) and a law of faith (Rom. 3.27), and they surpass natural law testified to by the conscience:

> However much the law of nature may offer testimony about good and evil according to the judgement of conscience, nevertheless it cannot be put on the

---

[60] Origen, *Romans* 5.6.3, p. 346. It is very likely that the *principali cordis* is Rufinus' translation of the *hēgemonikon* in Origen's original yet lost Greek version.

same level as the law of faith by which Abraham believed God and merited to be justified and to be named a friend of God.[61]

The difference between natural and spiritual conscience appears nowhere with the same clarity as in Augustine's refutation of Pelagius at the beginning of the fifth century. Augustine, too, believed that there is a an unchanging and stable order (*ordo*) of things called the cosmos, ruled by and flowed down from an eternal law of God in which man participates through the highest part of his soul on which this law is stamped (*quae impressa nobis est*) in the form of natural law.[62] In this highest part of the soul, the heart is the locus of natural law,[63] whilst the conscience is the means by which we become conscious of transgressions.[64] Yet Augustine was quite pessimistic about man's capacity to recognize the dictates of natural law. This pessimism which pertains to Augustine's conception of the ruinous effects of original sin did not remain unnoticed by Pelagius. It is not the original sin that we inherit from Adam, Pelagius argued against Augustine, but the innate capacity to make free choice between good and evil. This is the meaning of the phrase God created man in his own image: 'It is on this choice between two ways, on this freedom to choose either alternative, that the glory of the rational mind is based.'[65] Hence, even the capacity to do evil testifies to man's divine glory: 'To be able to do evil is good [*mala facere possumus bonum est*]', Pelagius maintains, 'because it makes the good part better by making it voluntary and independent, not bound by necessity but free to decide for itself.'[66] Of course, Pelagius did not argue that doing evil is good. He did not even maintain that avoidance of evil is easy, let alone doing what is good, for the habit of doing wrong has infected us from childhood. Yet it is not impossible either, because God has bestowed human nature not only with freedom of the will but also with the inner law and conscience:

> There is, I maintain, a sort of natural sanctity in our minds which, presiding as it were in the mind's citadel, administers judgement equally on the evil and the good and, just as it favours honourable and upright actions, so too condemns wrong deeds and, on the evidence of conscience, distinguishes the one side from the other by a kind of inner law.[67]

According to Pelagius, this inner law is the same law the Apostle Paul recalls in his Epistle to the Romans (2.14–16), the law written on the tablets of every heart (*tabulis*

---

[61] Origen, *Romans* 4.4.2, p. 253. Yet Origen also holds that once the law of faith (*nomos pisteōs*) or the spiritual law (*nomos pneumatikos*) is fulfilled by faith in God, the conscience does not cease to function, but is rather perfected by virtue of being governed by the Holy Spirit. According to Origen, in fact, the conscience becomes identical with it: 'In my opinion the conscience is identical with the spirit [*pneuma*].' Origen, *Romans* 2.9.3, p. 133.

[62] Augustine, *City of God* 19.13–14, in *NPNF1*, vol. 2, pp. 409–11.

[63] Augustine, *Confessions* 2.4, in *NPNF1*, vol. 1, p. 57.

[64] Augustine, *Our Lord's Sermon on the Mount* 2.9.32, in *NPNF1*, vol. 6, p. 44.

[65] Pelagius, 'To Demetrias,' in *The Letters of Pelagius and his Followers*, ed. B. R. Rees (Woodbridge: The Boydell Press, 1991), p. 38. Pelagius' letter to Demetrias (*Ep. ad Demetriadem*) is included in Migne's *Patrologia Latina* vol. 30 among works of Jerome.

[66] Pelagius, 'To Demetrias,' p. 38.

[67] Ibid., p. 40.

cordis),[68] whilst the conscience is like a court applying this law – though this court must be distinguished from the courts where the lawyers on opposing sides try to win the case by brilliant arguments, for the conscience rejects rhetoric and elaborate debates, seeking solely to know the truth of each and every situation.

It should be noted that there is no significant difference between Pelagius and the earlier teachings of the Fathers concerning the role of natural law and conscience. It is Augustine's pessimistic doctrine of man that appears to be a novelty. By the time he wrote Book X of his *Confessions* he had become convinced that the use of the free will cannot overcome the habit of sinning and in his later treatises, promulgated often against Pelagius and the so-called Pelagians, he began to hone his already existent pessimistic theory concerning man's natural capacities. In the human mind, he argues in *De Spiritu et littera*, there is but miserable darkness. Because we rely on our natural wisdom, we are prevented from perceiving the true wisdom of the Word.[69] Without doubt, Augustine still accepts that God had impressed the knowledge of good and evil, a spark of reason (*scintilla rationis*), in man's heart in the beginning. He also admits that this spark has not been utterly extinguished after the fall.[70] Yet this spark does not enable him to know good and evil by himself. At best, it enables him to be painfully aware of the loss suffered in the fall, making him thus capable of yearning for restitution. This very pain (*dolor*), in fact, is not only evidence of the good which has been forfeited, but also the only good which has been left: 'For, were nothing good left, there could be no pain on account of the good which had been lost.'[71]

This is not the whole truth, however. According to Augustine, the grace of God, infused in baptism and through faith, corrects the perverted natural conscience. In this respect, Augustine's interpretation of the Romans (2.14) in *The Spirit and Letter* is illuminating. In his reading, Augustine argues that the gentiles Paul is referring to in the Romans are those Christians in Rome who were already *converted* among the pagans.[72] In other words, Paul is not speaking about the gentiles in general, but of those gentiles whose nature is already reformed by the Spirit and grace through baptism and faith. They alone can do by nature what the law requires, for although Paul indeed says that gentiles do by nature (*physis*) what the law requires, this nature is not nature in its natural condition but nature infused by grace. Hence, without baptism and faith, there is no single conscience that could know the divine law of nature, let alone to follow it. With the help of Spirit, however, grace allows it to operate properly again so that it is able to tell right from wrong and good from evil. Grace restores the original right-eousness of conscience as the witness of natural law (*per gratiam reparata natura*),[73] which means that faith does not annul the law, but fulfils it, including the law of the

---

[68] Ibid.
[69] Augustine, *A Treatise on Nature and Grace* 47, in *NPNF1*, vol. 5, p. 137.
[70] Augustine, *City of God* 22.24, in *NPNF1*, vol. 2, p. 501; see also Augustine, *A Treatise on the Spirit and the Letter* 48, in *NPNF1*, vol. 5, p. 103.
[71] Augustine, *City of God* 19.13, in *NPNF1*, vol. 2, p. 409.
[72] Augustine, *Spirit and the Letter* 43–8, in *NPNF1*, vol. 5, pp. 101–3.
[73] Ibid. 47, in *NPNF1*, vol. 5, p. 103.

heart: 'The law is not made void [*exacuatur*], but is established [*statuitur*] through faith, since faith procures grace whereby the law is fulfilled.'[74] Through baptism and faith the conscience becomes the seat of God again.

Synderesis and conscientia: Scholasticism

I

In many respects, the medieval discourse on conscience followed the path delineated by the Fathers: conscience is the meeting place of God and man, the most secret sanctuary of man, the witness and the judge of natural law, perfect in Paradise but corrupted afterwards. If one listens to the voice of conscience, as Bernard of Clairvaux preached in 1140, one will learn the will and judgement of God, particularly when it comes to one's sins.[75] In *Summa Theologiae*, Thomas Aquinas concurs with this: 'God, in judging man, takes the sinner's conscience as his accuser' (*Deus in suo iudicio utitur conscientia peccantis quasi accusatore*).[76] Moreover, the medieval theologians agreed about Pelagius being erroneous when he claimed that Christians do not have a monopoly on virtue. According to the medievals, conscience does not operate properly unless it is regenerated by faith, infused by the Spirit, reformed by grace, and alike: conscience is 'implanted in us by nature, deformed by sin and reformed by grace', as Bonaventure put it in the thirteenth century.[77] This is not to say that there would have been no differences in the theological conception of conscience between Late Antiquity and the Middle Ages. For instance, the Scholastics no longer viewed the conscience primarily in terms of purity and impurity, seeking rather to establish what made it correct or erroneous. The reason for this is also quite evident. On the one hand, in Scholastic discourse the theme of law gained increasing importance, whereas the ancient idea of miasma receded into the background. On the other hand, although the Fathers had occasionally distinguished the Pauline law of the heart from conscience, this distinction remained by and large implicit and they were often spoken of as if they were interchangeable. The law of the heart is not only a law *for* the conscience, standing above it, but also the law *of* conscience, which implies that if the conscience is polluted, the pollution carries over to the law of the heart itself. In Scholasticism, notably in the writings of Aquinas, the distinction between conscience and the law of the heart becomes clear, because the conscience itself is divided into two: the *synderesis* and the *conscientia*. The *synderesis* corresponds to the law of the heart and the *conscientia* signifies the application of the precepts of this law in practice

---

74 Ibid. 52, in *NPNF1*, vol. 5, p. 106.
75 Bernard of Clairvaux, *On Conversion*, pp. 67–8.
76 Thomas Aquinas, *The Summa Theologica of St. Thomas Aquinas*, ed. Joseph Kenny (London: Burns Oates and Washbourne, 1920), IIa IIae, q. 67, a. 3, accessed 24 August 2012, http://www.newadvent.org/summa/
77 Bonaventure, *Soul's Journey into God* 1.6, p. 62.

– and whereas *conscientia* might become polluted ('erroneous'), *synderesis* is always pure and incorruptable.

Although the distinction between the *synderesis* and *conscientia* is medieval (it appears for the first time in Master Udo's commentary on Lombard's *Sentences*, written approximately in 1160–5), its textual origin can be traced back to Jerome's interpretation of the book of Ezekiel and especially the following passage (1.5–10):

> And from the midst of it came the likeness of four living creatures. And this was their appearance: they had the form of men, but each had four faces, and each of them had four wings. Their legs were straight, and the soles of their feet were like the sole of a calf's foot; and they sparkled like burnished bronze. Under their wings on their four sides they had human hands. And the four had their faces and their wings thus: their wings touched one another; they went every one straight forward, without turning as they went. As for the likeness of their faces, each had the face of a man in front; the four had the face of a lion on the right side, the four had the face of an ox on the left side, and the four had the face of an eagle at the back.

Jerome was not the first Christian to comment on the vision. It had enjoyed a high status already in the early Jewish mysticism (the so-called Merkavah mysticism).[78] As for Christianity, it became a central point of reference in the theology of Alexandrian Platonists, Origen being the first to give a comprehensive interpretation. Origen interpreted the four faces of the vision in terms of Plato's threefold division of the human soul: the man represents the rational soul (*logikon*), the lion the irascible emotions (*thymikon*) and the ox the concupiscent desires (*epithymētikon*). In addition to these three, however, there is a fourth element, the eagle, which does not have a counterpart in Plato. This fourth Origen described as an 'assisting power' (*boēthousan dynamin*), using the Stoic *hēgemonikon* (the ruling part of the soul situated in the heart) to clarify its meaning.[79] Both Ambrose and Jerome continued the tradition renaming, however, the face of the eagle. Ambrose used the term *to dioratikon* (*dioraō* = to see clearly),[80] whereas Jerome defined the eagle in terms of a *scintilla conscientiae* ('spark of conscience'), explaining that its meaning was identical to what certain (unidentified) Greeks had called *syntērēsis*, not put out even in the heart of Cain when he was driven from paradise:

> Some people interpret the man, the lion and the ox as the rational, emotional and appetitive parts of the soul, following Plato's division, who calls them the *logikon* and *thymikon* and *epithymētikon*, locating reason in the brain, emotion in the gall-bladder and appetite in the liver. And they posit a fourth part which is above and beyond these three, and which the Greeks call *syntērēsin*: that spark of conscience

---

[78] Merkavah mysticism flourished in the second century AD. The name Merkavah refers to an uncanny chariot seen by the prophet in a vision. On the movement, see Gershom Scholem, *Major Trends in Jewish Mysticism* (New York: Schocken Books, 1961), pp. 43–5.

[79] Origen, *Homiliae in Ezechielem* 1.16, in *PG*, vol. 13, p. 681b–c.

[80] Ambrose, *De Abraham Libri Duo* 2.8.54, in *PL*, vol. 14, p. 480a.

[*scintilla conscientiae*] which was not even extinguished in the breast of Cain after he was turned out of Paradise, and by which we discern that we sin [*nos peccatum sentimus*], when we are overcome by pleasures or frenzy and meanwhilst are misled by an imitation of reason. They reckon that this is, strictly speaking, the eagle, which is not mixed up with the other three, but correct them when they go wrong, and of which we read in Scripture as the spirit which 'intercedes for us with ineffable groaning' (Rom. 8.26).[81]

Characteristics of this ineradicable spark of conscience (*syntērēsis*) are, in other words, that it survived the fall, that it stands above all the other parts of the soul as the guardian, that it is non-discursive and ineffable (*inenarrabilis* – as Jerome translates Paul's word *alalēthos* in his quotation of the Romans 8.26), and that by it men discern when they sin.

The claim is sometimes made that there is no such word as *syntērēsis* in Jerome's original passage and that its appearance in the Scholastic corpus is due to a scribal error: the well-known *syneidēsis* (conscience) was accidentally copied as *syntērēsis*, which is a relatively uncommon word with an unclear meaning.[82] Be it as it may, it was this single citation of a Greek word in the year 415 that most profoundly influenced the later Christian conception of conscience, especially during the Middle Ages: it became the point of reference for the great majority of medieval authors dealing with the concept of conscience from Peter Lombard onwards. The most important reason for its influence was the fact that Lombard commented on it in his *Sentences* (1152), which became the basic textbook of theology in the era. Lombard, however, did not mention the term *syntērēsis*, or even *scintilla conscientiae*, but used the notion of 'spark of reason' (*superior scintilla rationis*).[83] In the meantime, Jerome's commentary on Ezekiel was incorporated in the *Glossa ordinaria*, which had become the basic text in biblical scholarship at the beginning of the century. Hence, theologians commenting on Lombard's *Sententiae* could pick up the original term from the *Glossa*.[84]

A modern reader may wonder why Lombard transformed the notion of *scintilla conscientiae* into *scintilla rationis*, but the reason is simple. In medieval theology, conscience was usually identified with reason, especially with practical reason. In this context, moreover, the most decisive expression is *scintilla*, expressing the highest capacities of the human mind nearest to divine nature. The meaning of *scintilla* as the image of God was established by Augustine in *The City of God* (*scintilla rationis*,

---

[81] Jerome, *In Ezekh.* 1.1.7, in *PG*, vol. 25, p. 22a–b. Cited and translated by Timothy C. Potts, *Conscience in Medieval Philosophy* (Cambridge: Cambridge University Press, 1980), p. 79. On the application of the Platonic division of the soul in the writings of Latin Church Fathers, see David N. Bell, 'The Tripartite Soul and the Image of God in the Latin Tradition,' *Rescherches de Théologie ancienne et medievale* 47 (1980): 16–52.

[82] On the lexical background of *syntērēsis*, see H. G. Stoker, *Das Gewissen* (Bonn: Verlag von Friedrich Cohen, 1925), pp. 25–30.

[83] Peter Lombard, *Sententiae in IV libris distinctae* (Grottaferrata: Collegium S. Bonaventurae ad Claras Aquas, 1971), lib. II, dist. 39. Hereafter *IV Sent.*

[84] On the reception of Jerome's Ezekiel commentary in the Middle Ages, see D. Odin Lottin, *Psychologie et morale aux XII et XIII siècles*, vol. 2 (Gembloux: J. Duculot, 1948), pp. 103–349. Lottin's *Psychologie* includes a comprehensive collection of Latin extracts related to the issues of *synderesis* and *conscientia* in the works of Scholastics from Lombard to Jean Gerson. See also Robert A. Greene, 'Synderesis, the Spark of Conscience, in the English Renaissance,' *Journal of the History of Ideas* 52:2 (1991): 195–219.

in qua factus est ad imaginem Dei).[85] This was also the immediate reference point of Lombard's *scintilla rationis*. It is not just reason but a higher reason distinct from and higher than the other three Platonic elements of the soul, as Master Udo says of *synderesis*, which became established as the Latinized version of the Greek word during the Middle Ages.[86] This *synderesis* is a special power of reason by which a man naturally hates what is evil, as Stephen Langton, Archbishop of Canterbury, put it a little later.[87] In the first Western treatise (1233) on the idea of conscience alone, Philip the Chancellor writes:

> For it is established that Adam [before the fall] was naturally righteous by virtue of his judgement, will and emotions: this righteousness was not completely taken away. Therefore, what remained can be called *synderesis*. For that of itself murmurs back against sin and correctly contemplates, and wants what is good as such.[88]

Certain exceptions aside, this idea was replicated by most of the Scholastics.[89] *Synderesis* is the uncorrupted part of the soul, the divine remnant of Adam's fall, which being incapable of error always tends towards good and away from evil in an infallible way.

This unanimity concerning the purity of *synderesis* does not mean that there would have been no disagreements regarding the finer points. One of the disputes concerned the locus of *synderesis*. Is it a part of reason or the will? Following Albert, Thomas Aquinas for one believed that the *synderesis* is located in reason as its highest part. Another disagreement raged over whether the *synderesis* should be classified as a disposition (*habitus*) or a potency (*potentia*). According to Aquinas, again, the *synderesis* is a disposition and, more precisely, an innate disposition. Hence, although Aquinas' psychology is otherwise mostly based on Aristotle's assumption in *De anima* (430a2), according to which the human mind is 'at first like a clean tablet on which nothing is written',[90] he asserted that this particular disposition is innate, and that it is this innate disposition that provides man with knowledge of universal principles of natural law. According to Aquinas, these immediately known principles are for practical reason as the first demonstrative principles are for theoretical reason:

> Just as there is a natural disposition [*habitus naturalis*] of the human soul by which it apprehends the principles of theoretical disciplines, which we call the understanding of principles, so too there is in the soul natural disposition of first principles of action, which are the universal principles of natural law [*universalia principia iuris naturalis*]. This disposition pertains to *synderesis*.[91]

---

[85] Augustine, *City of God* 22.24, in *NPNF1*, vol. 2, p. 502.

[86] '*Sinderesim ... id est superiorem rationem.*' Cited in Lottin, *Psychologie*, p. 107. According to Lottin, this is the first time that the term *synderesis/sinderesis* is employed in the Western tradition.

[87] Cited in ibid., p. 112.

[88] Cited in ibid., p. 147.

[89] On a detailed exposition, see ibid., pp. 103–349. One of the early Scholastics who rejected the idea that *synderesis* is infallible was William of Auvergne.

[90] Aquinas, *Summa Theologica*, Ia q. 79. a. 2.

[91] Aquinas, *De veritate*, q. 16, a. 1, co. See also *ST*, IIa Iae, q. 94, a. 1–2.

Franciscans, such as Philip the Chancellor, John de La Rochelle and Bonaventure, argued instead that the *synderesis* is located in the will. In his commentary on Lombard's *Sentences*, Bonaventure for instance emphasized that *synderesis*, being absolutely pure of sin, cannot be a part of reason, not even the higher part, because mortal sin (that of Adam) cannot occur without deliberation and hence without an actualization of the higher part of reason.[92] Therefore he established the *synderesis* in the will and the affective part of the soul, because 'sin does not occur in the act of will as it exists by nature or moves naturally but only as it moves deliberatively'.[93] Bonaventure went on to argue that the *synderesis* is not a disposition but rather a 'dispositional potency' (*potentia habitualis*), describing it as a sort of a natural weight (*pondus*)[94] that directs the will towards good and away from evil:

> Just as *conscientia* names that judicatory [a natural judicatory for the soul] only insofar as it directs us to moral actions, so *synderesis* names that weight of the will [*pondus voluntatis*], or the will with that weight only insofar as it inclines it to the morally honourable good.[95]

In spite of these differences of opinion, however, essentially all of the Scholastics were presupposed that such an innate, unerring and imperishable image of God does inhere in man's nature, no matter how morally corrupt a person might become: 'Its integrity cannot be violated even by demons', as Jean Gerson later wrote (1402).[96] Although the Scholastics rarely claimed that God speaks to man in the *synderesis* directly, it was nevertheless the means by which man participates in the divine order of things. The *synderesis* contains the basic precepts of natural law (*lex naturalis*) through which man participates in God's eternal law (*participatio legis aeternae in rationali creatura*), as Aquinas maintained.[97] The *synderesis*, Thomas continued, does not reach the heights of God but it ascends above mere human reality, coming 'near to something of what is proper to an angelic nature',[98] since angelic knowledge is 'midway between these two', that is, between God's immediate self-consciousness and the mediated human

---

[92] Bonaventure, 'Conscience and Synderesis,' in *The Cambridge Translations of Medieval Philosophical Texts, vol. 2: Ethics and Political Philosophy*, ed. A. S. McGrade, J. Kilcullen and M. Kempshall (Cambridge: Cambridge University Press, 2001), p. 198. Bonaventure's 'Conscience and Synderesis' is a translation of dist. 39, a. 1–2 in the second book of his commentary on Lombard's *Sentences*.

[93] Ibid., p. 197.

[94] The expression *conscientiae pondus* can be found already in Cicero's *De natura Deorum*: 'It is with reluctance that I enlarge upon this topic, since you may think that my discourse lends authority to sin; and you would be justified in so thinking, if the weight of conscience [*conscientiae pondus*], without any divine assistance, did not point out, in the clearest manner, the difference between virtue and vice. Without it everything collapses.' Marcus Tullius Cicero, *De Natura Deorum*, in Cicero, *De Natura Deorum and Academica with an English Translation*, trans. H. Rackham (London: William Heinemann, 1961), 3.35.85, p. 370. Translation modified.

[95] Bonaventure, 'Conscience and Synderesis,' p. 189. The source of Bonaventure's weight metaphor is Wisdom 11:20 where God is spoken of as arranging 'all things by measure and number and weight'.

[96] Jean Gerson, *Sermon on Saint Bernard*, in Gerson, *Early Works*, p. 144.

[97] Aquinas, *Summa Theologica* Ia IIae, q. 91, a. 2.

[98] Aquinas, *De veritate*, q. 16, a. 1, co.

consciousness of God.[99] Bonaventure, in his mystical treatise *Journey into God*, conceived the *synderesis* as the sixth and final stage in the mind's journey into God:

> Just as there are six stages in the ascent into God, there are six stages in the powers of the soul, through which we ascend from the lowest to the highest, from the exterior to the interior, from the temporal to the eternal. These are the senses [*sensus*], imagination [*imaginatio*], reason [*ratio*], understanding [*intellectus*], intelligence [*intelligentia*], and the summit of the mind [*apex mentis*] or the *synderesis scintilla*.[100]

In the last stage God is contemplated in His absolute goodness, whose essence it is to communicate itself in its fullness – after which comes the Sabbath of perfect ecstasy, in which all intellectual operations are suspended and the soul is wholly passive in its ineffable union with God.

I a

Although both Jerome's *scintilla conscientiae* and Augustine's *scintilla ratio* functioned as immediate reference points for Scholastic speculations concerning the *synderesis*, the spark as a metaphor for the divine part of the soul is not originally Christian. We find it already in Plato's *Seventh Letter* (341c–d) in which he describes philosophical knowledge of the absolute as follows:

> For this knowledge is not something that can be put into words like other sciences; but after long-continued intercourse between teacher and pupil, in joint pursuit of the subject, suddenly, like light flashing forth when a fire is kindled, it is born in the soul and straightway nourishes itself.

For Plato, in other words, the absolute reveals itself without words to the soul – especially to its highest part, called *nous*, which is beyond being (*ousia*), as he says in the *Republic* (505d–509b) – in the form of a sudden (*exaiphnēs*) intuition (*noēsis*), which is like a spark of fire. After Plato, the idea of divine spark resurfaces in the Stoic belief that the soul, especially the governing part of the soul (*hēgemonikon*) situated in the heart, is a fragment (*apospasma*) of cosmic fire (*pur*) called ether (*aither*),[101] although the Stoic conception owes more to Heraclitus' notion of cosmos as everliving fire kindling in measures than to Plato's speculations. It appears also in the Chaldean oracles, in pagan Neo-Platonism and in Gnosticism.[102] In the Gnostic tradition, the

---

[99] It must be conceded that Thomas is cautious to identify the *synderesis* with angelic knowledge (it only 'comes near' it), holding in addition that even an angel is not able to know God without the mediation of the concept (in contrast to man whose knowledge is after all mediated by his senses). See Aquinas, *Summa Theologica* Ia, q. 56, a. 3.

[100] Bonaventure, *The Soul's Journey into God*, 1.6, p. 62.

[101] Diogenes Laertius, *Lives of Eminent Philosophers*, 7.137–43, pp. 240–6. Diogenes (8.28) finds this idea also in Alexander Polyhistor's *Succession of Philosophers*, in which the latter is said to report that the Pythagoreans believed that the immortal 'soul is a fragment [*apospasma*] of ether'.

[102] On a detailed analysis of the historical background and development of the idea of the spark of the soul (*Seelenfünklein*) from Stoicism up to Meister Eckhart, see Heinrich Ebeling, *Meister Ekharts Mystik* (Stuttgart: W. Kohlhammer Verlag, 1941), pp. 212–347.

basic idea is that all humankind shares in the divine spark of God which is imprisoned in the body. The purpose of life is to enable the divine spark to be released from its captivity in matter and to re-establish its connection with or return to God, who is perceived as the source of this spark.[103]

In the Christian tradition, to my knowledge, the spark appears for the first time in Tatian's *Oratio ad Graecos*, written about AD 150. In this text Tatian interprets the beginning of John's Gospel, commenting on the condition of the human soul. According to Tatian, the soul is not, as the Greeks claimed, immortal as such but immersed in darkness. In the beginning, however, this was not the case, for the divine spirit was the soul's constant companion, only forsaking it when the soul was no longer willing to follow the spirit. Yet the soul retained a 'spark [*enausma*] of its power', which becomes manifest in its ability to seek the true spirit of God.[104] Since *Oration*, the metaphor occurs frequently in Christian literature. However, unlike Tatian, the early Church Fathers, such as Irenaeus and Tertullian, employed it in the critical context of denouncing Gnostic heresy. After Tatian, perhaps the first Christian who bestowed the metaphor of spark with a positive meaning was the Alexandrian Platonist Clement. In *Stromata*, he writes: 'Many things in life take their rise in some exercise of human reason, having received the kindling spark from God.'[105] If Clement's phrasing is still quite Platonic, in Origen's *De Principiis* we find a formulation that comes pretty close to Gnostic one. According to Origen, the soul which in the fall had 'waxed cold' from 'participation in the divine fire' has 'not lost the power of restoring itself to that condition of fervour in which it was at the beginning'.[106] Yet neither Clement nor Origen associates the spark with conscience, although they exalt conscience in other respects: it is the true pedagogue of the soul, absolutely holy and of divine origin.

II

Scholastics believed in the existence of an uncorrupted part of the soul, *synderesis*, in post-lapsarian man. This is that light of natural reason, as Aquinas writes, whereby we distinguish good and evil, which is the function of natural law, impressed upon us by the divine light.[107] In this mysterious *synderesis* we find absolute knowledge of good and evil, knowledge that cannot be extinguished, not even by demons – and many Scholastics believed that it is not extinguished even *from* demons.[108] I say mysterious, on the one hand, because the *synderesis* apprehends truth without inquiry, yet without telling us which particular act is good, as it merely forces us to recognize the difference between good and evil. On the other hand, the Scholastics, although admitting the existence of this absolute knowledge inscribed in the *synderesis*, nonetheless thought

---

[103] On the Gnostic idea of the spark, see Kurt Rudolph, *Gnosis: The Nature and History of Gnosticism* (San Francisco: Harper Collins, 1987), pp. 57–87.
[104] Tatian, *Addresses to the Greeks* 13.1, in *ANF*, vol. 2, pp. 70–1.
[105] Clement of Alexandria, *Stromata, or Miscellanies* 6.17, in *ANF*, vol. 2, p. 517.
[106] Origen, *De Principiis* 2.8.3, in *ANF*, vol. 4, p. 288.
[107] Aquinas, *Summa Theologica* Ia IIae, q. 91, a. 2.
[108] See Lottin, *Pscyhologie*, pp. 22, 159, 177–8.

that man is not necessarily aware of it. The *synderesis* did not designate as much an experience of conscience as an unspoiled and unerring disposition (Aquinas) or dispositional potentiality (Bonaventure) present in the nature of man. True, the Scholastics generally repeated Jerome's assertion that the spark of conscience murmurs against sin, which was the very proof that such a spark was left burning in Adam after the fall – he regretted the consequences of his transgression. Yet it was the conscience as *conscientia* rather than *synderesis* that designated the conscious experience of it, that is, the conscience that binds, incites, warns, accuses, torments, rebukes and so on.[109] This conscience did not have the purity of *synderesis* and none of the Scholastics ever claimed that *conscientia* was infallible. Compared to *synderesis*, it was a second-rate concept: '*Conscientia* is not the first rule of human acts, *synderesis* is.'[110]

This was the opinion of Aquinas in particular, who understood *conscientia* as an act of application of knowledge (*scientia*) to some special act, insofar as this knowledge concerns those general practical principles of natural law contained in the *synderesis*. The conscience was thus subjected to *synderesis* as a 'rule under a rule' (*regula regulata*).[111] Moreover, Thomas held, like virtually all the Scholastics, that *conscientia* may be erroneous. In Aquinas' view, the error of conscience can arise in two ways: 'In one way, because that which is applied contains an error in itself, in another way in this that it is not correctly applied.'[112] Hence, a person's *conscientia* is erroneous, for instance, if it accuses him even though he has not acted against the right principles of *synderesis* but merely thinks so. It may also be erroneous if one's *conscientia* approves a particular act that is contrary to the principles of *synderesis* though the person in question correctly contemplates the right principles of *synderesis*. Bonaventure formulates the same idea in less-technical terms:

> Although the act of *synderesis* cannot be entirely taken away or extinguished, it can nevertheless be impeded temporarily, by the darkness of blindness, the wantonness of pleasure, or the hardness of obstinacy.[113]

This is why all the Scholastics thought – regardless of their sometimes different views of the actual nature of the *conscientia* – that it has to be rightly informed and properly associated with the principles of *synderesis*. Respectively, the allocation of this information was seen as the duty of the church, inquisition being the harshest form, whereas pastoral direction of consciences was undoubtedly the most common.

---

[109] When Aquinas, for instance, refers to *conscientia* as an act (*actus*) by which the principles of *synderesis* are applied in particular case, he means such mental acts that we would nowadays call experiences of conscience. Aquinas mentions such acts of conscience as to bind, to incite, to accuse, to torment and to rebuke. See *Summa Theologica* Ia, q. 79, a. 13.

[110] Thomas Aquinas, 'On Conscience,' in Thomas Aquinas, *Selected Writings*, ed. R. McInerny (London: Penguin Books, 1998), p. 228. 'On Conscience' is a translation of *De veritate*, q. 17.

[111] Ibid., p. 228.

[112] Ibid., p. 226.

[113] Bonaventure, 'Conscience and Synderesis,' p. 193.

II a

As we know, pastoral examination, direction and education of consciences was one of the principal tasks of the church in medieval Catholicism. We also know that the Christians did not invent the examination of conscience: many pagan philosophers from Pythagoras to Marcus Aurelius had exercised it.[114] Moreover, it is not a secret that this was established as a regular practice in Christianity almost from the beginning. Unlike in philosophy, however, the initial impetus for the examination of conscience, which was first mainly self-examination, did not arise in Christianity from the desire to live in perfect harmony with (divine) reason but rather from the demand to have a pure conscience when engaging in religious rituals, such as the Eucharist. In quantitative terms, it seems to be in this context that the very word 'conscience' appears most frequently in the patristic writings. Yet although the practice of the examination of conscience was introduced very early (according to a manuscript attributed to Athanasius, Anthony the Hermit, born about the middle of the third century, examined his conscience every day),[115] it usually concerned the divines and monks alone. Moreover, although in monasteries the examination of conscience by another person was also introduced relatively early, it was rare elsewhere before the sixth century, that is to say, before the Celtic monastic movement extended the practice of recurrent private confession to apply also to the local Christian laypeople. Since then, regular and even obligatory confession became increasingly a rule, not only on the Isles but on the Continent as well.[116] Yet the practice of a regular obligatory confession for the laypeople was not established by a papal degree before the IV Lateran Council in 1215. Degree 21 of the IV Lateran begins as follows:

> On reaching the age of discernment, everyone of the faithful, of either sex, is faithfully at least once a year to confess his sin in private to his own priest, and is to take care to fulfil according to his abilities the penance enjoined on him, [otherwise] he is to be barred from entering the church in his lifetime and to be deprived of Christian burial at his death.[117]

According to the Council, this degree had to be published in every Church to prevent anyone from appealing to blindness of ignorance. The task of the priest was in turn to 'carefully inquire about the circumstances of both the sinner and the sin, so that he may prudently discern what sort of advice he ought to give and what remedy to apply, using various means to heal the sick person'.[118] Starting from the IV Lateran, it gradually became an uncontested truth among Catholics that the consciences of all men must be examined, directed and educated by the authorities of the church. Thus although the Scholastics stressed that there is a *synderesis* within man, the authorities

---

[114] On this see Michel Foucault, *The Hermeneutics of the Subject*, trans. G. Burchell (New York: Picador, 2006).

[115] In his cell, Anthony was 'daily a witness to his conscience [*martyrōn tē syneidēsei*].' Athanasius, *Life of Antony* 47, in *NPNF2*, vol. 4, p. 209. Translation modified.

[116] See John Mahoney, *The Making of Moral Theology* (Oxford: The Clarendon Press, 1987), pp. 5–17.

[117] Cited in Ibid., p. 17.

[118] Ibid., p. 18.

of the church (including the Scholastics themselves) were convinced that not every man is able to apply the infallible precepts of *synderesis* correctly. Therefore, people's consciences must be directed and educated: 'It is not enough in conscience for a man to judge by himself whether his actions are good or bad. In cases of doubt he must rely on the opinion of those authorized to resolve such doubts',[119] as Francisco Vitoria wrote in 1539, when pastoral direction of conscience had already been firmly established in Catholic practice. Hence, in the medieval Catholic tradition, the church stood between the *synderesis* and the *conscientia*, mediating the truth of the former for the latter – as it still stands today, at least if we are to believe Pope Benedictus XVI, according to whom the pope is the 'advocate of the Christian memory' of the good contained in the depths of the ontological conscience.[120]

III

Although the Scholastics considered *conscientia* as a second-rate concept, virtually all agreed that it is a sin to act against it. This idea relates to the interpretative tradition of the famous Pauline statement in Romans (14.23), according to which 'all that is not of faith is sin'. Clement of Alexandria had understood this statement in Aristotelian–Stoic terms ('everything that is contrary to *orthos logos* is sin'),[121] but it was not the Clementian formulation that the Scholastics usually adopted but rather the formulation of Anselm of Laon from the beginning of the twelfth century, offered in his commentary on the Scripture, *Glossa Interlinaeris*. In the *Glossa*, Anselm equates faith with conscience: against faith means against conscience.[122] A little later, Gratian made the same equation in his *Decretum*, declaring that everything done against conscience paved the way to hell ('*omne quod contra conscientiam fit, aedificat ad gehennam*'),[123] whilst Peter Lombard in his *Sentences* states: '*quod fit contra fidem, id est conscientiam*'.[124] As already said, practically all the Scholastics adopted this equation. Yet there was no absolute unanimity amongst them concerning the interpretation of this dictum. The majority of the schoolmen usually followed Augustine's doctrine, according to which the command of a subordinate authority is not binding if it runs counter to the command of a superior authority. The duty to disregard an erroneous conscience, contradicting the command of a superior – as Alexander of Hales, the first medieval Aristotelian Scholastic, explained – is more binding than the duty not to act against conscience.[125] This was the opinion of Bonaventure as well.

---

[119] Francisco Vitoria, *On the American Indians*, in *Vitoria: Political Writings*, ed. A. Pagden and J. Lawrence (Cambridge: Cambridge University Press, 1991), p. 236.

[120] Ratzinger, 'Conscience and Truth,' p. 36.

[121] Cited in Johannes Stelzenberger's, *Syneidesis, conscientia, Gewissen* (Paderborn: Ferdinand Schöningh, 1963), p. 100.

[122] See Eric D'Arcy, *Conscience and its Right to Freedom* (London: Sheed & Ward, 1961), p. 77.

[123] *Decretum magistri Gratiani*, Decreti Pars Secunda, Causa 28, q. 1, c. 14, accessed 24 August 2012, http://geschichte.digitale-sammlungen.de/decretum-gratiani/online/angebot

[124] Lombard, *IV Sent.*, dist. 39, c. 6.

[125] See D'Arcy, *Conscience*, pp. 77–9.

Although it is always a mortal sin to act against conscience, even if it is erroneous,[126] conscience cannot oblige us to act against the command of a superior: 'One ought to comply more with the command of a superior than with conscience, especially when superiors command what they can and ought to command.'[127] Also, Bonaventure's solution to this paradox is traditional: if conscience errs and dictates contrary to the command of a superior, one is obliged not to act against conscience, but to set it aside. Then one must 'consult those who are wiser, or, if human counsel is lacking, turn to God in prayer.'[128]

Although the majority of the schoolmen agreed with Alexander and Bonaventure, there were some who did not. Among them was Thomas Aquinas, according to whom conscience is always binding (a correct conscience binds per se, whereas an erroneous conscience binds accidentally, that is to say, as long as it endures), and its binding force is greater than the binding force of the command of a superior ('prelate').[129] Thomas's conclusion relates to his understanding of the relationship between conscience and truth. He admits that objectively speaking a conscience can be erroneous, but when it comes to the subject, the conscience never lies, for whatever it dictates, it dictates as true. Now, insofar as all truth is from God, even if it is held to be true erroneously, it binds more than the command of the prelate, because God is greater than the prelate.[130] Conscience is 'the arrival of the precept of God to the one whose conscience it is,'[131] and therefore conscience rather than the command of the prelate must be obeyed. This is not to say, of course, that God is not greater than conscience and inasmuch as God is greater it naturally follows that it is a duty of conscience to submit itself to the law of God. Yet whereas Bonaventure had argued that the divine law obligates one to set aside erroneous conscience, Aquinas remarks that the divine law obligates only if one *knows* the divine law: 'No one is bound by a precept except through knowledge of the precept.'[132] Hence, if the human conscience apprehends that to believe in Christ is evil, it is also evil, which means that it is evil and against the law of God to believe in Christ contrary to reason and conscience, which, for Thomas, is the judgement of reason: 'One who transgresses' the dictates of the erroneous conscience is 'effectively a transgressor of the law of God.'[133] However, although the erroneous conscience is binding, it does not follow that it is not erroneous. It is indeed erroneous, and furthermore, to follow one's erroneous conscience does not necessarily exonerate one from having sinned. For although Aquinas holds that no one is bound by a precept except through knowledge of the precept, he nonetheless maintains that there also is inexcusable ignorance, namely ignorance of those self-evident moral principles of Divine Law written in the *synderesis* and revealed in the Scripture. Aquinas calls this ignorance voluntary and continues that an error arising from ignorance of a

---

[126] Bonaventure, 'Conscience and Synderesis,' pp. 182–3.
[127] Ibid., p. 185.
[128] Ibid.
[129] Aquinas, 'On Conscience,' pp. 231–8.
[130] Aquinas, *Summa Theologica*, Ia IIae, q. 19, a. 5; Aquinas, 'On Conscience,' pp. 237–8.
[131] Aquinas, 'On Conscience,' p. 235.
[132] Ibid., p. 230.
[133] Ibid., p. 235.

circumstance alone is involuntary and therefore excusable.[134] We may wonder why the ignorance of the Divine Law is inevitably voluntary, but what is essential here is that none of the Scholastics, even though they believed that it was a mortal sin to act against conscience, held that conscience (*conscientia*) was incapable of error or that to act according to the dictates of conscience was necessarily virtuous.

III a

In his lectures on Plato's *Sophist* in winter semester 1924, Martin Heidegger translated Aristotle's *phronesis* as *Gewissen*. In his recollection of these lectures, which dealt with Aristotle's practical philosophy rather than Plato, Hans-Georg Gadamer, mentioning particularly Heidegger's analysis of *phronesis*, talks of how Heidegger liberated Aristotle 'profoundly and strikingly from the sedimentations of the Scholastic tradition'.[135] This may be true. Yet there is nothing strikingly anti-Scholastic to translate *phronesis* as conscience. As a specialist in Scholastic theology, Heidegger himself certainly knew that Aquinas translates *phronesis* as conscience and more precisely as *synderesis* in his *Summa Theologiae*. Referring to *Nicomachean Ethics* (1140b31–41a8), where Aristotle says that *phronesis* is 'a truth-attaining rational disposition [*hexis*], concerned with action in relation to things that are good and bad for human beings', Thomas equates *phronesis* with *synderesis*, translating *hexis* as *habitus*: 'The first practical principles, bestowed on us by nature, do not belong to a special power, but to a special natural habit, which we call *synderesis*'.[136] Thus, *phronesis* is ontological conscience already for Aquinas. In Thomas's discussion on *conscientia* in *Summa*, however, there is no allusion to an Aristotelian equivalent, but in his commentary on *Nicomachean Ethics* (1143a5–10) we find a notion that perfectly fits in Aquinas' definition of *conscientia*. This notion is *synesis*:

> *Synesis* does not deal with the things that exist for ever and are immutable, nor yet with all of the things that come into existence, but with those about which one may be in doubt and may deliberate. Hence it is concerned with the same objects as *phronesis*. *Synesis* is not however the same thing as *phronesis*, for *phronesis* issues commands, since its end is a statement of what we ought to do or not to do, whereas *synesis* merely makes judgements.

In his interpretation of this passage, Aquinas does not mention *conscientia*, but his definition of Aristotle's *synesis* is the same as his definition of *conscientia* in *Summa* and elsewhere. In the same way as *conscientia*, which is an act of judgement applying the principles of *synderesis*, also *synesis*, Aquinas writes, 'makes a judgement' using the intellectual habit of *phronesis*. Moreover, exactly like the *synderesis* with regard to *conscientia*, the intellectual habit of *phronesis* is 'more excellent than *synesis*'.[137]

---

[134] See Aquinas, *Summa Theologica*, Ia IIae, q. 19, a. 6.

[135] Cited in Stuart Elden, *Speaking against Number: Heidegger, Language and the Politics of Calculation* (Edinburgh: Edinburgh University Press, 2006), p. 55.

[136] Aquinas, *Summa Theologica*, Ia q. 79, a. 12.

[137] Thomas Aquinas, *Commentary on Aristotle's Nicomachean Ethics*, trans. C. J. Litzinger (Notre Dame: Dumb Ox Books, 1964), pp. 371, 391–2.

Divine instinct

The Scholastics did not consider the *synderesis* only as the apex of the mind placed above reason and will and containing the immutable principles of morality, but sometimes also as an instinct (*instinctus*). *Synderesis* is the 'virginal part of the soul' but it is also an 'ineradicable instinct' (*instinctus indelebilis*), according to Jean Gerson.[138] Strictly speaking, the textual genealogy of this natural instinct is not the same as the history of *synderesis*, the origin of which lies, as already noted, in Jerome's commentary on the book of Ezekiel. The history of the natural instinct can rather be traced back to Cicero's *De inventione*,[139] but especially to Ulpian's definition of the natural law in Justinian *Digest*, interpreted as 'natural instinct' (*instinctus naturae*) by Isidore of Seville in the seventh century. In *Digest*, Ulpian defines natural law as follows:

> *Jus naturale* is that which nature has taught to all animals; for it is not a law specific to mankind but is common to all animals – land animals, sea animals, and the birds as well. Out of this comes the union of man and woman which we call marriage, and the procreation of children, and their rearing.[140]

In his commentary on *Digest*, Isidore says that this law is universally held by the instinct of nature, not 'because of any enactment'.[141] With the discovery of a surviving manuscript of the *Digest* in 1070 and the reiteration and extension of Isidore's definition of natural law by Gratian in the *Decretum Gratiani* of 1140, the stage was set for the extensive series of commentaries by glossators and commentators that followed.[142] Gratian himself started his *Decretum* by quoting Isidore: 'The human race is ruled by two things, namely by natural law [*naturali iure*] and by usages [*moribus*]',[143] where 'usages' refers both to customary and written law. Gratian then continues that this natural law originates in the creation of rational being and that it is also contained in the Law and the Gospel – although he simultaneously indicates that not everything contained in the Scriptures constitutes natural law. Finally, Gratian raises this law above positive and customary law, stating that 'whatever has been recognised by custom, or laid down in writing, if it contradicts natural law, must be considered null and void'.[144]

---

[138] Gerson, *On Mystical Theology* 1.14, p. 280.

[139] 'The law of nature [*naturae ius*] is that which is not born of opinion, but implanted in us by a kind of innate instinct [*in natura vis insevit*].' Marcus Tullius Cicero, *De inventione*, in Cicero, *De invetione, De optimo genere oratorum, Topica with an English Translation*, trans. H. H. Hubbell (London: William Heinemann, 1960), 2.161, p. 329.

[140] *The Digest of Justinian* 1.1.1.3, ed. A. Watson, T. Mommsen and P. Krueger (Philadelphia: University of Pennsylvania Press, 1985), p. 4.

[141] Isidore of Seville, *The Etymologies of Isidore of Seville*, trans. S. Barney et al. (Cambridge: Cambridge University Press, 2006), 5.4, p. 117.

[142] See Robert A. Greene, 'Natural law, Synderesis, and the Moral Sense', *Journal of the History of Ideas* 58:2 (1997): 177.

[143] Gratian, *The Treatise on Laws*, in Gratian, *The Treatise on Laws with the Ordinary Gloss* (Decretum DD. 1–20), trans. J. Gordley (Washington, DC: Catholic University of America Press, 1994), 1.1, p. 3.

[144] Ibid., 8.11, p. 25.

Yet although Gratian, unlike Ulpian, clearly distinguishes the natural law of animals (the law of self-preservation and procreation) from the natural law of rational creatures (the moral law of good and evil), he did not solve the question as to on what grounds the distinction between the natural law common to all creatures and the natural law specific to man was to be made – the urgency of which stemmed from the fear that their inseparability would open the door to pantheism: if instinctual nature is the foundation of natural law which is same for all creatures, and natural law is of divine origin, then instinctual nature, nature tout court, is divine.[145] One solution to this problem was presented by a distinction that became famous later through Spinoza's *Ethics*, namely the distinction between 'creative nature' (*natura naturans*, sometimes also called *summa natura*), and 'created nature' (*natura naturata*). The idea of God as a creative nature (*summa natura*) was at least as old as Augustine (in fact, we find the expression *summa natura* in Cicero's *De legibus*, in which it refers to the natural law of divine origin),[146] but the particular terms had their origin in the first Latin translations of Averroes' commentaries on Aristotle. Especially such thirteenth-century civilian lawyers as Azo of Bologna, Accursius (the author of *Glossa ordinaria* for Justinian's *Corpus*) and Henry of Bracton (the author of *De Legibus et Consuetudinibus Angliae*) interpreted natural law to mean something that *natura naturans* (God) has implanted in man's mind (like the Scholastic *synderesis*) in the form of a natural instinct, distinguished from the *natura naturata* which defines the state of animals and man's state of corruption.[147] (For example, in *Glossa ordinaria* for Gratian's *Decretum*, the writer Johannes Teutonicus says that the natural law of men is based on an 'instinct proceeding from reason'.)[148] In principle, the *natura naturata* also originates from God (*Nature, id est Deus*, as Bracton wrote in *De Legibus*!),[149] but only the natural law peculiar to man is based on a 'divine' instinct, whereas the natural law common to all animals is based on evil instincts, equivalent to the Apostle Paul's 'other law in my members' (Rom. 7.23). (The 'evil' sense adhering to natural instincts can be traced back to Hilary of Poitiers, who in c. 350 argued in this Commentary on the Psalms that men are urged by an *instinctus naturae* to succumb to vices such as pride, greed, drunkenness, hypocrisy and lying. In *Contra Julianum*, Augustine quoted Hilary's argument as evidence of the church's teaching, against the Pelagians, arguing that human nature was 'vitiated by the transgression of the first man'.)[150] Yet, as already mentioned, also the 'divine' part of the natural law was defined as an *instinct*. William of Gascoigne, for instance, asserted in his treatise (1203–8) that natural law is an 'instinct of human nature', adding that its discovery arises from a 'contemplation of a

[145] See Brian Tierney, 'Natura id est Deus: A Case of Juristic Pantheism', *Journal of the History of Ideas* 24:3 (1963): 310.

[146] '*Lex est ratio summa insita in natura*.' Cicero, *De legibus*, 1.18, p. 316.

[147] See Greene, 'Natural Law', pp. 177–8.

[148] Gratian, *Ordinary Gloss*, in Gratian, *The Treatise on Laws*, 1.2.CC.6–7, p. 6.

[149] 'Ius naturale est quod natura, id est ipse deus, docuit omnia animalia.' Henry of Bracton, *De Legibus et Consuetudinibus Angliae*, ed. G. Woodbine (New Haven: Yale University Press, 1922), p. 26.

[150] Augustine, *Against Julian*, trans. M. Schumacher (Washington: The Catholic University of America Press, 2004), 2.8.28, p. 90.

unique sort'.[151] In the subsequent discussions by the canonists, natural law was as a rule associated with a natural instinct of this kind, differentiated from the animal instinct by emphasizing its connection to the 'divine' parts of man's soul, such as reason. And although some authors had rejected the notion of *instinctus*, notably Rufinus in his *Summa* (1157–9), even the latter refers to a 'natural force which had not been extinguished' after the fall and to 'sparks of justice', equating them with 'moral precepts of decent and honourable behaviour'.[152]

Thus there was nothing extraordinary in Gerson's definition of *synderesis* as an 'ineradicable instinct', which he had earlier in *Mystical Theology* described as follows:

> *Synderesis* is an appetitive power of the soul that comes immediately from God. It takes on a certain natural inclination to the good. Through this proclivity it is drawn to follow the moment of the good on the basis of the understanding presented to it in the simple intelligence.[153]

But Gerson was not the only Scholastic to define *synderesis* as an instinct. In the case of Bonaventure, for instance, the instinctual nature of *synderesis* is at least implicitly present, given the fact that it operates in the sphere of man's affective and emotional life, being a natural weight that directs man to good and away from evil without deliberation. Moreover, it would be a mistake to assume that Aquinas' intellectual *synderesis* had nothing to do with instincts. Although he is generally careful to identify natural instinctu and the intellect as opposites, in the case of *synderesis*, even though located in reason, this opposition is far from obvious: *synderesis* apprehends moral truth immediately without deliberation and examination (*sine inquisitione et discursu*).[154] And although he does not directly associate *synderesis* with *instinctus naturae*, he frequently associates the latter with natural law, the precepts of which were, as we remember, inscribed in the natural habit of *synderesis*. In *Summa contra Gentiles*, he writes:

> Now, laws that are established should stem from the instinct of nature [*ex naturali instinctu*], if they are human: just as in the demonstrative sciences, also, every human discovery takes its origin from naturally known principles. But, if they are divine laws, they not only express [*explicant*] the instinct of nature but also supplement [*supplent*] the deficiency of natural instinct, as things that are divinely revealed surpass the capacity of human reason.[155]

All in all, it seems that the entire medieval discourse on *synderesis* and natural law revolved around the idea of (rational) instinct rather than discursive reason. Hence, although the Scholastics turned to Aristotle in order to rationalize Christian theology and ethics, the ultimate authority of morality remained instinctual, ineffable and

---

[151] Cited in Greene, 'Natural Law,' p. 180.
[152] Cited in ibid., p. 178.
[153] Gerson, *On Mystical Theology* 1.14, p. 279.
[154] Aquinas, *De veritate*, q. 16, a. 1.
[155] Thomas Aquinas, *Summa contra Gentiles* (New York: Hanover House, 1955–7), 3.123, accessed 24 August 2012, http://dhspriory.org/thomas/ContraGentiles.htm. Translation modified.

heteronomous. According to the canonists and the Scholastics alike, there is within man a natural instinctual foundation of morality, separate from and above not only animal instincts (*natura naturata*) but discursive reason as well. It is the instinct, the 'instinct of conscience' (*instinctus conscientie*), as Albert the Great put it in *Summa de bono*,[156] that connects man to divine wisdom – to wisdom that cannot be communicated ('no one is able to express in words to another the *synteresis*', as the young Luther said),[157] but which nevertheless communicates, without words or ideas, to a man the fundamental principles of his life. Respectively, obeying these principles or more precisely this divine instinctual pressure (*pondus*) arising from within was the firm foundation of virtue.

The spark of the soul: Eckhart and Tauler

I

Jean Gerson was not only the last of the great Scholastics but also one of the most significant medieval mystics. It was he who defined the mystical union (*unio mystica*) as the perfection of a contemplative life in which a person becomes dead to the world and united with God, being so sated that he neither requires nor desires anything further.[158] Indeed, it was not only in the Scholastic and juristic speculations concerning the apprehension of natural law that the question of *synderesis* (divine instinct) became paramount. It was an essential issue for the medieval mystics as well – among them Meister Eckhart, Johannes Tauler and Gerson himself, who usually expressed the idea with notions such as the 'ground of the soul', (*grunt der sele*), the 'spark of the soul' (*vünkelin der sele*), the 'divine spark' and so forth. Like *synderesis*, this spark is the highest, noblest and the innermost part of the soul. It exists, as Eckhart writes, 'far above where the powers of intellect and will burst forth'.[159] It does not merely come to close to angelic nature, but it is 'formed like God'.[160] Apart from knowing God immediately (*âne mittel*), it knows everything like God knows everything: 'To know God and to be known by God, to see God and to be seen by God, are in reality one and the same', as one of Eckhart's most famous maxims goes.[161] Moreover, to the extent that God's knowing is his substance, nature and being, it follows, Eckhart writes, that in the knowing taking place in the ground of the soul 'his being, his substance, and his nature' also become mine.[162] Therefore, whenever a man

[156] See Lottin, *Psychologie*, p. 218, footnote 1.
[157] Martin Luther, 'Handbemerkungen zu Taulers Predigten', in *D. Martin Luther's Werke: Kritische Gesamtausgabe* (Weimar: Herman Böhlau, 1883–1966), vol. 9, p. 103.
[158] Jean Gerson, *The Mountain of Contemplation*, in Gerson, *Early Works*, pp. 92–3.
[159] Meister Eckhart, *Teacher and Preacher*, ed. B. McGinn (New York: Paulist Press, 1986), sermon 7, p. 254.
[160] Ibid., sermon 3, p. 245.
[161] Ibid., sermon 76, p. 327.
[162] 'Because his knowing is mine and because his substance, his nature and his being are his knowing, it follows that his being, his substance, and his nature are mine.' Ibid., sermon 76, p. 329.

acts on account of the innermost and highest part of his soul, he is actually carrying out the creative work of God:

> There, where time never entered nor image shined in, in this innermost and highest [part] of the soul, God creates this whole world. Everything that God created six thousand years ago when he made the world and everything he will yet create in a thousand years (if the world lasts that long), all this he creates in the innermost and in the highest of the soul.[163]

Eckhart has many names for this highest part. It is not only a ground and a spark but also a power and a light. Yet all these names are misnomers ('whatever words we use, they are telling lies'). The highest part is free of all names, and cannot even be called a part: 'It is neither this nor that, neither here nor there.'[164] It is 'completely mysterious',[165] for unlike all the other creatures on earth it is 'wholly empty and free'.[166] It is empty and free, Eckhart writes, as God himself is empty and free. It is utterly one and simple and so 'exalted above every manner and every power, that no power, no manner, not God himself may look at it'.[167] It is in this absolutely naked and empty part of the soul, invisible even to God, that man meets his God, becoming not only like Him but one with Him, as naked as 'he is in himself'.[168]

In fact, the ground of the soul, the highest part of the soul without a part, is always already naked, empty and free, and hence one with God. The problem is just that a man is not aware of the empty part in his soul. How then does he become aware of it? By emptying himself: 'The more a person lays himself bare, the more he is like God.'[169] Such emptying entails the suspension of all normal sensory, rational and volitional activities, a shutting down of all the regular processes of the soul. It requires that sense and reason, knowing trough sensible images and through concepts, are held in abeyance. It requires all this because these normal ways of knowing conceal the true knowing from us: 'As long as the soul is not laid bare and stripped of every kind of medium, no matter how small it may be, it will not see God.'[170] The act of emptying the soul is what Eckhart famously calls 'detachment' (*abegescheidenheit*) and 'letting go' (*gelâzenheit*). It is only in such detachment, in the standstill when it becomes like nothing, that the soul is capable of sharing God's knowledge, performing his work and judging like him, that is to say, to become 'all in all' like God. Eckhart writes:

> When I come to the point that I form myself into nothing and form nothing into myself, and if I remove and throw out whatever is in me, then I can be placed into the bare being of God, and this is the bare being of the spirit. Everything must be driven out that is likeness, so that I can be placed above into God and become one

---

[163] Ibid., sermon 30, p. 292.
[164] Ibid., sermon 24, p. 285.
[165] Ibid., sermon 7, p. 254.
[166] Meister Eckhart, *The Essential Sermons, Commentaries, Treatises, and Defence*, trans. E. Colledge and B. McGinn (New York: Paulist Press, 1981), sermon 2, p. 180.
[167] Ibid., sermon 2, p. 181.
[168] Ibid., sermon 48, p. 198.
[169] Eckhart, *Teacher and Preacher*, sermon 40, p. 301.
[170] Ibid., sermon 69, p. 312.

with him, on substance, one being, one nature, and the Son of God. And after this has happened, nothing in God is hidden that does not become revealed or that does not become mine. Then I become wise, powerful, and all that he is – and one and the same with him.[171]

II

In *Either/Or* Søren Kierkegaard criticizes the mystic as one who chooses himself abstractly rather than concretely, assuming no responsibility for himself as this particular individual: 'His love for God reaches its highest expression in a feeling, a mood: in the dusk of evening when fogs prevail he melts with vague movements into one with his God.'[172] According to Sonya Sikka, however, at least Johannes Tauler, arguably Eckhart's most famous disciple, should be excluded from such a definition of the mystic, for there is an ethical kernel in Tauler's preaching.[173] Generally speaking, to be sure, Tauler's doctrine is well in line with Eckhart. The goal of existence is to attain union with God and it takes place at the innermost part of the soul called the spark (*vünkelin*), the ground (*grunt*), or the spirit (*gemüte*) of the soul. This divinely hued part of the soul is 'more intimate and closer to us than we are to ourselves',[174] but it is also the strangest and least known to us, for it is above the senses, reason and will: 'What the soul encounters there soars above all the senses. Reason [*vernuft*] may not touch it.'[175] And like for Eckhart, the prerequisite for reaching this ground is the emptying of the soul in 'total detachment'.[176] If one has accomplished this successfully and denied 'himself utterly',[177] one merges into the abyss of God, becoming oneself with it:

> The breadth which opens up here has neither form nor image nor any other mode or manner; nor are there any concepts of space. For it is an unfathomable abyss [*ein unsprechenliches abgrunde*], poised in itself, unplumbed, ebbing and flowing like the sea.[178]

Finally, like for Eckhart, this loss is simultaneously the most wonderful gain. In the ineffable abyss of God, men become godlike beings, enjoying utter bliss whilst performing the works of God:

> Ah, how glorious such men are! They are raised to a supernatural, a divine level, and none of their work is ever done without God. And if one may dare to utter it, they themselves no longer work, but God works in them. How blessed they are!

---

[171] Ibid., sermon 76, p. 239.
[172] Søren Kierkegaard, *Either/Or*, trans. H. and E. Hong (Princeton: Princeton University Press, 1971), vol. 2, p. 252.
[173] Sonya Sikka, *Forms of Transcendence: Heidegger and Medieval Mystical Theology* (New York: State University of New York Press, 1997), p. 187.
[174] Johannes Tauler, *Sermons*, trans. M. Shrady (New York: Paulist Press, 1985), sermon 35, p. 118.
[175] Ibid., sermon 11, p. 60.
[176] Ibid., sermon 5, p. 47.
[177] Ibid., sermon 5, p. 49.
[178] Ibid., sermon 44, p. 147.

They are the lofty pillars of the universe [*edele sülen der welte*], on whom rests the weight of the whole world.[179]

Yet rather more emphatically than Eckhart, whose vantage point is usually that of eternity, Tauler stresses the experience of anguish arising from the fact that man is posited between time and eternity. The earthly journey toward heavenly joy is not easy but full of struggle. It entails humiliation and, what is even more distressing, cannot fully take place as long as the soul is also part of this world.[180] Tauler admits that the soul can get a glimpse of divinity and dwell in its intimacy with God, but this is a mere 'foretaste of eternal life'.[181] However, to the extent that the soul does foretaste this life, it is capable of good works and just deeds, for dwelling in the unfathomable and ineffable abyss of the soul is not only the bliss of man but also the condition of his ethicality.[182] Hence, at stake is not passive dwelling in a mood. On the contrary, when the soul has forsaken everything that is in it, its empty kernel thus reaching the dwelling-place of God, it becomes pure activity: 'Since God has made His creatures in His likeness, activity is inherent in all of them', yet less in plants and animals than in man who, being the image of God, is the most active.[183] In its purity, this activity is inward but it also can – and indeed must – be transformed into outward activity ('to the benefit and good of all').[184] In the final instance, these two forms of activity are merely two aspects of the same general divine activity in which the interior aspect operates as if a guardian of the exterior, 'just as a master workman who has many young apprentices and servants under him' working according to his instructions.[185] In other words, the interior activity of dwelling in the inexpressible abyss of the ground of the soul is the foundation of all ethical activity, all justness and goodness, just deeds and good works, even to the extent that the men capable of reaching the ground are, as already said, the pillars of the universe on whom the weight of the whole world rests.[186]

In truth, the mystical union with God is not a mere subjective mood without ethical dimension for Eckhart either. Rather, it marks the very condition of possibility for ethics and ethical action. The more a person lays himself bare, the more just he becomes and the more able to perform good works: 'The just man is one with God'.[187] This is not to say that a just man is fulfilled by good intentions. For Eckhart, the presence of very intention (be it selfish or altruistic) thwarts the justness of an act: 'If you want to be informed by and transformed into justice, have no intention in your works and form no "why" in yourself, either in time or in eternity, either reward or happiness, either this or that'.[188] Just works emanate only from the total absence of intention, because every intention admits the presence of the self, and the

---

[179] Ibid., sermon 5, p. 48.
[180] Ibid., sermon 11, p. 60.
[181] Ibid., sermon 2, p. 60.
[182] Ibid., sermon 1, p. 35.
[183] Ibid., sermon 40, p. 138.
[184] Ibid., sermon 40, p. 140.
[185] Ibid.
[186] Ibid., sermon 5, p. 48.
[187] Eckhart, *Teacher and Preacher*, sermon 10, p. 265.
[188] Ibid., sermon 39, p. 296.

presence of the self entails sin.[189] In order to do just works, a man must be dead to all things, lose everything and become like nothing, stripped of everything. According to Eckhart, such a man, in the deepest inwardness of his soul, is stripped even of goodness, because the ground of the soul that perceives God, perceives Him as totally bare, 'stripped of goodness and being'.[190] In fact, he is stripped even of God, because things like goodness, being, and God are mere garments behind which the true 'God', namely Godhead, is hidden. This Godhead is not a thing but an unfathomable abyss, ultimately a negation of God, a 'non-God' (*ein nit-got*).[191] Yet it is precisely this nothing, the absolute annihilation of every thing in the depths of the soul, that is the condition sine qua non not only of God but also of true goodness and justice. Although we do not encounter anything in this depth, it is this nothing that enables everything, including everything good.

* * *

In spite of the difference in language and style, it would be a mistake to assume that there is a huge difference between the German mystics and the Scholastics like Bonaventure and Aquinas concerning the fundamentals of ethics. They all, like the medieval jurists, founded ethics on a ground inaccessible to discursive reason – on a power of the soul that is 'completely mysterious and hidden', as Tauler put it.[192] The Scholastics just called this mysterious anthropological foundation of morality and politics the *synderesis*, an angelic part of the soul beyond rational reflection and individual volition. In his Latin commentary on Genesis, Eckhart himself writes of *synderesis*:

> Neither in Cain nor in any other sinner is *synderesis* silent, but it always calls out in opposition to evil and in inclination to good with an appropriate voice that neither time nor place ever interrupts or diminishes. This is so even though its external voice is not audible in time and place, because it is neither temporal nor material.[193]

Without doubt, Aquinas' *synderesis* operates in the form of law, whereas the theme of law and obligation is conspicuously absent in mystical theology. Similarly, Aquinas was very cautious about envisioning a mystical union of man and God in the *synderesis* which for him was a created thing, unlike Eckhart's eternal spark of the soul. Despite these differences, both Scholastics and mystics – not forgetting the instinct of reason of the medieval canonists – believed that the foundation of morality, even if it resides in the human soul, is far beyond the sensual nature of man and yet impenetrable also to his discursive reason. Moreover, for the mystics and the Scholastics alike, the authority of this mysterious element over the self was unconditional – and perhaps

---

[189] Ibid.
[190] Ibid., sermon 9, p. 258.
[191] Eckhart, *Essential Sermons*, sermon 83, p. 208.
[192] Eckhart, *Teacher and Preacher*, sermon 7, p. 254.
[193] Eckhart, *Essential Sermons*, 3.164, p. 121.

being shrouded in mystery was the very condition of its moral authority. Anyone who has experienced the ground is not only incapable of expressing it in words but even if he could, he must remain silent:

> What it is that He does in those depths of the soul which have been touched by Him directly, no one can say. Nor can any man tell another, and even he who has experienced it must remain silent.[194]

We cannot and should not speak of this experience and yet we must surrender to its measureless authority, for although it is measureless, or perhaps because of that, it is the true measure (*mosse*) of everything else: 'It measures everything else, giving it its form, stability and weight.'[195]

II a

Today the most common metaphor attached to conscience is 'voice', but the medieval authors we have hitherto dealt with relied mostly on the metaphor of light. This metaphor – to which we shall return – has several origins, including Platonism ('sun'), Stoicism ('cosmic fire'), Gnosticism ('divine light') and the Old Testament images of God as light and fire. As to the voice of conscience, to my knowledge the metaphor is employed for the first time by Seneca the Elder in his *Controversiae* – *confessio conscientiae vox est*[196] – but given the fact that this is the only occurrence of the phrase in the survived Roman literature, it is probable that the metaphor was not very common. It was not common among the Fathers either. Hilary of Poitiers uses the metaphor *vox conscientiae* in his commentary on the Psalms,[197] written circa 365, but I have not detected other occurrences of the phrase in Patristic literature. Of course, the idea that God 'speaks' to men with an ephemeral voice is very old, and arguably more common in the Hebraic than the Greek and the Roman tradition. In the Old Testament, there are a number of cases when God approaches men through voice. In the early Christian theology, moreover, there are many attempts to explain the nature of this voice, the common denominator usually being the observation that God's speech through voice must be decisively distinguished from human speech. The conscience is also quite frequently mentioned as the place where God's speech takes place. As we perhaps recall, in his commentary on the Sermon of the Mount, Augustine, referring to the Pauline law of the heart, writes: 'There is no soul ... in whose conscience God does not speak' (*in eujus conscientia non loquatur Deus*). Finally, it is easy to find passages in the writings of the Fathers in which the conscience is said to speak. In *De officiis*, Ambrose

---

[194] Tauler, *Sermons*, sermon 5, p. 49.

[195] Cited in Steven E. Ozment, *Homo Spiritualis: A Comparative Study of the Anthropology of Johannes Tauler, Jean Gerson and Martin Luther (1509–1916) in the Context of Their Theological Thought* (Leiden: J. J. Brill, 1969), pp. 15–16.

[196] The Elder Seneca, *Controversiae*, books 7–10, in *Declamations in Two Volumes*, vol. 2, trans. M. Winterbottom (Cambridge, MA: Harvard University Press, 1974), 8.1, p. 184.

[197] '*Magnae et securae conscientiae vox est, judicii sui judicium postulare: ut ad id quod statutum a se sibique complacitum est, etiam divinae sententiae examen exoptet.*' Hilary of Poitiers, *Tractatus super Psalmos* 20.3, in *PL*, vol. 9, p. 633A.

of Milan maintains that the conscience speaks without audible voice (*conscientia loquebatur, ubi vox non audiebatur*).[198] In *Stromata*, Clement of Alexandria says that both volition and conscience speak to God, 'sending their voice' (*proieisai tēn phōnēn*) to him.[199] Yet except Hilary, none of the Fathers seemed to use an exact metaphor the voice *of* conscience, and to my knowledge the metaphor becomes popular only after the Reformation.

The fact that Reformation marks the shift from 'light' to 'voice' suggests that the displacement relates to the emergence of voluntarism in Scholasticism. From this perspective, the metaphysical foundation of the metaphor of light would lie in the idea that man (micro-cosmos) participates in the 'light' of God (macro-cosmos) through his own 'spark'. Voluntarism called this idea of participation into question – if not always explicitly, at least by implication. The created order is absolutely contingent, since God may suspend the order of the macro-cosmos by his omnipotent divine will, thus removing the divine light in which man is supposed to participate through the spark implanted in him. Yet even if, as a corollary, participation in God's divinity became impossible, such impossibility does not explain why the metaphor of voice became popular. Does not 'voice' imply participation as well? Is not the very word 'harmony' (supposed to prevail between the micro-cosmos and the macro-cosmos) an expression derived from voice? Furthermore, sometimes both metaphors are used interchangeably. One of the earliest is Bernard of Clairvaux's discussion on God's voice in his sermon *On Conversation* (1140). Here Bernard first tells us that when God speaks we hear his words in our consciences. Yet we do not hear them as words but precisely as a voice – as a voice that springs from within. If we listen to this 'inner voice', we will learn the will of God:

> I admonish you, therefore, to lift up the ears of your heart to hear this inner voice [*ad hanc ergo interiorem vocem aures cordis erigi admonemus*], so that you may strive to hear inwardly what is said to the outward man. For this is the voice of magnificence and power (Ps 28.4), rolling through the desert (Ps 28.8), revealing secrets, shaking souls free of sluggishness.[200]

But Bernard does not make a distinction between the inner voice and the inner light. For him, they are identical: 'There is no difference between this inner voice and light, for they are one and the same Son of God and Word of the Father and brightness of glory (Heb. 1.3).'[201] Bernard's comment – which is surprisingly rare in the history of Western conscience – on these metaphors does not mean, however, that they are generally speaking employed in a random fashion. The dividing line runs, it seems to me, not between the intellectualists ('great chain of being') and voluntarists ('great gap in being'), but rather between the mystics and the jurists: the more mystical one's approach in theology (God as a lover), the more one is inclined to use the metaphor of light, whereas the more juridical the approach (God as a judge), the greater is the

---

[198] Ambrose, *On the Duties* 1.3.9, in *NPNF2*, vol. 10, p. 2.
[199] Clement of Alexandria, *Stromata* 7.7, in *ANF*, vol. 2, p. 533.
[200] Bernard of Clairvaux, *On Conversion*, p. 67.
[201] Ibid., p. 67.

propensity to employ the metaphor of voice. Yet even this argument is a bit sketchy and easily contested – and it can be contested by appealing to Bernard himself who was, besides an enthusiastic supporter of the crusades against the heretics, one of the great mystics of the high Middle Ages.

A voluntarist bias of William of Ockham?

I

Although the doctrine of *synderesis* was popular among the Scholastics, the belief in such an inborn disposition/potentiality was not universally shared. The most notable example is William of Ockham. For anybody who knows anything about medieval theology, this cannot come as a surprise, since Ockham – together with Duns Scotus – is usually blamed for the destruction of the harmonious Christian order of nature, reason and grace. This accusation was mostly made due to the emphasis they put on the freedom of the divine will and the absolute contingency of the created order. Moreover, inasmuch as Ockham held virtue to mean exclusively obedience to the divine will that is free to will anything not involving contradiction, it has been argued that he would have to forgo nature and reason as the foundation for ethics and politics, paving the way for scepticism and fideism: Ockham cut morality off from nature, casting man 'adrift in an infinite cosmos with no natural law'.[202] In a certain sense such an argument is also justified because Ockham did maintain that no contradiction would arise if God were to command that the Ten Commandments were no longer in force and that from then on people would be obliged to obey their opposites, including the hypothetical command to hate God.[203] We may thereby assume that Ockham had drawn the conclusion that human nature does not contain absolutely valid moral principles inscribed in the *synderesis*.

Yet the issue is not necessarily as simple as it seems. Although Scotus affirms the absolute freedom of the divine will as well to the extent that God is able to use his absolute power (*potentia absoluta*) to save Judas, even retroactively, since there is no contradiction in his doing so,[204] he nevertheless employs the language of *synderesis* in the same way as the earlier Scholastics. To be sure, contrary to Aquinas, Scotus does not believe that a man who heeds the principles of *synderesis* inevitably also follows them, since the will is absolutely free. It can freely choose not to observe the dictates of *synderesis*. Yet he was as convinced as Thomas that the *synderesis* exists and that the will, although free, has an inclination (*inclinatio*) to follow the principles of *synderesis*.[205] On the other hand, even though Ockham does not use the notion of *synderesis*,

---

[202] Michael Allen Gillespie, 'The Theological Origins of Modernity', *Critical Review* 13:1–2 (1999): 10.
[203] See William of Ockham, *Quodlibetal Questions*, trans. A. Freddoso and E. Kelley (New Haven: Yale University Press, 1991), vol. 1, III, q. 14, pp. 213–14.
[204] Duns Scotus, *On the Will and Morality*, ed. A. B. Wolter (Washington, DC: The Catholic University of America Press, 1986), ord. I, dis. 44, a 16, pp. 256–7.
[205] Ibid.

this does not entail that he would have not believed in universal moral principles. Such principles do exist and they are naturally and self-evidently known by all reasonable creatures, even without any knowledge of Scripture: 'In moral philosophy there are many principles that are known per se.'[206] God can change these principles whenever He wills, but this is merely an abstract possibility contained in the concept of omnipotent God.

This does not mean that there would be no differences between Ockham and his predecessors in terms of the principles of morals. First, it seems that Ockham did not believe that the dictates of right reason, even if self-evidently known, are inborn.[207] In this sense, Ockham was perhaps a better Aristotelian than those Scholastics who denied the Aristotelian theorem of the soul as tabula rasa.[208] Right reason must develop as human capacities in general, through experience and education. Second, although Ockham agreed with Scotus that one can freely will against the dictates of right reason, since the will is absolutely free, he went further than Scotus. Whereas the latter argued that the will has a natural inclination to follow the dictates of *synderesis*, Ockham denies the existence of such an inclination.[209] The human will is free in the radical sense that it can even choose the opposite of blessedness.[210] In the third place, like the Scholastics usually, Ockham argues that the obligation to obey the dictates of conscience (*conscientia*) holds true in the case of erroneous conscience: 'It is impossible that an act of will which is elicited against conscience and against the dictate of the reason, whether right or in error, be virtuous.'[211] To this effect, he cites the words of Gratian in *Decretum*: 'Everything done against conscience builds towards hell' (*Sed omne, quod contra conscientiam fit, aedificat ad gehennam*).[212] However, Ockham's argument seems to go a bit further. Whereas the previous Scholastics had usually argued that an act based on an erroneous conscience is merely excusable, Ockham holds that such an act is virtuous: 'A created will which follows an invincibly erroneous conscience is a right will.'[213] Hence, not only should we abstain from acting against conscience, but we should also always follow the dictates of conscience – though it must be added here that Ockham, like the Scholastics in general, was convinced that the conscience can be erroneous and that it is one's duty to correct such a conscience, unless the error is invincible. Finally, the earlier Scholastics had usually referred also

---

[206] Ockham, *Quodlibetal Questions* II, q. 14, p. 149.

[207] See William of Ockham, *Quaestiones in quattuor libros sententiarum*, in *Opera philosophica et theologica* (St. Bonaventure, NY: The Franciscan Institute, 1967–88), vol. 1, III, q. 11. Hereafter *Sent.* See also Michael G. Baylor, *Action and Person: Conscience in Late Scholasticism and the Young Luther* (Leiden: E. J. Brill, 1977), pp. 78–9.

[208] Bonaventure, for instance, rejected the idea of tabula rasa straightforwardly, arguing that such conception does not accord even with Aristotle's own words. Aquinas, on the other hand, was a borderline case, for although he explicitly accepted Aristotle's definition of the soul as a blank tablet, he did not reject the idea of *synderesis* as an inborn habit.

[209] Ockham, *Sent.* III, q. 13. See also Ockham, *Quodlibetal Questions* I, q. 14, pp. 68–72.

[210] See Ockham, *Sent.* I, q. 6. See also *Sent.* IV, q. 14.

[211] Ockham, *Sent.* III, q. 13.

[212] William of Ockham, *A Short Discourse on Tyrannical Government*, ed. A. S. McGrade (Cambridge: Cambridge University Press, 1992), III, c. 12, p. 97.

[213] Ockham, *Sent* III, q. 13.

to the beneficial consequences of obedience, such as the common good, happiness and beatitude, whilst Ockham emphasized that a man has the duty to obey the judgement of conscience regardless of the consequences: we ought to do what we know to be right for the reason that we believe it is right and here not even risking death would make ignoring the dictates of conscience acceptable.[214] Despite these differences, we can conclude that Ockham did not break up with the Scholastic moral tradition, but rather confirmed it inasmuch as he erects morality more firmly and steadfastly than ever before on the obligation to obey the voice of conscience.

* * *

Although Ockham did not use the notion of *synderesis*, it did not disappear from the historical stage of Western conscience. Even his most famous disciple and the last of the great Scholastics, Gabriel Biel, although otherwise a faithful follower, treated *synderesis* and *conscientia* as if nothing much had changed since Aquinas. According to Biel, the *synderesis* or 'the spark of conscience' (*scintilla conscientiae*) is found in everyone, is inextinguishable, and naturally inclines to good and murmurs against evil. It is not an inborn disposition, like it was for Aquinas, but rather an inborn potency or faculty (*potentia*), as for Bonaventure, but its way of relating to the conscience is similar to Aquinas' theory: conscience is the particular application of the principles assented to by the *synderesis*.[215] Catholics subscribe to this twofold conscience still today, but it also survived in Protestantism, particularly in Anglicanism and mysticism but to some extent even in orthodox Lutheranism and Calvinism.[216] Even such a forerunner of techno-scientism as Francis Bacon, regardless of his sarcasm towards medieval metaphysics, assumed the Scholastic doctrine of *synderesis*. According to him, namely, there is a light of nature imprinted on the 'spirit of man by an inward instinct, according to the law of conscience, which is a sparkle of the purity of his first estate'.[217] This is not to say that the Christian tradition of conscience would have continued without interruption: Martin Luther dealt a blow against the *synderesis* in the turn of the 1520s. Therefore – and for the reason that Luther became one of the main originators of one of the greatest upheavals in the tradition of the West – it is worth examining Luther's views in greater detail.

---

[214] William of Ockham, *On the Virtues*, ed. Rega Wood (West Lafayette: Purdue University Press, 1997), 2.125–8, p. 83.

[215] On Biel's views on the *synderesis* and the *conscientia*, see Baylor, *Action and Person*, pp. 91–118.

[216] Among the seventeenth-century moralists of the Church of England, the Thomistic view of conscience was a standard. Like Aquinas, these Anglicans, such as Robert Sanderson and Jeremy Taylor, divided conscience in two parts: the superior and the inferior conscience. The former, which contains the universal laws of morality, is divine and infallible, whilst the latter can be erroneous and it is erroneous whenever 'a strong vice or malicious heart draws a veil over' the principles of the superior conscience. Jeremy Taylor, *The Rule of Conscience: Bishop's Taylor's Ductor Dubitantium Abridged in Two Volumes* (London: Bollingsley, 1725), vol. 1, p. 27. See also Robert Sanderson, *Bishop Sandersons Lectures on Conscience and Human Law*, ed. C. H. R. Wordsworth (London: Rivingtons, 1877), pp. 18–28.

[217] Francis Bacon, *Advancement of Learning* (Oxford: Clarendon Press, 1869), p. 254.

The Lutheran revocation

I

Luther's critique of *synderesis* has not remained unnoticed by the scholars. In his early writings, as Michael J. Baylor has pointed out,[218] Luther still employed conventional word references that were fully consistent with the Scholastic teaching:

> The *synteresis* of the reason pleads inextinguishably for the best, the true, the right, and the just. For this *synteresis* is a preservation [*conservatio*], a remainder [*reliquiae*], a residue [*residuum*] and a survivor [*superstes*] of our nature … in the corruption and faultiness of perdition.[219]

According to Baylor, Luther's drift away from the doctrine of *synderesis* takes place around 1515 and can be illustrated by his reaction to a verse in Psalms (4.6) that had become a customary reference for Scholastic commentators, who interpreted it as a revelatory confirmation of *synderesis*: 'The light of Thy countenance, O Lord, is signed upon us.'[220] In his commentary on the Psalms written in 1513–15, Luther omitted any reference to *synderesis* and by 1518 this silence had hardened into an explicit rejection of that interpretation:

> This verse cannot be understood of natural reason, *synderesis*, as it is the opinion of many who say that first principles in morals are self-evident, as in matters of speculation. This view is false. Faith is the first principle of good works.[221]

After 1519 the term disappears altogether, best explainable by Luther's increasingly pessimistic anthropology. Radicalizing the Augustinian position, Luther asserted that man is a sinner through and through. Naturally, he knows nothing of true righteousness, let alone self-evidently, as the Scholastics including Ockham thought. The fall and the devil have corrupted reason and conscience to such a degree that man has not even a capacity to will such righteousness.[222] The Scholastics believed that the testimony of natural conscience is not infallible, but Luther believed that it is always fallible: 'No act is done according to nature that is not an act of concupiscence against God'[223] for there is 'no moral virtue without sin'.[224] Hence, acting in concert with one's conscience is never enough.[225]

---

[218] See Baylor, *Action and Person*, pp. 157–208.
[219] Martin Luther, *Sermone aus den Jahren 1514–1517*, in *D. Martin Luthers Werke*, vol. 1, p. 32, 1–6.
[220] The quotation is from the Catholic Douay-Rheims Bible, which is a translation of Vulgate. In Vulgate, the phrase goes as follows: *leva super nos lucem vultus tui Domine dedisti laetitiam in corde meo*. In both the King James Version and the Revised Standard Version the sentence has the form of an appeal: light your countenance upon us. This implies that the light is not yet on us but will be if God so wishes.
[221] Martin Luther, *Operationes in Psalmos*, in *D. Martin Luthers Werke*, vol. 5, p. 119, 12–15.
[222] Man's will is 'innately and inevitably evil and corrupt'. Martin Luther, *Disputation against Scholastic Theology*, in *LW*, vol. 31, par. 9, p. 9.
[223] Ibid., par. 21, p. 10.
[224] Ibid., par. 38, p. 11.
[225] God does not and will not act 'according to your will or your conscience'. Martin Luther, *Sermons on the Gospel of John 6–8*, in *LW*, vol. 23, pp. 65–6.

This does not mean that conscience (*conscientia* or *Gewissen*) has no role to play in Luther's thought. Even in his soteriology, conscience is indispensable. Yet the Lutheran conscience is quite different from the Scholastic one. Whilst many Scholastics thought that a conscience without faith is easily in error when it comes to moral judgements, Luther holds that such a conscience is never reliable ('everyone who is lacking in faith sins even when he does a good work'),[226] for without faith we are 'unable to judge about anything at all'.[227] But the real difference between the Scholastics and Luther lies rather in the *message* of conscience, especially when awakened by faith. Although Luther, too, believes that conscience bears witness to the law of nature, it does not indicate whether one has acted according to this law, as the Scholastics thought, condemning transgressors and excusing the obedient. The Lutheran conscience, when awakened by faith, does not excuse, since it bears witness nothing but to the *inherent, all-pervasive and permanent sinfulness of man*: 'The moment you begin to have faith you learn that all things in you are altogether blameworthy, sinful, and damnable.'[228] For Luther, in other words, conscience is no longer a guide of life but an instance which reproduces the divine judgement of absolute condemnation, revealing to the believer his absolute sinfulness, 'blindness, misery, wickedness, ignorance, hate, and contempt of God'.[229] Furthermore, it is precisely because the conscience bears witness to the natural law that a man becomes conscious of his fate as a sinner who is 'subject to death and worthy of eternal wrath'.[230] It is the law that bruises and beats down the believer with his 'false confidence, wisdom, righteousness and power',[231] forcing him to acknowledge that sin pervades him, his senses, will, reason and works: 'When he has been crushed and humbled this way, he acknowledges that he is truly miserable and damned.'[232] Thus, whilst the Scholastics thought that natural law written in the *synderesis* of man draws him closer to God, Luther believed that it marks the point of *absolute separation* between the sinful man and righteous God. Man does not participate in the eternal law of God through natural law but, on the contrary, this law reveals that there is a maximum dissimilarity between him and his Lord.[233]

Yet, as already said, Luther conceives such a law-bound conscience indispensable and he does so because a conscience terrified by the law alone makes a man realize that he needs Christ and the grace of God. That is to say, the guilty conscience prepares us for faith: 'It humbles us and thus makes us ready for the grace and blessing of Christ.'[234] Hence, although the law reveals God's wrath, thereby terrifying the conscience, this trembling conscience is nevertheless the very the condition of possibility of faith which creates in man a yearning for Christ and redemption:

---

[226] Martin Luther, *Lectures on Romans*, in *LW*, vol. 25, 14:23, p. 507.
[227] Martin Luther, *Lectures on Galatians*, in *LW*, vols. 26–7, 4:6, p. 375.
[228] Martin Luther, *The Freedom of a Christian*, in *LW*, vol. 31, pp. 346–7.
[229] Luther, *Galatians* 3.19, p. 309.
[230] Ibid., p. 314.
[231] Ibid.
[232] Ibid., p. 239.
[233] 'Not being God is what being man means,' as Steven Ozment aptly summarizes Luther's anthropology. Ozment, *Homo Spiritualis*, p. 138
[234] Luther, *Galatians* 3.21, p. 331.

When the conscience has been terrified this way by the Law, there is a place for the doctrine of the Gospel and of grace, which raises it up again and comforts it; it says that Christ did not come into the world to break the bruised reed or to quench the dimly burning wick (Isa. 42.3) but to announce the Gospel to the poor, to bind up the brokenhearted, and to proclaim liberty to the captives (Isa. 61.1).[235]

Moreover, the guilty conscience begot through the law is indispensable only at the beginning as one starts to believe.[236] It is the first step on the path towards faith and, more precisely, it is the first *act* of faith, since whoever acknowledges his sinfulness is no longer a mere sinner but also not a sinner. By consciously becoming the sinner that one always already unconsciously is, one is already starting to become righteous. What, then, does it mean to become righteous? It means the fading away of guilty conscience. In righteousness, there is no longer guilt or sin. Thus, although the Christian conscience must first be terrified by the law and sin, eventually it must be free from both of them. This is the principal meaning of the famous Lutheran *Gewissenfreiheit*: 'Sin has been forgiven and the conscience has been liberated from the burden and the sting of sin.'[237] And the conscience becomes free by detaching itself from the law through faith in Christ and in God's forgiveness of sins as it is announced in the Gospel: 'The Law oppresses the conscience with sins, but the Gospel frees the conscience and brings peace through faith in Christ.'[238] Therefore, the conscience of the faithful must be liberated from all laws, not only from the ceremonial and civil, but also from natural moral and divine positive laws. Christ has indeed always already liberated the conscience from all of them, as the entire law (*toto Lex*) is completely abrogated (*abrogata*) in Christ.[239] Luther writes: 'By this victory of His, Christ has driven the Law to flight out of our conscience, so that it can no longer bring us to despair and condemn us.'[240] The Christian conscience must be 'dead to the law',[241] Luther continues, because sin is not annulled by a lawful living, for nobody is able to live up to the law: 'It is impossible for you to fulfil the Law.'[242] Sin and law are inseparable, as the very function of the law is to incur sin: 'It not only reveals sin but causes it to abound.'[243] Justification does not come from the law but from faith alone – faith in Christ and the grace of God as it is announced in the word of Gospel (*sola scriptura*).

For the Scholastics, liberating conscience from the divine positive law would have been a blasphemous suggestion, whereas liberating conscience from the natural moral law would have been a contradiction in terms inasmuch as the very function of the conscience was to bear witness to this law. What about Luther? Does his liberated conscience have a function at all? It does, for it becomes a source of peace and

---

235 Ibid., 3.19, pp. 314–15.
236 Ibid., 3.23, p. 337.
237 Ibid., 2.16, p. 133.
238 Luther, *Romans* 10.15, p. 416.
239 Luther, *Galatians* 2.19, p. 156.
240 Ibid., 4.4, p. 371.
241 Ibid., 2.19, p. 158.
242 Ibid., 5.14, p. 53.
243 Ibid., 3.20, p. 326.

heavenly joy – almost in the same way as the ground of the soul was for the German mystics. It does not know sin, has no sense of guilt, for they are 'engulfed in the unfathomable depths [*abysso*]' of God's righteousness,[244] where there is nothing but the 'the glory of the conscience before God'.[245] Such a conscience knows only Christ,[246] for where Christ is, there is 'a good conscience and joy'.[247] Eventually, the conscience of a Christian becomes one with Christ: 'Christ and my conscience must become one body',[248] whereby I attain a state comparable to that of Adam and Eve in paradise:

> We should think of the works of a Christian who is justified and saved by faith because of the pure and free mercy of God, just as we would think of the works which Adam and Even did in Paradise, and all their children would have done if they had not sinned.[249]

Yet we must notice that Luther says a Christian *should* be regarded from this perspective. Namely, according to Luther, the nature of a Christian is twofold. His conscience is liberated from the law, which means that he has become just, even a saint (*sanctus*), but given the fact that he continues to live in his body and flesh, he is simultaneously a sinner (*simul peccator et iustus*). Perfect righteousness does not become a reality in this life, because remnants of sin cling to the sinful nature of man. In other words, although the one who believes in Christ and forgiveness of sins is truly faithful, he does not become righteous as Adam before the fall, but remains necessarily a sinner – not because a mere remnant of Adam's rationality remains in him, as the Scholastics said, but rather because reason itself, 'God's bitterest and most harmful enemy',[250] is not completely killed in this life. In effect, he must also suffer the sense of sin in his conscience, because it is, according to Luther, 'very beneficial if we', namely the faithful, 'sometimes become aware of the evil of our nature and our flesh'.[251] It is beneficial because it is, according to Luther, 'impossible for you to follow the Spirit as your guide through everything without some awareness of hindrance by the flesh', that is to say, awareness of one's sinful nature.[252] The awareness of sinfulness reminds that one has not reached the state of perfect righteousness yet and that one must continue to struggle against sin: 'A Christian struggles with sin continually.'[253] Without such a struggle, without the constant threat of sin and Satan, men's conscience becomes careless, negligent and sluggish. So, Luther writes, 'it is all right for sin to stir them up, provided that they do not gratify it'.[254]

What, then, is the glory of conscience, if sin assails even the consciences of the faithful? The glory of conscience is this: the Christian no longer interprets the sense of

---

[244] Luther, *Romans* 2.15, p. 188.
[245] Luther, *Romans* 15.20, p. 522.
[246] 'For here the conscience should consider and know nothing except Christ alone.' Luther, *Galatians* 4.3, p. 365.
[247] Ibid., 2.17, p. 151.
[248] Ibid., 2.20, p. 166.
[249] Luther, *Freedom of a Christian*, p. 360.
[250] Luther, *Galatians* 3.6, p. 228.
[251] Ibid., 5.17, p. 74.
[252] Ibid., p. 72.
[253] Ibid., 5.19, p. 87.
[254] Ibid., 5.17, p. 74.

guilt as a sign of his condemnation.[255] The glad tidings are not that the Christian has become free of sin. Everybody is a sinner and sins all the time. The glad tidings are that these sins are no longer *counted*: 'A Christian is not someone who has no sin or feels no sin; he is someone to whom, because of his faith in Christ, God does not *impute* his sin.'[256] In his commentary on the Galatians, Luther writes: 'I know I have committed many sins, and I continue to sin daily, but that does not bother me.'[257] It does not bother him because he believes in the forgiveness of sins. Like the Fathers, Aquinas thought the one having 'a sin on his conscience cannot make satisfaction to God',[258] but Luther believed that such a sin does not deprive a man of God's grace. This is what makes the conscience of the Christian peaceful, secure and good. The faith of the true Christian in the grace of God is so strong that he may face the admonishing voice of conscience without fear and trembling. This belief makes him 'stand bravely against all the dangers of death and the terrors of conscience and of sin, no matter how much they attacked him, accused him, and wanted to drive him to despair'.[259] The Christian is not immune to the guilty conscience, but he faces the pangs of conscience peacefully and without fear, because he is assured of God's grace. In point of fact, the true Christian may joyfully accept the accusations of conscience, because God is gracious to sinners who feel their sins. What he does not accept is the false assumption that this would be the sign of his perdition. Therefore, it is not the testimony of conscience the Christian believes in.[260] When the conscience accuses you, Luther continues, it is time to turn your eyes away from the 'sense of your conscience' to the Word of God which preaches the forgiveness of sins. It is not conscience but faith in grace announced in the Word that paves the way for salvation:

> We must not consult the consciousness of our own heart [*cordis nostri sensum*]. No, then we must consult the Word of God which says that God is not wrathful, but that he has regard for those who are afflicted, are contrite in spirit, and tremble at his Word.[261]

I a

Luther's interpretation of the law and conscience is based almost entirely on his reading of the Apostle Paul's Epistles. What about Paul himself? What is his conception of conscience and how does it relate to the law and especially to the law of the heart? Generally speaking, conscience (*syneidēsis*) is a much less crucial concept for Paul than for Luther, although he does employ it more frequently than any of the New

---

[255] On this point see also Randall C. Zachman, *The Assurance of Faith: Conscience in the Theology of Martin Luther and John Calvin* (Minneapolis: Fortress Press, 1993), p. 65.

[256] Luther, *Galatians* 2.16, p. 133.

[257] Ibid., 2.19, p. 158.

[258] Aquinas, *Summa Theologica* suppl. IIIae, q. 14, a. 1.

[259] Luther, *Galatians* 2.19, p. 161.

[260] 'In temptation we must not on any account decide this matter on the basis of our feeling [*ex sensu nostrum*].' Luther, *Galatians* 4.6, p. 384.

[261] Ibid., 5.5, p. 27.

Testament authors. In the undisputed Pauline letters, *syneidēsis* occurs fourteen times, whilst the New Testament as a whole includes twenty-two occurrences, all of them in the letters attributed to Paul.

As to the Bible in general, it must be noted that in Hebrew there is no word for 'conscience'. However, *syneidēsis* appears once in the Septuagint, namely in Ecclesiastes 10.20: 'Even in your thought [*en syneidēsei*], do not curse the king.' It occurs twice in Apocrypha as well. In Ecclesiasticus, it is said that the 'most high knows all knowledge [*pasan syneidēsin*]' whereas in the Wisdom of Solomon (17.11) we read: 'For wickedness is a cowardly thing, condemned by its own testimony; distressed by conscience [*syneidēsis*].' In addition, the verbal compound *synoida emautō* ('I know with myself') from which the noun *syndeidēsis* derives appears once in the Septuagint, in the book of Job, 27.6, where the Hebrew 'heart' (*lēb*) is translated as *synoida emautō* ('my heart does not reproach me for any of my days'). Also, Paul occasionally uses the term 'heart' (*kardia*) as if it were an equivalent to *syneidēsis*, but more often conscience appears, like in 2 Corinthians (1.12), as a witness (*martys*) testifying to the condition of the soul:

> For our boast is this, the testimony of our conscience [*to martyrion tēs syneidēseōs hēmōn*] that we have behaved in the world, and still more toward you, with holiness and godly sincerity, not by earthly wisdom but by the grace of God.

Yet the context where the term occurs most frequently relates to food offered to idols. These occurrences in 1 Corinthians tell us that Paul is not categorical with regard to the dictates of conscience, for he exhorts the Corinthians to put the conscience aside and not to disturb peace among the believers for the sake of food, which is a morally neutral thing. On the one hand, Paul says 'eat whatever is sold in the meat market without raising any question on the ground of conscience' (1 Cor. 10.25), because for those who live in Christ everything is permitted (1 Cor. 10.23) but, on the other, he maintains (1 Cor. 10.28–9) that if someone else in the company is offended by the fact that food is offered in sacrifice, one should not eat it for the sake of 'other's conscience' (Paul calls him the 'weak brother'). However, insofar as it is Romans 2.14–15 that has figured most prominently in the Western history of conscience, let us briefly analyse how Paul himself conceives that conscience which bears witness to the law of the heart.

Let us begin with the theme of the law as such. We know what Paul says about the law (*nomos*): 'All who rely on works on the law are under a curse' (Gal. 3.10); 'The power of sin is the law [*nomos*]' (1 Cor. 15.56); 'If it had not been for the law [*nomos*], I should not have known sin' (Rom. 7.7), and so on. But what is the law Paul is speaking about? Most obviously, it is the Mosaic Law, both ceremonial and Ten Commandments, but he also refers to Genesis (Gal. 4.21) and cites prophets and psalms as words of *nomos* (1 Cor. 14.21 and Rom. 3.10–18). Hence, the word *nomos* in Paul seems to refer to the whole of Israel's sacred tradition.[262] It is only from this perspective that we can understand Paul's statement in the Philippians (3.5–8) in

---

[262] See also Heikki Räisänen, *Paul and the Law* (Tübingen: J. C. B. Mohr, 1983), p. 16.

which he counts as a loss the entire way of life (the Hebrew *nomos*) he had practiced before his conversion. Yet this is not necessarily the point where Paul's critique ceases. At least Origen, in his commentary on the Romans, stresses that when Paul speaks about law (*nomos*) he means also natural law. Examining the passage 5.13 where Paul says that 'sin is not imputed when there is no law', Origen asserts that he cannot refer to the Mosaic Law alone, since otherwise the Gentiles would be sinless. Therefore, 'Paul is speaking of natural law',[263] the law that has been universally in force ever since Adam. What, then, does the phrase 'when there is no law' mean? And, especially, what is the meaning of Paul's words in the Romans 7.9, where he speaks about himself as living without law ('I was once alive apart from the law')? At first, Origen thinks that at issue is only the first period of childhood when one's conscience, meaning one's capacity to distinguish between good and evil, is not yet fully developed.[264] But Origen also notices that in the Romans 3.21 Paul speaks about the righteousness of God manifesting itself 'apart from the law'. Hence, not only the natural children but also the children of God – those who live in Christ – are free from all laws. In Christ, in other words, even the natural law, as Origen is forced to conclude, is rendered inoperative.[265]

Let us assume that Origen is right. The Pauline critique of the law concerns also the law written in the heart – even especially, because of the late date of the Mosaic Law. The whole world is under the law and becomes guilty before God (Rom. 3.19), but this cannot be the case if the law was the Mosaic Law. The whole world may be guilty only because there is a law written in the heart of every man conscience as its witness. It is thus this law that must be rendered inoperative. Perhaps the very reason why Paul wanted to render the law inoperative relates to the accusations of conscience: 'The law brings wrath' (Rom. 4.15) and God's wrath is the cause of the sense of guilt and bad conscience ('through the law comes the knowledge of sin', Rom. 3.20). It is this conscience and knowledge Paul abhors and not, for instance, the punishments that law proscribes. The end of law means consequently the end of bad conscience and the birth of a good one (1 Tim. 1.3–20). Therefore, natural law cannot be in force when we are living in Christ. The law is the power of sin (1 Cor. 15.56) and hence the source of guilt and debt, but now Jesus Christ has discharged us from the law and debt through the redemption, literarily ransoming (*dia tēs apolutrōseōs*), which is in him (Rom. 3.24).[266]

Yet we must be precise here. Paul is not saying that we must get totally rid of the law, let alone conscience. The law can be useful and it is useful prior to the emergence of faith: 'The law was our custodian [*paidagōgos*] until Christ came, that we might be justified by faith' (Gal. 3.24). The law is a *paidagōgos* for those who have no faith and nobody is born with faith. In Christ, however, there is no use for the law and hence, for the conscience that bears witness to it. But this does not signify that the

---

[263] Origen, *Romans*, 3.2.9, p. 192.
[264] Ibid., 3.2.7–9, pp. 191–2.
[265] Ibid., 3.7.5, p. 210.
[266] This did not remain unnoticed by Origen: 'The term "redemption" refers to that which is given to enemies for those whom they are keeping in captivity, in order that they might restore them to their original freedom.' Ibid., 3.7.14, p. 215.

conscience as such is forsaken in Christ, for now on it bears witness to the Holy Spirit: 'My conscience bears me witness in the Holy Spirit' (Rom. 9.1). The Holy Spirit is neither the law of conscience nor does it mark the point of the absence of conscience. The Holy Spirit marks the point of conscience's freedom: 'For freedom Christ set us free' (Gal. 5.1). The freedom of conscience is freedom from the law and sin and this is the realm of grace: 'You are not under law but under grace' (Rom. 6.14). This does not entail, however, that the man of faith, living without the law (*nomos*), becomes immoral (*anomos*). On the contrary, it is precisely now that he becomes moral in the proper sense of the word: 'The fruit of the Spirit is love, joy, peace, patience, kindness, generosity, faithfulness, gentleness, and self-control' (Gal. 5.22). True morality is not the fruit of the law, be it natural, habitual or positive (as they all are included in the Greek concept of *nomos*) but of freedom in righteousness (*dikaiosynē*) that comes through faith in Christ:

> For his sake I have suffered the loss of all things, and count them as refuse, in order that I may gain Christ and be found in him, not having a righteousness of my own, based on law, but that which is through faith in Christ. (Phil. 3.7–9)

II

Let us return to Luther. Although Luther launched an attack on the Scholastic conception of *synderesis*, he did not reject the Christian assumption that the conscience has a central role to play in the economy of salvation. We must consult the conscience tormented by the law because it is the tormented conscience that drives a man to Christ for help – and given the fact that the human nature will always remain sinful, this tormenting conscience cannot cease to operate even among the faithful. Furthermore, even though the dictates of conscience cannot reveal anything about the true will of God, especially when it comes to his acceptance, these dictates remain fully effective in the mundane life of man. In point of fact, the dictates of conscience do reflect, as they do in the Scholastic discourse, those basic moral principles that are written in the heart of every man – though Luther often asserts, like Augustine, that the law of the heart is written in the heart for the first time when a person is born again through his faith in Christ.[267] In other words, although Luther criticized the Scholastic notion of *synderesis*, he did not deny the existence of an inborn knowledge of good and evil even in his later writings. Inborn knowledge exists and it is precisely this knowledge that is the true foundation of human law and good works:

> All men have a certain natural knowledge implanted in their minds (Rom. 2.14–15), by which they know naturally that one should do to others what he wants done to himself (Matt. 7.12). This principle and others like it, which we call the law of nature, are the foundations of human law and of all good works.[268]

---

[267] See for instance Martin Luther, 'Answer to the Hyperchristian, Hyperspiritual and Hyperlearned Book by Goat Emser in Leipzig,' in *LW*, vol. 39, pp. 175–203.
[268] Luther, *Galatians* 5.14, p. 53.

The most fundamental principle of the law of nature is the command of love and this law is established in the human heart, which is 'the loveliest and best of books about all laws'.[269] According to Luther, the Christian must compare 'all the acts, words, and thoughts of his whole life with this commandment as a rule'.[270] Hence, the Christian freedom is not 'carefree fleshly freedom which is not obligated to do anything'.[271] Every Christian is obliged to heed the law of the heart: 'I am bound to commandments of that law that is implanted in everyone by nature and written in everyone's heart'.[272]

Surely, more vehemently than his Catholic predecessors, Luther emphasized the impotence of human reason to recognize the inborn knowledge of good and evil: 'Human reason is so corrupted and blinded by the malice of the devil that it does not understand this inborn knowledge; or, even if it has been admonished by the Word of God, it deliberately neglects and despises it'.[273] He stressed, in addition, that this impotence is universal. No one is able to love his neighbour the law requires: 'There is no one who keeps the law'.[274] Although this may be occasionally and partially possible for the most saintly of Christians, it is not possible fully and all the time, which is to say that even the most pious men sin: 'Even the Saints love in an imperfect and impure way in this present life'.[275] Love becomes perfect only in the life to come, where faith, consequently, has become useless. Finally, it is the *body* of a Christian that is bound by the law, including the law of the heart. Christians are ready to serve other people with love, but they know that they are debtors to the brethren 'according to the flesh' alone,[276] not inwardly. They do not serve others under the obligation of conscience but that of the body:

> The godly should remember that for the sake of Christ they are free in their conscience before God from the curse of the law, from sin, and from death, but that according to the body they are bound; here each must serve the other through love, in accordance with this commandment of Paul. Therefore let everyone strive to do his duty in his calling and to help his neighbour in whatever way he can.[277]

In other words, although the Christian is bound to commandments of that law that is written in everyone's heart, the conscience of a Christian is not obliged by any law. Therefore, for the Christian conscience, the law of the heart is not, in the final analysis, a proper law at all but rather a law without a law, without measure, without end, without limit (*lex sine lege, sine modo, sine fine, nesciens limitem*).[278] It is a proper law only to the body. However, to the extent that it indeed lays an obligation on the

[269] Ibid., pp. 57–8.
[270] Luther, *Romans* 13.10, p. 476.
[271] Martin Luther, 'Preface to the Epistle of St. Paul to the Romans,' in *LW*, vol. 35, p. 376.
[272] Martin Luther, *Predigten über des zweite Buch Mose 1524–1527*, in *D. Martin Luthers Werke*, vol. 16, p. 380.
[273] Luther, *Galatians* 5.14, p. 53
[274] Ibid., 3.12, p. 273.
[275] Ibid., 5.16, p. 64.
[276] Ibid., 5.13, p. 51.
[277] Ibid., pp. 49–50.
[278] Luther, *Romans* 2.14, p. 187.

body and because, as Luther adds, righteous works emanate from the true Christian like good fruits grow from a good tree,[279] a true Christian is outwardly like any good and virtuous person: 'Externally there is not much difference between the Christian and another socially upright human being.'[280]

The return of the repressed: Spiritualists and pietists

I

Although Luther did not, as the Catholic authors presumed, abandon the idea of natural law and conscience bearing witness to it, it is not a great wonder that the Counter-Reformation saw an arch-heretic in him. The first theoretical attack came from the Catholic circles in the middle of the sixteenth century, notably by such neo-Thomists as Domingo de Soto, Luis de Molina, Cardinal Bellarmine and Francisco Suárez. According to Suárez, for example, it is a heresy to maintain that all the works of the just are sinful and that it is impossible even for them to fulfil the law of God. Likewise, it is a heresy to deny the necessity of works for the attainment of justice. The same can be said of the Lutheran doctrine that a just man is not bound by any law, provided that he remains steadfast in his faith – a doctrine based on the assumption that sins are not imputed to a believer and do not incur any punishment, whatever the works performed by him, due to Christ's merits.[281] According to Suárez, God does not command anything that it would be impossible for man to carry out, just works are necessary for salvation, sins are imputed to sinners, and the obligation of law is by no means 'rendered ineffective' (*impedire*) by faith as the Lutherans hold, but on the contrary, the very opposite is true: 'All men in this life are subject to law to such an extent, that they are bound to obey it, and become legal culprits in the sight of God, if they do no voluntarily observe the law.'[282] In Suárez' view, there is no exception to this obligation ('these laws were not less binding upon the just than upon the unjust'), an actuality that can be inductively proved from the fact that men have been subject to natural law from the beginning of creation, including popes and emperors.[283] Even God will grant (even if he surely can) no dispensation from this law, written in the hearts of men and testified to by their consciences.[284]

However, the Catholics were not the only ones to criticize Luther, this *scandalum* for Rome. Perhaps an even more vehement attack came from Luther's own ranks years before

---

[279] 'When Christ has thus been grasped by faith and I am dead to the Law, justified from sin, and delivered from death, the devil, and hell through Christ – then I do good works, love God, give thanks, and practice love toward my neighbour.' Luther, *Galatians* 2.19, p. 161.

[280] Ibid., 4.6, p. 376.

[281] Francisco Suárez, *A Treatise on Laws and God the Lawgiver*, in Francisco Suárez, *Selections from Three Works*, ed. by G. L. Williams et al., vol. 2 (Oxford: The Clarendon Press, 1944), 1.18.2, p. 132.

[282] Ibid., 1.18.3, p. 132.

[283] Ibid., pp. 132–3.

[284] 'We shall declare the opinion of Occam and of others to be false.' Ibid., 2.15.5, p. 288 and 2.15.26, p. 304.

the Catholic reaction, spearheaded by such reformed radical mystics and spiritualists as Thomas Müntzer, the famous leader of the peasant rebellion. Certainly, Müntzer's criticism was not directed exclusively at Luther. According to Müntzer, the church as a whole had been an unfaithful whore since the death of the followers of the original Apostles, because it had alienated the people from the experience of the living word of Law that God had inscribed in the hearts of men. For Müntzer, however, Luther represented the culmination of this alienation. This 'ambassador of the devil'[285] claimed that the living law had now been set aside – and if it is explained to him how the law is 'written in the heart' and how one must be 'attentive to its teachings in order to see the right path', then this 'godless one attacks the righteous and drags Paul around with such an idiotic comprehension that even to a child it becomes as ridiculous as a puppet show'.[286] According to Luther, Müntzer continues, one should simply believe but he does not say how one must proceed in order to do this. Müntzer's own stated view – in fact very Lutheran – is that faith presupposes the experience of the law from the beginning to end:

> For the spirit punishes unbelief only after there is a knowledge of the law, an unbelief no one knows unless he has previously acknowledged it in his heart passionately, like the most unbelieving heathen.[287]

Therefore, Müntzer asserts, the law 'should be enforced with the greatest strictness, as Paul instructs his disciple Timothy, and through him all pastors of souls'.[288] This must be done because the fear of God's law alone empties the soul and it is only in empty soul, as Eckhart and Tauler had taught, that man is able to receive the 'unending wisdom' of God.[289]

On the other hand, Luther had argued that *sola fide* was inseparable from *sola scriptura*, whereas Müntzer believed that only Pharisees, including Luther himself, rely on the Scripture alone. Without the living spirit the Word of God has no significance.[290] Even more: it is poison. Indeed, Müntzer argued, Scripture itself stands firmly against *sola scriptura*:

> If one had throughout his entire life neither heard nor seen the Bible, he could still have a sincere Christian faith through the true teaching of the Spirit, as all those have who, without any books, have written the Holy Scripture.[291]

According to Müntzer, Luther lacked such Spirit. Therefore, also, the Bible remained incomprehensible to him. Without Spirit, nobody understands the Bible even if he 'swallowed a hundred thousand of them'.[292] Certainly, Müntzer knew what Luther

---

[285] Thomas Müntzer, *Highly Provoked Defence*, in *Revelation and Revolution: Basic Writings of Thomas Müntzer*, ed. Michael G. Baylor (Bethlehem: Lehigh University Press, 1993), p. 150.

[286] Ibid., p. 141.

[287] Ibid.

[288] Ibid., p. 143.

[289] Cited in Ozment, *Mysticism*, p. 83.

[290] See Thomas Müntzer, *The Prague Protest*, in *Revelation and Revolution*, pp. 56, 62.

[291] Cited in Ozment, *Mysticism*, p. 88.

[292] Müntzer, *Sermon to the Princes*, in *Revelation and Revolution*, p. 105. This insult was soon returned in kind with Luther replying that Müntzer seemed to have swallowed the Holy Ghost, feathers and all. See Roland H. Bainton, *Here I Stand: A Life of Martin Luther* (New York: Meridian, 1995), p. 203.

had said of faith and the Spirit: 'It makes us altogether different in heart and spirit, mind and powers.'[293] Müntzer also knew that Luther was a great admirer of Tauler and edited in 1518 the *Theologia Germanica*, which became a sort of second Bible for mystical German theology, and in the preface of which he wrote: 'No book except the Bible and St Augustine has come to my attention from which I have learned more about God, Christ, man, and all things.'[294] Yet Müntzer (the storey goes that Müntzer always carried Tauler's sermons around with him) was convinced that Luther did not fully endorse these teachings. By emphasizing the primacy of the Word, Luther forgot the Spirit, and so doing relativized the experience of the Holy Spirit emanating from the 'abyss of the soul',[295] where we may expect God's present revelations. We also must expect these revelations,[296] because they are these revelations, pertaining to knowledge rather than faith,[297] which make men 'certain of their cause'.[298]

Spiritualists agreed with Müntzer. The mere letter of the Scripture without living Spirit is the spawn of Satan, as Sebastian Franck asserted. You should not read the Bible in order to teach your conscience, but on the contrary, you must listen to the teaching of the Spirit and to 'interpret the Scripture as a confirmation of thy conscience'.[299] Whereas Luther had held that the conscience must be guided by the Scripture, Franck now suggests that the Scripture has to be studied in order to confirm what the conscience already knows. The truth can be found in the conscience alone whereas the Scripture, even the historical Christ himself, is a mere witness of that inner truth: 'Although one may be able to take a Bible in hand and, without a single error, explicate its contents, he still does it in vain and preaches absolutely nothing. For God is not in what he says.'[300] God is not present in written books but in the book of the heart which is the 'living office of the Holy Spirit and a basic library, bookstore, and Bible'.[301] This book is learned by listening to the voice of the Word within. It is this voice rather than the Scripture, baptism, or even Christ himself that makes men Christians,[302] for, in the final analysis, this inner Word is identical with God:

> The inner, truly living, natural, and almighty word of the Father, which in recent times has become flesh, and is taken to be the seed of Abraham and named 'Christ' in the New Testament, is that which goes forth directly from the mouth of God, through which everything is created, sustained, nourished, and preserved. This word is eternal; indeed, it is God himself, free from all created things, and

---

[293] Luther, 'Preface to the Epistle of St Paul to the Romans,' p. 370.
[294] Martin Luther, 'Preface to the complete edition of A German Theology,' in *LW*, vol. 31, p. 75.
[295] Müntzer, *Sermon to the Princes*, p. 105.
[296] Ibid., p. 101.
[297] 'We must know and not only believe.' Ibid., p. 104.
[298] Müntzer, *Prague Protest*, p. 55.
[299] Sebastian Franck, 'A Letter to John Campanus,' in *Spiritual and Anabaptist Writers*, ed. G. H. Williams (Philadelphia: The Westminster Press, 1957), p. 159.
[300] Cited in Ozment, *Mysticism*, p. 155.
[301] Cited in ibid., p. 150.
[302] 'Consider as thy brothers all Turks and heathen, wherever they be, who fear God and work righteousness, instructed by God and inwardly drawn by him, even though they have never heard of baptism, indeed, of Christ himself, neither of his storey of scripture, but only of his power through the inner Word perceived within and made fruitful.' Franck, 'A Letter to John Campanus,' p. 156.

incapable of being spoken and written. God must himself utter it in our soul and heart so that the word may also become flesh and Christ be born in us.[303]

Anabaptists, such as Hans Denck, joined the chorus. Not the Bible but the inner truth spoken and written by Christ 'from the beginning until the end of the world in the hearts of men'[304] has the supreme authority on earth: 'Whenever it directs me, I will go, according to its will; and where it prevents me, I will flee.'[305] It is called *synderesis* as well as *fünklin* and it is a 'mediator between God and men'.[306] It drives me 'without my willing and doing',[307] or better still, it drives me only when my willing and doing cease, when I hold still and lose myself in the standstill (*gelassenhait*) of the soul. Salvation is not of us, Denck admits, but it is in us – and if salvation is in me, so is God and everything that belongs to God: 'Omnipotence, righteousness, mercy.'[308]

To put it bluntly, these radicals and mystics were Catholics without the Church and Protestants without the Word. Like Catholics, they believed in the spark of God's light operating in the heart of every man, but like good Lutherans they refused to subject this spark to the authority of the Church. Like Luther, moreover, they admitted that the Bible is important, but they believed that Scripture bears witness to God's truth only mediately, whilst the experience of the inner Word is its immediate expression. Through this experience the Christian becomes free and autonomous, even omnipotent, albeit not the originator of his law, for although the word of truth and law are within me, they are not mine: they emanate from 'the will of the Other'.[309]

II

Müntzer was killed and the peasant rebellion crushed. With the help of the German princes, Lutheran orthodoxy was established. Yet mysticism was also kept alive, for instance by theologians such as Johann Arndt. In his *Four Books on True Christianity* (1605–9), read widely in the seventeenth century – more widely than any of Luther's books – Arndt returned to medieval themes, writing that God allowed there to remain, even after the fall, a 'spark of natural life or a tract and sign of natural testimony', namely a natural testimony for the existence of God, final judgement, and the law of nature or 'natural righteousness by which honour and shame might be distinguished and joy and sorrow may be discovered'.[310] According to Arndt, whoever is called a Christian by word and is not internally converted must necessarily feel a terrible pain in his conscience that the eternal perdition will only multiply, but this same fate awaits pagans as well, not because they have not been called by word but because they have

---

[303] Cited in Ozment, *Mysticism*, p. 160.
[304] Cited in ibid., p. 129.
[305] Cited in ibid., p. 121.
[306] Hans Denck, 'Whether God is the cause of Evil', in *Spiritual and Anabaptist Writers*, p. 95.
[307] Cited in Ozment, *Mysticism*, p. 122.
[308] Denck, 'Whether God is the cause of Evil', pp. 93–4.
[309] Ibid., p. 95.
[310] Johann Arndt, *True Christianity*, ed. P. C. Erb (New York: Paulist Press, 1978), p. 52.

not 'followed the small, inner light that is in them from nature'.[311] God planted this light in the human conscience and therefore, the conscience is 'always and internally directed to God',[312] being the true meeting place of man and Him.[313]

In the seventeenth century these themes continued to have currency in Pietism, which was a heterogeneous cluster of different discourses marginalized by orthodox Lutheranism. But it was not until the emergence of the so called radical Pietism in the eighteenth century that a whole-hearted mystical theology based on the inner experience evolved in the wake of the medieval German mystics such as Tauler and Arndt. A good example of this trend is Gottfried Arnold and his phantasmagorical reading of the divine voice in his *Mystery of the Divine Sophia*.[314] According to Arnold, this divine voice was fully present in the innocence of the first man, awakening in him all imaginable joy in and desire for God. When Adam fell – that is, turned outward with doubt and desire toward creatures – the divine Sophia turned away from him and from the whole world. The creation of Eve from Adam's rib had been the first indication of this turn, but the voice did not cease to speak to each child of Adam internally in their hearts and to bid them re-establish the lost treasure. This voice – Arnold also calls it the call, the inner word and the hidden inner speech – communicates Sophia's secret activity in the soul which no man can either deny or completely rule out, but only hinder or put out for a time. It occurs from youth onwards and it remains with a person as long as it is not opposed. The first activity and instruction of this divine and secret voice of Sophia is punishment: 'First, it punishes the person, makes him troubles and sorrowful internally concerning all that is evil as often as it find him in such thought, words, or deeds.'[315] But to the extent that this punishment leads to remorse and repentance, it is followed by Sophia's other secret and inexpressible works and instructions to the effect that the final outcome is the wedding of man and Sophia, so blissful that only angelic tongues can describe it:

> In truth, all the desire of youth and all the supposed fulfilment of physical marriage are less than nothing with reckoned against this heavenly joy. It is an actual power of paradise when the most beautiful bride meets a spirit. It is a sweet transport and filling of all the power of the soul and the sinking of all though into the flood of love.[316]

The *Mystery* was published in 1700. Nearly 400 had passed since 1329, when Pope John XXII had issued a bull in which a series of statements by Eckhart was denounced as heretical. Nearly 200 years had passed since Luther, who, in spite of his admiration

[311] Ibid., p. 54.
[312] Ibid., p. 53.
[313] Ibid., p. 248.
[314] Arnold is also the author of the widely read *Theologia Experimentalis*. The German subtitle of the book brings to light something essential of author's approach: 'Spiritual Doctrine of Experience, or Experiential Knowledge [*Erkäntnisz*] and experience [*Erfahrung*] concerning the preeminent aspects of living Christianity from the Beginning of Conversion to is Perfection.'
[315] Gottfried Arnold, *The Mystery of the Divine Sophia*, in *Pietists: Selected Writings*, ed. P. C. Erb (Mahwah: Paulist Press, 1983), p. 222.
[316] Ibid., p. 226.

of the mystics such as Tauler, condemned all Enthusiasts to hell. Despite these and many other setbacks, mysticism was alive and kicking, and with it the belief in the inner light of God as the sole and authoritative guide of man in this life and also in the hereafter. As Johan Christian Edelmann, a pietist theologian in the beginning of the eighteenth century, put it:

> Because the sensation I experience now in my ground [*Gemüte*] is indisputably more familiar to me than that experienced by some other outside me and it touches me much more convincing a manner than that which takes place in another than me, thus I also must infallibly accept it as a norm [*Norm*] of my conscience [*Gewissen*] rather than a sensation of some other outside me. For why should my God, he who is for me in me myself [*in mir selber*] closer than anyone else, want me to understand his will through a stranger rather than through myself?[317]

Calvin's compromise

I

The basic tenets of Calvin's theology are so close to Luther's that there is no point in going into details here. Calvin agrees with Luther that man is corrupt almost to the bone. It is not only the flesh that is corrupt but also and even predominantly humanity's will and reason: 'Everything which is in man, from the intellect to will, from the soul to the flesh, is defiled and pervaded with concupiscence.'[318] Like Luther, Calvin thinks that justification does not come from works of law but from faith alone, and therefore that the Christian conscience must be free from all laws: 'The consciences of believers, whilst seeking the assurance of their justification before God, should rise above the law, and think no more of obtaining justification by it.'[319] Likewise, for Calvin, as for Luther, the principal commandment of the law established in conscience is love, but it is impossible to keep this law because of the corrupt human nature. For the non-regenerated this keeping is absolutely impossible, since the works of unbelievers are necessarily counted as sins,[320] whilst the small number of regenerated, strictly separated from the rest of humankind by God, can at times perform acts required by this law, at least in part.[321] Yet although the law is of no use with regard to justification, it is not thereby rendered inoperative. It is still useful and even

---

[317] Cited in Heinz D. Kittsteiner, *Die Entstehung des Modernen Gewissens* (Frankfurt am Main: Suhrkamp, 1995), p. 113.

[318] Calvin, *Institutes*, 2.1.8, p. 218.

[319] Ibid., 3.19.2, p. 131.

[320] Ibid., 2.5.1, p. 273. 'Man is so enslaved by the yoke of sin that he cannot of his own nature aim at good either in wish or actual pursuit.' Ibid., 2.4.1, p. 265.

[321] Ibid., 3.14.3–5, pp. 75–7. According to Calvin, Adam's righteousness, vitiated and almost destroyed by the fall, is 'partly seen in the elect, insofar as they are regenerated by the Spirit'. Ibid., 1.15.4, p. 165.

indispensable, especially the natural law established in the 'conscience which God has engraved on the minds of men'.[322] The first use of the law of conscience is to deprive man of 'all pretext of ignorance',[323] 'to render man inexcusable'[324] and to incur a sense of guilt,[325] in order for man, who is blinded by self-love, to be brought at once to know and to confess his weakness and impurity, which is the condition for receiving the grace of Christ.[326] This is the very definition of conscience: it is a sense which does not allow men to conceal their sins, 'but drags them forward as culprits to the bar of God'.[327] The second use of the law is to kerb those who, unless forced, have 'no regard for rectitude and justice',[328] although mere natural law is not sufficient here but requires that its precepts are written down and implemented by magistrates. In fact, natural law, although 'true and eternal rule of righteousness',[329] is not adequate even for the first use of the law, which is why the Mosaic Law was given. In other words, although this law established in the conscience is a true and eternal rule pronouncing a universal judgement on good and evil, we should not thereby suppose that this judgement is in every respect sound and complete – not only by virtue of man's utter corruption, but also because a man, when it comes to a particular case, easily forgets the rule he had laid down for the general case, as Calvin put it, echoing Aquinas.[330]

Yet there are also differences between Luther and Calvin, at least in tone. First, Luther emphasized that the law was established by God primarily to inculcate humility and prevent crimes, whereas Calvin stresses that for the believers the law, first and foremost the Mosaic Law (which 'removes the obscurity of the law of nature'),[331] also functions as a rule and a guide. In other words, Calvin fully accepts the so-called third or pedagogical use of the law. In his view, in fact, this third use of the law forms its principal use and is most closely connected with its proper end:

> There are two ways in which they [the regenerated] still profit in the law. For it is the best instrument for enabling them daily to learn with greater truth and certainly that will of the Lord in which they aspire to follow, and to confirm them in this knowledge ... Then, because we need not doctrine alone, but exhortation also, the servant of God will derive this further advantage from the Law: by frequently meditating upon it, he will be excited to obedience, and confirmed in it, and so drawn away from the slippery path of sin.[332]

Second, whereas Luther believed that the Mosaic and natural law obliges the body whilst the soul and the conscience remain eternally free, Calvin thought that

---

[322] Ibid., 4.20, pp. 650–76. According to Calvin, the second tablet of the Mosaic Law is 'nothing else than the testimony of natural law'. Ibid., p. 4.10.16, p. 664.
[323] Ibid., 2.2.22, p. 242.
[324] 'Finis legis naturalis est, ut redattur homo inexcusabilis.' Ibid., 2.2.22, p. 241.
[325] Ibid., 2.7.3, p. 302.
[326] Ibid., 2.7.6–8, pp. 304–6.
[327] Ibid., 3.19.15, p. 141.
[328] Ibid., 2.7.10, p. 307.
[329] Ibid., 4.20.15–16, pp. 663–4.
[330] Ibid., 2.2.23–4, p. 242.
[331] Ibid., 2.8.1, p. 317.
[332] Ibid., 2.7.12, p. 309.

these laws, even if it is impossible to observe them fully, are indeed binding to the conscience.[333] As a matter of fact, even the laws of men bind the conscience, at least at in the general sense that men are bound to obey magistrates as the Romans 13 implies – only individual positive laws 'do not reach the conscience'.[334] Thus, whereas Luther thought that no law, whether divine, natural or human, bind the conscience, extending only to the body, Calvin believes that they all do, excluding individual positive laws which reach the 'external forum' but not the 'forum of conscience'.[335]

I a

The third use of law was not Calvin's invention. This pedagogical use was originally formulated by Melanchthon and it became established as a doctrine in the *Formula of Concord* (*Formula Concordiae*), written a generation after Luther's death with the aim of settling the serious controversies that had arisen among the theologians of the Augsburg Confession. Following Melanchthon, the *Concord* declares that the law is not given only as a torment to the conscience or a restraint to the wicked but also as a rule of life. Although Luther had not said anything opposed to Melanchthon's inclusion, the introduction of this new application of the law nevertheless marked a shift of emphasis in the Lutheran teaching. In the final instance, it entailed that the Christian life as a whole became articulated in terms of observing the law. As the *Formula of Concord* declares: 'Although the truly believing and truly converted to God and justified Christians are liberated and made free from the curse of the Law, yet they should daily exercise themselves in the Law of the Lord'.[336] Justified Christians should mediate the law day and night, 'live and walk in the law',[337] for the law is a mirror in which the will of God and what pleases Him are exactly portrayed and therefore, it 'should be constantly held up to the believers and be diligently urged upon them without ceasing'.[338] In this way, the consciences of true Christians were again entirely bound to a law which they could not avoid because the 'Law of God has been written in their heart'.[339] Faith does not replace the law of the heart and the conscience as its living witness and judge, because faith does not exist alongside the immoral intention to 'act against the conscience'.[340] In this respect, Lutheranism does not mark such a radical rupture in the Western tradition of conscience as the Catholic critics claimed: the conscience still bears witness to the law of the heart which, together with the Mosaic Law, the written version of natural law, must pervade the life of a true Christian as a 'fixed rule according to which they are to regulate and direct their whole life'.[341]

---

[333] Ibid., 3.19.16, p. 142. Calvin repeats this argument in 4.10.3–4, pp. 415–16.

[334] Ibid., 4.10.5, p. 417.

[335] Ibid., 4.10.5, p. 415.

[336] *The Solid Declaration of the Formula of Concord* 6.7, accessed 24 August 2012, http://bookofconcord. org/sd-preface.php

[337] Ibid., 6.1.

[338] Ibid., 6.7.

[339] Ibid., 6.5.

[340] *Epitome of the Formula of Concord* 3.11, accessed 24 August 2012, http://bookofconcord.org/fc-ep. php

[341] *Formula of Concord* 4.1.

II

There is still one feature related to conscience that seems to distinguish Calvin from his predecessor from Eisleben. Although Calvin's condemnation of natural man is as harsh as Luther's, he continues to employ the traditional vocabulary of remainders, seeds and sparks of Adam's original righteousness. The nature of man is not utterly base but contains some 'notions of justice and rectitude' the Greeks called *prolēpseis*, which are 'implanted by nature in the hearts of men'.[342] There are still 'some sparks' which show that he is a rational animal, 'some residue' of rectitude in intelligence and in will, 'seeds' and 'impressions' of civil order and honesty, 'some remains of the divine image', as Calvin repeatedly asserts in his *Institutes*.[343] On the one hand, these notions, seeds and impressions, the conscience as their living witness, pertain to the natural knowledge of natural moral law that stands as the sole 'aim, the rule and the end of all laws'.[344] On the other hand, they give rise to the sense of deity:

> That there exists in the human mind and indeed by natural instinct [*instinctus*], some sense of deity, we hold to be beyond dispute, since God himself, to prevent any man from pretending ignorance, has endued all men with some idea of his Godhead, the memory of which he constantly renews and occasionally enlarges.[345]

According to Calvin, in other words, 'nature herself' has sown a seed of deity and religion in all men, which is 'indelibly engraven on the human heart' and 'thoroughly fixed as it were in our very bones'.[346] This is attested to especially by the contumacy of the wicked who, though struggling furiously against this sense, unavoidably fall victim to the 'worm of conscience' gnawing them on the inside keener than a burning steal.[347] Whilst Luther maintained that by nature man 'cannot find in himself one spark of the love of God',[348] Calvin thus believed not only that such sparks, inclinations and surviving traces of Godhead exist in the natural soul of man but also that it is, at least to some extent, capable of deciphering them. Finally, whilst Luther warned not to confuse the voice of conscience with God's will, Calvin conceived conscience as a privileged locus of the Christian God-consciousness, in fact a middle place (*medium*) between God and man.[349] In the conscience, God reveals his will to man, if not immediately then at least as hints and allusions, for it 'bears reference' (*refertur*) to God.[350] In the case of sin, this reference is direct:

---

[342] John Calvin, *Commentary on the Romans*, in *Calvin's Bible Commentaries: Romans*, trans. John King (Forgotten Books, 2007), 2.14–16, pp. 68–70.
[343] Calvin, *Institutes* 2.2.12–13, pp. 233–5 and 2.2.17, p. 238.
[344] Ibid., 4.10.15–16, pp. 663–4. On the role of natural law in early Protestantism more generally, see Stephen J. Grabill, *Rediscovering the Natural Law in Reformed Theological Ethics* (Grand Rapids: Eerdmans, 2006).
[345] Ibid., 1.3.1, p. 43.
[346] Ibid., 1.3–4, pp. 44–7.
[347] Ibid., 1.3.3, pp. 44–5.
[348] Luther, *Galatians* 2.16, p. 87.
[349] Calvin, *Institutes* 3.19.15, p. 141 and 4.10.3, p. 415.
[350] Ibid., 3.19.16, p. 142.

As often, then as the secret compunctions of conscience invite us to reflect upon our sins, let us remember that God himself is speaking with us. For that interior sense by which we are convicted of sin is the peculiar judgement seat of God, where he exercises his jurisdiction.[351]

The Puritan God within

I

If the German spiritualists radicalized Luther's teachings, the English Puritans did the same to Calvin by adopting the Protestant doctrine of inner freedom but combining it with the more traditional notion of conscience. In a widely used casuistic treatise written in 1630, the Puritan divine William Ames, for instance, conceives the conscience in terms that are in many ways identical with those of Aquinas. First, Ames says that the conscience belongs to the understanding. Second, he divides the conscience in two and uses the technical term *synderesis* to denote those habitual principles of moral obligation that are written in man's heart, referring both to natural and God's law. The *synderesis* is, as Ames writes, the 'storehouse' of moral principles, which cannot be utterly lost, although it may for a time be hindered from acting.[352] Furthermore, he describes, like Aquinas, the conscience as the act of application of these principles and more precisely, as an act of practical judgement. However, whilst Aquinas thought that *synderesis* was 'merely' the angelic part of the soul, in Ames discourse it had become already the vicar of God that possesses 'the power of a will of God'.[353] Virtually all the noteworthy Puritans agreed with Ames. There is no authority that surpasses the authority of conscience in the human sphere. This was the opinion of William Perkins as well. For although he abandoned the twofold conscience and asserted that 'every particular man hath his own particular conscience',[354] he did not deny the divinity of conscience but on the contrary underlined it more fervently than anyone before him.

It is hard to overestimate Perkins' influence on the religious thought of his time. The sales of the works of this early Puritan divine from Cambridge surpassed even those of Calvin himself. His nickname, 'Calvin of England', is also telling. Like Calvin, he maintains that man's nature, both the body and the soul, is absolutely corrupted by the fall, so much so that the restoration of its original integrity is entirely dependent on faith and God's grace.[355] Yet although human nature is totally corrupt, Perkins maintains, like Calvin, that there are still 'some remnants of the light of nature' in

---

[351] Cited in Zachman, *The Assurance of Faith*, p. 100.

[352] William Ames, *Conscience with the Power and Cases Thereof* (Leyden: W. Christiaens, E. Griffin, J. Dawson, 1639), 1.2, pp. 4–5.

[353] Ibid., 1.3, p. 7.

[354] Perkins, *Discourse of Conscience*, p. 6.

[355] William Perkins, *The Foundation of the Christian Religion gathered into Six Principles*, in *The Work of William Perkins*, ed. Ian Breward (Appleford: The Sutton Courtenay Press, 1970), p. 150.

human nature, 'showing us what is good and evil'.[356] He also believes, as Calvin did, that God is universally known through the testimony of natural conscience. Namely, when a man sins, he will have a 'griping in his conscience', which is 'a strong reason to show that there is a God, before whose judgement seat he must answer for his fact'.[357] According to Perkins, the living conscience itself is a special kind of judge, namely a judge appointed by God to 'declare and put in execution his just judgement against sinners'.[358] Referring to the by-now-familiar 'books' in the Revelation, Perkins writes:

> The books of every man's doings shall be laid open, men's consciences shall made either to accuse them or excuse them, and every man shall be tried by the works which he did in his life time, because they are open and manifest signs of faith or unbelief.[359]

Moreover, like Calvin, Perkins considers the conscience a 'thing placed of God in the middle between him and man'.[360] It is even more than that since Perkins maintains that conscience, though God does not have one,[361] is of 'divine nature',[362] even 'a little God sitting in the middle of men's hearts'.[363] Therefore, it is the wisest guide and the highest judge of all human affairs, the supreme authority on earth:

> God in the heart of every man has erected a tribunal seat, and in his stead has placed neither Saint or Angel, nor any other creature whatsoever, but conscience itself, who therefore is the highest judge that is or can be under God; by whose direction also courts are kept, and laws are made.[364]

Of the relationship between the law and conscience, Perkins first states that Christ has set our consciences free from the law but then immediately adds that the law of God, both written and natural, binds the conscience universally and at all times. In other words, although Perkins admits that the Gospel, which was never impressed in man's nature, liberates man from the law,[365] he simultaneously holds that in addition to certain articles of faith also the keeping of the laws of God is necessary to a Christian and his salvation, because the 'Gospel does not abolish the law of nature, nor the positive laws of all countries, but it does establish them'.[366] To be sure, following these laws perfectly is not possible for a man and therefore it is not required from him, but this does not mean that he is not bound by them.[367] According to Perkins, the 'drowsy Protestants and lukewarm gospellers' who believe that faith in the free remission of

---

[356] Perkins, *Discourse of Conscience*, p. 68.
[357] Perkins, *Foundation of the Christian Religion*, p. 149.
[358] Perkins, *Discourse of Conscience*, p. 3.
[359] Perkins, *Foundation of the Christian Religion*, p. 166.
[360] Perkins, *Discourse of Conscience*, p. 6.
[361] Ibid., p. 9.
[362] Ibid., p. 6.
[363] Ibid., p. 9.
[364] Ibid., p. 32.
[365] Ibid., p. 31.
[366] William Perkins, *The Whole Treatise of the Cases of Conscience*, in *William Perkins 1558–1602*, ed. Thomas F. Merrill (Nieuwkoop: B. De Graaf, 1966), p. 178.
[367] Perkins, *Discourse of Conscience*, p. 11.

sins is adequate by itself should therefore be rejected.[368] It is only half of the truth that one can be saved by faith alone, without any works of the law. The works of the law do not earn salvation, but this does not entail that the binding power of the law would cease. The Gospel liberates the conscience but by liberating it the Gospel also binds it, not only to the law but also to the Gospel itself: 'The Gospel does as well bind conscience as the law, and if it be not obeyed, will as well condemn.'[369] Perkins' interpretation of 1 Corinthians 4.4 illustrates this well. According to Perkins, all men must 'labour that they may say with Paul "I know nothing by my self," that they may stand before God without blame for ever', although what Paul seems to be saying here is that despite the absence of a guilty conscience (*ouden emautō synoida*), he is not necessarily innocent since God alone is his judge. Luther, in any case, read this Pauline passage from this perspective, believing that salvation is a matter of faith and not of conscience. But for Perkins it is through the experience of conscience that an 'infallible certainty of his own salvation' becomes both ordinary and possible for man.[370] In the final analysis, obedience to conscience under the auspices of law is more important for one's salvation than faith itself.[371]

II

Thomas Hill, a Roman Catholic exile, argued in 1600 that one of the great disadvantages of Protestantism was that it, unlike Catholicism, did not teach 'cases of conscience' in which 'is set down what is sin, and what not'. In other words, Hill was concerned about the lack of casuistry in Protestantism, a form of analysis in which a priest attempts to solve the moral problems of his parishioners by applying general rules to particular cases through reasoning. Because the Protestants do not deal with these problems of conscience, he argued, they not only remain utterly ignorant of the nature, difference and quality of sins, but also seem to think, being predestined, that they are immune to these very sins.[372] In a sense, Hill was right, as there indeed was a general distaste for the guidance of conscience in early Protestantism and especially in Lutheranism. According to the Lutherans, the Catholic guidance of conscience was not only a means of the Catholic priests to torture people's consciences,[373] but it also included, especially since the introduction of probabilism in casuistry by Jean Gerson, a precarious tendency to allow consciences to remain uncertain. Gerson

---

[368] Ibid., p. 11.

[369] Ibid., p. 15.

[370] Ibid., p. 22.

[371] On conscience that goes further than faith, see ibid., p. 6

[372] Cited in Ian Breward, introduction to *The Work of William Perkins*, ed. Ian Breward (Appleford: The Sutton Courtenay Press, 1970), p. 61.

[373] It is told that Luther, when he burnt the papal bull of excommunication directed against him, also threw a manual of confession, *Summa Angelica* of Angelus de Clavasio, into the flames. 'We believe and are at peace,' William Tyndale says of Lutherans, 'in our conscience, we run not hither and thither for pardon, we trust not in this friar or that monk neither in anything save in the word of God only.' William Tyndale, *The Obedience of A Christian Man*, ed. D. S. Daniel (London: Penguin Books, 2000), pp. 101–2, 147.

had suggested that a good Christian may act with a safe conscience even if the moral legitimacy of a course of action could not be established with absolute certainty: it suffices that the conscience is merely probable.[374] According to Luther, this is false. The conscience of a Christian must always be certain and secure, even if it occasionally feels scruples. This does not mean, however, that Hill would have been entirely correct in his estimation. As we have seen, Lutheranism and Protestantism more generally developed in the direction of legalism. The law is made inoperative by faith and yet a Christian must observe it day and night, as the *Formula of Concordia* demanded. This demand, together with the doctrine of the pedagogical use of law, introduced by Melanchthon, epitomized the need of guidance and casuistry.[375] This need was met particularly in sixteenth-century English Puritanism.

Like the majority of Protestants, Puritans believed in the idea of the priesthood of all believers, but they also saw it necessary to promote and develop casuistry and to write casuistic manuals for the priests. Yet the *raison d'être* of Puritan casuistry was different from the Catholic one. The aim was not to heal the scruples of conscience by lowering the standards of morality, but to raise them, to make people more rule-abiding and conscientious. This moralism is visibly present in Perkins, too, who, as a matter of fact, was responsible for introducing casuistry into the Puritan discourse.[376] This moralism also explains his stance against both Lutherans and Catholics. Perkins argued against the Lutherans because they allegedly neglected the law, but he polemicized against the Catholics too, primarily because of the laxity of their casuistic practices. In his view, the Church cannot grant dispensations of God's laws, as often happens when a casuist calculates the probabilities of sins. It is not possible, he argues, that God should liberate a conscience from the moral law and hence from the bondage of sin, but keep it subjected to the laws and the ordinances of the Church. In his view this is absurd.[377] Moreover, Perkins angrily rejects, not unlike the Lutherans, the Catholic assumption according to which it is not a sin to do something with a doubting conscience.[378] The Council of Trent had considered being assured of one's personal election as an inexcusable presumption, but the only conscience that Perkins sees to please God is the conscience that is perfectly assured of the remission of its sins and the forthcoming everlasting life. A Christian is also bound in his conscience to be infallibly certain of his salvation.[379] Without such conscience, there is neither justification nor sanctification and therefore, whomever the Gospel has been revealed must

---

[374] See Rudolf Schüssler, 'Jean Gerson, Moral Certainty and the Renaissance of Ancient Scepticism,' *Renaissance Studies* 23:4 (2009): 445–54.

[375] Indeed, much of Melanchthon's second book of the *Epitome of Moral Philosophy* consists of applied ethics in which he tests his moral theory by evaluating a wide range of contemporary problems according to it. See Ralph Keen, 'Defending the Pious: Melanchthon and the Reformation in Albertine Saxony, 1539,' *Church History* 60:2 (1991): 180–96.

[376] Perkins published two tracts on casuistry during his lifetime. *A Case of Conscience – the Greatest that Ever was* appeared in 1592 and *A Discourse of Conscience* in 1595. Some minor works were published also earlier, but without much impact, including J. Woolton, *Of the Conscience* 1575 and A. Hume, *A Treatise of Conscience* 1594.

[377] Perkins, *Discourse of Conscience*, p. 31.

[378] Ibid., p. 41.

[379] Ibid., p. 61.

strive incessantly to obtain such a conscience. And if the way to heaven was opened up by a certain conscience, was it not necessary to teach to the priests and pastors how to deal with the cases of conscience of their parishioners – despite the fact that they already had the Bible as a guide? According to Perkins, it was. On the one hand, the Bible is the true anchor of conscience: 'Search the scriptures', Perkins wrote, 'to see what is sin and what is not sin in every action', admonishing the believer to do 'nothing at any time against thy conscience, rightly informed by the word'.[380] On the other hand, however, even if everybody could grasp the message of the Ten Commandments, it was not easy to decipher, on account of the Word alone, that pastimes like dancing and dicing, even if not forbidden either by the Word or any human laws, can still count as acts against the law of God.[381]

III

Perkins' *Discourse of Conscience* was published in 1595. It was not the first English treatise on the subject with a Protestant leaning, but it was one of the most influential. Moreover, it ushered in an animated period in the publication of books and pamphlets on conscience at the turn of the century and right afterwards. By the beginning of the seventeenth century, the conscience had become, as the historians tell us, a sort of catchword ringing on everyone's lips. The conscience discussed was usually that conscience of Perkins.[382] In a sermon given in 1616 and published under the title *Balm from Gilead to Recover Conscience*, Samuel Ward of Ipswich, for instance, made use of many Perkinsian ideas and metaphors: 'Conscience is God's lieutenant, and under him the principal commander and chief controller of man's life, yea every man's god in that sense that Moses was Aaron's'.[383] According to Ward, the conscience is a 'small god within', subject to God but nobody else, to which God has allotted more 'force and power' than 'all other agents', including angels, kings, magistrates, fathers, mothers and any superiors.[384] Indeed, the conscience makes man a godlike, self-sufficient and independent being, even an automaton. Ward writes:

> [The conscience in man is] the principal part of God's image, and that by which he resembles most the autarchy and self-sufficiency of God, which I grant is proper to this infiniteness, to be content and complete within itself; but under him, and with his leave and love, this faculty makes man self-sufficient and independent of other creatures, like unto those self-moving engines, which have their principle of motion within themselves.[385]

Because of this faculty, in other words, man no longer needs any external guidance, not to mention external authority. The force and power of conscience is greater than

---

[380] William Perkins, *A Grain of Mustard Seed*, in *The Work of William Perkins*, p. 407.

[381] Perkins, *Discourse of Conscience*, p. 46.

[382] On the post-Perkinsian Puritan conscience, see John S. Wilks, *The Idea of Conscience in Renaissance Tragedy* (London: Routledge, 1990), pp. 34–43.

[383] Samuel Ward, *Balme from Gilead to Recouer Conscience* (London: Roger Jackson, 1616), pp. 21–2.

[384] Ward, *Balme*, pp. 19, 21.

[385] Ibid., pp. 18–19.

any other power on earth and even the power of angels, not because it truly has this power on earth but because this power is the most authoritative. Eventually, its authority surpasses even the authority of the Word, since, as Ward writes, we must follow, as the Apostle Paul suggested, the dictate of conscience rather than the dictates of angel, potentate or prelate, ending his list with 'yes, even of Apostle himself'.[386]

Historians have paid a lot of attention to the fact that the increasing demands for liberty of conscience since Luther form one of the cornerstones for the subsequent development of the political culture in the West, but they rarely emphasize that this liberty was a mere logical outcome of the Christian doctrine of the *sovereignty* of conscience. Already the Scholastics had reasoned that the compulsion of conscience meant a compulsion to sin. Yet they as a rule believed that Church authority ultimately surpasses the authority of conscience – if not in principle then at least in practice. In point of fact, the same holds true with Lutheranism and Calvinism once they were established as national churches. Luther had claimed the right to freely interpret the Bible, but it did not take long before this very interpretation became regarded as the final word of truth: *Gottes Wort ist Luthers Lehr* was the credo of the orthodox, engraved on a memorial coin of the year 1617 – and any deviation from it was conceived as heresy. Hence, as soon as Lutheranism, or Calvinism for that matter, became established as a church with its own doctrine, the freedom of conscience was immediately severely diminished, if not entirely abolished. In *Temporal Authority*, Luther had written that heresy can never be restrained by force and that everybody is entitled to preach as he or she likes regardless of the opinion of princes, but already Melanchthon thought that it is entirely within the prince's rights to control the impious forms of worship.[387] However, Luther's basic message that no church authority can overcome the authority of conscience when properly anchored in the word of God was not forgotten. This was the message of various Protestant groups all around the Europe from Anabaptists and spiritualists to Huguenots and English dissenters. Moreover, as we have already seen, the most radical of them refused to subordinate conscience even to the Bible. For them, the authority of the Bible was merely external authority, because the true authority resides within: 'The pre-eminent and supreme authority', John Milton wrote, 'is the authority of the Spirit, which is internal, and the individual possession of each man.'[388] It is in the light of this spirit that the Word can and must be understood:

> Every believer is entitled to interpret the scriptures; and by that I mean interpret them for himself. He has the spirit, who guides truth, and he has the mind of Christ. Indeed, no one else can usefully interpret them for him, unless that person's interpretation coincides with the one he makes for himself and his own conscience.[389]

---

[386] Ibid., p. 49.
[387] See Keen, 'Defending the Pious,' p. 184.
[388] John Milton, *Complete Prose Works*, ed. M. Kelley, vol. 6 (New Haven: Yale University Press, 1973), p. 587.
[389] Ibid., pp. 583–4.

Philip the Chancellor had argued that the erroneous conscience is like someone who knows in general that every she-mule is sterile but who nevertheless believes that this she-mule is pregnant on account of his *conscientia*.[390] If the radical Protestant conscience dictated that this she-mule is pregnant, it indeed was pregnant, because the inner light of conscience – which was the sanctuary of God – convinced him to believe so: 'Whosoever hath the divine light of faith in him, that man hath no need of man's law to be his rule, but he is law unto himself',[391] as the co-founder of the Muggletonian movement John Reeve asserted. Some of the most radical Protestants went so far as to declare that swearing, drunkenness, adultery or theft were no more sinful than prayer, if the inner light was informing the soul, or, in the words of Laurence Clarkson: 'No matter what Scripture, Saints, or Churches say, if that within you do not condemn you, you will not be condemned.'[392] Yet none of these radicals suggested that man, let alone an individual, was the origin of this thing within, for it comes from God. It is God's lieutenant, a ray of divine light, but it is not self-legislating, for even if it is the legislating faculty, even the supreme faculty of earthly legislation, it is not self-sufficient, because the source of this voice resides outside the self. Yet it *makes* a man self-sufficient and it does so *because* it is the voice of the Other.

On the modern protestant conscience

I

There is a remarkable continuity in the history of Christian conscience. With the exception of the Jansenists (condemned by Pope Innocent X in 1655), whose conception of conscience resembles the Lutheran one, the Catholic doctrine of conscience has remained almost the same throughout centuries: 'One is always bound to follow conscience when it feels certain about its immediate duty', as it is said in the *Theologiae Moralis Principia* from the 1920s, which was one of the manuals commonly used as textbooks in seminaries training men for priesthood.[393] In the Pastoral Constitution on the Church in the Modern World from 1965 (II Vatican: *Gaudium et Spes* 1.1.16), we find the following:

> In the depths of his conscience [*conscientia*], man detects a law which he does not impose upon himself, but which holds him to obedience. Always summoning him to love good and avoid evil, the voice of conscience when necessary speaks to his heart: do this, shun that. For man has in his heart a law written by God; to obey it is the very dignity of man; according to it he will be judged. Conscience is the

---

[390] Cited in Lottin, *Psychologie*, p. 155.
[391] Cited in Edward G. Andrew, *Conscience and its Critics: Protestant Conscience, Enlightenment Reason, and Modern Subjectivity* (Toronto: University of Toronto Press, 2001), p. 31.
[392] Cited in ibid., p. 31.
[393] Cited in D'Arcy, *Conscience*, p. 122.

most secret core and sanctuary of a man [*nucleus secretissimus atque sacrarium hominis*]. There he is alone with God, Whose voice echoes [*resonat*] in his depths.

Even the technical term *synderesis* features sometimes in contemporary Catholic texts, including the Catechism of the Catholic Church (paragraph 1780) published in 1992:

> Conscience includes the perception of the principles of morality (*synderesis*); their application in the given circumstances by practical discernment of reason and goods; and finally judgement about concrete acts yet to be performed or already performed.[394]

Admittedly, there have been numerous struggles centring on the freedom of conscience in Catholicism – the idea that was more than often condemned by the popes but that nonetheless has appealed to many Catholics throughout the centuries.[395] The most famous example is undoubtedly Cardinal Newman's defence of this freedom in the middle of the nineteenth century, but because Newman does not add anything substantial to the traditional understanding of conscience, a couple of representative passages suffice here: 'The rule and measure of duty is not utility, nor experience, nor the happiness of the greatest number, nor State convenience, nor fitness, order, and the *pulchrum*.' The rule and measure of duty is conscience, for it is 'a messenger from Him, who, both in nature and in grace, speaks to us behind the veil, and teaches and rules us by His representatives.' Newman summarizes:

> Conscience is the aboriginal Vicar of Christ, a prophet in its informations, a monarch in its peremptoriness, a priest in its blessings and anathemas, and, even though the eternal priesthood throughout the Church could cease to be, in it the sacerdotal principle would remain and would have a sway.[396]

II

Among the Reformed, the theme of natural law fades gradually away, but not the idea that the experience of conscience is a privileged religious experience. It bears reference to God even in Søren Kierkegaard's theology, though devoid of foundation in nature. It is true that in Kierkegaard's estimation the conscience (*Samvittighed*) that people usually call 'conscience' is not conscience at all, but rather 'moods, stomach reflexes, vagrant impulses' and so on.[397] In addition to this conscience, however, there exists a

---

[394] *Catechism of the Catholic Church* 3.1.6.1.1780, accessed 24 August 2012, http://www.vatican.va/archive/ENG0015/_INDEX.HTM

[395] In the Encyclical *Mirari Vos* (15 August 1832), Pope Gregory XVI for instance proclaims: it is 'absurd and erroneous proposition' that 'liberty of conscience must be maintained for everyone' for it 'spreads ruin in sacred and civil affairs', as 'thence comes transformation of minds, corruption of youths, contempt of sacred things and holy laws – in other words, a pestilence more deadly to the state than any other'. Accessed 24 October 2012, http://www.papalencyclicals.net/Greg16/g16mirar.htm

[396] Newman, 'A Letter Addressed to His Grace the Duke of Norfolk,' p. 449.

[397] Søren Kierkegaard, *Søren Kierkegaard's Journals and Papers*, vols 1–5, ed. H. and E. Hong (Bloomington: Indiana University Press, 1967), vol. 1, p. 321.

genuine conscience. Everyone has this conscience, but people do not usually know anything about it, because they are deafened by the noise of the crowd: 'If we are part of a group it means good-night to conscience.'[398] Indeed, the very substance of public life is the 'lack of conscience'.[399] The genuine conscience is heard only in solitude and silence, in the stillness of the soul: 'Without stillness conscience does not exist at all.'[400] Yet once we attune to the voice of conscience in solitude, silence, and stillness, it does speak to us. What, then, does it say to us? Like the Heideggerian call of conscience, it summons us to become individuals. Unlike in Heidegger, however, this silence and stillness of conscience is not the silence of death, but on the contrary, 'it is the transition to life',[401] namely to eternal life. It is eternity that speaks in conscience – and it is precisely eternity that 'takes hold of each one separately with the strong arms of conscience, encircles him as the single individual, sets him apart with his conscience'.[402] Moreover, to the extent that it is eternity that speaks in conscience, conscience is man's God-relationship: 'A man could not have anything on his conscience if God were not present, for the relationship between the individual and God, the God-relationship [*Guds-Forholdet*], is conscience.'[403] Such a conscience must pervade the walk of whole life of the Christian, or as Kierkegaard in the *Works of Love* writes:

> It is in the nature of the inner power of conscience to spread abroad just like God's omnipresence, which one cannot restrict to a certain place and then say that God is everywhere present by being in this particular place, for that is to deny his omnipresence. In the same way to restrict the conscience-relationship to something in particular is to deny altogether the conscience-relationship.[404]

As to the nature of this relationship – the God-relationship called conscience – Kierkegaard holds that it is a relationship of debt. It is a relationship of debt because with it the heart becomes infinitely bound to God and his law of love. However, inasmuch as God is omnipresent, every relation between man and man is also 'a relationship of conscience [*Samvittigheds-Forhold*]'[405] and thereby a relationship of debt. Every Christian must conceive every other human being in terms of infinite debt. He is infinitely bound by the divine law of love to love everybody infinitely, that is, 'to remain in the debt of love to everybody'.[406] The psychological manifestation of this debt is anguished conscience: 'Remove the anguished conscience and you may as well close the churches and turn them into dance halls.'[407] Anguished conscience is the very essence of Christianity and thus, without the anxiety of anguished conscience,

[398] Ibid., vol. 2, p. 417.
[399] Ibid., vol. 3, p. 320.
[400] Søren Kierkegaard, *Three Discourses on Imagined Occasions*, ed. H. and E. Hong (Princeton: Princeton University Press, 1993), pp. 11–12.
[401] Kierkegaard, *Three Discourses*, p. 12.
[402] Søren Kierkegaard, *Upbuilding Discourses in Various Spirits*, ed. H. and E. Hong (Princeton: Princeton University Press, 1993), pp. 128–9.
[403] Søren Kierkegaard, *Works of Love*, trans. H. and E. Hong (New York: Harper & Row, 1962), p. 143.
[404] Ibid., p. 140.
[405] Ibid., p. 137.
[406] Ibid., p. 174.
[407] Kierkegaard, *Journals and Papers*, vol. 3, p. 63.

one 'will never become a Christian'.[408] Luther knew it, but his mistake was to believe that Christ removes the anguished conscience. According to Kierkegaard, Luther in fact turns Christianity upside down, as it becomes 'an optimism anticipating that we are to have an easy life in this world'.[409] Christ does not remove anguished conscience but confirms it. God is love, but because we know that we are unconditionally loved by God, we also know that we are infinitely indebted to Him and through him to the whole humankind, so that nothing can remove our anguished conscience. Without such a conscience, man knows nothing about the love of God – which does not remove guilty conscience, but requires that we unconditionally and without reward sacrifice ourselves to Him.

III

Let us lastly briefly examine the concept of conscience in the *Ethics* of the most eminent twentieth-century Protestant theologian, Karl Barth, one of the fiercest enemies of natural theology. Consistent with his aversion to such theology, Barth rejects what he calls the Catholic conception of conscience as the voice of truth naturally immanent in man as well as the alleged Enlightenment view according to which the voice of conscience is the voice of humanity within each particular conscience.[410] According to Barth, we all have a conscience as fallen creatures (Adam and Eve had no conscience in the Paradise), and therefore each individual has an own idiosyncratic conscience which speaks solely to him or her.[411] With Barth, in other words, the conscience becomes, in principle, entirely subjectivist and therefore an object of great suspicion:

> Even though the voice of my heart or conscience be ever so loud and credible, who has given to it the authority of a final word, the authority of God's command? What kind of an equation has preceded this bold equation? Might it be the equation of God and myself, i.e., the true and typical equation of sin in which we do not love God but want to be God?[412]

Yet not even Barth wants to dispense with conscience. According to him, in fact, the voice of conscience (*Stimme des Gewissens*), our own voice, is 'undoubtedly God's voice'.[413] In what sense, then, can the voice of conscience be God's voice, if the gap between God and natural man is absolute and unbridgeable, as Barth believes? Let us examine the analysis of conscience he gives in his *Ethics*.

Barth starts with an assumption that the voice of conscience is usually conceived as an alien inner voice addressing the one who encounters it: 'When my conscience speaks to me, I am addressed. Someone encounters me.'[414] But it is not God who is

---

[408] Ibid., vol. 1, p. 199.
[409] Ibid., vol. 3, p. 103.
[410] See Barth, *Ethics*, p. 278.
[411] Ibid., p. 493.
[412] Ibid., p. 295.
[413] Ibid., p. 480.
[414] Ibid.

addressing me. This someone is not somebody else than me. In the voice of conscience, I judge myself, being simultaneously the judge and the judged, the addressee and the addressed: 'I find that I am on both sides.'[415] Yet the 'I' on these sides is not the same 'I'. There are two separate selves, says Barth, the 'I' in my present state and the 'I' in a state of 'pure futurity' (*in reinen zukünftigkeit*).[416] In the voice of conscience, it is the 'I' of pure futurity that speaks to me, passing judgement on the 'I' in its present state. But the 'I' of this pure futurity is not the 'I' of tomorrow or next year, for it is nothing less than the 'I' of Judgement Day. This 'I' judges me in my present state from the point of view of eternity: 'Conscience is the living and present message of the coming kingdom of God.'[417] Thus, when the conscience condemns us, it condemns us to eternal death:

> When we really regard ourselves as condemned by our conscience, we know very well that this condemnation, providing we have heard it aright, is not just any condemnation but a final judgement on us, not just any restraint that might be placed upon us but the restraint that is placed upon us when we are condemned to death.[418]

At the same time the message of conscience is the living and present message of the promise of the coming redemption: 'In conscience I hear my voice as that of the redeemed child of God.'[419] The 'I' of pure futurity, the voice of conscience, has thus two possible messages: the message of condemnation and the message of redemption. According to Barth, this is how the message of the voice of conscience must be understood – eschatologically.

Consistently with this, Barth denies that people who have not heard the Word of God would have a conscience in the first place: 'We have conscience as a judicial authority within us to the extent that God has us in his Word.'[420] It is thanks to this Word that conscience may attain truth:

> A conscience which tells us the truth has to be the conscience which is captive to the Word of God, and this captivity has to signify no more and no less than its elevation to participation in the truth itself.[421]

To those who do have the Word of God in themselves, Barth continues, the judgement of conscience is an unconditional judgement. It must be obeyed unconditionally, because its authority is absolute. Yet this obedience does not make us slaves to conscience, because its voice is always mine – the voice of my pure futurity. In point of fact, obedience to this voice entails unconditional *freedom*. When I subject myself to the unconditional judgement of conscience, I become absolutely free and cannot be conditioned by anything or anybody else. Therefore, the voice of conscience is

---

[415] Ibid., p. 480.
[416] Ibid.
[417] Ibid., p. 487.
[418] Ibid., p. 482.
[419] Ibid., p. 486.
[420] Ibid., p. 481.
[421] Ibid., p. 477.

revolutionary through and through. According to Barth, however, this revolutionary freedom does not imply autonomy – that 'mad autonomism [*Autonomismus*] which has come to characterise the deeschatologized consciousness in both its modern and its Roman Catholic version.'[422] True freedom is not autonomous because freedom is possible only by virtue of one's decision to be an obedient child of God bound by his word: 'As a captive to the Word of God, he is free.'[423] Only submission to the Word of God which contains the promise of final judgement liberates man from all other authorities, states and churches – from all claims made by others. To be bound by God's promise announced in the Word is to be liberated in the world: 'Proclaiming the absolute future, conscience proclaims the relativity of everything present [*die Relativität alles gegenwärtigen*].'[424]

Now we know why the voice of conscience is undoubtedly God's voice. Inasmuch as conscience is knowledge shared by the present 'I' with the 'I' of pure futurity, that is, with the 'I' that has found its home in God's Word, conscience is 'co-knowledge with God'. Yet this co-knowledge is completely different from the co-knowledge with God in the Scholastic *synderesis*. This knowledge is entirely situational: 'The pronouncement of conscience may be very different today from what it was yesterday, just as today is not yesterday.'[425] Conscience is not a store-house of moral principles. 'Even the most authentic pronouncement of conscience', Barth writes, 'cannot be stored and then unthinkingly brought out and proclaimed as the truth the next day or twenty years later because it was once so authentic and powerful.'[426] In effect, conscience is not an entity (*Sache*), but an event (*Ereignis*). It is like the manna given to the Israelites in the wilderness: it cannot be laid in store but 'rings forth afresh each unrepeatable today'.[427] It is an event in which we have to tell ourselves something as children of God. What we have to say to ourselves, however, has nothing to do with moral principles and convictions. The Christian conscientiousness does not mean, Barth tells us, that we follow such and such holy principles, not even the so-called law of the heart. In fact, this law has no other meaning than that people accuse and excuse themselves individually, which is an 'arrogant and unauthoritative affair'.[428] The event of conscience means fundamental openness and willingness to be guided by the conscience, which in its openness to the Word and to God's promise has something *new* to say at every moment – also to the sum total of our shared human morality.[429] This is not to say that there is nothing constant in the message of the Christian conscience. On the one hand, when the conscience speaks, it involves a categorical command to wait and seek for the coming kingdom in God.[430] On the other hand, it drives us

---

[422] Ibid., p. 285.
[423] Ibid., p. 482.
[424] Ibid., p. 487.
[425] Ibid., p. 496.
[426] Ibid., p. 495.
[427] Ibid.
[428] Ibid., p. 477.
[429] Ibid., p. 496.
[430] Ibid., p. 489.

outside ourselves to engage in responsible action here on earth, for the call of conscience is also a call for responsibility, as it makes 'each individual responsible as such'.[431]

---

[431] Ibid., p. 494.

4

Conscience in Early Modern Moral and Political Philosophy

In *Beyond Good and Evil*, Friedrich Nietzsche writes:

> To figure out and determine, for example, what kind of history the problem of science [*Wissen*] and conscience [*Gewissen*] has so far had in the soul of *homines religiosi*, one might perhaps have to be as profound, as wounded, as monstrous as Pascal's intellectual conscience was.[1]

Nietzsche may be right. But it would be a mistake to assume that conscience had been a problem or a question for *homines religiosi* alone. It was a problem and a question, usually also a solution, for the philosophers of the Enlightenment as well. At least, it was a solution for the first openly atheist movement in the West after Christianity, the so-called *Gewissener* founded by the radical democrat Matthias Knutzen (Cnuzen) in 1673: 'They asserted' as Pierre Bayle tells us, 'that there is no other God, no other Religion, no other lawful Magistracy, but *Conscience*'.[2] This is indeed what Knutzen preached:

> We deny the existence of God; we deeply despise the authorities [*Magistratum*] and also reject the churches with all their priests. To *Conscientiariis* one is not sufficient but many [*Plurimorum*] … Here is our conscience that is given to all men by the generous Mother Nature. It [conscience] replaces Bible (Rom 2.14–15) as well as authority, being the true judge [*Tribunal*], as Gregory of Nazianzen says … and it replaces the priest, because it performs the works of the doctor, teaching us to harm nobody, to live in honesty, and to give everybody what is his. If we do evil, it brings us thousand tortures, even Hell, but if we live well, it becomes our Heaven in this life which is the only one there is. This same conscience comes into existence with our birth and it disappears when we pass into death. These are the principles that are innate in us: whoever rejects them rejects himself.[3]

4

---

1 Friedrich Nietzsche, *Beyond Good and Evil*, trans. W. Kaufmann (New York: Dover Publications, 1997), §45, p. 33.
2 Pierre Bayle, *A General Dictionary, Historical and Critical* (London: James Bettenham, 1734–41), vol. 6, p. 554.
3 Matthias Knutzen (Cnuzen), 'Amicus Amicis Amica!' Originally published in 1675 and reprinted in Veyssière La Croze, *Entretiens sur divers sujets d'histoire et de religion, entre My Lord Bolingbroke, et Isaac D'Orobio, rabin des Juifs portugais à Amsterdam* (London, 1770), pp. 413–14. On *Gewissener*, see Kittsteiner, *Die Entstehung des modernen Gewissens*, pp. 101–56.

What is remarkable here is that it was the very same Pauline conscience of the Romans (2.14–15) that had hitherto borne witness to the existence of God that now testified to his non-existence. The authority of conscience not only surpasses the opinion of men and the Bible but also God himself. Otherwise, however, Knutzen's doctrine of conscience is perfectly in line with the Christian tradition of conscience since the Fathers, not only because the authors Knutzen cites are Christian but also because the substance of the argument is inherently Christian. What are absent are the external authority of the church and the state, the entire tradition of the Romans 13 as well as God and the afterlife, that is to say, the rewards of heaven and punishments of hell by means of which the Christian conscience was traditionally pacified and terrified. In other words, Knutzen contracts the vast Christian game of elemental spiritual forces within the soul. What is perhaps most interesting here, however, is that not even all Christians denounced Knutzen. One of his defenders was the above-mentioned pietist theologian J. C. Edelmann. His support for Knutzen was not of course based on the latter's denial of God but on Knutzen's belief in the supreme authority of conscience in human life: for this reason he could not be, Edelmann argued, an atheist at all, since the conscience is the living God within us.[4]

The witness of natural law from Suárez to Pufendorf

I

Before analysing the history of this godless conscience, we must return to the early modern philosophy, first shortly to the early modern Catholic theory of natural law and then to its Protestant variants. To the Catholic theorists, it was self-evident that there is a direct link between the dictates of conscience and natural law. As already mentioned, the Catholic natural law theorists, such as Francisco Suárez, argued that from the beginning of the world all men have been universally subject to natural law, that the obligation this law lays on the conscience is absolute, and that all those who fail to observe it inevitably transgress, becoming thus 'legal culprits in the sight of God'.[5] God, who in his own moral acts is guided by his 'eternal reason as by law',[6] has inscribed this law in the hearts of men and it can be found in the *synderesis* which is one and the same in all men.[7] Moreover, it is precisely in the experience of conscience (*conscientia*) the precepts of this law are discerned, independently of any knowledge of the revelation or the scriptures:

> Conscience [*conscientia*] bears witness to and reveals the work of the law written in hearts of men, since it testifies that a man does ill or well, when he resists or obeys the natural dictates of right reason [*dictamen naturale rectae rationis*], revealing also, in

---

[4] See ibid., p. 113.
[5] Suárez, *On Laws* 1.18.3, p. 132.
[6] Ibid., 2.2.3, p. 153.
[7] Ibid., 2.8.5, p. 220.

consequence, the fact that such dictates have the force of law over men, even though, they may not be externally clothed in the form of written law.[8]

Insofar as the conscience reveals the dictates of right reason and natural law, men are always bound to obey their consciences.[9] According to Suárez, in effect, to act against conscience incurs eternal punishment,[10] and, conversely, by obeying it a man paves his way to heaven: 'Observance of a just law is essentially conducive to salvation.'[11] Suárez admits that someone may be ignorant of the precepts of natural law, but such ignorance cannot exist without guilt, not at least for any great length of time: 'For knowledge of these precepts may be acquired by very little diligence; and nature itself, and conscience, are so insistent in the case of the acts relating to those [precepts] as to permit no inculpable ignorance of them.'[12] He also admits that the conscience is wont to apply not merely true law but reputed law as well, in which sense it sometimes occurs that 'conscience is in error'.[13] But where the conscience bears witness to a reputed law, it must be guided towards the true law. This is the law as it is taught by the Catholic Church, whose interpretation of the law of nature is the best, as 'the Universal Church cannot err in those matters which pertain to faith and morals'.[14]

Suárez assumed that the Protestant did not believe in the law written in the heart but, as we have seen, this was not the case, neither with Luther nor with Calvin. The subsequent generations of reformed theologians and philosophers were even more convinced of the existence of this law witnessed by conscience. Let us start with Jerome Zanchi, the leading Reformed political theorist before Johannes Althusius. According to him, the law of nature law is the foundation of all legislation. This law is inscribed in all hearts and it is the conscience that bears witness to it, to the effect that 'sinning against conscience is sinning against God who teaches and advises us from within'.[15] Contrary to Aquinas and Suárez, however, Zanchi holds that we do not carry a seed of Adam's original rectitude in conscience, for the natural law is inscribed 'in the minds and hearts of human beings *after* the fall'.[16] On the other hand, unlike Augustine, who argued that the law of the heart is imprinted only in those Gentiles who were converted to the Gospel, Zanchi maintains that this must have taken place before the Gospel, otherwise all people, including the Old Testament prophets, would have wandered in total darkness before the first coming of Christ.[17] Hence, Zanchi introduced a third alternative between the two extremes: the rectitude of the present

---

[8]   Ibid., 2.5.10, p. 184.
[9]   Ibid., 2.9.6, pp. 226–7.
[10]   It does so 'even if the transgressor be ignorant of every supernatural law'. Ibid., p. 225.
[11]   Ibid., 1.9.10, p. 113.
[12]   Ibid., 2.9.7, pp. 221–2.
[13]   Ibid., 2.5.15, p. 187.
[14]   Ibid., 3.23.13, p. 696.
[15]   Hieronymus Zanchi, 'On the Law in General', trans. J. Veenstra, *Journal of Markets & Morality* 6:1 (Spring 2003): 331. *On the Law in General* (*De lege in genere*) is Chapter X of the fourth volume of Zanchi's eight-volume *Operum theologicorum*, published 1617.
[16]   Ibid., p. 329. Italics mine.
[17]   On this subject Zanchi agreed with his contemporary Peter Martyr Vermigli, also an Italian Reformed theologian of a Thomistic persuasion. On Vermigli's position, see Grabill, *Rediscovering the Natural Law*, pp. 199–220.

conscience does not relate to the remnant of Adam's original righteousness,[18] but neither does it relate to the regeneration through the Gospel. Rather, it pertains to the secret reworking of God in the hearts of men right after and since the fall.[19] Although this law is distributed by God as he sees fit, it does not follow that it would be given to some and denied from others. It is written more fully and effectively in the hearts of the elect,[20] but it is nonetheless inscribed in all hearts – so forcefully that it 'cannot be altered by anyone or completely blotted out'.[21]

Johannes Althusius' account of conscience in *Politica* (1603) resembles a lot that of Zanchi. Althusius first affirms, like Protestants in general, the corruptness of man, declaring that the knowledge of natural law is not so firmly established there that it would be sufficiently efficacious in restraining men from doing evil and impelling them towards good. It merely teaches, inclines and accuses men, but it does not enforce its subjects as a positive or proper law does. Yet it is nonetheless the knowledge of natural law (*jus naturale*), 'imprinted within us by God',[22] on which positive laws of men must be based. This knowledge is exposed in conscience (*conscientia*), for it is by virtue of conscience that 'man knows and understands law [*jus*]', as also Romans 2.14–15 indicates. According to Althusius, all men possess such knowledge of conscience. It is an 'innate inclination' (*inclinatione innata*) and a 'secret instinct of nature' (*arcane naturae instinctu*),[23] urging man to perform what he understands to be just and to avoid what he knows to be unjust. Contrary to Zanchi, however, Althusius believes that this secret instinct is a relic of Adam's original righteousness in the fallen man. Yet Althusius was not entirely in agreement with the Thomist position either, for although the knowledge of natural law imprinted in the consciences of men is 'communicated more abundantly to some and more sparingly to others', it is not so because some think about it more profoundly, as Aquinas thought, but 'according to the will and judgement of God'.[24]

Althusius' views were affirmed in numerous subsequent Reformed reflections on the subject. Even the earnest defenders of Calvinist orthodoxy were convinced of the existence of natural law and the conscience as its witness. In his *Institutes of Elenctic Theology*, Francis Turretin writes:

> There is a natural law not arising from a voluntary contract or law of society but from a divine obligation being impressed by God upon the conscience [*conscientia*] of man in his very creation, on which the difference between right and wrong is founded and which contains the practical principles of immovable truth [*principia practica immotae veritatis*].[25]

---

[18] Zanchi, 'On the Law in General', pp. 328–9.
[19] Ibid., p. 327.
[20] Ibid., p. 335.
[21] Ibid., p. 336.
[22] Johannes Althusius, *Politica: Politics Methodically Set Forth and Illustrated with Sacred and Profane Examples*, trans. F. Carney (Indianapolis: Liberty Fund, 1995), 21.20, pp. 139–40.
[23] Ibid., 21.20, p. 140.
[24] Ibid., 21.21, p. 140.
[25] Francis Turretin, *Institutes of Elenctic Theology in 3 vols*, ed. J. Dennison (New Jersey: Presbyterian and Reformed Publishing Company, 1992–7), 11.1.7.

Right and wrong do not depend upon man's will, but they do not depend on the free will of God either, because something is not good because God wills it but rather God wills it, Turretin argues, because it is intrinsically good, founded on the nature of God.[26] He admits that the fall severely corrupted the rectitude of the original conscience and hence the knowledge of the practical principles of immovable truth, but some remnants of it survived, as for instance the remorse of conscience after a crime committed in secret shows. In fact, this remorse bears witness not only to the existence of these immovable principles, but also to the existence of God himself.[27] Hence, the pangs of conscience lay the foundation for natural law and for natural theology alike – law and theology which are 'derived from the book of conscience by means of common notions'.[28]

Given the Roman Stoic background of the doctrine of natural law known through the dictates of conscience, it is not surprising that we also encounter it in the work of the neo-Stoic philosopher Justus Lipsius. Lipsius first asserts that the conscience is an offshoot of faith, but assents that 'even where there is no religion or the fear of the Divine at all, there is still a tiny spring of conscience, in danger, so to speak, from the bad soil'.[29] He then goes on to quote approvingly both Christian writers and Roman authors with Stoic persuasion, including Cicero, Juvenal, Seneca, Origen and others, praising the conscience on account of its divinity, ineradicable nature, right guidance and so on.[30] His own definition of conscience is a combination of Scholastic and Stoic elements as he describes it as a 'small spark of right reason left in man [*reliqua in homine rectae rationis scintilla*], the judge and indicator of good and evil deeds'.[31] Finally, he juxtaposes conscience with reputation, asserting that a good man is not characterized by his reputation but by a good conscience, as Pliny and Seneca tell us.

What we have said of other early modern thinkers by and large also applies to Hugo Grotius, the main theorist of early modern international law. In the famous *De jure belli ac pacis* (1625), Grotius first affirms that natural law is the unalterable foundation of justice and virtue, 'so unalterable that it cannot be changed even by God himself'.[32] This law is the rule and dictate of right reason:

> Natural law [*ius naturale*] is the rule and dictate of right reason [*recta ratio*], showing the moral turpitude, or moral necessity, of any act from its agreement or disagreement with the rational nature, and consequently, that such an act is either forbidden or commanded by God, the author of nature.[33]

---

[26] Ibid., 11.2.11.

[27] Ibid., 3.1.14.

[28] Ibid., 1.3.4.

[29] Justus Lipsius, *Politica: Six Books of Politics or Political Instructions*, trans. J. Waszink (Assen: Uitgeverij Van Gorcum, 2004), 1.5.5, pp. 276–7.

[30] Ibid.

[31] Ibid.

[32] Hugo Grotius, *On the Law of War and Peace*, trans. A. C. Campbell (Kitchener: Batoche Books, 2001), 1.1.10, p. 10. According to Grotius, God would contradict himself if he transformed what is intrinsically evil into good.

[33] Ibid., 1.1.10, p. 9.

Second, the conscience is what bears witness to this law.[34] It is a judicial power by means which we discern right and wrong and therefore, the sovereign guide of man: 'God has given conscience a judicial power to be the sovereign guide of human action.'[35] Because it is such a God-given power, bearing witness to natural law, it is free from the judgement of men and under the dominion of God alone. Finally, Grotius equates the Pauline dictum 'against faith' with 'against conscience', saying that we should not do anything against conscience, mitigating the burden of conscience by suggesting that in case of doubt it is better not to act at all – and if this option is not available, the lesser evil should be chosen.[36]

Samuel Pufendorf, arguably the most celebrated of the early modern Protestant theorists of natural law, developed his theory on the firm foundation of the Western tradition. According to him, there exists a natural law that is both immutable and eternal – yet changeable at God's will, for Pufendorf is an ardent voluntarist – known to man through his reason, which God has promulgated by the 'force of the innate light'.[37] Therefore, these laws, being 'dictates of right reason [*recta ratio*]',[38] are easily known to men at least in their common and most important precepts. Particularly, the stirrings of conscience (*conscientiae vellicationes*) attest to the existence of these laws, for these stirrings arise at the moment when men 'sin against natural law'.[39] In addition, they certify God as the author of this law, as the bites of conscience are felt even if no human being is bearing witness to one's transgression:

> Among other arguments for this fact are those bites of conscience with which the wicked are seized, even when they have hope of deceiving men and escaping human punishment; and that such a fear springs from no higher principle, from no realization of the divine sovereignty, but can be traced to mere simplicity, habit, or the fear of human punishment, no pious man is convinced.[40]

Hence, the voice of conscience is, as it were, the voice of God, but it is not such a voice only when it is biting but also when it is happy:

> For the happy conscience after the fulfilment of one's duty, and the internal torments and accusations consequent to wrongdoing, all come – we piously acknowledge – from the strength of Almighty God, for Whom it is easy to punish through themselves those who are unimpressed by other men's power.[41]

---

[34] Ibid., 1.1.16, p. 15.
[35] Ibid., 2.23.2, p. 233. Grotius does not use the word *conscientia* but *animus* here. In this context, however, I think that *animus* can and indeed should be translated as conscience, as the translator has done.
[36] Ibid., 2.23.2, pp. 233–4.
[37] Samuel Pufendorf, *On the Duty of Man and Citizen*, ed. J. Tully (Cambridge: Cambridge University Press, 1991), 1.3.10, p. 36.
[38] Samuel Pufendorf, *Two Books of the Elements of Universal Jurisprudence*, ed. T. Behme (Indianapolis: Liberty Fund, 2009), 1.8.14, p. 216.
[39] Pufendorf, *On the Duty of Man and Citizen*, 1.3.11, p. 37.
[40] Samuel Pufendorf, *Of the Law of Nature and of Nations*, trans. B. Kennett (London: J. Walthoe et al., 1729), 3.4.6, p. 256. Translation modified.
[41] Pufendorf, *Of the Law of Nature and Nations*, 1.6.12, p. 68. Translation modified.

As to the anatomy of conscience, Pufendorf's account owes much to the Scholastics' understanding of it: the conscience (*conscientia*) is the judgement passed on moral actions by the understanding (*intellectus*), it is subject to a law, it is accountable to the lawgiver, be it God or the sovereign, it can be right or erroneous, the error can be vincible or invincible, ignorance voluntary or involuntary, and so forth.[42] Moreover, like most Scholastics, Pufendorf maintains that a person who follows the instructions of the erroneous conscience necessarily sins and is therefore obliged to correct his conscience by conforming it to a law promulgated by a superior, be it God or the sovereign. At the same time he holds, stumbling upon the same double bind as the medieval schoolmen, that even if erroneous, the conscience still binds, because 'to do a thing against conscience is nothing else but to commit a voluntary evil'.[43] Unlike a number of his Protestant predecessors, however, Pufendorf does not believe in the innate knowledge of natural law. He admits that this law, as the Scripture says, is written in the heart, but it is not inborn for we are imbued with a sense of it from childhood onward by the 'discipline of civil life [*vitae civilis disciplina*]'[44] Yet even though Pufendorf believes, as did Origen and Ockham, that the sense of natural law is acquired in childhood, like one's mother tongue, it does not entail that this sense would be unstable or extinguishable. According to Pufendorf, once the conscience is formed, the principles of natural law become 'so ingrained in our minds that they can never thereafter be wiped away from them, however the impious man may strive wholly to extinguish his sense of them'.[45]

* * *

There are certain tendencies that distinguish Pufendorf from Suárez, Althusius and Grotius. They had emphasized that the authority of natural law is independent of divine will and derives from the order of things themselves. Grotius formulated this following Gregory of Rimini's suggestion that natural law would be valid even if God did not exist,[46] whilst Suárez and Althusius argued that the authority of natural law does not derive from its being given by a superior, but from its being the right measure of moral conduct. According to Pufendorf, however, conscience as a sense of sin and duty is entirely inoperative without the assumption that the law of nature is a command of God and that the transgression of this law entails divine punishment: 'Ultimate sanction of duties towards other men comes from religion and fear of the

---

[42] Ibid., 1.3.4, pp. 26–7.
[43] Ibid., 1.3.5, p. 27. See also 1.3.13, p. 32: 'If the conscience entertain a vincible error about an evil thing, the man sins, as well as he acts for it, as if he acts against it.'
[44] Pufendorf, *On the Duty of Man and Citizen*, 1.3.12, p. 37.
[45] Ibid.
[46] In his commentary on *Sentences*, Rimini had suggested that even if God did not exist, or if he did not make use of reason, or if he did not judge things correctly, the dictates of right reason dwelling within man would have the same binding force as they have under the sovereignty of God. Gregory of Rimini, *Lectura super primum et secundum sententiarum* (St. Bonaventure, NY: Franciscan Institute, 1955), sent. II, dist. 34, q. 1, art. 2.

Deity.[47] Man would not be even sociable (*socialitas*), which is for Pufendorf, as it was for Althusius and Grotius, one of the two fundamental laws of nature, if he were not imbued with religion, particularly with a fear of divine punishment. Second, even such fear does not suffice to make men sociable, not to mention that they would obey other laws of nature derived from this fundamental one. A truly effective remedy for suppressing the evil desires of men, 'the remedy perfectly fitted to the nature of man', is found in the state (*civitas*).[48] Echoing the teaching of Jean Bodin and Thomas Hobbes, Pufendorf argues that the consciences of many must be submitted to the conscience of the sovereign, so that his conscience is taken as the will of all and everyone (*omnes & singuli*).[49]

The candle of the Lord: Cambridge platonists

I

Perhaps the most notable group among early modern Protestant philosophers to defend the place of conscience at the heart of ethics was the Cambridge Platonists. Like many early modern Protestant theorists of natural law, they outlined their theories of morality in response to sceptics such as Michel Montaigne but also against those Protestants who subordinated the natural knowledge of good and evil to the Word. This criticism was present already in the theory of morality based on the intuitive knowledge of conscience set forth by Lord Herbert of Cherbury, a sort of precursor of the Cambridge Platonists. In fact, Herbert's criticism was targeted at Scholastics as well. Ockhamite voluntarism was a self-evident adversary, but Herbert accused even Aquinas for neglecting to acknowledge the authority of natural conscience. Although Aquinas, as the majority of Scholastics, had believed in the angelic nature of conscience (*synderesis*), he had also argued that the efficaciousness of such a conscience presupposes God's agency in the form of grace. Without God's grace and the assistance of the Church, the principles of *synderesis* remain hidden in the corrupted nature of man. Herbert disagreed. There is, he argues in *De Veritate* (1624), an innate knowledge 'imprinted on the soul [*foro interiore*] by the dictates of Nature herself'.[50] This knowledge consists of 'common notions' (*Notitiae Communes*) and although these notions are surely hidden within us, there is no such corruption in our nature that it would prevent us from grasping them. They reveal themselves fully whenever we are stimulated by objects. When an appearance given in experience conforms to a faculty within us, this faculty is activated by what Herbert calls a natural

---

47　Pufendorf, *On the Duty of Man and Citizen*, 1.3.13, p. 37.
48　Ibid., 2.5.9, p. 134.
49　Ibid., 2.6.5, p. 136.
50　Herbert von Cherbury, *De Veritate* (Stuttgart: Friedrich Frommann Verlage, 1966), p. 29. The analysis of *De Veritate* is based here mainly on J. B. Schneewind's interpretation in his *Invention of Autonomy: A History of Modern Moral Philosophy* (Cambridge: Cambridge University Press, 1998), pp. 179–83.

instinct (*instinctus naturalis*) which, without reason (*ratio*) or deliberation (*discursus*), brings into play the appropriate faculty to respond to a given experiential stimulus.[51] In a sense, discursive reason is the least useful of the faculties, because it is the source of all error. Reason affords a mere means in enabling us to draw conclusions from the general principles of the common notions.

In matters of morality, these general principles are called the common notions of conscience (*conscientia*). These notions, like all common notions, are instinctual and constituents of all men independently of revelation. According to Herbert, however, the conscience is the highest faculty, to the effect that its common notions should control all the inner forms of consciousness. It is the highest, first, because unlike the other common notions the 'inner truths which refer to Conscience' do not answer merely the question of the actual nature of a thing but the question of 'whether the thing *ought* to exist in the given way'.[52] Second, the concepts and principles of morality are in a different category from all others, because they cannot be derived from the senses. It is not from the external world that we learn what we ought to follow and what to avoid: such knowledge is within ourselves. This alone explains why, concerning morality, there exists among peoples a consensus comparable to mathematical truths. This alone, moreover, explains why each of us must be authorized to make moral or religious decisions independently, without the interference of external authorities: 'Justice and religion do not depend upon the behest of priest or judge, but upon the commands of conscience.'[53] When we obey these commands, we not merely become virtuous but godlike, since through the commands of conscience we are partaking of God's cogitations.

I a

Like the Christian natural law tradition in general, the doctrine of common notions (*communis notitia*/*koinai ennoiai*) can be traced back to the Stoics, playing an important role in the Stoic epistemology. Its starting point is the Epicurean theory according to which the repetition of perceptions brings about mental preconceptions called *prolēpseis*, but it became established as a doctrine by Zeno, a contemporary of Epicurus, who employed the term *ennoia* in the same context. Diogenes Laertius describes these notions as follows: 'By preconception [*prolēpseis*] they mean a sort of apprehension of a right opinion or notion [*ennoia*], or universal idea stored in the mind.'[54] According to the Stoics, these preconceptions are present in the mind in the mode of potentiality, as 'seeds of knowledge' (*logoi spermatikoi*) or 'sparks of fire' (*ingiculi*), which themselves are fragments of divine Logos/Fire permeating the whole universe, as they had learned from Heraclitus. Because they are present only in the mode of potentiality, activation of these seeds and sparks resulting in common notions

---

[51] von Cherbury, *De Veritate*, pp. 37–44.
[52] Ibid., p. 105.
[53] Cited in Schneewind, *Invention of Autonomy*, p. 181.
[54] Diogenes Laertius, *Lives of Eminent Philosophers*, 10.33–4, pp. 562–4.

presupposes teaching, training and practice. Although no Stoic stated it explicitly, they are likely to have thought that these notions also provide the foundation for man's knowledge of natural law. Through the common notions a man, if he has teaching and training, naturally and spontaneously comes to know the good, the wise, the just, the beautiful and God.[55] At any rate, this was the opinion of Epictetus, who in his *Discourses* considered *prolēpseis* as natural moral ideas which are equally distributed in all human beings, moral errors and disputes being due to misguided application of these conceptions in particular cases.[56]

It was this Epictetian conception transmitted by such Roman authors as Cicero, Seneca and Marcus Aurelius that became prevalent among the theologians. Both Augustine and Aquinas refer to common notions in their speculations on morality, the former emphasizing that these notions are impressed on the mind during illumination,[57] whereas the latter holds that they are innate and imprinted in natural reason at the moment when God created humankind.[58] Likewise, Calvin refers to *prolēpseis* in speaking about the Pauline law of the heart, asserting that God implanted an understanding of right and wrong in the consciences of pagan nations before these received the Gospel.[59] Also, such neo-Stoics as Lipsius and Jean Bodin employed the language of common notions and it remains valid in seventeenth-century theological, ethical and political thought as well. Conscience is, as Robert Sanderson wrote, the application of the light of nature, that is, those 'common notions impressed upon the soul by the dictates of nature, and reserved in the Synteresis, as a brand snatched from the common fire'.[60] In fact, this language remains valid even in eighteenth-century thought, for instance in Thomas Reid's common sense theory of morality in which these notions are understood as intuitively known principles of morality arising from an instinct.

II

Thus, if Herbert's theory of morality based on the common notions of conscience had a long tradition behind it, this tradition continued after him. Virtually all of the seventeenth-century Cambridge Platonists also subscribed to the idea of common notions, that is, innate moral truths inscribed in people's minds and known by reason and conscience. We find these innate moral truths already in the first published treatise of the Cambridge Platonists, Nathanael Culverwel's *An Elegant and Learned Discourse of the Light of Nature* of 1652. In his treatise, Culverwel first defends freedom of the will and the innate light of reason, placed in the soul by God in the beginning of creation to enable man to naturally understand God's moral law. For him, moreover, no absolute

---

[55] On the Stoic origin and the Christian heritage of common notions, see Maryanne Cline Horowitz, *Seeds of Virtue and Knowledge* (Princeton: Princeton University Press, 1988), pp. 21–56.
[56] See Epictetus, *Discourses* 1.22, pp. 142–9 and 2.17, pp. 337–49.
[57] Augustine, *On the Holy Trinity* 8.3.4, in *NPNF1*, vol. 3, p. 237.
[58] Aquinas, *Summa Theologica* Ia IIae, q. 94, a. 4.
[59] Calvin, *Romans*, p. 68.
[60] Sanderson, *Lectures on Conscience*, pp. 24–5.

difference can be made between faith and the light of reason, for even if distinct, they are complementary and harmonious. Culverwel calls this light of reason the 'Candle of the Lord' and rather than for discursive reason this candle stands for an intuitive and instinctual knowledge of the natural moral law. Culverwel writes:

> The Law of Nature is a streaming out of Light from the Candle of the Lord, power-fully discovering such a deformity in some evil, as that an intellectual eye must needs abhor it; and such a commanding beauty in some good, as that a rational being must needs be enamoured with it; and so plainly showing that God stamped and sealed the one with his command, and branded the other with his disliking.[61]

According to Culverwel, Adam and Eve discovered their folly and nakedness by means of the Candle of the Lord. It flamed in Cain's conscience and it was owing to it that the Gentiles came to know the law of the heart. Actually, Culverwel was more a Thomist than a Platonist, relying heavily on Aquinas himself but particularly on Suárez. In his view, man participates in the eternal law through natural law, which is known by means of the Candle of the Lord, called also the *scintilla divinae lucis* – which is an inborn, infallible and divine remnant of the fall. Culverwel's concept of *conscientia* also comes from the Scholastics. First, he describes it following Herbert:

> The law of nature as it is thus branched forth, does bind in *foro conscientiae*; for as that noble author [Herbert of Cherbury] speaks very well in this; natural conscience is the *centrum notatiarum communium*, and it is a kind of *sensus communis* in respect of the inward faculties, as that other is in respect of the outward senses. It is a competent judge of this law of nature: it is the natural pulse of the soul, by the beating and motion of which the state and temper of men is discernible. The Apostle Paul thus felt the heathen's pulse, and found their consciences sometimes accusing them, sometimes making apology for them.[62]

Culverwel continues by arguing, not unlike Aquinas and Suárez, that the conscience is 'a practical dictate about particulars' (*dictamen practicum in particulari*), that is, an execution and application of natural law, 'as Providence is of that eternal law'.[63]

Culverwel was the first Cambridge Platonist to be published, but Benjamin Whichcote, the founding father of the movement, was the first to publicly preach the doctrine of the candle of the Lord in Protestant England.[64] Arguing against the voluntarists, Whichcote insists that the moral part of religion never alters, that moral laws are not imposed by the divine will but originate in the immutable divine intellect, and that the most important part of this immutable morality can also be known. He believes that this immutable good and evil is known by a special instinctual capacity, different from discursive reason and our grasp of what is useful or harmful, specifying

---

[61] Nathanael Culverwel, *An Elegant and Learned Discourse of the Light of Nature* (Oxford: Williams, 1669), p. 35.

[62] Ibid., p. 47.

[63] Ibid., p. 48.

[64] These sermons were delivered at the Trinity Church in the 1630s.

that this awareness is 'God's vice-regent' and His 'dwelling in us'.[65] In his posthumously published *The Use of Reason in Matters of Religion* (1698), edited by Shaftesbury, Whichcote calls this capacity 'the light of reason and conscience'. It is by this capacity that we discern the difference between good and evil, as this distinction appears naturally to the light of reason, whilst the conscience, as the guardian of this light, punishes a man whenever he is about to transgress the immutable laws of morality.[66]

Henry More agreed with his colleagues. According to More, as he writes in his major work on moral philosophy, *Enchiridion Ethicum* (1667), our mind contains unchangeable ideas or 'impressions' of good and evil, like figures in mathematics.[67] These impressions enter into the consciousness mainly through the judgement of conscience, which is why More insists that in all actions the appeal should be to the judgement-seat of good conscience. He then opposes the judgement of conscience to the feelings of shame and fame, arguing that shame does not drive us from what is substantially unjust, nor does fame impel us toward the substantially just: only the conscience can do that.[68] In *An Antidote to Atheism* (1653), in turn, More argues that a man without conscience must be a monster and that man's natural conscience, which 'puts him upon hope and fear of good and evil from what he does or omits, though those actions and omission do nothing to change of the course of nature or the affairs of the world', testifies that there is an Intelligent Principle over universal nature that 'takes notice of the actions of men'.[69]

More situated the conscience in the so-called 'boniform faculty', that is, 'a faculty of that Divine composition and supernatural texture' that 'enables us to distinguish not only what is simply and absolutely best, but to relish it, and to have pleasure in that alone'.[70] Ralph Cudworth, the leader of Cambridge Platonists, situates it within the economy of the Stoic *hēgemonikon*, the 'ruling, governing, commanding, and determining' part of the soul by which 'every man is self-made'.[71] Like More, Cudworth maintains that there are special moral ideas in God's mind guiding him in his creative activity and guiding us as well. In his defence of the freedom of the will and human responsibility, not only against Hobbesian determinism but also against Thomist intellectualism according to which the will inevitably consents to the ideas of the intellect, Cudworth argues that these ideas are inscribed in our nature as specific natural instincts which are plainly sensed, for instance, when the conscience blames and accuses us. In addition, these accusations prove that we are free beings not determined by nature, beings who have something *eph hemin*, *in nostra potestate*, 'in our own power',[72] as Cudworth says, using the Stoic notion to denote moral responsi-

---

[65] Benjamin Whichcote, *Moral and Religious Aphorisms*, in *The Cambridge Platonists*, ed. C. A. Patrides (Cambridge, MA: Harvard University Press, 1970), p. 335.

[66] Benjamin Whichcote, *The Use of Reason in Matters of Religion*, in *The Cambridge Platonists*, p. 51.

[67] Henry More, *An Account of Virtue* (London: Benj. Tooke, 1701), 1.12.7, p. 81.

[68] Ibid., 1.11.13, p. 76.

[69] Henry More, *An Antidote against Atheism*, in *The Cambridge Platonists*, p. 237.

[70] More, *An Account of Virtue*, 1.2.5, p. 6.

[71] Ralph Cudworth, *A Treatise of Free Will*, ed. J. Allen (London: Parker, 1838), 1.8, p. 32 and 1.10, p. 37.

[72] Ibid., 1.11, p. 43.

bility, a term transmitted to Christians by Origen.[73] Cudworth also cites Origen, fully affirming the passage in *Contra Celsum* where Origen argues that evil actions result from each person's mind and that each person is responsible for the evil that exists in him (*nam sua cuique ratio cause est existentis in ipso malitiate*),[74] continuing that the accusations of conscience would be nonsensical without the freedom of the will, since the conscience never accuses man of anything that he has not freely done. And to the extent that it indeed accuses him, it must be that he has freely done something wrong, even if he feels himself to have been compelled to act:

> And that we have a power more and less to exert ourselves to resist lower incli-
> nations, or hinder the gratification of them, and to compel with the dictate of
> conscience or honesty, we being not wholly determined therein by necessary
> causes antecedent, but having something at least of it *eph hemin*, in our power,
> every man's own conscience bears witness, in accusing and condemning him
> whenever he does amiss.[75]

II a

Even though the technical term *synderesis* by and large disappeared from early modern Protestant discourse, the idea of innate moral knowledge itself did not vanish. Now this idea was expressed either with such Stoic notions as seeds and impressions or such biblical metaphors as light and candle. We have already seen that Calvin spoke about seeds and impressions of the original rectitude of Adam. Similarly, William Perkins asserts that naturally every man has in him 'some remnants of the light of nature, showing us what is good and evil'.[76] We find these ideas and metaphors also in early modern philosophical discourse, not only in the writings of Cambridge Platonists, but also in the texts of such voluntarists as John Locke who, despite his conviction that there are no such things as inner ideas, asserts that the majority of humankind would live in 'Egyptian darkness, were not the candle of the Lord set up by himself in men's minds, which it is impossible for the breath or power of man wholly extinguish'.[77] Even Immanuel Kant, regardless of his repudiation of nature as the foundation of morals, admits that there is a germ of goodness left in every man: 'Surely we must presuppose in all this that there is still a germ of goodness [*ein Keim des Guten*] left in its entire purity, a germ that cannot be extirpated or corrupted'.[78] As to biblical metaphors, a customary reference in the case of light was Psalms 4.6 ('the light of Thy countenance, O Lord, is signed upon us'), and we have already seen that this was employed in

---

[73] In *De Principiis*, Origen writes that it lies within our power (*eph hemin*) to devote ourselves to life worthy of praise or of blame. Origen, *De Principiis* 3.1.1, in *ANF*, vol. 4, p. 302.

[74] Origen, *Against Celsus* 4.66, in *ANF*, vol. 4, p. 527.

[75] Cudworth, *Treatise of Free Will*, 1.11, p. 43.

[76] Perkins, *Discourse of Conscience*, p. 68.

[77] John Locke, *An Essay Concerning Human Understanding* (Oxford: Clarendon Press, 1975), 4.3, p. 552.

[78] Immanuel Kant, *Religion within the Boundaries of Mere Reason*, ed. A. Wood and G. di Giovanni (Cambridge: Cambridge University Press, 1998), p. 66.

Scholastic discourse as a revelatory confirmation of the *synderesis*. The metaphor of candle originates in turn from Proverbs 20.27 ('the spirit of man is the candle of the Lord'), and although the *Glossa Ordinaria* had already spoken about the candlelight as '*lumen naturale rationis*', it was not until Denys Ryckel (Dionysius the Carthusian), a Flemish theologian from the fifteenth century, that the candle became identified with the *synderesis*. Candlelight is, according to him, '*res illuminata a Deo lumine intellectuali, continens in se lumen ingenii atque synderesis*'.[79]

A crisis of conscience: Hobbes, Spinoza, Locke

I

Although the eulogy of conscience was as fervent in early modern and Enlightenment philosophy as it was in theology, it was not universal. The first explicit philosophical critique of conscience in the Western tradition since antiquity appears with Renaissance scepticism and more precisely in Michel Montaigne's *Essays*. Montaigne's attitude towards natural law is telling: there is no such a thing as natural law, for the laws that oblige man in his conscience are the laws of his country, nothing else. According to Montaigne, the conscience itself is a mere reflection of custom and habit, an expression of the norms of context and community. What looks like a natural inclination of an innate and universal moral sense, allegedly bearing witness to natural law, is nothing more than an expression of sanctioned and localized social conduct:

> The laws of conscience [*les loix de la conscience*], which we say are born of nature, are born of custom [*coustume*]. Each man, holding in inward veneration the opinions and the behaviour approved and accepted around him, cannot break loose from them without remorse, or apply himself to them without self-satisfaction.[80]

Montaigne paved the way, but the first major assault on conscience was that undertaken by Thomas Hobbes. In the sixth chapter of *De Corpore Politico*, Hobbes presents a radically redefined version of the medieval natural instinct, dropping out the Pauline law of the heart (*synderesis*) whilst basing his argument entirely on the lower law of the limbs, that is, on the law of self-preservation. Moreover, contrary to the higher natural instinct, this law does not incline one to seek the good and avoid evil but by necessity forces one to seek what is good for oneself alone – first and foremost, to preserve one's life. In *Leviathan*, Hobbes goes so far as to proclaim that the conscience people are talking about is a mere metaphor for the original meaning of the word, which stands for 'co-knowledge' (*syn-eidēsis/con-scientia*) one shares with others, that is, when two or more people are said to be conscious of something together. According to Hobbes,

---

[79] Cited in Robert A. Greene, 'Whichcote, the Candle of the Lord, and Synderesis,' *Journal of the History of Ideas* 52:4 (1991): 621.

[80] Michel de Montaigne, 'On Habit,' in *The Complete Essays of Montaigne*, trans. D. Frame (Stanford: Stanford University Press, 1958), 1.23, p. 83.

this is not only the original but also the true meaning of the word. It was only later (Hobbes does not specify when) that 'conscience' was used metaphorically to denote a knowledge of men's own 'secret facts' and 'secret thoughts'. Ultimately – Hobbes is referring to his own time – men have given the 'reverenced name of conscience'[81] to their private judgements and opinions.

With this etymological deconstruction of the notion of conscience, beyond doubt, Hobbes wanted to deprive the individual conscience of all political authority, honour and glory. In this respect, however, the most remarkable gesture was his assertion that the doctrine *contra conscientiam facere peccatum est*, one of the most firmly established Christian truths, is one of the most *repugnant* doctrines for civil society. According to Hobbes, it installs the individual as absolute judge of good and evil, whereby he is authorized to reflect and resist the laws of the commonwealth. Such reflection entails the destruction of civil society because no one obeys the law 'farther than it shall seem good in his own eyes'.[82] In *De Corpore Politico*, Hobbes similarly writes: 'If every man were allowed this liberty of following his conscience, in such difference of consciences, they would not live together in peace an hour'.[83] Indeed, if every man were allowed this liberty, the result would be anarchy, the war of all against all in the famous Hobbesian state of nature where man is wolf to man. Hence, instead of raising man above the beasts, as was usually believed, the conscience reduces him to the same level as them. Therefore, Hobbes thought, the individual conscience must be deprived of its authority and replaced by the authority of 'public conscience', that is, by the positive civil law,[84] identical with the command of the sovereign. It is this law that must be conceived as the sole measure of good and evil in the commonwealth.[85]

I a

Although Hobbes is correct in claiming that conscience (*syneidēsis/conscientia*) has signified knowledge one shares with others, it is contestable whether this is the original meaning of the word. The very first document where the Greek word for conscience (*syneidēsis*) is mentioned, namely Democritus' fragment no. 297 (Diels), shows that the knowledge that is shared is not shared with others but denotes secret thoughts: 'Some people, ignorant about the decomposition of mortal nature and in the *syneidēsis* of evil-doing in life, endure the time of their lives in confusion and fear because of inventing lies about the time after death.'[86] Moreover, even if we accept the assumption according to which *syneidēsis* derives from the verb *sydoida*, a compound of *syn*, signifying 'with', and *oida*, which is the perfect indicative active of the verb *eidenai*, signifying to 'see', to 'perceive' and to 'know', especially intuitively, as opposed

---

[81] Thomas Hobbes, *Leviathan* (Cambridge: Cambridge University Press, 1991), 1.7, p. 48.
[82] Ibid., 2.29, p. 223.
[83] Thomas Hobbes, *The Elements of Law Natural and Politic*, ed. J. C. A. Gaskin (Oxford: Oxford University Press, 2008), 24.2, p. 137.
[84] Hobbes, *Leviathan*, 2.29, p. 223.
[85] Ibid.
[86] Cited and translated by Bosman, *Conscience in Philo and Paul*, p. 61.

to acquiring knowledge through reasoning (*noein*), it does not follow that this knowing was originally knowing with someone else. Here again the first proven occurrences of the word in the Greek literature denote secret thoughts, not shared knowledge. We find it in a fragment of Sappho as well as in Solon's *Eunomia* (fragment 4.15–16), in which it is said that *Dikē* 'in silence knows [*synoide*] what happens and what has been and in the course of time comes without fail to exact the penalty'.[87] Certainly, *synoida* was also used to denote knowledge one shares with others, particularly in contexts suggesting complicity in conspiracies,[88] but it seems that this meaning is no more original than the one denoting so called secret thoughts. Furthermore, even though the Latin *conscientia* was also used in the sense of shared knowledge, here again the first attestable case which appears in the *Rhetorica ad Herennium* (2.5.8) refers to one's guilty conscience, not knowledge one shares with others. Advising the prosecutor to take notice of and appeal to the visible signs of guilt, the author of the *Rhetorica* writes:

> For subsequent behaviour we investigate the signs which usually attend guilt or innocence. The prosecutor will, if possible, say that his adversary, when come upon, blushed, paled, faltered, spoke uncertainly, collapsed, or promised to be somehow; which are signs of conscience [*signa conscientiae*].[89]

As to the noun *syneidēsis*, it is not until the first century BC that it came into more frequent usage, although fragmentary transmission from the third and second century BC renders any final conclusion impossible.[90] Yet the Greeks also used other nouns such as *synesis* to denote the phenomenon of conscience and specifically bad conscience. *Locus classicus* is a passage in Euripides's *Orestes* (392–7) in which Orestes complains about the inner suffering caused by the killing of his mother: 'What sickness is destroying you?' asks Menelaus, and Orestes replies: 'My *synesis*, I am aware [*synoida*] that I have done something terrible.' On the other hand, and more commonly, the Greeks used the verbal compound *synoida emautō* ('I know with myself') in order to express bad feelings aroused by an evil deed. To be sure, *synoida emautō* could also have a neutral meaning, signifying that one is conscious of something concerning oneself. Yet it could involve a moral meaning as well, expressing negative judgement concerning one's own moral state as a man and a citizen. The earliest instance of such a case can be found in the *Thesmophoriazusae* (476–7) of Aristophanes: 'I know

---

87　Cited and translated by ibid., p. 51. The Sappho fragment containing the verb *synoida* from the early sixth century BC is older than the earliest non-reflective phrase denoting knowledge one shares with others. On the use of *synoida* word group in Classical period, see ibid., pp. 49–105; Antonia Cancrini, *Syneidesis: Il tema semantico della 'con-scientia' nella Grecia antica* (Roma: Edizioni dell'Ateneo Roma, 1970).

88　In the ninth oration of Isaeus ('On the Estate of Astyphilus,' 20), for instance, we read: 'To prove that he remained throughout his life at variance with Cleon, I will produce as witnesses before you those who know with [*syneidotas martyras*]'. *Isaeus with an English Translation*, trans. E. S. Forster (London: William Heinemann, 1962), pp. 338–9.

89　Anonymous, *Rhetorica ad Herennium*, trans. Harry Kaplan (Cambridge, MA: Harvard University Press, 1954), pp. 72–3. Translation modified. *Rhetorica* is sometimes wrongly attributed to Cicero.

90　Even during this period *syneidēsis* is found very sporadically, twice in the writings of Diodorus Siculus and four times in Dionysius Halicarnassus. See Bosman, *Conscience in Philo and Paul*, p. 63; Marietta, 'Conscience in Greek Stoicism,' p. 178.

with myself of many terrible things [*ksynoid' emautē polla dein*].[91] Since then, the compound occurs in numerous documents used in this specific sense. In his letter to Demonicus (*Orationes* 1.16), Isocrates writes: 'Never hope to conceal any shameful thing which you have done. Even if you do conceal it from others, you still know with yourself [*seautoi syneidēseis*].'[92] In *Anabasis* (1.3.10), Xenophon likewise says: 'I decline to go, chiefly, it is true, from a feeling of shame, because I know with myself [*synoida emautō*] that I have proved utterly false to him.'[93] In Plato's *Republic* (331a), we can read: 'Someone who is conscious of no wrong [*mēden heautōi adikon syneidoti*] has sweet good hope as his constant companion – a nurse to his old age, as Pindar too says.'

II

John Locke seldom agreed with Hobbes, but the case of conscience seems to be an exception. Although in *An Essay concerning Toleration* written in 1667 Locke defended the idea of toleration, in his early works he seems uncomfortable with the idea that the conscience would be the final arbitrator in morals and politics, and even with the very idea of the liberty of conscience. In the *Second Tract on Government* written circa 1662, for instance, Locke argues that the liberty of conscience is a dangerous idea used by the religious zealots, such as Puritans and other dissenters, in order to arm the reckless foolishness of the ignorant and passionate multitude with the authority of conscience, kindling thus 'a blaze among the populace capable of consuming everything'.[94] In *An Essay Concerning Human Understanding*, he maintains that the notion of innate moral ideas, naming particularly that of Herbert of Cherbury, is politically a highly flammable one. Men use the theory of innate ideas and standards allegedly 'set up by God in his mind' to support the doctrines of their particular churches, thus stamping the 'character of divinity upon absurdities and errors'.[95] Therefore, it is not a surprise that Locke denied the very existence of innate moral ideas. Like Pufendorf, he argues that the conscience is not innate and that, originally, the human mind is an 'empty cabinet'[96] and a 'white paper'.[97] There is no such thing as conscience understood as an inborn sense of right and wrong. The conscience is, as Montaigne and other sceptics had maintained, a product of people's 'education, company, and customs of their country',[98] becoming ultimately reduced to 'our own opinion or judgement of the

---

[91] Aristophanes, *Thesmophoriazusae*, pp. 170–1. Translation modified.

[92] Isocrates, 'To Demonicus', in *Isocrates with an English Translation in Three Volumes*, vol. 1, trans. G. Nordin (London: William Heinemann, 1961), pp. 12–13. Translation modified.

[93] Xenophon, *Anabasis*, in Xenophon, *Hellenica (6–12) and Anabasis (1–3)*, trans. C. L. Brownson (Cambridge, MA: Harvard University Press, 1961), pp. 268–9. Translation modified.

[94] John Locke, *Second Tract on Government*, in *John Locke: Political Writings*, ed. John Wootton (Indianapolis: Hackett Publishing Company, 2003), p. 153.

[95] Locke, *Human Understanding*, 1.2.26, p. 83.

[96] Ibid., 1.1.15, p. 55.

[97] Ibid., 2.1.2, p. 104.

[98] Ibid., 1.2.8, p. 70.

moral rectitude or depravity of our own actions'.[99] It is, in other words, a custom and education that echo in the voice of conscience, nothing more.

Moreover, although Locke's theory of natural law owes much to Pufendorf and he certainly affirms the existence of natural law, Locke does not give any credit to the conscience with respect to man's endeavour of deciphering the divine law of nature. The conscience does not bear witness to natural law, he writes in his early *Essays on the Law of Nature*, not even in the mode of negative judgement. There are men who have committed many crimes and still have no pangs of conscience. It is reason and particularly discursive reason that perceives the law of nature, building its arguments on the foundation of sense-perception.[100] The first truth that reason concludes from sense-experience is that there is a deity, the author of all things, and as soon as this is laid down, the notion of a universal law of nature 'binding all men necessarily emerges'.[101] Unfortunately, Locke does not say anything about this sense-experience. He merely observes that the law of nature is not known by means of tradition and that 'on the evidence of the senses it must be concluded that there is some maker of all these things, whom it is necessary to recognise not only powerful but also wise'.[102] Finally, it is similarly evident that this wise maker intends man to act, namely to preserve life in society with other men, but no explanation is given on what grounds this intention is disclosed to man. Indeed, Locke time and again stresses that it does *not* become evident to the majority of the people at all. In general people are unaware of it, which is why in moral matters one should consult those who 'are more rational and perceptive than the rest'.[103] Most people, Locke argues, are guided not as much by reason as either by the example of others, or by the customs and fashion of the country, or finally 'by the authority of those whom they consider good and wise'.[104]

III

Yet it must be noted that none of these scholars repudiated conscience altogether. If the custom and tradition have the highest authority and if the voice of conscience stems from custom, as Montaigne believed, then it would be inconsistent for him to disregard it: the conscience is the very guarantee of the continuation of tradition. Indeed, in the very same essay in which Montaigne argues that conscience is the outcome of the local customs and education, he asks whether there are any worse sorts of vices than those committed against a man's own conscience and the natural light of his own reason, answering with an emphatic 'no'. Such a positive attitude towards conscience becomes manifest particularly in his late additions to the *Essays*, by which time Socrates had become his intellectual inspiration. After praising Socrates, Montaigne writes:

---

[99] Ibid.
[100] John Locke, *Essays on the Law of Nature*, ed. A. J. Allan (Oxford: The Clarendon Press, 1954), p. 149.
[101] Ibid., p. 133.
[102] Ibid., p. 157.
[103] Ibid., p. 115.
[104] Ibid., p. 135.

It is a ruinous teaching for any society, and much more harmful than ingenious and subtle, which persuades the people that religious belief is enough, by itself and without morals, to satisfy divine justice. Practice makes us see an enormous distinction between devoutness and conscience.[105]

From the conscience arises morality, from faith stupidity – and even honour is despicable compared to the value of conscience, at least among women: 'Every woman of honour will much rather choose to lose her honour, than to hurt her conscience.'[106]

III a

Surprisingly, Socrates' famous daemon does not play an important role in the history of Christian conscience, although nowadays it is quite often held that his daemon was a personification of moral conscience.[107] I say Christian conscience, because there have been pagan scholars in whose opinion the Socratic daemon is precisely conscience. Perhaps the first to identify a conscience in the Socratic daemon was Apuleius. In his *De deo Socratis* (16), he first writes:

> From this more elevated order of demons, Plato is of opinion that a peculiar demon is allotted to every man, to be a witness and a guardian of his conduct in life, who, without being visible to any one, is always present, and is an overseer not only of his actions, but even of his thoughts.[108]

He continues by asserting that this demon that sees and understands all things, dwells in the most profound recesses of the mind in the place of conscience (*in ipse peritissimis mentibus vice conscientiae diversetur*), guarding and observing us, reproving if we do evil, approving if we do good, and so on.[109] Similarly, in his commentary on the *First Alcibiades* of Plato, Olympiodorus the Younger writes:

> It must be said, therefore, that the allotted demon is conscience, which is the supreme flower of the soul, is guiltless in us, is an inflexible judge, and a witness of Minos and Rhadamanthus of the transactions of the present life. This also becomes the cause to us of our salvation, as always remaining in us without guilt, and not assenting to the errors of the soul, but disdaining them, and concerning the soul to what is proper. You will not err, therefore, in calling the allotted demon conscience.[110]

---

[105] Michel de Montaigne, 'Of Physiognomy,' in *Complete Essays*, 3.12, p. 881.

[106] Michel de Montaigne, 'Of Glory,' in ibid., 2.16, p. 477.

[107] This is not to say that the Christian theologians would have been ignorant of Socrates' daemon. They indeed knew it but they did not equate it with a conscience but with an evil demon. In this respect, Augustine's interpretation of the Socratic voice in *The City of God* (8.14–15) has been the most influential.

[108] Apuleius, *On the God of Socrates*, in *The Works of Apuleius* (London: Georg Bell and Sons, 1878), p. 365.

[109] Ibid.

[110] Ibid., footnote 2.

In Olympiodorus' commentary – though pagan himself, he lived in a world surrounded by Christians – there is already a visible Christian element in his interpretation. Conscience is no longer a mere guardian of the soul but appears as the cause of salvation, and what is more important, it is defined as a guiltless part of the soul like Jerome's *scintilla conscientiae*. Yet Christians themselves, as already said, have not usually referred to Socrates' daemon in their discussions on conscience, not even those like Montaigne, who identified in Socrates the ideal type of moral man. Moreover, even if they have on occasion done so, like Shaftesbury in his *Soliloquy*, they have usually denounced the daemon as a mythical guise of conscience, in truth nothing more miraculous than a mere effect of self-reflection.[111]

IV

To be honest, not even Hobbes was an unequivocal opponent of conscience, nor was he someone who would have taken a 'momentous step'[112] with his concept of conscience. He does abandon the concept of *synderesis*, but we have seen that the early Protestants had already become increasingly suspicious with regard to it. Furthermore, it has never been a secret that the word conscience denotes co-knowledge, though it must be admitted that Christians usually understood this co-knowledge as knowledge we share with God rather than with other people. The same can be said of Hobbes' insight that the conscience is a mere judgement and opinion, for what else is the Thomistic *conscientia* except one's private judgement of good and evil? Moreover, if we examine the *use* of the concept of conscience in the Hobbesian corpus, it soon becomes apparent that Hobbes does not use it in the sense he implies in his etymology, that is, as knowledge one shares with others, not even in the sense of mere opinion. When Hobbes uses the concept, he uses it in a very traditional way. In *The Elements of Law Natural and Politic*, Hobbes speaks about the tribunal of conscience.[113] He also asserts that no human law is intended to oblige the conscience of man.[114] He even subscribes to the Scholastic doctrine according to which whatsoever is against conscience is against the law of nature:

> Seeing the laws of nature concern the conscience, not he only breaketh them that doth any action contrary, but also he whose action is conformable to them, in case he think it contrary. For though the action chance to be right, yet in his judgement he despiseth the law.[115]

In *De Cive*, likewise, Hobbes maintains that divine law of nature (*lex naturalis*) lies in right reason (*recta ratio*) and that this reason gives rise to an obligation in the internal

---

[111] See Anthony Ashley-Cooper, Third Earl of Shaftesbury, *Soliloquy* (London: John Morphew, 1710), 1.2, pp. 16–17.
[112] This is Jürgen Habermas's expression when he describes the Hobbesian reduction of conscience to opinion. Jürgen Habermas, *Structural Transformation of the Public Sphere*, trans. T. Burger (Cambridge, MA: The MIT Press, 1991), p. 90.
[113] Hobbes, *The Elements of Law*, 1.18.10.
[114] Ibid. 2.6.3.
[115] Ibid., 1.17.13.

court (*Foro interno*), that is (*sive*), in conscience (*conscientia*).[116] Moreover, Hobbes holds that the laws of nature which bind conscience may be violated not only by an action contrary to them but by an action consonant with them if the agent believes he is acting against them: 'For although the act itself is in accordance with the laws, his conscience is against them.'[117] Thus, it is evil to act against conscience, that is, to do something that one believes to be evil, even though it is not evil according to the law. Hence, also in *De Cive*, Hobbes seems to agree with the Scholastic doctrine *contra conscientiam agere peccatum est*. In fact, he repeats the doctrine verbatim: 'Whatever one does against conscience is a sin [*peccatum est quicquid quis fecerit contra conscientiam*]; for to do such a thing is to reject the law.'[118]

Similar arguments can be found in *Leviathan*. Although it is precisely here that Hobbes introduces his idea that conscience is a mere metaphor that should be restored to its original use as co-knowledge, he does not use it as a metaphor attached to one's private opinion, let alone in the sense denoting co-knowledge. Like his Christian contemporaries, Hobbes speaks about a troubled conscience referring to man's perplexed mind.[119] He says, moreover, that the laws of nature oblige *in foro interno*, which is a classical definition of conscience.[120] He mentions the safety of conscience,[121] and laments that in the state of nature man has no other accuser than his conscience.[122] He speaks about a crime against conscience,[123] and refers to conscience as a judge.[124] He tells us that conscience can be bound[125] and as the Scholastics had done uses the notions of reason and conscience as if they were interchangeable.[126] In fact, he goes so far as to assert, like Aquinas,[127] that conscience is the court of natural justice where God reigns: 'There … is no Court of Naturall Justice, but in the Conscience only; where not Man, but God raigneth.'[128] We must of course be precise here: although the conscience is such a court universally, in civil society it is the sovereign alone who is entitled to act according to his conscience, because the sovereign's command is the law for the subjects' action. Moreover, Hobbes maintains that sovereigns 'may ordain the doing of many things' 'contrary to their own consciences'.[129] But Hobbes does not mean that such action contrary to conscience is neutral in terms of morality. On the contrary, he states that it is a 'breach of trust and of the law of nature'.[130] Inasmuch as it is a breach of the law of nature, which is eternal and immutable, it is also evil.

---

[116] Thomas Hobbes, *On the Citizen*, ed. R. Tuck (Cambridge: Cambridge University Press, 1998), pp. 54, 59.
[117] Ibid., p. 54.
[118] Ibid., 12.2, p. 132.
[119] Hobbes, *Leviathan*, 1.2, p. 18.
[120] Ibid., 1.15, p. 110.
[121] Ibid., 2.23, p. 172.
[122] Ibid., 2.27, p. 202.
[123] Ibid., 2.27, p. 209.
[124] Ibid., 2.30, p. 231.
[125] Ibid., 3.33, p. 260.
[126] Ibid., 3.37, p. 306.
[127] See Aquinas, *Summa Theologica* IIa Iae, q. 94, a. 4.
[128] Hobbes, *Leviathan*, 2.30, p. 244.
[129] Ibid., p. 172.
[130] Ibid.

This implies that, even in *Leviathan*, Hobbes believes that it is evil to act against one's conscience. Certainly, in all the works just mentioned Hobbes maintains that the *contra conscientiam* doctrine neither gives licence to ignore or to act contrary to sovereign's commands, but this does not mean that Hobbes had introduced an unprecedented conception of conscience into the history of the West. What he does is that he calls into question the authority of the subjects' consciences. Now it is the conscience of the sovereign alone that is sovereign.

What about John Locke? As already stated, Locke's theory of natural law owes much to Pufendorf, including the conclusion that it is not conscience but the fear of the deity, the 'rewards and punishments of another life',[131] that is the true foundation and the principal motive for moral action.[132] There are nevertheless certain ambiguities here. Although Locke emphasizes the powerlessness of conscience, it ceases to be so if man is conscious of these rewards and punishments – eternal bliss and eternal misery – which the Almighty has established and which 'nobody can make any doubt of'.[133] According to Locke, namely, the mere hope of heavenly pleasure is enough to compensate for the possible miseries of virtuous life, whereas the mere fear of everlasting pain is enough to render vicious life painful even on earth. And it is here that the conscience enters the game: it is the terrified conscience of a criminal facing the vision of hell that is the cause of pain in him, the most awful suffering imaginable here on earth.[134] Hence, the conscience has after all a function in Locke's theory of morality, namely the terrified conscience, but contrary to many Scholastics and even to many early modern Protestants, such as Perkins and Ward, let alone a number of early modern philosophers, Locke's conscience has no autonomous power, not to mention that it would render man autonomous: it does not work until the fear of hell is living presence to it. In this, too, he agrees with Pufendorf. Unlike Pufendorf, however, Locke does not seem to give any credit to the conscience with respect to man's endeavour of deciphering the law of nature.

Yet there are certain ambiguities here as well. In the *Essay on the Law of Nature*, for instance, Locke maintains that the duty to preserve not only one's own life but peaceful life with others is 'very much urged by an inward instinct [*interno instinctu*].'[135] In the conclusion of this *Essay*, he states that the natural law is so firmly rooted in human nature that human nature must be changed 'before this law can be either altered or annulled',[136] adding that there are some definitive duties that result from man's inborn constitution (*ex nativa constitutione*).[137] Hence, although Locke in this early manuscript already holds that the law of nature is not written in the hearts of men (if this were the case, then it would be found undiminished and unspoiled among the primitives peoples, but this is clearly false, because there 'appears not the slightest

---

[131] Locke, *Human Understanding*, 2.21.72, p. 281.
[132] Ibid., 2.28.7–8, p. 352.
[133] Ibid., 2.21.72, p. 281.
[134] Ibid., 2.21.72, p. 282.
[135] Locke, *On the Law of Nature*, p. 159.
[136] Ibid., p. 199.
[137] Ibid., p. 198.

trace or track of piety, merciful feeling, fidelity, chastity, and the rest of virtues' among such peoples),[138] he continues to employ the dogmatic notions of natural instincts and inborn constitutions in the context of his moral and political reflections. Similar accounts can be found in his later works as well. Although Locke emphatically rejects inborn ideas in *An Essay Concerning Human Understanding*, he nonetheless writes in the same treatise that there is a Candle of the Lord installed in men's minds, 'which it is impossible for the breath or power of man wholly to extinguish'.[139] In *Two Treatises*, finally, he states that it is written in the hearts of all mankind that in the state of nature everyone has a right and is also obliged to punish those who have transgressed the law of nature,[140] concluding his consideration on natural law with the remark that it is 'nowhere to be found but in the minds of men'.[141]

V

Although certain seventeenth-century philosophers, notably Hobbes and Locke, attempted to move beyond the Christian heritage of conscience, mainly because of the 'flammable' consequences that this doctrine (it is a sin to act against conscience, the conscience is a demigod within, and so on) presumably had on the civil order of society, their attempts were only partially successful, to say the least. Yet there was at least one philosopher in the seventeenth century whose thought represents a definitive break in the long tradition of conscience, and that is Baruch Spinoza. Surely, Spinoza is not that far removed from the tradition, since he employs the Stoic idea of common notions, speaks about the inborn light of nature, and distinguishes between the inferior and superior reason, identifying the former with discursive and the latter with intuitive knowledge (*scientia intuitiva*), which, operating without words and images (*extra verba et imagines*), bears a close resemblance even to the medieval *synderesis*.[142] Yet unlike the majority of his predecessors Spinoza did not see anything redeemable in conscience (*conscientia*), particularly in bad conscience. Bad conscience (*conscientiae morsus*) is nothing but a source of pain, 'accompanied by the idea of a past thing whose outcome was contrary to our hope'.[143] As such, this was not of course anything new. The painful aspect of conscience had been universally recognized since the Greeks. In the Christian tradition, in fact, one of the most common metaphors for conscience has been the worm. Both Origen and Augustine interpreted the worm in Isaiah (66:24), the immortal worm inhabiting the dead bodies of men who had repelled against the Lord, as the worm of conscience. According to Aquinas, the worm of conscience is the punishment reserved for unbaptized children who have departed this world

---

[138] Ibid., p. 141.

[139] Locke, *Human Understanding*, 4.3.20, p. 552.

[140] John Locke, *Two Treatises of Civil Government*, ed. P. Laslett (Cambridge: Cambridge University Press, 2003), 2.11, p. 274.

[141] Ibid., 2.136, p. 358.

[142] Benedict de Spinoza, *The Tractatus Theologico-Politicus*, in *Benedict de Spinoza: The Political Works*, ed. A. G. Wernham (Oxford: The Clarendon Press, 1958), p. 81.

[143] Benedict de Spinoza, *Ethics*, trans. A. Boyle (London: Everyman's Library, 1989), book 3, 'Definition of the Emotions,' 17, p. 132.

without any other than the original sin.[144] Thus, identifying conscience with pain was a commonplace with a long history. Yet the theologians did not want to dispense with the pain of conscience, because it is necessary for sincere repentance and thus is a stage on the road to knowledge of God. Satan might be the cause of this pain, but simultaneously the one who attempts to make it numb: 'Satan for his part goes about by all means he can to benumb the conscience', as Perkins wrote.[145] The same holds true for the early modern philosophers: the reproach of conscience is a sane and thus indispensable reaction to the transgression of natural law and therefore one of the principal means of knowing this law. In Spinoza's theory of ethics, however, there is no role for the pain of conscience, because all pain, even all spiritual pain, is always directly evil (*malum*).[146] Pain brings about sadness and all sadness is, by definition, bad and evil. Sadness is evil because it diminishes our power (*potentia*) to act, which is the sole source of joy as well as that of virtue.

To be sure, not all the early modern philosophers did think highly of guilty conscience. According to René Descartes, for instance, there is nothing beneficial in the remorse of conscience, because nothing can be made undone. Therefore, one should try to avoid remorse as well as one can. On the other hand, however, Descartes believed that the best means to avoid the remorse of conscience is to 'accustom ourselves to form certain and decisive judgements'[147] based on the testimony of conscience itself: 'It suffices that our conscience testifies that we have never lacked resolution and virtue to execute all the things that we have judged to be the best.'[148] Contrary to Descartes, Spinoza does not find the remedy for the remorse of conscience in the testimony of good conscience. The sole remedy is that we understand everything correctly. We must understand, first, that everything is absolutely determined by logical connections and causal relations and, second, that it is precisely this understanding that relieves us from sadness. When we understand the cause of an emotion – for instance of the painful emotion of bad conscience – through the adequate use of our reason we gain more power, virtue and joy, which to Spinoza are identical. We understand, for instance, that evil is not a transgression of a law, be it natural or divine, but something that harms our well-being. According to Spinoza, in effect, it is impossible to transgress natural qua divine laws because they are causal and it is impossible to transgress causal laws. Therefore, if Adam had used his reason freely without the constraint of emotions, he would have acknowledged that God's prohibition to eat the fruit was not a moral prohibition in the form of law at all but an eternal and necessary truth that

---

[144] 'These children will have the worm of conscience.' Aquinas, *Summa Theologica* suppl. IIIae, app. 1, q. 1, a. 2. During the Renaissance, the metaphor became popular especially among the poets and playwrights. Shakespeare uses it in *Richard III* and in *Macbeth*. In his *Pelerinage de l'Ame* (1355–8), the French poet Guillaume de Deguileville pictured conscience as a human-headed bodiless creature with a worm's tail. See Greene, 'Synderesis', p. 202.

[145] Perkins, *Discourse of Conscience*, p. 3.

[146] Spinoza, *Ethics*, book 4, prop. 41, p. 170.

[147] René Descartes, *Passions of the Soul*, trans. S. H. Voss (Indianapolis: Hackett Publishing Company, 1989), p. 113.

[148] René Descartes, *The Correspondence between Princess Elisabeth of Bohemia and René Descartes*, trans. L. Shapiro (Chicago: University of Chicago Press, 2007), p. 99.

the fruit was dangerous to one's well-being and happiness: 'Hence that revelation was a law, and God a legislator or king, only in Adam's eyes, and only because of his lack of knowledge did he conceive them in this way.'[149] For Spinoza, in point of fact, the very idea of evil is an inadequate idea and thus contrary to reason: 'The knowledge of what is evil is inadequate knowledge.'[150] Thus, if a man lives according to his reason alone, which means that he would have only adequate ideas in his mind, his mind 'would form no notion of evil'.[151] And to the extent that good and evil are correlates, he would have no conception of good either. A reasonable man, which is the same as a free man, 'would form no conception of good and evil as long as they were free'.[152] Hence, it is conceivable that Spinoza, unlike all the other philosophers discussed so far, has no need for the experience of conscience, not even the alleged experience of good conscience.

VI

The early Enlightenment campaign against the authority of conscience was first of all a political campaign attempting to kerb those sixteenth- and seventeenth-century religious upheavals in which each faction appealed to the religious truth revealed to it by conscience. It is against this background that the Hobbesian dictum *auctoritas, non veritas facit legem* becomes understandable. It is also in this political context that the Lockean assault on innate ideas must be situated: if each party appeals to a religious truth within, revealed by the dictates of inborn conscience, the battle of consciences becomes a battle between infallible divine natures, not between fallible men. Yet the early Enlightenment critique of conscience did not entail the eclipse of conscience, not even in the writings of the critics themselves. The impact of Locke's critique of the innate ideas lay elsewhere. Once the conscience became perceived as acquired rather than innate, the *formation* of conscience became one of the most essential questions for mankind: 'Locke had demonstrated', Voltaire wrote in his *Dictionary*, 'that we have no innate ideas or principles', but this should not drive us to despair, because just ideas and good principles can and indeed must be instilled (*mettre*) 'into the mind as soon as it acquires the use of its faculties'.[153] In fact, such a formation of conscience, installation of just ideas, had started a good deal earlier. During the Reformation various corrective, disciplinary and educational projects had already been launched all over Europe, the Huguenots, Puritans and Pietists being at the forefront of the movement. Theologians soon became pedagogues – like Johan Amos Comenius, whose work greatly inspired August Hermann Francke's famous experiments in education and schooling in the pedagogical institutions he had established in 1695 (*Franckesche Stiftungen*) – but so did philosophers, like Locke himself. The logic was simple: if there are no principles of good and evil within to be awakened by the proper guidance of the

---

[149] Spinoza, *Tractatus Theologico-Politicus*, pp. 77–8.
[150] Spinoza, *Ethics*, book 4, prop. 64, p. 185.
[151] Ibid., corollary.
[152] Ibid., prop. 68, p. 186.
[153] Voltaire, 'Conscience', in *Oeuvres complètes de Voltaire* (Paris: Furne, 1835), vol. 7, p. 368.

church, they must be imprinted from without (and this is possible because the mind of a child is, as Locke put it, like 'wax to be moulded and fashioned as one pleases'),[154] not as much by irregular guidance as by continuous and strict discipline.[155] 'Man is truly called *animal disciplinabile*, since he cannot truly become a man except through discipline', as S. S. Laurie describes Comenius' view on the subject.[156] Yet Comenius was not a critic of conscience. In his opinion, in fact, conscience alone can save us from evil and establish a 'true order in the world'.[157]

Actually, the seventeenth-century philosophical critique of conscience was as wavering as it was short lived. What followed Hobbes, Spinoza and Locke was a revival of conscience with authors such as Anthony Ashley-Cooper (the third Earl of Shaftesbury), Francis Hutcheson, Samuel Clarke, Joseph Butler, Georg Berkeley, Richard Price, Thomas Reid and Adam Smith in Britain, G. W. Leibniz, Christian Wolff, Christian August Crusius, Immanuel Kant and J. G. Fichte in Germany, and Pierre Bayle, Jean-Jacques Burlamaqui and Jean-Jacques Rousseau in France. All of them, one way or another, restored the conscience to the heart of ethics – and more often than not this revaluation of conscience was accompanied by a scathing critique of Hobbes and Locke, as well as of the thinkers who were seen as their followers. Conscience is the 'noblest and most divine of all our senses' (Hutcheson);[158] it is the 'only tribunal God has erected here on Earth' (Matthew Tindal);[159] it is our proper governor endowed with sacred authority (Butler);[160] it is a 'demigod within the breast' (Smith);[161] it is 'far superior to every other power of the mind' (Reid);[162] the will of God is revealed to man in his conscience (Coleridge);[163] it is divine instinct and immortal voice from Heaven making man like to God (Rousseau);[164] it is a wonderful capacity and 'the condition of all duties as such' (Kant);[165] it must always be followed and every

---

[154] John Locke, *Some Thoughts Concerning Education* (Dublin: J. Kiernan, 1712), par. 21, p. 324.

[155] In Locke's view, this discipline consists of rewards and punishments, because rewards (pleasure) and punishments (pain) are the only motives of a rational creature (the 'spur and reins whereby all mankind are set on work') and such discipline must be practiced in all education, because children are rational creatures too. Locke, *Some Thoughts Concerning Education*, par. 54, pp. 54–5.

[156] S. S. Laurie, *John Amos Comenius: Bishop of the Moravians, His Life and Educational Works* (New York: Lennox Hill, 1972), p. 80.

[157] Comenius, *Labyrinth of the World*, p. 205.

[158] Francis Hutcheson, *A Short Introduction to Moral Philosophy* (Hildesheim: Georg Olms Verlag, 1990), 1.1.10, pp. 16–17.

[159] 'The only tribunal God has erected here on Earth (distinct from that he has mediately appointed by men for their mutual defence) is every man's own conscience; which, as it can't but tell him, that God is the author of all things, so it must inform him, that whatever he finds himself obliged to do by the circumstances he is in, he is obliged by God himself; who has disposed things in that order, and placed him in those circumstances.' Matthew Tindal, *Christianity as Old as Creation* (London, 1730), pp. 106–7.

[160] Joseph Butler, *Fifteen Sermons Preaches at the Rolls Chapel* (Cambridge: Hillard and Brown, 1827), sermon 2, p. 56.

[161] Smith, *Theory of Moral Sentiments*, 3.2, p. 208.

[162] Thomas Reid, *Essays on the Active Powers of Man* (Edinburgh: John Bell, 1788), 3.6, p. 238.

[163] Samuel Taylor Coleridge, *Essay on Faith*, in *The Literary Remains of Samuel Taylor Coleridge*, ed. H. N. Coleridge (London: Pickering, 1839), vol. 4, p. 437.

[164] Jean-Jacques Rousseau, *Émile*, trans. B. Foxley (London: Orion Publishing Group, 2004), p. 304.

[165] Kant, *Metaphysics of Morals*, p. 534.

omission in this respect is an 'absolute sin' (Fichte),[166] and so forth. At this time, at the latest, it was also clear that the conscience is not a battlefield of extraordinary forces, be they divine or satanic. Whilst it is true that the conscience was still often conceived as the voice of God, this voice now echoed unceremoniously in nature, bearing witness to the unchangeable moral order of the universe. Ultimately, even this assumption became refuted, but not, as we will see, the conscience itself as the source of human morality.

---

[166] Johann Gottlieb Fichte, *The System of Ethics*, ed. T. Breatzeale and G. Zöller (Cambridge: Cambridge University Press, 2005), p. 168.

5

The Conscience of the Enlightenment

Although the late seventeenth- and the eighteenth-century discussions on conscience were characterized by its praise and defence against the sceptic, hedonistic and utilitarian understating of morality, the grounds for this defence were not always the same, but varied depending on the approach. Very roughly speaking, the eighteenth-century apology of conscience can be divided into two categories. On the one hand, there were the moral rationalists whose theories were embedded in the millennial tradition starting from the Roman Stoics and continuing through the Fathers and medieval Scholasticism up to the early modern and Catholic theories of natural law. On the other hand, there were the so-called moral sense theorists represented by authors such as Shaftesbury, Hutcheson and Adam Smith.

The moral sense from Shaftesbury to Smith

I

Shaftesbury was educated after childhood by John Locke, but he did not adopt Locke's view of morality, mostly because he disliked Locke's voluntarism. Moreover, although he posited feelings, mainly approbation and disapprobation, at the centre of his moral theory, he did not conceive that man's motivation to do well and to avoid evil corresponds to his tendency to seek pleasure and to avoid pain. Likewise, instead of attempting to dispense with the experience of conscience, he understood it as one of the most important moral feelings, even *the* moral feeling as such. There is of course nothing new in such identification. The entire Christian tradition had identified pangs of conscience with feelings, namely those of pain, whereas a clear conscience was seen as one of the most significant sources of Christian joy. We have also seen that Bonaventure and his Franciscan followers located conscience in the affective part of the soul. The novelty of Shaftesbury's view of conscience is that he elevates what he calls the natural moral conscience above the religious conscience. Whereas the majority Christian theologians and political theorists, such as Pufendorf, had argued that a conscience without faith is ineffective ('without religion there could be no conscience', as Pufendorf said, emphasizing the fear of hell as the necessary motive for moral conduct),[1] Shaftesbury considers the natural moral conscience to come first: without conscience there is neither religion nor fear of hell.[2]

---

[1] Pufendorf, *On the Duty of Man*, 1.4.9, p. 44.
[2] Anthony Ashley-Cooper, Third Earl of Shaftesbury, *Characteristics of Men, Manners, Opinions, Times*, ed. L. E. Klein (Cambridge: Cambridge University Press, 1999), p. 209.

According to Shaftesbury, the foundation of morality consists of natural generous affections residing within us, affections directed towards the good of the public. Yet we do not know that these affections are beneficial unless we have what he calls a 'moral faculty' or 'moral sense'. Also this moral sense induces a feeling, but this feeling is not an immediate moral instinct, such as a sudden feeling of sympathy. The object of this moral feeling, invoked by the moral sense, is affections, passions and desires themselves – our own or those of others. In other words, the affection of the moral sense arises through reflection. This reflection does not necessarily involve any deliberation, designating instead a sort of second-order feeling, namely the feeling of approval or disapproval concerning the first-order affections, passions and desires, not so much as separate impulses but rather from the point of view of their totality. It is this totality of passions and desires that the moral faculty either approves or disapproves – and it approves or disapproves them on account of their mutual harmony or disharmony. When the inner affections are in harmony, the moral sense apprehends it and this brings about happiness. These affections are in harmony when they so to speak reflect – this reflection being the task of a well-functioning moral faculty – the harmony of the objective moral universe manifesting itself in the nature of a given creature ('there is in reality a right and a wrong state of every creature').[3] The nature of man is so constituted, Shaftesbury argues, that everything virtuous or done for the good of the others accords with such harmony.

As part of the moral faculty, the role of the conscience – Shaftesbury also calls it the 'natural sense of the odiousness or crime and injustice'[4] – is to inform man when he breaks with this natural harmony. We find such a conscience in every rational creature to whose shame and regret it bears witness whenever these have transgressed the natural, harmonious order.[5] Shaftesbury admits that there may be men who are incapable of shame and regret, but if so, they are totally devoid of natural affection. Therefore, they are not capable of happiness either: 'So to want conscience', Shaftesbury writes, 'is to be most of all miserable in life.'[6] Such a 'man without conscience' is not a creature devoid of all affections, but his affections are not natural but 'horrid, unnatural and ill' – although these terrible affections derive from the very same fact that made a man with conscience to tremble, that is, from the fact that he has transgressed the harmonious order of nature.[7] Therefore, we should not envy those without a conscience. Even if there are men who lack this painful experience, it does not prove that they are happy. Men without conscience are monsters and monsters cannot be happy because unhappiness is inscribed in their very nature which is horrid, unnatural and ill.

Francis Hutcheson agreed with Shaftesbury. Virtuous life alone can be happy life. Similarly, Hutcheson thought that this virtuous happy life is attainable by following an inborn moral sense residing within each of us and impelling us to virtue. This

---

[3]   Ibid., p. 167.
[4]   Ibid., p. 209.
[5]   Ibid.
[6]   Ibid.
[7]   Ibid., p. 210.

inborn moral sense is the product of the 'wise order of nature',[8] which itself is and remains 'stable and harmonious'.[9] This 'divine sense' is called conscience. In *A Short Introduction to Moral Philosophy* (1747), Hutcheson writes:

> To regulate the highest powers of our nature, our affections and deliberate designs of action in important affairs, there's implanted by nature the noblest and most divine of all our senses, that conscience by which we discern what is graceful, becoming, beautiful and honourable in the affections of the soul, in our conduct of life, our words and actions. By this sense, a certain turn of mind or temper, a certain course of action, and plan of life is plainly recommended to us by nature; and the mind finds the most joyful feelings in performing and reflecting upon such offices as this sense recommends; but is uneasy and ashamed in reflecting upon a contrary course.[10]

Inasmuch as the conscience is implanted in us by nature and hence by immutable 'divine wisdom and goodness',[11] it does not reflect merely our subjective opinion and it plainly excludes selfishness 'aiming solely at its own interests or sordid pleasures'.[12] The conscience does not approve of virtuous action because such action is profitable to the one who approves of it, for we equally praise and admire, Hutcheson explains, any glorious actions of ancient heroes from which we derive no advantage.[13] Hutcheson holds that the sense of conscience is also an instinct, not of the body but of the soul, specifying that it is the judge seated in the soul that 'naturally and immediately' determines and pronounces its infallible sentence on our affections and actions, either by approving or condemning them.[14] In the former case, a man is made stronger by the conscience because he knows that he has acted virtuously, whereas in the latter case, when he has omitted his duties, it punishes him with severe remorse.[15] According to Hutcheson, moreover, 'reasoning' is subservient to this inborn and universal sense of conscience in moral matters. In fact, the reason why morality varies so much between nations is due to different reasoning, whilst if all the nations were governed by the moral sense of conscience, which by its nature is the sovereign governor, their views on moral matters would coincide perfectly.[16] Hence, unlike Shaftesbury's conscience, which was only a part of the moral faculty, the sentinel of transgressions, Hutcheson's divine sense of conscience can be found at work everywhere and in all conditions of life. Like the Stoic *hēgemonikon*, it is the 'governing power in man'[17] and must be seen

---

[8]   Francis Hutcheson, *On Human Nature*, ed. T. Mautner (Cambridge: Cambridge University Press, 1993), pp. 99–100.

[9]   Hutcheson, *A Short Introduction*, 1.1.10, p. 20.

[10]   Ibid., 1.1.10, pp. 16–17.

[11]   Ibid., 1.1.10, p. 21.

[12]   Ibid., 1.1.10, p. 17.

[13]   Ibid., 1.1.10, p. 19.

[14]   Francis Hutcheson, *A System of Moral Philosophy* (London: Poulis, 1755), 1.4.4, p. 58.

[15]   Hutcheson, *A Short Introduction*, 1.1.12, p. 24.

[16]   That this sense is implanted in nature is evident, according to Hutcheson, from the fact that in all ages and nations certain tempers and actions are universally approved and their contraries condemned. Ibid., 1.1.10, p. 18.

[17]   Ibid., 1.1.12, p. 24.

as 'the judge of the whole of life, of all the various powers, affections and designs', which 'naturally assumes a jurisdiction over them'.[18]

II

Although David Hume's theory of morality is usually categorized as a moral sense theory, there are some elements in it that are at odds with the theories of his predecessors. As meticulously as Shaftesbury and Hutcheson, Hume distinguishes judgements of reason from moral sentiments: 'Moral distinctions, therefore, are not the offspring of reason.'[19] Unlike his predecessors, however, Hume identifies moral sentiments with simple and non-reflective feelings of pleasure and displeasure: if we feel pleasure from agreeing with someone's action, it is virtuous, and whenever we disapprove of it with displeasure, it is vicious – at least these are what we call virtue and vice. Moreover, whilst Hutcheson thought that we do not approve virtuous action because it brings about happiness but because it is virtuous, Hume argues that we consider virtuous action virtuous because of its profitable consequences, including happiness and even gaiety. Finally, although Hume occasionally identifies the moral sense with conscience in his *Treatise on Human Nature*,[20] the concept is conspicuously absent in Hume's main treatise on morality, *Enquiry Concerning the Principles of Morals*.

Why is this? I believe Hume abandoned the concept of conscience because he conceived the Western ethics of conscience antithetical to his own conception of ethics and virtue. In *An Enquiry*, on the one hand, Hume decisively attempts to emancipate his theory of morality from the 'monkish virtues' of Christian ethics, including celibacy, fasting, penance, mortification, self-denial, humility, silence, solitude and so on,[21] disposing them in his catalogue of vices. He admits that 'a gloomy, hair-brained enthusiast' may have a place in the calendar, but he will scarcely ever be admitted, whilst alive, into intimacy and society, 'except by those who are as delirious and dismal as himself'.[22] To the extent that such a humble enthusiast can be identified with the man of conscience, it explains why such a ('monkish') notion is left aside. On the other hand, Hume's own catalogue of virtues consists of good manners, politeness and decency (his exemplary man of virtue being a 'good-natured, sensible fellow'),[23] whilst the true motive for becoming such a man of good manners is based, according to him, on the love of fame and reputation.[24] This is diametrically opposed to the traditional

---

[18] Ibid., 1.1.11, p. 23.
[19] David Hume, *A Treatise on Human Nature*, ed. L. A. Selby-Bigge (Oxford: Clarendon Press, 1896), 3.1.1, p. 458.
[20] Ibid., 3.1.1, p. 458.
[21] David Hume, *An Enquiry Concerning the Principles of Morals*, ed. T. L. Beauchamp (Oxford: Clarendon Press, 1988), 9, p. 73.
[22] Ibid.
[23] Ibid., 8, p. 68.
[24] Ibid., 9, p. 77. Already Locke had spoken about the law of reputation and fashion and argued that this law based on the economy of public praise and blame is much more effective means of preserving virtue in a country than the laws of God, even more effective than the fear of Hell. Locke, *Human Understanding*, 2.28, pp. 10–12.

Christian ethics of conscience. For a Christian, as Augustine among many others believed, the repugnant glory of men is the opposite of the 'glory in God, the witness of a good conscience'.[25] In his *Consolation of Philosophy*, Boethius likewise writes that the wise man does not 'measure his good by popular repute, but by the truth of conscience [*conscientiae veritate*]'.[26] Finally, when we take into account that Hume formulated his theory of moral sentiments, in which general social utility is also seen as the sole foundation of justice, as a response to such moral rationalists as Samuel Clarke, it is all the more likely that he left 'conscience' aside on purpose. Clarke had argued that the conscience, as the judgement of reason, lays the 'greatest and strongest of all obligations' on the subject, regardless of the consequences of his action,[27] whereas Hume believed that morality, particularly justice, can only be measured by the sum total of utility of its consequences for society.

III

Being a moral sense theorist of sorts Adam Smith accepted many of Hume's assumptions, including the idea that morality is based on sentiments. Yet contrary to Hume, Smith did include the conscience in his theory, arguing that the source of all morality and, more specifically, all altruism stems from the 'inhabitant of the breast, the man within, the great judge and arbiter of our conduct' called conscience.[28] It is not the source of fanaticism as Hobbes and Locke claimed but a guardian of morality against the fanatical opinions of the party-men and factions.[29] It is not an expression of self-love but the sole instance which is capable of counteracting its impulses:

> It is he [the man within] who, whenever we are about to act so as to affect the happiness of others, calls to us, with a voice capable of astonishing the most presumptuous of our passions, that we are but one of the multitude, in no respect better than any other in it.[30]

It is from this inner man, this 'demigod within the breast',[31] when we prefer ourselves to others that we learn the 'real littleness of ourselves' and become worthy of resentment, abhorrence and execration. The inner man shows us the 'propriety of generosity and the deformity of injustice'.[32] Smith also calls this inner man the 'great guardian' and the 'impartial spectator', arguing that a wise man constantly heeds the judgement of this awful and respectable judge:

---

[25] Augustine, *City of God* 14.28, in *NPNF1*, vol. 2, p. 283.
[26] Boethius, *The Consolation of Philosophy*, trans. V. Watts (London: Penguin Books, 1999), 3.6, p. 58. Translation modified.
[27] Samuel Clarke, *A Discourse Concerning the Unalterable Obligations of Natural Religion* (Glasgow: Griffin, 1823), p. 211.
[28] Smith, *Theory of Moral Sentiments*, 3.3, p. 216.
[29] Ibid., 3.3, p. 246.
[30] Ibid., 3.3, p. 216.
[31] Ibid., 3.2, p. 208.
[32] Ibid., 3.3, p. 216.

He has never dared to forget for one moment the judgement which the impartial spectator would pass upon his sentiments and conduct. He has never dared to suffer the man within the breast to be absent one moment from his attention. With the eyes of this great inmate he has always been accustomed to regard whatever relates to himself. This habit has become perfectly familiar to him. He has been in the constant practice, and, indeed, under the constant necessity, of modelling, or of endeavouring to model, not only his outward conduct and behaviour, but, as much as he can, even his inward sentiments and feelings, according to those of this awful and respectable judge.[33]

A wise man not only constantly obeys this judge for eventually, he becomes almost one with it: 'He almost becomes himself that impartial spectator and scarce even feels but as that great arbiter of his conduct directs him to feel.'[34] Yet we must not ignore Smith's choice of word 'almost' here, for a full identification with this great guardian is not desirable, because, as Smith explains, the separation between a man and his inner judge is established by nature to ensure that one take proper care of oneself. It is this very separation that guarantees that a man does not lapse but keeps heeding the judgements of the demigod within. A wise man enjoys complete self-approbation because he does and feels what the inner spectator requires, but he does not become one with the spectator, this inner all-seeing eye, because if he did, he would have no motive 'for avoiding an accident'.[35] Although a man who is essentially identical with the judge-spectator within is perfectly virtuous and enjoys tranquillity of mind, there is a danger that such tranquillity makes him careless of mistakes. The conscience is the guardian of man, but if a man becomes one with his guardian, who guards him then?

The judgement of intuitive reason

I

Although both Shaftesbury's and Hutcheson's theories of morality are based on the moral sense of conscience, they put more emphasis on social and public approbation and disapprobation than the Christian tradition of conscience had done, the tradition which, in the footsteps of Cicero and Seneca, had usually seen these two as opposites. Conscience has nothing to do with men's approval or disapproval but only with God. Yet there were moral and political theorists in eighteenth-century Britain who clearly preferred the more traditional view of morality with the conscience as its heart. One of them was a moral rationalist Samuel Clarke. Despite his Newtonian view of the

---

[33] Ibid., 3.3, pp. 230–1.
[34] Ibid., 3.3, p. 231.
[35] Ibid., 3.3, p. 233. Although accident here refers to a physical accident (if one becomes as mentally hardened against pain as the Stoics required, one becomes careless regarding accidents), Smith means moral failures as well.

world, Clarke's moral theory, presented most consistently in *The Evidences of Natural and Revealed Religion* (1705), resembled more that of Aquinas than that of Thomas Hobbes. Indeed, Clarke considered Hobbes as his principal intellectual adversary, although his critique was aimed at Spinoza as well. Whilst Hobbes believed that the positive law sets the standards for good and evil, Clarke was assured that they can be apprehended from the nature of things. Clarke writes:

> If there be no such thing as good and evil in the nature of things, antecedent to all laws, then neither can any one law be better than another, nor any one thing whatever, be more justly established, and enforced by laws, than the contrary: nor can any reason be given, why any laws should ever be made at all.[36]

Paraphrasing Cicero, Clarke affirms that there is a natural and eternal difference between good and evil – as certain as the most fundamental mathematical truths and independent from revelation – and this difference is perceived by the right reason which God has implanted in human nature. This reason is the law of nature, universally valid and eternal. This lawful order cannot be abrogated and every effort to act against it is an attempt to destroy the 'order by which the universe subsists'.[37] He then goes on to cite Romans 2.14–15, asserting that it is the conscience that most clearly testifies to this order by accusing man when he transgresses it. Moreover, although external rewards and punishments are necessary for the government of frail and fallible creatures, the most effectual means of control have little to do with rewards or punishments. These as well as considerations concerning the consequences of actions are secondary to the original obligation deriving from the eternal reason of things that echoes in the conscience of man. Clarke admits that there are some men who 'by means of a very evil and vicious education' or through a 'long habit of wickedness and debauchery' have corrupted their nature and who thereby are deaf to the voice of conscience, but argues later that absolute corruption is impossible and that even such irredeemable individuals sometimes feel the pangs of consciences, 'however industriously they endeavour to conceal and deny their self-condemnation'.[38]

If Clarke had criticized Hobbes for neglecting right reason and conscience, in his *Fifteen Sermons Preached at the Rolls Chapel* (1726) Bishop Joseph Butler criticizes Shaftesbury for reducing the voice of conscience and the obligation it imposes on a man to mere feeling and taste. To be sure, also Butler speaks about feelings, for instance about shame, which was given to man to prevent him from performing shameful actions,[39] but for Butler, the core of ethics does not lie in feelings, such as sympathy or love. It does not lie in the rewards and punishments we feel or calculate either, but in the notion of duty – and it is conscience that discloses our duty to us. According to Butler, obeying the voice of conscience is itself an absolute duty:

> Conscience does not only offer itself to show us the way we should walk in, but it likewise carries its own authority with it, that it is our natural guide, the guide

---

[36] Clarke, *A Discourse Concerning the Unalterable Obligations*, pp. 161–2.
[37] Ibid., p. 169.
[38] Ibid., pp. 172–3.
[39] Butler, *Sermons*, sermon 2, p. 48.

assigned us by the Author of our nature: it therefore belongs to our condition of being, it is our duty, to walk that path, and follow this guide, without looking about to see whether we may not possibly forsake [our thoughts and acts] with impunity.[40]

Butler admits that those who maintain that there are instincts, dispositions and propensities in human nature which lead man to do what is good are perfectly right, these instincts and propensities relating to what the Apostle Paul calls the law of the heart. In fact, even those who emphasize the natural selfishness of man, focusing on his evil instincts and passions, pertaining to what Paul calls the law of the members, are right. Human nature is double, containing opposite instincts and propensities, as if a battlefield.[41] According to Butler, however, all these instincts are not only distinct from but inferior to the faculty of conscience,[42] for conscience is the supreme judge of human life. It is such a judge as it passes infallible judgement upon man's feelings, thoughts and actions when he comes to reflect on them – conscience itself being a 'particular kind of reflection'.[43] It is by virtue of such reflective conscience and not that of the law of the heart that 'every man is naturally a law to himself'.[44] In real life, Butler concedes, the conscience is clearly not always respected, owing especially to the natural power of instincts and passions which often or even most of the time surpass its power. Whenever this happens, however, the natural moral constitution of man is out of order, since there is a natural hierarchy of principles within man, conscience being the supreme one. Only if the other principles are under 'absolute and entire direction' of conscience, the character of man is not only good, worthy and virtuous,[45] but his actions are natural in the proper sense of the word because they correspond to man's true nature.[46] Therefore, even if the power of instincts and passions surpass the power of conscience, the ultimate authority remains in this faculty and 'had the conscience power, as it has manifest authority, it would absolutely govern the world'.[47]

> This faculty was placed within to be our proper governor; to direct and regulate all under principles, passions, and motives of action. This is its right and office: thus sacred is its authority. And how often soever men violate and rebelliously refuse to submit to it, for supposed interest which they cannot otherwise obtain, or for sake of passion which they cannot otherwise gratify; this makes no alteration as to the natural right, and office of conscience.[48]

Whilst Butler attacked the moral sense theorists for reducing the conscience to taste, the moral sense theorist Henry Home – Butler's contemporary and a relative of David

40 Ibid., sermon 3, p. 61.
41 Ibid., sermon 2, pp. 51–2.
42 Ibid., sermon 2, pp. 49, 53.
43 Ibid., sermon 2, p. 49.
44 Ibid., sermon 2, pp. 51, 53.
45 Ibid., sermon 3, p. 59, footnote 1.
46 Ibid., sermon 3, p. 64.
47 Ibid., sermon 2, p. 56.
48 Ibid., sermon 2, p. 56.

Hume, whose theory of morality he criticized on the same grounds as Butler had criticized Shaftesbury – berated Butler for reducing the conscience to mere reflection. The voice of conscience, Home explains, is indeed the 'voice of God within' which, rather than consisting merely in an act of reflection, arises immediately. Its authority, Home argues, lies in the fact that we immediately perceive certain action to be our duty.[49] In one respect, however, Butler, Home and the moral sense theorists all agreed. All of them emphasized the happy coincidence of virtues and happiness. In other words, not even Butler, an orthodox Anglican priest, disagreed here. For him, obedience to the dictates of conscience does not mean sacrificing happiness, even if this happiness is thought to be based on self-love. According to Butler, namely, self-love ('cool self-love' as Butler calls it) and the conscience are always in agreement with each other. Duty and the authentic interest of man coincide perfectly – since a man, even if he gives up all the 'advantages of the present world' because of the dictates of his conscience, has 'infinitely better provided for himself and secured his own interest and happiness'.[50]

II

Joseph Butler's impact on the development of moral thought in Britain was significant. Adam Smith was influenced by him but not as much as Richard Price, a democrat and an ardent defender of American independence and the French Revolution. As a moral philosopher, Price was a rationalist and moral intuitionist – probably the first to apply the term intuition to moral judgement. In his *Review of the Principal Questions in Morals* (1787, the first edition was published in 1757), Price argues, like Butler, that ethics and justice cannot be based either on utilitarian calculations or on mere feelings, but are a matter of reason/reflection and must include a moment of absolute obligation. Arguing against Locke, moreover, he states that right and wrong have nothing to do with the feelings of pleasure and pain, but have their basis in reality – and that it is from reality that the absolute obligation arises. Thus, some actions are intrinsically right and some are intrinsically wrong and it is not even difficult to discern between them, for we know them by our immediate but rational intuitions of right and wrong.[51] These intuitions arise from the nature of man anchored in the eternal and immutable law ruling the universe and even God himself, insofar as this law is nothing but God in his infinite, eternal and all-perfect understanding.[52] We become conscious of these intuitions in the forum of conscience, which presents them to us as obligations: do what is right, avoid what is wrong. Therefore, as Price asserts, the voice of conscience is the 'voice of eternal wisdom' from heaven.[53]

According to Price, we must obey the dictates of conscience, although we do not know the consequences of our doing so. The voice of conscience is thus beyond all

---

[49] Henry Home, *Essays on the Principle of Morality and Natural Religion* (Hildesheim: Georg Olms Verlag, 1976), 1.2.3, pp. 44–5.

[50] Butler, *Sermons*, sermon 3, p. 65.

[51] Richard Price, *A Review of the Principal Questions in Morals* (Strand: T. Cadell, 1787), p. 59.

[52] See ibid., pp. 181–8.

[53] Ibid., pp. 245, 248.

calculations as it is beyond all considerations of happiness. Indeed, the most virtuous men (those who have 'established the sovereignty of conscience in themselves')[54] are not always the happiest in this life, but often the greatest sufferers (because they rather sacrifice their lives than their consciences), whereas the most vicious may sometimes be the least unhappy.[55] We also have an absolute obligation to obey the dictates of conscience even if these were erroneous, as it were, because there is no difference between such conscience and the right conscience, for nothing but the conscience can tell us our duty and hence, if we fail to do what our conscience asks, we are doing something intrinsically evil.[56] This does not mean that for Price every conscience is on equal level since some consciences are better informed of the universal rules of virtue than others. Therefore, not only is there an obligation to obey the voice of conscience but also an obligation to inform it as well as possible: 'Our rule is to follow our consciences steadily and faithfully, after we have taken care to inform them in the best manner we can.'[57] Price admits that the conscience may be hardened, but he points out that it cannot be altogether duped, because the 'grand lines and primary principles of morality are so deeply wrought into our hearts, and one with our minds, that they will be forever legible'.[58] This is already evident from the fact that even the most morally depraved individual may pass moral judgements on the actions of others (particularly when he comes to realize that he himself is treated unjustly), but it is also evident that nobody, however morally corrupt, is so corrupt that he would never feel the remorse of conscience. Hobbes thought that if every man were allowed the liberty of following his conscience, men would not live together in peace for an hour, but Price was convinced that 'every man ought to be left to follow his conscience, because then only he acts virtuously'[59] – which is the true condition of lasting peace. Therefore, Price concludes, everyone should yield himself '*entirely* and *universally* to the government of conscience ...'[60]

Thomas Reid, the founder of the Scottish school of common sense (*sensus communis*) who followed Adam Smith as the professor of moral philosophy at the University of Glasgow, was influenced by Butler's moral teaching as well. Unlike Smith, however, Reid was widely read and taught during his lifetime, both in Britain and in France, but especially in the United States, where his common sense theory of morality was practically adopted as a national doctrine, advocated by authors such as Thomas Paine: 'Were the impulses of conscience clear, uniform and irresistibly obeyed,' Paine writes at the beginning of his *Common Sense* (which was published anonymously in 1776, becoming immediately a national bestseller with more than fifty editions), 'man would not need any lawgiver ...'[61] This had been one of Reid's chief arguments since the publication of his first major work, *An Inquiry Into the Human*

---

54   Ibid., p. 349.
55   Ibid., p. 446.
56   Ibid., p. 300.
57   Ibid., p. 302.
58   Ibid., p. 292.
59   Ibid., p. 303.
60   Ibid., p. 380.
61   Thomas Paine, *Common Sense* (New York: Dover Publications, 1997), p. 3.

Mind on the Principles of Common Sense (1752), although the fullest presentation of his theory can be found in his principal work on ethics, *Essays on the Active Powers of Man*, published in 1788. Like his Butlerian predecessors, Reid is notably critical of the utilitarian theory of morality, particularly that of Hume. Arguing against him, Reid maintains that if moral approbation and disapprobation were mere feelings or sensations, there would be no difference between animals and men, since feeling distinguishes animal nature from the inanimate, but not men from animals. What distinguishes men from animals is men's capacity to judge. Indeed, it would be absurd to say, Reid argues, that when a man condemns another man for what he has done, the former does not pass judgement on the latter at all, but only expresses 'some uneasy feeling'.[62] According to Reid, judgement and feeling are entirely different from each other, although they may coexist. In the approval of a good action, for instance, feeling is present, but there is also esteem and the esteem is a matter of judgement, not of feeling. The same goes for blame.[63] In fact, Reid seems to maintain that even very simple feelings, when they are recognized as particular feelings, involve a judgement, for such recognition has the form of judgement and not of feeling. What then is this judgement and especially, Reid asks, how do we learn to judge and determine that this is right and that is wrong? Here Reid is unequivocal: we learn because our Creator has planted in our nature an 'imperceptible seed' which is either aided or hurt by education and which is called conscience.[64] Indeed, if God had not given to man this power called conscience man would be a mere brute, similar to 'an ox that eats grass'.[65] This power of conscience is 'far superior to every other power of the mind',[66] for other principles of action may have more strength, but only the conscience has authority, as Reid paraphrases Butler. Other principles may urge and impel, but this alone author-izes.[67] It is the candle of the Lord set up within us, to guide our steps. Reid writes:

> It is evident, that this principle [conscience] has, from its nature, an authority to direct and determine with regard to our conduct; to judge, to acquit, or to condemn, and even to punish; an authority which belongs to no other principle of the human mind.[68]

Reid also calls it moral sense and moral faculty, but of importance is its unquestionable authority as well as its infallible character. For the conscience is as infallible as all the external senses, which do not deceive as Descartes and his followers had claimed, but on the contrary, are the very foundation on which all knowledge of external bodies is based:

> As we rely upon the clear and distinct testimony of our eyes, concerning the colours and figures of the bodies about us, we have the same reason to rely with

---

[62] Reid, *Active Powers*, 5.7, p. 467. A little later Reid wonders ironically why a person holding an office in the court house is called a 'judge' and not a 'feeler', as this would be more appropriate if Hume was right about the nature of morality and justice. Reid, *Active Powers*, 5.7, p. 486.
[63] Ibid., 5.7, p. 485.
[64] Ibid., 5.1, p. 378.
[65] Ibid., 5.5, p. 413.
[66] Ibid., 3.6, p. 238.
[67] Ibid., 3.8, p. 261.
[68] Ibid., 3.8, p. 261.

security upon the clear and unbiased testimony of our conscience, with regard
what we ought and ought not to do.[69]

Whatever is immediately perceived to be just, honest and honourable by the testimony
of conscience carries moral obligation and it is from these immediately perceived
obligations that all other moral obligations are and must be deduced by reasoning. This
immediate perception of conscience is based on a sentiment, but this sentiment is not
a mere feeling. Rather, it is a judgement of reason without the 'labour of reasoning',[70]
accompanied with feeling, heeded most properly when a person is simultaneously
calm and dispassionate, unbiased by interest, affection, or fashion.[71] For Reid, the
sentiment of conscience accompanied with the feeling of guilt is particularly significant. This sentiment is unique because contrary to the other feelings, which testify
to human slavery, the feeling of guilt testifies to his freedom. It testifies that man is a
moral and accountable being, capable of acting rightly and wrongly, and answerable for
his conduct to Him who created him and assigned him a part to act upon the state of
life. If there is no freedom, there is no guilt and if there is guilt, there must be freedom
– at least so we must think if we are to preserve the morality and accountability of man.

Yet Hume's theory of moral feelings is not Reid's only disagreement with the fellow
Scotsman. His criticism is also directed at Hume's idea of utility and the general
good of society as the foundations of justice. Were this correct, the majority of men
would never have a clue of justice, since only few of them think of the general good of
society. Furthermore, the temptation to injustice, Reid argues, is the strongest among
the majority, meaning the lowest class of men. This entails that if nature had not
provided any other motive to oppose those temptations than the sense of public good,
there would not be a single just and honest man in that class.[72] Good music or good
cookery, Reid continues, have the merit of utility in procuring what is agreeable both
to ourselves and to society, but they have not obtained among humankind the denom-
ination of moral virtues.[73] Justice is certainly useful, but it is not based on usefulness. It
is based on the judgement of conscience developed in people through upbringing and
education. The conscience alone can distinguish between just and unjust, being the
ground of all moral obligations without which morality would be unimaginable *tout
court* – the conscience that in the final analysis is 'a faint but true copy' of the moral
excellence of our Creator, the image of God in man's soul.[74]

III

Butler's and Reid's ethics of conscience was adopted later by the representatives of the
Scottish School of ethics, such as Dugald Stewart, John Abercrombie, Thomas Brown

---

[69] Ibid., 3.6, p. 242.
[70] Ibid., 3.7, p. 251.
[71] Ibid., 3.6, p. 242.
[72] Ibid., 5.5, p. 416.
[73] Ibid., 5.5, p. 424.
[74] Ibid., p. 5.7, p. 493.

and others and subsequently, through the influence of Samuel Taylor Coleridge, by the nineteenth-century Cambridge moralists. As to Coleridge himself, his view of man is more traditionally Christian than that of Reid, but the role of conscience is almost identical. Coleridge starts his study of morality by asserting that reflection is the alpha of all human life. A man must fix his attention on the world within him, study the processes and superintend the works which he is carrying on in his own mind.[75] This world within is conscience – the only 'practical contradistinction of man from the brutes'.[76] It is not a faculty or a habit, Coleridge explains, but it is not synonymous to human consciousness in general either. Rather, it is 'the *ground* and antecedent of human (or *self-*) consciousness',[77] not as its transcendental condition, but as a peculiar experience:

> The conscience is neither reason, religion, [n]or will, but an *experience* (sui generis) of the coincidence of the human will with reason and religion. It might, perhaps, be called a spiritual sensation; but that there lurks a contradiction in the terms, and that it is often deceptive to give a common or generic name to that, which being unique, can have no fair analogy. Strictly speaking, therefore, the conscience is neither a sensation nor a sense; but testifying state, best described in the words of our liturgy, *as the place of God that passes all understanding*.[78]

Hence, although conscience is an experience, it is an incomprehensible experience, or rather the experience of the incomprehensible, the experience which yields no sensation but nonetheless somehow bears witness to God's supreme intelligence: 'The will of God, which is one with the supreme intelligence, is revealed to man through the conscience'.[79]

* * *

One of the main intellectual enemies of Coleridge and the Cambridge Moralists was Jeremy Bentham, perhaps the most vociferous critic of conscience in eighteenth-century England. According to him, conscience is a 'thing of fictitious existence, supposed to occupy a seat in the mind'.[80] In the common use of the phrase, Bentham admits, it is implied that the rule of conduct of a person is correct if he heeds the voice of conscience, but in his estimation nothing in conscience guarantees such correctness.[81] It does not lead us to virtue, not to mention happiness, for it is imbued with insoluble contradictions:

> I ought to keep my promise. Why? Because my conscience bids me to do so. How do you know that your conscience bids you? Because I am prompted by a certain

[75] Samuel Coleridge, *Aids to Reflection* (Burlington: Chauncey Goodrich, 1829), p. 3.
[76] Coleridge, *Essay on Faith*, p. 426.
[77] Coleridge, *Aids to Reflection*, p. 76.
[78] Ibid., p. 374.
[79] Coleridge, *Essay on Faith*, p. 437.
[80] Jeremy Bentham, *Deontology*, vol. 1 (London: Longman, 1834), p. 137.
[81] Jeremy Bentham, *Principles of Legislation*, in Bentham, *Theory of Legislation*, ed. C. M. Atkinson, vol. 1 (London: Oxford University Press, 1914), p. 10.

internal feeling. Why ought you to obey your conscience? Because God is the author of my being, and to obey my conscience is to obey my God. Why ought you to obey God? Because it is my first duty. How do you know that? Because my conscience tells me so, etc.[82]

In fact, conscience is not only incapable of preventing evil, but according to Bentham's assessment of his time, is predominantly employed in the service of evil. Thus if we are to avoid evil in society, we cannot rely on the inner voice of conscience. In Bentham's view, evil can only be avoided by means of public disapprobation, legal punishment and the fear of hell, for true morality cannot be based on nothing else than utilitarian calculations on pleasure and pain. But why did Bentham reject conscience? Richard Cumberland did not reject it, although it was precisely him that introduced the principle of greatest happiness of the greatest number of people in the Western philosophy.[83] Neither did Pierre Gassendi, whose Epicurean ethics was profoundly hedonistic and utilitarian. According to him, namely, the conscience is the best and most excellent councillor a man can have.[84] This was the opinion of Erasmus of Rotterdam as well, also a defender of Epicurean ethics. Time and again he stresses, like the Fathers, that a guilty conscience is not only the highest form of pain, but also the enemy of God and a foretaste of the torments of hell, whereas a clear conscience is the highest form of pleasure and happiness. Therefore, no one is more truly an Epicurean than a bare-footed Franciscan, for if he has a good conscience, he lives a thousand times more hedonistically than the most honoured king or pope.[85] Not even J. S. Mill was ready to abandon conscience. According to Mill, in fact, nothing was 'more curious' than the absence of recognition in any of Bentham's writings of the existence of conscience.[86] Mill admits that utilitarian calculation may pave the way for the dismissal of the dictates of conscience, but so do all other theories of morality.[87] In the final instance, Mill argues, the basic principles of utilitarianism are compatible with the essence of conscience, which is a feeling of pain connected with the pure idea of duty,[88] but this remained unnoticed by Bentham because of his ignorance of human life: 'He saw in man little but what the vulgarest eye can see,'[89] as was Mill's verdict of him.

---

[82] Ibid., p. 25.
[83] In his *Treatise of the Laws of Nature*, Cumberland writes: 'Great are the Powers of this Principle [conscience], both to the Formation and Increase of Virtue, to the erecting and preserving Civil Societies, both among those who are not subject to the same Civil Power, and among Fellow-Subjects.' Richard Cumberland, *A Treatise of the Laws of Nature*, trans. J. Maxwell (Indianapolis: Liberty Fund, 2005), 2.12, p. 390.
[84] See Lisa T. Sarasohn, *Gassendi's Ethics: Freedom in a Mechanistic Universe* (Ithaca: Cornell University Press, 1996), p. 165.
[85] Erasmus, *The Epicurean*, in *The Colloquies of Erasmus*, ed. E. Johnson (London: Reeves & Turner, 1878), vol. 2, p. 337.
[86] J. S. Mill, *Bentham*, in J. S. Mill and Jeremy Bentham, *Utilitarianism and Other Essays*, ed. A. Ryan (London: Penguin Books, 1987), p. 152.
[87] J. S. Mill, *Utilitarianism* (Indianapolis: Hacket Publishing Company, 2001), p. 25.
[88] Ibid., p. 29.
[89] Mill, *Bentham*, p. 150.

The French experience: From Bayle to Rousseau

I

In France, the ethics of conscience went through the same crisis in the beginning of the eighteenth century as it had done in Britain at the end of the seventeenth century. Claude Adrien Helvétius, Julien Offray de la Mettrie, Baron d'Holbach, Voltaire, Condillac and others fashioned their ethics after Montaigne, Hobbes and Locke, that is to say, in terms of scepticism, self-preservation, self-interest and rational calculus, rather than in terms of conscience. Yet the majority of the French *philosophes* believed in the existence of natural moral law and few of them wanted to disrepute conscience entirely. One of those who did it was La Mettrie, the author of the (in)famous *L'homme machine* (1748). According to him, conscience varies according to an individual and even according to climate bearing thus no witness to any law, not to mention natural moral law. In his view, in fact, conscience is the greatest enemy of man. It brings about remorse and for La Mettrie, remorse is as useless as it was for Spinoza. It is even worse than useless because remorse makes the virtuous miserable, since only they are aware of it, whereas it cannot prevent the vicious from doing ill, since they do not suffer the pangs of conscience.[90] Helvétius agreed with La Mettrie on this subject – and even though Baron d'Holbach, for instance, maintains that the conscience is the true guide of man, he also adds that it does not reside in everybody's heart, but is 'infinitely rare and is found only in a small number of select men'. It is found in those who are 'well born, provided with a lively imagination or a sensible heart, and fittingly modified', whereas the common people have no conscience at all, or if they do, it is necessarily erroneous, 'one that judges in a manner little in accord with the nature of things or with truth'.[91]

Yet not all of the *philosophes* agreed with the critics of conscience. The *Encyclopédie* exemplifies this well. In the Preliminary Discourse of the Editors for the *Encyclopédie*, d'Alembert writes that there is knowledge (*connaissance*) based on the testimony of mere senses that often produce in us a persuasion that is as forceful as if it were an axiom. Such sentiments are of two kinds: one concerns aesthetic and the other moral truths. This second sentiment which can be found universally in all hearts is called conscience (*conscience*), and it is described as follows:

> It [conscience] follows from the natural law [*loi naturelle*] and from the idea we hold of good and evil; it could be called the testimony of the heart [*évidence*

---

[90] Julien Offray de la Mettrie, 'Anti-Seneca or the Sovereign Good', in La Mettrie, *Machine Man and Other Writings*, ed. A. Thomson (Cambridge: Cambridge University Press, 1996), pp. 135–8. See also Schneewind, *Invention of Autonomy*, p. 464. It should be noted here that French *conscience* means both consciousness and conscience, but usually the context of the noun reveals its meaning.

[91] Baron d'Holbach, *Universal Morality: or, The Duties of Man, Founded on Nature*, in *Moral Philosophy from Montaigne to Kant: An Anthology*, ed. J. B. Schneewind (Cambridge: Cambridge University Press, 1990), vol. 2, p. 436.

du Coeur], because different though it is from the testimony of the spirit that is attached to the speculative truths, it subjugates us with the same force.[92]

In his article on atheists in the *Encyclopédie*, Yvon claims that only atheists have no principles of conscience, though they are nevertheless condemned by their consciences. In his entry on happiness, Pestre in turn maintains that true happiness is the result of moderation, wellbeing, temperance and conscience, whereas Jacourt states in his article on conscience that it is the immediate rule of our actions. This was the opinion of the French natural law theorist Jean Jacques Burlamaqui in *The Principles of Natural and Politic Law* (1747–51) in addition. True, neither of these men claims that conscience is the law of our actions, because natural law is such a law. This universal and immutable law is, as Burlamaqui argues, the dictate of right reason engraved on men's hearts, whereas conscience is the judgement of action in reference to that law.[93] Yet Burlamaqui admits, as had Thomas Aquinas, that this law must first be acknowledged as law, for otherwise it would be nonsensical to speak about the obligation it lays on the conscience, the obligation without which no law can have authority over the subject as it ought to in order to be effective. Burlamaqui writes:

> Conscience supposes, therefore, a knowledge of the law, and particularly of the law of nature, which, being the primitive source of justice, is likewise the supreme rule of conduct. And as the laws cannot serve us for the rules, but inasmuch as they are known, it follows, therefore, that conscience becomes thus the immediate rule of our actions, for it is evident we cannot conform to the law, but so far as we have notice thereof.[94]

Hence, although the conscience does not dictate the law but merely judges an act by comparing it to the law, in the final analysis it is the conscience which stands as the immediate rule of action for us. For the same reason, the first duty of man is to enlighten the conscience, that is to say, to become increasingly conscious of the precepts of the law, without which the conscience leads us astray: 'Conscience has no share in the direction of human actions, but inasmuch as it is instructed concerning the law, whose office it properly is to direct our actions.'[95] Thus, Burlamaqui agrees with the Scholastics and the early modern theorists of natural law, such as Pufendorf: the conscience may be right or erroneous depending on how it conforms to the law. Yet this does not entail that we may dispense with the counsel of conscience. The urgings of conscience lay an 'indispensable obligation' on us,[96] not only because human laws have very little force were they not founded on the principles of conscience, but also because it is the conscience that is, at any given moment, the best judge of law and hence of the proper rule of life. Burlamaqui concludes: 'We ought always to follow

---

[92] Jean le Rond d'Alembert, 'Discours Preliminaire,' in M. Diderot and M. d'Alembert, ed., *Encyclopédie* (Paris, 1775–92), 1.14, accessed 24 August 2012, http://encyclopedie.uchicago.edu/
[93] Jean-Jacques Burlamaqui, *The Principles of Natural and Politic Law*, ed. P. Korkman (Indianapolis: Liberty Fund, 2006), 2.9.1, pp. 196–7.
[94] Ibid., 2.9.3, p. 197.
[95] Ibid., 2.9.5, p. 199.
[96] Ibid., 2.9.4, p. 198.

the dictates of conscience, even when it is erroneous',[97] for even if our actions do not become categorically excusable thereby, an act against any dictate of conscience is necessarily wrong.

Burlamaqui was not the first French philosopher to acknowledge the rights of the erroneous conscience. The first was Pierre Bayle.[98] According to him, even tempting a person to act against his conscience is wrong, regardless of whether the conscience is correct or erroneous, because to force conscience is to cause a person to act contrary to what he believes is the voice of God: 'Commanding to act against Conscience, and commanding to hate or contempt God, is one and the same thing.'[99] What, then, is conscience? According to Bayle, the conscience is an instinct God has established on the souls of all men as a means of naturally discerning what is right and wrong. In terms of morality and religion, it surpasses even the Revelation, because conscience precedes it historically. God addressed Adam through the voice of conscience before He spoke to him through external voice:

> I am verily persuaded, that Almighty God, before ever he spoke by an external voice to *Adam,* to make him sensible of his duty, spoke to him inwardly in his conscience, by giving him the vast and immense idea of a being sovereignly perfect, and printing on his mind the eternal laws of just and honest.[100]

Conscience surpasses the Revelation ontologically as well, because the knowledge given in conscience is much more unequivocal than the words of the Bible. Indeed, it is through the voice of conscience that we primarily discern the true law of God:

> If we examine this matter ever so little, we shall find, that conscience, with regard to each particular man, is the voice and law of God [*la Voix & la Loi de Dieu*] in him, known and acknowledged as such by him, who carries this conscience about him: so that to violate this conscience is essentially believing, that he violates the law of God.[101]

Bayle admits that man's capacity to heed the dictates of conscience was radically diminished by the fall, which is why the Revelation was needed, but this does not remove the obligation to follow the voice of conscience. On the contrary, all biblical truths must pass the test of natural light and conscience before they can be truly believed in. It is not the Bible that lays an obligation on the conscience, but the other way around: one is obliged to interpret the Bible in the light of nature and conscience.

---

[97] Ibid., 2.9.10, p. 203.
[98] See Pierre Bayle, *A Philosophical Commentary on These Words of the Gospel, Luke 14:23, 'Compel Them to Come In, That My House May Be Full,'* ed. J. Kilcullen and C. Kukathas (Indianapolis: Liberty Fund, 2005), 1.6, pp. 82–9.
[99] Ibid., 1.6, p. 81.
[100] Ibid., 1.1, p. 49.
[101] Ibid., 1.6, p. 81.

II

Though Bayle's ethics is ethics of conscience to the bone, the most famous eighteenth-century French defence of conscience was presented by Jean-Jacques Rousseau. In book IV of *Émile*, we find the following remarkable passage, a sort of summary of the Western tradition of conscience from the Fathers up to Rousseau himself:

> Conscience! Conscience! Divine instinct [*instinct divine*], immortal voice from heaven; sure guide for a creature ignorant and finite indeed, yet intelligent and free; infallible judge of good and evil, making man like to God! In thee consist the excellence of man's nature and the morality of his actions; apart from thee, I find nothing in myself to raise me above the beasts – nothing but the sad privilege of wandering from one error to another.[102]

Many of the traditional components of conscience are present here and the same book IV contains many more. Apart from the idea that the conscience is not the remnant but a result of the fall,[103] the Rousseaun eulogy of conscience voiced through his protagonist, a vicar from Savoy, fits perfectly in the Western tradition of conscience. First, the conscience is an innate instinct, an instinct of nature, but it is not an instinct of the body. Rather, as with the canonists and Hutcheson, it is an instinct of the soul.[104] Hence, according to Rousseau, there are in man's constitution two distinct instinctual foundations, one resembling the Pauline law of the members and another that can be identified with the law of the heart and conscience, one the animal, the other angelic. Second, the conscience is – as the Franciscans and the moral sense theorists had emphasized – a feeling rather than a judgement of reason: 'The decrees of conscience are not judgements but feelings.'[105] Moreover, these feelings and hence the conscience are independent of and above reason, correcting it when it goes astray, like Jerome's *scintilla conscientia*. Sure, Rousseau argues that reason is able to know the good and the evil as well, but because it is precisely conscience that impels man to love good and hate evil, the conscience is more reliable than reason: 'Too often does reason deceive us; we have only too good a right to doubt her; but conscience never deceives us; she is the true guide of man.'[106] Third, arguing against the sceptics, the conscience is not an expression of one's prejudices and it is, as the Fathers had already emphasized, clearly distinct from self-interest, even the very opposite of it. We do not hate evil, Rousseau explains, because evil would personally harm us in some way, otherwise it would be ridiculous to feel contempt for a Catiline or a Caesar. Besides, no one is willing to die from self-interest, although it is self-evident that sacrificing oneself for the sake of

---

[102] Rousseau, *Émile*, p. 304.
[103] If man's soul had remained in a state of freedom and innocence, Rousseau argues, he would certainly be happy, but his happiness would not attain the highest level, the witnessing of a good conscience within him: 'He would be but as the angels are, and no doubt the good man will be more than they.' Ibid., p. 306.
[104] Ibid., p. 298.
[105] Ibid., p. 303.
[106] Ibid., pp. 298–9.

others is a virtuous act of conscience.[107] Fourth, as a legion of theologians and philosophers had argued, it is through the remorse of conscience that we know that we have
done something wrong, not only against men but first of all against nature herself,
since it is a secret punishment of nature for hidden crimes.[108] This is evident also from
the fact that evil men ceaselessly attempt to escape the voice of conscience and since
this voice is the voice of their very soul, from themselves:

> The wicked fears and flees from her; he delights to escape from himself; his
> anxious eyes look around him for some object of diversion; without bitter satire
> and rude mockery he would always be sorrowful; the scornful laugh is his one
> pleasure.[109]

Fifth, the conscience is all that is required for a man to become virtuous. It is a sure
guide through the labyrinth of thought and it must be followed. It provides us a
guardian against bad laws, manners and opinions of men: 'It may be you will stand
alone, but you will bear within you a witness which will make the witness of man of
no account with you.'[110] In other words, the man of conscience cares little what people
think of him, as long as his conscience approves of him. Indeed, why should one
believe men rather than conscience, since conscience is the witness of divine nature,
whereas the society of men is in a state of chaos? Rousseau writes: 'Nature showed me
a scene of harmony and proportion: the human race shows me nothing but confusion
and disorder.'[111] Finally, the conscience, which is easily confused by noise and crowds,
can only be heard in solitude and silence, because the voice of conscience, the sacred
voice of nature, is a timid and vulnerable voice, easily dumbed by every form of
fanaticism.[112]

Why then, if there was nothing new as regards the Christian heritage, did
Rousseau's eulogy of conscience become so famous, inspiring both Romantics and
Idealists alike? Did it become famous because it was neither a critique of orthodox
Christianity from the viewpoint philosophy nor a critique of philosophy from the
perspective of orthodox Christianity but challenged these two rivals at once? For,
even though the vicar's conscience resembles the Christian conscience, particularly
the conscience of the Puritans and Pietists, the vicar himself is a Deist to the bone:
there exists a God by whose wise and powerful will the world is governed, but we
do not need books and dogmas in order to know that. It is visible to us through his
effects in the external nature but specifically within us. True religion is the religion of
the heart: 'Do not let us confuse the outward forms of religion with the religion itself.
The service God requires is of the heart.'[113] On the other hand, the vicar attacks the
Enlightenment *philosophes*, disdaining their dogmatism and reliance on calculating

---

[107] Ibid., p. 302.
[108] Ibid., pp. 300–1.
[109] Ibid., p. 301.
[110] Ibid., p. 332.
[111] Ibid., p. 288.
[112] Ibid., p. 304.
[113] Ibid., p, 310.

reason: 'Let us consult the inner sentiment; it will lead me astray less than they [philosophers with their reasonings] lead me astray.'[114] Besides, philosophy, even dogmatic philosophy, presupposes continuous doubt, but the vicar does not understand how to doubt sincerely and on principle: 'The mind', Rousseau writes, 'prefers to be deceived rather than to believe nothing.'[115] Hence, it is neither reason nor revelation that serves the vicar's cause, but something that lies between and above them, namely the divine instinct of conscience. But as we have seen, even orthodox Christians and Enlightenment philosophers preached the primacy of conscience, for although its dictates do not necessarily surpass the written Word of God or the demonstrations of reason, they agreed that the Word and reason remain powerless without the confirmation of conscience. Perhaps this was the reason why the vicar's eulogy became so famous: instead of introducing anything radically new into the Western tradition of ethics, the vicar merely consistently summarized the basic principles of the Western ethics of conscience, albeit liberating it, once again, from the prison of the Word and futile demonstrations of reason.

* * *

There has been lot of discussion about the status of chapter IV of *Émile*. Why did Rousseau put the eulogy of conscience in the mouth of a fictitious vicar from Savoy? Does it express Rousseau's own opinion at all? I believe it does. On the one hand, right after the vicar's confession the governor of Émile asserts that the vicar has shown how Émile is provided with a real motive for being good.[116] On the other hand, Rousseau had already in the *Discourse on the Arts and Sciences* stated that in order to learn the laws of virtue, we only need to 'examine ourselves, and listen to the voice of one's conscience, when the passions are silent'.[117] Moreover, in a letter to his Genevan friend, written shortly before the publication of *Émile*, Rousseau openly admits that the 'profession of faith' is his own, and many years later, in *The Reveries of the Solitary Walker*, he explains that it had been the result of an attempt to establish once and for all the beliefs and principles on which he would base the rest of his life.[118]

The German model: Wolff versus Crusius

As to the German eighteenth-century philosophy of ethics, it suffices to mention three pivotal figures before Immanuel Kant: Gottfried Wilhelm Leibniz, Christian Wolff and Christian August Crusius. As we very well know, Leibniz was a devout rationalist, and

[114] Ibid., p. 269.
[115] Ibid., p. 276.
[116] Ibid., p. 333.
[117] Jean-Jacques Rousseau, *A Discourse on the Arts and Science*, in *The Social Contract and Discourses by Jean-Jacques Rousseau*, trans. G. D. H. Cole (London: J. M. Dent & Sons, 1923), p. 154.
[118] Jean-Jacques Rousseau, *The Reveries of the Solitary Walker*, trans. C. E. Butterworth (Indianapolis: Hackett Publishing Company, 1992), pp. 34–5.

although he did not write much about morality, he did not deviate from his general line of thought in the writings dealing with this topic. First of all, Leibniz believes in the immutability of natural law established in the precepts of right reason (*recta ratio*).[119] He also severely criticizes both Hobbes and Pufendorf for dismissing this reason and claiming that law is nothing but a command of a superior. The efficient cause of natural law, Leibniz argues in his commentary on Pufendorf, is not an external command but lies within, being the light of eternal reason, 'kindled in our minds by the divinity'.[120] In the *New Essays Concerning Human Understanding*, written in French in the beginning of the eighteenth century but not published until 1765, Leibniz point by point argues against Locke's *Essays* concerning the same understanding, including Locke's claim that there are not innate notions in the human mind. In contrast to this, Leibniz not only insists that such notions exist, but asserts that these innate notions constitute the standards of morality. First he notes that if moral knowledge would be innate only in the same way that arithmetic is depending on demonstration, people would rarely be able to tell right from wrong, not at least without a great effort and time. Moral knowledge can be attained through demonstrations, but it is not based on them because moral knowledge arises immediately: 'Since morality is more important than arithmetic, God has given to man instincts which lead, straight away and without reasoning, to part what reason commands'.[121] Leibniz calls these instincts the instincts of conscience (*instincts de la conscience*). These instincts do not irresistibly impel men to act, inasmuch as their passions lead them to resist them, their prejudices obscure them and their contrary customs distort them. Yet the largest and soundest part of humankind accedes to them, as the authority of these instincts is recognized and respected virtually universally: by the Orientals, the Greeks and the Romans alike. Both Bible and Quran bear witness to them. Even animals know these gentle instincts, except spiders who consume each other. Yet in men they are the most efficacious, not only because men are concerned about their reputation, but also and above all because they are capable of remorse and the pangs of conscience. True, the instincts of conscience are no more than aids to reason, but Leibniz at the same time asserts that they are absolutely indispensable aids. Without them, discursive reason remains powerless, as these 'innate truths' relate to the light of reason as a genus relates to its species.[122]

As a Leibnizian, it is not a surprise that Christian Wolff believed in the unalterable and eternal law of nature. In his opinion, this is the only law man truly needs, because it is implanted in reason. Citing first the Apostle Paul (Rom. 2:14–15), Wolff writes: 'Because we know through reason what the law of nature [*das Gesetze der Natur*]

---

[119] G. W. Leibniz, *Opinion on the Principles of Pufendorf*, in *Leibniz, Political Writings*, ed. E. Riley (Cambridge: Cambridge University Press, 1998), p. 70.

[120] Ibid., p. 75.

[121] G. W. Leibniz, *New Essays on Human Understanding*, ed. B. Remnant and J. Bennet (Cambridge: Cambridge University Press, 1996), p. 93.

[122] Ibid., p. 94.

requires, a reasonable man needs no further law, for because of his reason he is a law unto himself.'[123] External punishments and rewards have no place in this configuration:

> Because a reasonable man is a law unto himself [*ihm selbst ein Gesetze ist*] and, besides natural obligation, needs no other, neither rewards nor punishments are, for him, motives to do good acts and avoid bad ones. So the reasonable man does good acts because they are good and does not do wicked ones because they are wicked. In his case he becomes like God, who has no superior who can obligate him to do what is good or not do what is wicked, but does the one and not the other simply because of the perfection of his nature.[124]

Also the role of conscience in Wolff's theory of morality by and large corresponds to the role Leibniz had assigned to it in his *New Essays*. Although reason provides knowledge what the law of nature requires, the conscience is needed for us to be able to judge whether we have acted according to the dictates of reason. Conscience is this judgement: 'The judgement of whether our actions are good or bad is called conscience [*Gewissen*].'[125] Therefore, the law of nature can also be called a law of conscience (*ein Gesetze des Gewissens*).[126] As to the definition of conscience, Wolff distinguishes antecedent from subsequent conscience and argues that in order to become happy a man must conform his consequent conscience with the antecedent conscience so that there is no contradiction between them, since it is this contradiction what causes pangs of conscience.[127] He also makes a distinction between 'teaching' (*lehrende Gewissen*) and 'moving' (*antreibende Gewissen*) conscience, specifying that the teaching conscience gives us information about the action, whereas the moving conscience moves us to carry out the action.[128] Yet Wolff does not believe that the teaching conscience automatically and immediately provides the right information needed to act well. This conscience may be erroneous and therefore, it must be rightly informed by reason, particularly about the consequences of action, because actions are judged by the consequences they bring. Hence, although Wolff says that the law of nature can be called a law of conscience, it does not follow that the dictates of conscience are inevitably in conformity with the natural law. The law of nature is what reason teaches, demonstration being the true means of deciding whether a conscience is right. Therefore, the art of demonstration is the foundation for the judgement of conscience. This also explains, according to Wolff, why the erring conscience was so widespread a phenomenon in his times: few people know the art of demonstration and those who do not understand demonstrations are not convinced by them.[129]

[123] Christian Wolff, *Vernüfftige Gedancken von der Menschen Thun und Lassen zu Beförderung ihrer Glückseeligkeit* (Frankfurt, 1736), 1.1.24, p. 18. Wolff translations from *Moral Philosophy from Montaigne to Kant: An Anthology*, ed. J. B. Schneewind (Cambridge: Cambridge University Press, 1990), vol. 1, p. 336.
[124] Wolff, *Vernüfftige Gedancken*, 1.2.38, pp. 28–9.
[125] Ibid., 1.2.73, p. 46.
[126] Ibid., 1.2.137, p. 76.
[127] Ibid., 1.2.112, pp. 66–7.
[128] Ibid., 1.1.78, p. 48.
[129] Ibid., 1.1.96, p. 58.

Contrary to Wolff, who maintained that man is law to himself, Christian August Crusius stressed, not unlike Locke and Pufendorf, the importance of deliberate obedience to the laws of God. Crusius also agreed with Locke and Pufendorf that morality is more about obligation than perfection as Leibniz and Wolff thought. Contrary to them all, however, Crusius argues that there is no need to *demonstrate* the basic dictates of the divine moral law, not to mention its existence. Even a man of moderate understanding knows them:

> A man of moderate understating will soon become aware in the hardest and most confused actions of what would be right or wrong, even without being able to give clearly any sufficient grounds for his judgement or even to defend it. From this it is evident that there is a natural sensation [*eine naturliche Empfindung*] of justice and propriety in us that has something more than a mere judgement of the understanding as its ground.[130]

Indeed, it is a valid complaint, according to Crusius, that the worst proofs of natural law are found in the writings of moral philosophers. All decent people know this law and this is a testimony that the 'truth of the law is hidden within ourselves'.[131] The law of nature can be known by arguments, too, but there is also a 'shorter path to knowledge' of it, independent of proofs and arguments.[132] The shorter path to this knowledge is the drive of conscience (*Gewissenstrieb*).[133] True, the drive of conscience does not tell us directly what we should do and avoid because it is, as it were, a drive and not a judgement of understanding. Yet it reveals that we are indebted to God and obliged to obey his law – and insofar as such indebtness-obligation is, according to Crusius, the very essence of morality, the drive of conscience constitutes the anthropological foundation of all morality.[134] Crusius then continues pointing out that a genuine obligation excludes compulsion, because obligation can concern free beings alone.[135] It must be distinguished from what one does out of fear or hope as well, because these feelings may cause us to do what we have no obligation to do. Furthermore, it must be distinguished from the situation in which an act is done out of love: in love we act as we prefer to act, but a genuine obligation may require us to act contrary to our preferences.[136] Finally, as already said, it is precisely because men have a drive of conscience that such a pure obligation can arise:

> The drive of conscience is ... a drive to recognise certain indebtedness [*Schuldigkeiten*], that is, such universal obligations [*Verbindlichkeiten*] as one must

---

[130] Christian August Crusius, *Anweisung, vernünftig zu Leben* (Leipzig: J. F. Gleditsch, 1767), 1.7.136, p. 187.
[131] Ibid., 1.7.136, p. 188.
[132] Ibid., 1.7.135, p. 186.
[133] Ibid., 1.7.132, p. 180.
[134] Ibid., 1.7.176, p. 579.
[135] Ibid., 1.3.40, p. 50. This is why Crusius time and again emphasizes the unconditional freedom of man.
[136] Ibid., 1.7.133, pp. 182–3.

observe even if one does not wish to consider the advantages and disadvantages deriving from them.[137]

Immanuel Kant and the infinite guilt

I

It is said that Crusius' ethics is a vital part in the transition from the earlier philosophy of German Enlightenment to the work of Immanuel Kant. This is certainly true, especially when it comes to the interdependence of obligation and freedom. However, as to the Kantian theme of autonomy – autonomy more radical than any of his Christian predecessors had been able to conceive inasmuch as Chrysostom and others had thought that the law of conscience makes man autonomous but not that it is man himself who makes the law – it was Rousseau who influenced him most. According to Rousseau's famous theorem, a man can be free only if he subjects himself to a law that he himself creates ('obedience to a law which we prescribe to ourselves is liberty'),[138] but whilst Rousseau understood this autonomy in collective political terms, Kant transposed the whole problematic into the sphere of individual morality. According to Kant, man is and must be autonomous, a legislator of his own law, in order to be moral: 'Moral personality is nothing other than the freedom of a rational being under moral laws',[139] as Kant writes, reiterating the basic tenet of Western tradition of ethics. Kant maintains, however, that moral laws are not given to the subject, but the subject must give them to himself: 'A person is subject to no other laws than those he gives to himself.'[140] Yet, although Kant adopted Rousseau's idea of autonomy, he did not accept Rousseau's view that morality is based on feelings. From the very start, when Kant started to reflect on the issues of morality, he argues that a mere feeling cannot serve as a criterion of what is objectively good, since feelings vary but objective good must necessarily be the same for all. Nor was he enthusiastic about Rousseau's belief that being virtuous makes man happy, the idea that was shared, if not by all then at least by the majority of the Enlightenment philosophers. From the moral point of view, Kant argued like Crusius, all considerations of happiness, in fact, all considerations concerning the consequences of actions, are plainly immoral, including even the fear of guilty conscience, for whatever is done out of fear has nothing to do with morality.

Now, if morality has nothing to do with feelings and excludes even the fear of guilty conscience, is there room for conscience in Kant's moral theory? At first sight, it seems that its role is minimal. In point of fact, he mentions conscience only twice in the *Groundwork for the Metaphysics of Morals*, whereas in the *Critique of Practical Reason* we find only one occurrence. The only place he discusses it at any length in his critical period are *Religion within the Boundaries of Mere Reason* and *The Doctrine*

---

[137] Ibid., 1.7.133, p. 183.
[138] Jean-Jacques Rousseau, *The Social Contract*, trans. M. Cranston (London: Penguin, 1968), 1.8, p. 65.
[139] Kant, *Metaphysics of Morals*, p. 378.
[140] Ibid.

of Virtue – and even here his remarks are sporadic rather than systematic. Does this imply that, for Kant, conscience is a metaphysical entity incommensurable with his critical philosophy? This is not the case. Instead of abandoning conscience, Kant in a sense rehabilitates the medieval twofold conscience. What else is the Kantian practical reason, the moral law as its 'fact',[141] than the Scholastic *synderesis*? Indeed, like the Scholastics and canonists, Kant distinguishes between two natures and two laws. Whilst the Scholastics and canonists spoke about angelic *summa natura* ('law of the heart') and bestial *natura naturata* ('law of the limbs'), seeing them as antithetical to each other, Kant speaks about the unsurpassable difference between the absolutely amoral world under causal laws of nature and the intelligible, noumenal and super-sensible world of *corpus mysticum*,[142] from which all morality emanates. Moreover, like the medieval *summa natura*, or *synderesis*, which cannot be spoken or written being neither temporal nor material, the Kantian *corpus mysticum* is immaterial, timeless and remains incomprehensible to theoretical understanding. In the *Religion within the Boundaries of Mere Reason* Kant even speaks about a 'germ of goodness' that has remained in man's heart after the fall. This germ is not only inborn but also, like the medieval *synderesis*, inextinguishable and incorruptible:

> Surely we must presuppose that there is still a germ of goodness left in its entire purity, a germ that cannot be extirpated or corrupted. And it certainly cannot be self-love, which, when adopted as the principle of all our maxims, is precisely the source of all evil.[143]

True, Kant does not argue that God has written a law in the heart of man by means of which right and wrong can be distinguished. Instead, he argues that in order to explain such feelings as remorse, we must presuppose the existence of moral law within, for otherwise this feeling would make no sense. Hence, even though we cannot know that a *noumenal* world and thereby the moral law exist, it is rational to believe so. Of importance here is, however, that the *effects* of this rational belief are the same as the effects of *synderesis* in Scholastic discourse. On the one hand, as Kant writes, 'the moral law commands that we ought to be better human beings'.[144] On the other hand, and more importantly, the moral law calls out in opposition to evil, bringing about humiliation and guilt whenever an act of will does not conform to the law: 'No human being, to whom morality is not indifferent can take pleasure in himself, or can even avoid a bitter sense of dislike about himself', when his act of will he is conscious of does not agree with the moral law in him.[145] I say more importantly because in the case of Kantian moral law dissatisfaction becomes first. According to Kant, as we know, the moral law produces respect (*Achtung*) by being recognized as a law: 'What

---

[141] Immanuel Kant, *Critique of Practical Reason*, in Kant, *Practical Philosophy*, p. 164.
[142] Corpus mysticum is Kant's definition of the moral world in the *Critique of Pure Reason*. Immanuel Kant, *Critique of Pure Reason*, ed. M. Weigelt (London: Penguin Books, 2007), p. 838.
[143] Kant, *Religion within the Boundaries*, p. 66.
[144] Ibid., p. 70.
[145] Ibid., p. 66, footnote.

I cognize immediately as a law for me I cognize with respect.'[146] On the other hand, it brings about humiliation (*Demütigung*): 'The moral law unavoidably humiliates every human being.'[147] Of these affects, however, humiliation comes first because it is only through humiliation that the feeling of respect can arise: 'If something represented as a determining ground of our will humiliates us in our self-consciousness, it awakens respect for itself.'[148] In other words, first the law 'strikes down my pride' and then I start to respect it, recognizing its 'solemn majesty'.[149] Indeed, what else can it do, as the Kantian moral law does not contain determinate commands? In fact, it has no content whatsoever, for, as Kant explains, all material practical principles 'come under the general principle of self-love or one's own happiness'.[150] The Kantian moral law is and can be nothing but a mere form of the law (*das bloße Form des Gesetzes*), and inasmuch as it is nothing but such a form, it cannot be but a certain force that this law forces upon us.[151] Hence, the law, not unlike the Franciscan weight (*pondus*) of *synderesis*, or the Crusian drive of conscience for that matter, does nothing but impose a certain pressure on the human being: a feeling of constraint and necessity (*Nötigung*), a feeling of dependence (*Abhängigkeit*), and a feeling that one is being bound by something, as the notion of obligation (*Verbindlichkeit*) implies.

II

Now, if the Kantian practical reason is, in a sense, equivalent to Scholastic *synderesis*, what about conscience (*Gewissen*)? Before we can address this question, we must take a closer look on the concept of conscience in Kant's works. Let us start with Kant's posthumously published lectures, particularly with the Collins notes, representing perhaps the basics of Kant's teaching for the nine years from 1775 until 1784.[152] Kant's remarks on conscience start with a notice that there exist two kinds of courts, *forum externum* and *forum internum*. The first one is the *forum humanum* where the human law reigns and the second *forum conscientiae* which is the court of divine moral law. Therefore, he calls it also *forum divinum*, 'for in this life our *facta* can be imputed before the *forum divinum*, not otherwise than *per conscientiam*'.[153] Yet although conscience is the court of divine moral law, it is not a faculty by means of which we judge whether a thing is right or wrong. This faculty resides in the understanding which we can use or not use, but conscience operates involuntarily: 'It must have power to compel us to judge our actions involuntarily, and to pass sentence on them, and be able to acquit and condemn us internally.'[154] Neither is it a faculty of liking and

---

[146] Immanuel Kant, *Groundwork for the Metaphysics of Morals*, in Immanuel Kant, *Practical Philosophy*, p. 56, footnote.
[147] Kant, *Critique of Practical Reason*, p. 200.
[148] Ibid.
[149] Ibid., p. 202.
[150] Ibid., p. 155.
[151] The moral law 'forces itself upon us of itself'. Ibid., p. 164.
[152] See J. B. Schneewind, introduction to Kant, *Lectures on Ethics*, p. xvi.
[153] Ibid., p. 88.
[154] Ibid., p. 88.

disliking in moral matters, because this is the moral feeling.[155] Conscience, on the contrary, is 'an involuntary and irresistible drive [*Trieb*] in our nature, which compels us to judge with the force of law concerning our actions',[156] a drive which 'sets the law before us, and obliges us to appear before the court'.[157] But it is also the very court itself and the prosecutor in particular – and it is precisely the existence of this prosecutor within us that testifies to the existence of the moral law.[158]

In the Collins notes, we thus find a very traditional storey of conscience: it is an instinct and a drive, but also an inner 'divine tribunal within us',[159] it has the power to compel us contrary to our will, and finally it is an instance which sets the moral law before us, making us recognize the force of law. No wonder Kant maintains in lectures that conscience is of 'the greatest importance in morals'.[160] Why then does Kant mention conscience only twice in the *Groundwork*, written probably during the same winter semester he gave the Collins lectures?[161] Is this so because he now holds that moral philosophy must be 'completely cleansed of everything that may be only empirical and that belongs to anthropology'?[162] I do not think so. Not even the fact that conscience is mentioned only once in the *Critique of Practical Reason* attests to its insignificance in Kant's moral theory, especially when we take into account that Kant there asserts that the juridical sentences of the 'wonderful capacity' of conscience are in 'perfect agreement' with the fact that a rational being is not determined by the natural necessity.[163] In other words, the experience of conscience bears witness to man's freedom – and nothing is more important than freedom for Kant. Conscience does so particularly in relation to time: a painful feeling of conscience arises in a man every time he recollects his past misconduct regardless of the time that has passed since the unlawful deed. In a practical sense, such a feeling is totally empty, since neither it nor repentance can serve to undo what has been done, but for Kant it is not

---

[155] Ibid.
[156] Ibid.
[157] Ibid.
[158] Ibid., p. 132.
[159] Ibid., p. 134.
[160] Ibid., p. 357.
[161] When Kant mentions conscience for the first time in the *Groundwork*, it appears as something with which the faculty of judgement (*Beurteilungsvermögen*) can quarrel with. Kant, *Groundwork*, p. 59. The second case is more interesting. Here Kant speaks about a man who finds himself urged by need to borrow money. Yet he well knows that he will not be able to repay it but sees also that nothing will be lent him unless he promises firmly to repay it within a determinate time. Kant then continues: 'He would like to make such a promise, but he still has enough conscience to ask himself: is it not forbidden and contrary to duty to help oneself out of need in such a way?' (p. 74). In other words, conscience makes him to hesitate between these two alternatives, between self-love and duty. The example is interesting, because Kant repeats it in the *Critique of Practical Reason* in the context where he attempts to prove the existence of the moral law. If a man is asked by his prince to give false testimony against an honourable man, the moral law causes him to at least momentarily suspend his self-love and to consider what his duty would be, this *suspension* of the decision being an empirical confirmation that the moral law exists, that is, a law that for Kant is nothing but the law of freedom itself. Kant, *Critique of Practical Reason*, pp. 163–4. Yet Kant does not mention the word conscience here.
[162] Kant, *Groundwork*, pp. 44–5.
[163] Kant, *Critique of Practical Reason*, p. 218.

without significance, because it shows that through this mere feeling a human being imputes the deed to himself as a free subject and cannot do otherwise, since he 'can by no means reduce to silence the prosecutor within him'.[164] In other words, the judicial sentences of conscience bear witness to man's freedom and responsibility, and to the extent that Kantian freedom and responsibility are inseparable from the idea of moral law, the conscience bears witness to the moral law itself, enforcing its supersensible precepts in sensible world.

Unlike in the second *Critique*, conscience is mentioned many times in the *Religion within the Boundaries of Mere Reason* (1793) published five years later. It appears in various contexts, for instance when Kant attempts to repudiate the claim that the idea of divine judgement would be more efficacious than the judgement delivered by reason through the reproaches of conscience, by arguing that it is precisely the 'judge within' that is the strictest judge, whereas the image of God as a judge still gives a chance to think that one can deceive the judge by appealing to human frailty.[165] Here Kant also severely criticizes the common practice of summoning a clergyman at the end of life to pacify the conscience of a dying man afraid of death. Instead of administering 'opium to the conscience' of a dying man, the conscience of the dying 'ought rather be *stirred up* and *sharpened*, in order that whatever good yet to be done, or whatever consequences of past evil still left to be undone (repaid for), will not be neglected'.[166] In addition, Kant takes up the idea of erring conscience, arguing that such conscience is an absurdity (*Unding*), because the conscience does not refer to my judgement on whether something is right or wrong – for this belongs to the understanding – but to my judgement on whether I truly believe rather than just pretend to believe in my judgement concerning right and wrong.[167] Hence, the judgement of conscience is always correct, for it does not relate to what is objectively right or wrong, but to subjective certainty of rightness of action. We also must obey the judgement of conscience, because it is a moral principle requiring no proof that we ought to venture nothing where there is a danger that our action might be wrong. In other words, we must be certain of the rightness of the action and we can be certain of that only after we have, with all possible diligence, examined that the action we are going to undertake is right. The conscience is the guardian of this diligence and it calls upon a human being to testify for or against himself as to whether such diligent examination has taken place, passing its 'judgement upon judgement itself'.[168] This also explains why Kant speaks here about the lack of conscience rather than about the erroneous conscience, implying that those who do evil whilst believing that they are passing judgement according to their conscience (Kant mentions an inquisitor as an example) do not possess a conscience that is in error (although it might be in error, too) but rather, an inoperative conscience. They pass judgement on others but forget to pass judgement upon their own judgements in a conscientious way and therefore,

---

[164] Ibid.
[165] Kant, *Religion within the Boundaries*, p. 93.
[166] Ibid., p. 93, footnote.
[167] Ibid., p. 27.
[168] Ibid, p. 179.

inasmuch as conscience is the scrutinizer of the sincerity of this self-judgement, their consciences remain asleep.

In the *Religion*, conscience appears as a scrutinizer of sincerity, but in Kant's *Doctrine of Virtue* (*Tugendlehre*) we encounter a conscience that resembles more the one we found in the Collins notes. In the book, the conscience is discussed in two places, first in the Introduction, then in the chapter entitled Doctrine of the Elements of Ethics. In the Introduction, the conscience is first defined as a moral endowment (*moralische Beschaffenheit*) and a natural predisposition of the mind (*Gemütsanlagen*).[169] It is, like moral feeling, love of one's neighbour and respect for oneself, the subjective condition of morality as such, for it is the condition of receptiveness to the concept of duty. Yet the conscience is not an endowment by means of which one knows whether something is or is not a duty. It is again the understanding that knows that, whilst conscience knows what duty is, for it is a consciousness of *dutifulness as such*: 'Conscience is practical reason holding the human being's duty before him for his acquittal or condemnation in every case that comes under a law.'[170] Therefore, it alone is capable of judging whether a human being conforms to a duty he knows to be a duty. Without conscience nobody would neither impute anything to himself as conforming to duty nor reproach himself with anything as contrary to duty. According to Kant, however, such a case is merely hypothetical, for there are no people without conscience. Every human being has a conscience as an unavoidable fact (*eine unausbleibliche Tatsache*) and when it is said that a certain human being has no conscience, what is meant is that he pays no heed to its verdict.[171] Yet although conscience is an empirical fact, it is completely different from other empirical facts, for the dictates of conscience are not empirical in origin but follow from the consciousness of the supersensible moral law, 'as the effect [*Wirkung*] this has on the mind'.[172] Hence, conscience is natural, but does not originate in nature. Like other moral endowments, such as love of one's neighbour and respect for oneself, it originates in the supersensible realm of moral law which executes itself through conscience.

In the Introduction, Kant also reiterates the view that 'an erring conscience is an absurdity',[173] specifying that it is possible for the understanding to misjudge whether something is a duty, whereas it is impossible to be mistaken about whether one has conformed to a duty, because conscience, as the sense of dutifulness in general, speaks

---

[169] Kant, *Metaphysics of Morals*, p. 528.

[170] Ibid., p. 529. In his book on religion, Kant had put it as follows: 'Conscience is a consciousness which is of itself [*für sich selbst*] a duty.' Kant, *Religion within the Boundaries*, p. 178. In Vigilantius' notes taken on a course given in 1793–4 when Kant had just finished his book on religion and was preparing the *Metaphysics of Morals*, we can read that conscience 'equals a consciousness of what duty is, for itself'. Kant, *Lectures on Ethics*, p. 357.

[171] Kant, *Metaphysics of Morals*, p. 529. In the *Lectures on Ethics*, Kant admits that there are people who consider conscience as a product of art and education that judges and speaks in a merely habitual fashion (*conscientia artificialis*), but in his view, this conscience is not a proper conscience at all, because a person lacking such training and education would be able to escape its pangs. This is not the case, however. Therefore, conscience must be natural (*conscientia naturalis*) disposition of the mind. Kant, *Lectures on Ethics*, p. 134.

[172] Kant, *Metaphysics of Morals*, p. 528.

[173] Ibid., p. 529.

involuntarily (*unwillkürlich*) and unavoidably.[174] Following this, Kant asserts that 'if someone is aware that he has acted in accordance with his conscience, then as far as guilt or innocence is concerned nothing more can be required of him'.[175] In other words, Kant argues, not unlike Knutzen or Butler, that one's guilt and innocence depend entirely on whether one has acted according to the judgement of conscience. Yet Kant simultaneously insists that to act in accordance with conscience cannot itself be a duty, because, on the one hand, there is no higher instance than conscience, which can judge whether an autonomous human being has acted in accordance with his duty, and, on the other hand, to act in accordance with conscience cannot itself be a duty, because a duty to act in accordance with conscience would require a second conscience in order for one to become aware of the actions of the first.[176] Yet, although to act in accordance with conscience cannot be a duty, it does not follow that we would not have duties towards the conscience. We do have such a duty, although this duty is merely indirect. This duty is to 'cultivate one's conscience, to sharpen one's attentiveness to the voice of the inner judge and to use every means to obtain a hearing for it'.[177]

After the Introduction, we encounter the concept of conscience in Part I of the *Doctrine*, entitled Doctrine of the Elements of Ethics. Here, in the first subsection, where Kant speaks about duties to oneself, we find the most extensive treatment of conscience in the works of Kant published during his lifetime. Kant starts by observing that practical understanding provides the rule of action, continuing that the internal imputation of a deed, as a case falling under a law, belongs to the faculty of judgement, upon which follows the conclusion of reason, the verdict that either condemns or acquits the result of the action. Kant then goes on to explain that '*all this* takes place before a tribunal [*coram iudicio*], which, as a moral person giving effect to the law, is called a court [*forum*]', and that the consciousness of this internal court (*innerer Gerichtshof*) in the human being is conscience.[178] Hence, conscience no longer is a moment in the moral decision-making process, but rather the instance which renders the operations of the court personnel *effective* bestowing them with the force of law. Kant continues:

> Every human being has a conscience and finds himself observed, threatened, and, in general, kept in awe (respect coupled with fear) by an internal judge [*innere Richter*]; and this authority watching over the law in him is not something that he himself (voluntarily) [*willkürlich*] *makes*, but something incorporated in his being. It follows him like his shadow when he plans to escape. He can indeed stun himself or put himself to sleep by pleasures and distractions; but he cannot help coming to himself or waking up from time to time; and when he does, he

---

[174] Ibid., p. 530.
[175] Ibid., p. 530.
[176] Ibid.
[177] Ibid.
[178] Ibid., p. 560. Emphasis mine.

hears at once its fearful voice [*die furchtbare Stimme*]. He can at most, in extreme depravity, bring himself to *heed* it no longer, but he still cannot help *hearing* it.[179]

Yet although Kant maintains that there is an internal judge within me whose judgements are not passed by me, he does not argue, like Adam Smith, that there is, within me, an impartial inner spectator. Instead, he argues that we must suppose the presence of such an alien person within ourselves, for otherwise the moral predisposition of conscience would be an absurdity. For if a human being who is accused by his conscience is understood as the same person as the prosecutor, the result of the trial would always be the same: the prosecutor would lose. Therefore, the person within the person must be another, or at least this is what we must think:

> A human being who accuses and judges himself in conscience must think of a dual personality in himself, a doubled self [*doppelte Selbst*] which, on the one hand, has no stand trembling at the bar of a court that is yet entrusted to him, but which, on the other hand, itself administers the office of judge that it holds by innate authority.[180]

According to Kant, however, such a doubled or split self does not yet fully explain the authority of the inner judge or the prosecutor, for even if there were two persons within me, nothing explains what makes the accused heed the judgement of the accuser. Therefore, Kant argues that the accuser must be thought of as an ideal person that reason creates for itself. Yet to the extent that no ideal person short of God can have the sufficient authority to judge the person as a whole and to make him accountable for all his deeds, as the conscience does (by 'watching over the law in him', conscience 'must be thought of as the subjective principle of being accountable to God for all one's deeds'.[181] Hence, reason necessarily creates for itself, if it is not to contradict itself, an idea and an image of God, not only in order to explain the factual authority of conscience to prosecute men without their consent but also in order to strengthen that authority.[182] Yet the creation of this idea does not presuppose that a human being is entitled to assume the independent existence of a supreme being outside himself, still less that he would be bound by his conscience to do so. The image of God here is nothing but a substitute for the *homo noumenon*, which in itself 'is distinct from us yet present in our inmost being',[183] understood as the lawgiving reason. In other words, the authority of conscience depends on human beings conceiving their lawgiving reason itself *as* God. The conscience is in turn the medium through which the law of this inner God becomes effective with regard to the *homo phenomenon*, the human being as a sensible being.[184]

---

[179] Ibid.
[180] Ibid, footnote.
[181] Ibid., p. 561.
[182] 'The reproaches of conscience will be without effect if it be not considered the representative of God.' Immanuel Kant, *Thoughts on Education*, trans. A. Churton (Boston: D. C. Heath & Co, 1906), p. 113.
[183] Kant, *Metaphysics of Morals*, p. 561.
[184] Ibid., p. 560, footnote.

Now, perhaps, the role of conscience in the Kantian moral theory begins to take shape. The conscience, particularly the accusing conscience, is the medium by means of which the force of the noumenal law reaches the human being as the *homo phenomenon*, for the conscience is the sensible expression of that force.[185] Without the voice of conscience, in other words, the moral law remains without force – and to the extent that such force is the fundamental prerequisite of law's existence, even its very essence, the voice of conscience is constitutive of the law, or to put it bluntly, the voice of conscience *is* the force of law. For Kant, the conscience is thus what it had been for Western thought for a millennium, that is, the 'necessary condition of the law's reaching the subject', as Walter of Château-Thierry, the Chancellor of the Archdiocese of Paris, described it in the middle of the thirteenth century.[186] As the medieval *conscientia*, it is an act of application of the general practical principles of natural law – with the difference that the Kantian conscience does not apply the principles of moral law but ensures that the subject recognize its *weight*. I refer specifically to the accusing conscience, because the advocate of the *homo phenomenon* accused in the court of conscience does not belong to the personnel of that court at all. For although Kant says that 'an advocate has been appointed to it', this advocate represents, as Kant notes elsewhere, self-love,[187] and to the extent that conscience in his view has nothing to do with self-love, the advocate of the accused *homo phenomenon* cannot belong to the personnel of the court of conscience. In this court, there is but a prosecutor-judge who accuses and judges unless something silences its accusations. For Kant, this something cannot be self-love, because self-love always stands defenceless before the judge: a human being cannot help hearing its voice from time to time – for the simple reason that he is a rational being that upon using his reason becomes conscious of the force of law through the voice of conscience. How, then, can the accusation of conscience be silenced? By virtue itself, that is to say, by obeying the authority watching over the law in man. This silence is also the only reward of virtue, for virtue does not bring about happiness or joy, but by silencing the inner prosecutor, it relieves the subject from anxiety (*Bangigkeit*).[188]

II a

Conscience was a judge, an accuser and a witness already for the Roman Stoics, but to my knowledge none of them spoke of conscience as an inner court of law. We cannot find this idea in the New Testament either, although the Greek translation of Job 27:6 as well the Pauline conscience as witness may imply such a court. Probably the first to use the court metaphor referring to conscience is Philo of Alexandria, the most notable non-Christian Greek-speaking author in antiquity when it comes to the history of Western conscience. In Philo's writings, 'conscience' occurs more frequently

---

[185] See also Jason J. Howard, 'Kant and Moral Imputation: Conscience and the Riddle of the Given,' *American Catholic Philosophical Quarterly* 78:4 (2004): 621.
[186] Cited in D'Arcy, *Conscience*, p. 80.
[187] Kant, *Lectures on Ethics*, p. 133.
[188] Kant, *Metaphysics of Morals*, p. 562.

than in any previous author. The noun *syneidos*, which is the Attic form of *syneidēsis*, occurs thirty-two times, whereas in the whole body of Greek literature prior to him only one incidence has been transmitted.[189] Like many of his contemporaries, Philo also speaks about conscience as a witness, an accuser, and a judge,[190] but in his treatise on Flaccus he introduces a new metaphor, that of the inner court: 'He who does wrong knowingly has no excuse, as he is already condemned by the court of conscience [*en tō tou syneidotos dikastērion*].'[191] As to the function of conscience, Philo usually maintains that it is *elengkhein* ('to reprove', 'to disgrace', 'to shame' and 'to accuse'), but he also frequently describes *syneidos* as a reliable *elengkhos*. Hence, for Philo, unlike for Socrates, elenchus (*elengkhos*) is not a philosophical 'method', but rather a part of the soul, the meaning of which is almost synonymous to that of *syneidos* itself:

> For innate and living in every soul is the *elenghkos* whose way it is not to admit anything that calls for censure, by nature always hating evil and loving virtue, itself being both a prosecutor [*katēgoros*] and a judge [*dikastēs*]. When activated as prosecutor, it lays charges, accuses and makes ashamed; as judge it rebukes, instructs and exhorts to change, and if he be able to persuade him, he is with you reconciled to him, but if he be not able to do so, then he wages an endless and implacable war against him, never quitting him neither by day, nor by night, but pricking him, and inflicting incurable wounds on him, until he destroys his miserable and accursed life.[192]

Yet the Kantian metaphor of the inner court is not the only modern metaphor of conscience that can be found in Philo. In his interpretation of Genesis 37.12–17 in *Quod deterius potiori insidiari solet* ('why the worse attacks the better'), there is a figure that is almost identical with Adam Smith's impartial spectator, this inhabitant of the breast and the great judge and arbiter of our conduct:

> This man, dwelling in the soul of each individual, is found at one time to be a king [*arkhon*] and ruler [*basileus*], and at another time to be a judge [*dikastēs*] and umpire [*brabeutēs*] of the contests which take place in life. At times also he takes the place of a witness [*martus*] and accuser [*katēgoros*], and without being seen he corrects us from within, not suffering us to open our mouths, but taking up, and restraining, and bridling, with the reins of conscience [*syneidos*] the self-satisfied and restive course of the tongue.[193]

---

[189] In Demosthenes' oration *De Corona*, we read: 'Though I say nothing further about the rest of my policy, your *syneidos* will serve my purpose equally as well.' Demosthenes, *De corona and De falsa legatione*, trans. C. A. and J. H. Vince (London: William Heinemann, 1926), 18.110, pp. 90–1.

[190] For a detailed study, see Bosman, *Conscience in Philo and Paul*, pp. 107–74.

[191] Philo of Alexandria, *In Flaccum* 2.6, in *The Works of Philo*, trans. C. D. Yonge (Peabody, MA: Hendrickson Publishers, 1993), p. 725. Translation modified.

[192] Philo, *De Decalogo* 87, in ibid., p. 526. Translation modified.

[193] Philo, *Quod deterius potiori insidiari solet*, in ibid., p. 114. Translation modified.

III

It is not easy to distinguish Kant's reason from his concept of conscience. In the Introduction to the *Doctrine of Virtue*, Kant names four feelings through which the mind became receptive to duty, a concept which stands in immediate relation to the moral law: conscience, moral feeling, love and self-respect. By virtue of all these 'sensuous pre-concepts' (*Ästhetische Vorbegriffe*) a human being can be put under obligation, which is, for Kant, the very condition of morality. These preconceptions are phenomenal links between the supersensible and the sensible, being themselves sensible experiences, but originating in the supersensible. Yet, although Kant groups these four together under the same rubric of sensuous pre-concepts, conscience clearly differs from the others, for unlike moral feeling, love or respect, conscience is not a feeling at all.[194] Rather, the conscience is, as Kant writes, directed to the subject 'to affect moral feeling by its act'.[195] In other words, moral feelings are effects of conscience, whereas conscience itself is not a feeling but the cause of the purely moral feelings, originating in the supersensible realm of reason and freedom.

Perhaps the real reason why Kant did not write so much about the voice of conscience in the second *Critique* pertains to the fact that there he used the expression 'voice of reason' (*die Stimme der Vernunft*) in the sense he used the expression 'voice of conscience' in the *Doctrine of Virtue*. We have already seen that in the *Doctrine* it is the inner judge of conscience that yields respect coupled with fear when the subject recognizes the moral law within. In the second *Critique*, this same effect is produced by the voice of reason. The conflict between the principle of morality and the principle of happiness would ruin morality altogether, Kant writes in the second *Critique*, 'were not the voice of reason [*die Stimme der Vernunft*] in reference to the will so distinct, so irrepressible, and so audible even to the most common human beings'.[196] Little later he continues that this voice, the voice of reason, 'makes even the boldest evildoer tremble and forces him to hide from its sight'.[197] What else is this voice but the voice of conscience asserted by the entire Western tradition and even Kant himself in his lectures and later writings? Audible to the most common of human beings, making even the boldest evildoer tremble, it is clearly the voice of conscience that Kant has in mind. In his *Opus Postumum*, in fact, Kant describes this phenomenon without referring either to 'reason' or to 'conscience', replacing them both by a mysterious 'being' (*Wesen*) within:

> There is a being [*Wesen*] in me which, though distinct from me, stands to me in relations of causal efficacy, and which, itself free, i.e., not dependent upon the law of nature in space and time, inwardly directs me (justifies or condemns), and I, as

---

[194] Kant usually considers all feelings pathological from the point of view of morality 'No moral principle is based, as people sometimes suppose, on any feeling [*Gefühl*] whatsoever.' Kant, *Metaphysics of Morals*, p. 510. Yet the above mentioned moral feelings are not pathological, but, as already said, necessary conditions of morality as such.

[195] Ibid., p. 529.

[196] Kant, *Critique of Practical Reason*, p. 168.

[197] Ibid., 204.

man, am myself this being. It is not a substance outside me; and what is strangest of all, the causality is a determination to action in freedom, and not as a necessity of nature.'[198]

Although Kant, not unlike the Scholastics, distinguished the lawgiving reason from the conscience applying the law, it seems that eventually they became almost inseparable. This is not to say that it is this inseparability that distinguishes Kant from the tradition. We recall that the Fathers habitually muddled up the law of the heart and the conscience. Not even the distinction between *synderesis* and *conscietia* was always clear-cut in Scholasticism, for as we have seen, also the *synderesis* murmurs back against sin. What distinguishes Kant from the majority of Fathers and Scholastics, but not of course from Luther, is the assumption that the fulfilment of the moral law is *impossible*. For although I stated that the Kantian law is known primarily through transgression incurring guilt (if we consider a maxim that does not agree with the moral law as a transgression of the law), it is strictly speaking not transgression but the very impossibility of its fulfilment that reveals the existence of such a law. It is this impossibility itself that is the source of guilt. In other words, the guilt still bears witness to the existence of moral law, but the source of guilt is displaced from transgression to the very being of the law. For, although Kant argues above that no man can escape bitter dissatisfaction in becoming conscious of maxims which do not agree with the moral law in him, we must note that, according to Kant, no single maxim ever agrees with the moral law: 'No example of exact observance of it can be found in experience.'[199] This is Kant's message throughout his works: we are obliged to obey the moral law even if the best efforts to obey it inevitably fail, being blameworthy even in our own eyes, 'if we do not strife our inner tribunal, which judges according to this law'.[200]

Instead of interpreting this impossibility merely as Kant's complaint about human frailty, we should interpret it as an insight on the *very condition of possibility of all morality*. Without this discrepancy between the law and the act of will, there would be no need for morality at all. It is precisely this discrepancy that is the origin of the force of law Kant refers to – of the force arousing the feeling of dependence, indebtedness and 'infinity of guilt'.[201] This is also the basic reason why man is, according to Kant, radically evil. For although Kant says that this evilness is a natural propensity of man, it follows from the consciousness of the law, not from his nature per se: '"That the human being is evil," cannot mean anything else than that he is conscious of the moral law'.[202] Admittedly, the passage continues 'and yet has incorporated into his maxim the (occasional) deviation from it', but we must bear in mind that maxims always deviate from the moral law and thus, it is the moral law itself that is responsible for man's radical evilness and his infinite guilt. Hence, rather than providing a universal

---

[198] T. M. Greene, ed., *Kant Selections* (New York: Scribner, 1929), p. 373.
[199] Kant, *Critique of Practical Reason*, p. 177.
[200] Kant, *Lectures on Ethics*, p. 104.
[201] See Kant, *Religion within the Boundaries*, p. 89.
[202] Ibid., p. 55.

law of objective good and evil, Kant's moral law, like that of Luther, provides man only with an awareness that he is always already guilty. For Kant, morality means the assumption of this guilt, whereas immorality is defined, not by any objective criteria, but by one's *unwillingness* to assume this primordial guilt. It is precisely guilt that is the *ratio conoscendi* of freedom as freedom is the *ratio essendi* of guilt – of which we become conscious of in the court of conscience: 'Who can say that he morally innocent? We may be innocent enough *coram foro externo*, but not here, in the court of conscience.'[203]

Obviously, Kant also insists that an act of will may approximate the moral law. For according to him, the will operates on subjective principles of volition called maxims. Hence, Kant believes that in any act of willing one relies on maxims one draws up for oneself, these maxims operating as the motivational ground of the will. The content of these maxims is not set since they are nothing but practical rules I myself create for my conduct in order to will and act at all. However, the maxims are not all equal. According to Kant, it is possible to postulate a formula for the creation of the maxim that corresponds to the very lawfulness of the moral law, namely to the empty form of law. This famous formula goes as follows: 'Act only in accordance with that maxim through which you can at the same time will that it become a universal law.'[204] Yet, we must note that this formula is not itself a moral law, not to mention a maxim that agrees with the formula. Indeed, it would be nonsensical to claim that a formula or a maxim summons up humiliation, respect, remorse and so on. Not even Kant would make such a claim, emphasizing instead ceaselessly the unsurpassable difference, not only between the law and the maxim but also between the maxim and the actual deed. It is practical reason judging through conscience that brings about all these effects, and it does so regardless of whether one wills that his maxim should become a universal law. On the contrary, the formula merely guarantees, if one attempts to apply it in practice, that one is using his reason, which in turn renders the moral law and the inner court of conscience operative. For whenever a human being uses his reason, he at once hears the fearful voice of conscience. Upon hearing it, it is no longer possible for him to escape his internal judge, this authority watching over the law in him and judging him guilty, irremediably and definitely, before any transgression or omission, for there is no morality, no freedom, no responsibility, not, as we will see, even true happiness, in the sphere of innocence.

I said even true happiness, for although Kant was a rigorist, he was not a sadist. The subjective idea of God was not necessary for him only for the reason that the judge of conscience would thus acquire the weight it requires but also in order to alleviate the negative consequences of moral freedom, the ensuing infinite guilt. Namely, Kant acknowledged that human life is impossible without a certain amount of happiness and that infinite guilt is of course bound to radically deprive man of happiness: 'Because of this infinite guilt all mankind must look forward to endless punishment

---

[203] Kant, *Lectures on Ethics*, p. 193.
[204] Kant, *Groundwork*, p. 73.

and exclusion from the kingdom of God.'[205] How, then, does the idea of God alleviate these negative consequences of human freedom, the infinite guilt resulting from man's absolute accountability? On the one hand, the idea of God calls forth the idea of the final judgement. One day each of us will stand before the judgement seat of the infallible judge. Hence, even if the earthly life of a moral man may be full of sorrow and renunciation, he can find consolation in the hope that he will be compensated for his renunciations and the accounts will be settled. Although this hope, contrary to Luther's opinion, should not be taken for granted because in these matters there is no certainty,[206] it still alleviates the pain of infinite guilt felt by the moral man, making him if not happy then at least content. On the one hand, a man may rely on the idea of God's grace. This grace does not entail that the guilt is removed once and for all when one begins to believe, but that the inevitable failure to become guiltless in terms of morals is not counted as one's fault. The fault is only counted if one does not even try to become better, that is to say, if one is not willing, as Kant writes in the *Religion*, to sacrifice the old man of inclinations in the revolutionary conversion in which the 'subject dies unto sin in order to live unto justice'.[207] True, this conversion does not remove the pain of infinite guilt, but it transforms its meaning – and this is the effect of the idea of grace. Whilst the old man of inclinations understands the punishment of guilt merely as punishment, the new man, heeding the voice of reason alias conscience, willingly takes it upon himself, because he knows that it is the cause and at the same time the effect of his disposition for the good. Hence, whereas the old man reads the guilty conscience as a mere punishment, the new man also finds in it 'contentment and moral happiness',[208] something that pleases God and the given human being, too – at least in the mode of self-esteem.[209] Although it is impossible for anybody to become guiltless in this world, the mere willingness to progress towards goodness removes guilt – guilt as punishment – if the person both admits his guilt and sees it from the perspective of God's grace:

> So man finds himself very defective in terms of moral law. But belief in a heavenly supplement to our incompleteness in morality makes up for our want. If only we cultivate good dispositions, and bend all our efforts to fulfilment of the moral law, we may hope that God will have the means to remedy this imperfection. If we do this now, we are also worthy of divine assistance.[210]

[205] Kant, *Religion within the Boundaries*, p. 89.
[206] See ibid., p. 92.
[207] Ibid., p. 90.
[208] Ibid., p. 91, footnote.
[209] We may wonder how the 'old man' recognizes his guilt in the first place inasmuch as the pain of guilt arises only in a man who heeds morality, whereas a villain is always already content with himself, since he does not give a toss about morality. Probably Kant's reply to this objection would have been twofold: insofar as a rascal is a human being, he cannot escape the fearful voice of conscience infinitely, but even if he somehow could, the moral contentment ensuing from the sacrifice of the old man is twice as 'pleasing' as the happiness following from sensuous pleasure; not only because it is the universal condition for his being worthy of happiness but also because nothing is more uplifting than the feeling of this worthiness, self-esteem.
[210] Kant, *Lectures on Ethics*, p. 104.

Contrary to Luther, however, for Kant this grace is not God's gift to the one who believes in his grace, but to the one who intends to become morally better and thereby, to 'make himself antecedently worthy of receiving' grace.[211]

IV

From early on, commentators of Kant's moral philosophy noticed a certain paradox in his theory, including Kant's follower Karl Leonard Reinhold. In the *Groundwork of the Metaphysics of Morals*, Kant had written that the only truly free act is an act of will that is in conformity with the law: 'A free will and a will under moral laws are one and the same.'[212] He went as far as to assert that the moral law leaves the 'will no discretion with respect to the opposite',[213] although this law is precisely the law of freedom. To this effect, Reinhold asked: if the will is free only when one acts in conformity with the moral law, then all immoral acts are obviously involuntary and hence, the doer of the immoral deeds is not accountable for his acts.[214] Moreover, Kant had also claimed in the second *Critique* – not mentioned by Reinhold, however – that no example can be found of exact fulfilment of moral law in experience, which means, if Reinhold's view holds true, that *all* deeds are involuntary and hence their doers unaccountable. To the extent that it was obviously one of the main aims of Kant's theory to abolish the very possibility of unaccountability, he must have felt anxious in facing this objection. In any case, he seems to have taken it seriously, especially if we interpret his *Religion within the Boundaries of Mere Reason* as an attempt to address this challenge. In this book, he famously distinguishes between two aspects of the will, namely the will (*Wille*) and the power of choice (*Willkür*), arguing that they both originate in the supersensible realm, but whereas the will is always rational, the power of choice, even though it has the same source as the will and does not originate in the sensible realm, is not a fact of reason but designates pure arbitrariness in terms of volition. Although it is not entirely clear what the exact relationship between these two is, the aim of this distinction is nevertheless apparent. With the distinction, already introduced in the second *Critique*, Kant attempts to make it clear that the human will is never determined by nature – natural impulses, desires and so on. When a human being acts, his action is always absolutely free:

> Whatever his previous behaviour may have been, whatever the natural causes influencing him, whether they are inside or outside them, his action is yet free and not determined through any of these causes.[215]

Therefore, Kant continues, the human being must make or have made himself into whatever he is or should become in a moral sense, good or evil:

[211] Kant, *Religion within the Boundaries*, p. 65.
[212] Kant, *Groundwork*, p. 95.
[213] Ibid., p. 72.
[214] On this debate, see for instance Michelle Kosch, *Freedom and Reason in Kant, Schelling, and Kierkegaard* (Oxford: Oxford University Press, 2006), pp. 44–65.
[215] Kant, *Religion*, pp. 62–3.

These two must be an effect of his free power of choice, for otherwise they could not be imputed to him and, consequently, he could be neither morally good nor evil.[216]

In the history of Western ethics, man's accountability has always been one of the central issues, but it is not until the eighteenth century that it becomes *the* question of ethics. This question forms the backdrop to Kant's moral philosophy from the very beginning. His reason for insisting that every reasonable being is free is not to cherish human mastery over nature. His aim was to make it crystal clear that man cannot escape his absolute accountability: he is and must be guilty for everything in him and he also knows it thanks to the heteronomous voice of reason that ineluctably forces the concept of freedom upon him. Here repentance has no meaning, for now guilt has become irreducible, not as punishment but as a disposition of a moral being.

German idealism: Conscience as conviction

I

It is no secret that Johann Gottlieb Fichte's theory of morality is profoundly Kantian. Like Kant, Fichte argues that man can and must legislate the law of his own conduct, that the will is absolutely free, that he has no excuse but is accountable for everything he is and does, and that he can make himself into whatever he chooses, at least in moral terms, being 'thoroughly his own creation'.[217] Yet, for Fichte, Kant's categorical imperative is 'purely heuristic' and 'by no means constitutive' of morality.[218] According to Fichte, if it were constitutive, then mere reflection of the maxim given in the consciousness of man would be enough to generate moral action. This is not the case, however. In Fichte's view, mere reflection leads nowhere. If, as Fichte believes, determinism, materialism and realism destroy human freedom and thereby all morality, idealism, although preserving freedom, cannot preserve morality, because morality is not an operation of the intellect reflecting on a categorical imperative but concrete action based on firm conviction. Reflection produces mere images, neither conviction nor action.[219] It is conviction that leads to moral action and such conviction emanates only from the reality of concrete life.

If the Kantian categorical imperative is not constitutive for morals, then what is? Fichte is here absolutely unambiguous: the voice of conscience (*die Stimme des Gewissens*). In the similar manner as Kant, Fichte understands conscience as the witness of the supersensible world, that is to say, as consciousness of our higher nature and of absolute freedom.[220] However, whilst Kant held that to act according

---

[216] Ibid., p. 65.
[217] Fichte, *The Vocation of Man*, p. 73.
[218] Fichte, *The System of Ethics*, p. 222.
[219] Fichte, *The Vocation of Man*, p. 63.
[220] Fichte, *The System of Ethics*, p. 140.

to one's conscience cannot itself be duty, as we would need a second conscience to instruct us to do so, Fichte proclaims that it is the absolute duty of man.[221] It is man's only duty, because there are no and cannot be higher judges than conscience in moral matters – and to the extent that moral matters are the most decisive matters in human life, conscience is the supreme judge of life as a whole. Conscience, which 'never errs and cannot err',[222] has, always and without exception, 'final jurisdiction and is subject to no appeal'.[223] All attempts to go beyond conscience are necessarily unethical and lead to an error fundamental to all dogmatism. Going beyond conscience entails that the ultimate ground of morals is supposed to be found outside the moral self, but such an externalization of the ground amounts to depriving the self of its morality, freedom and responsibility. In *The System of Ethics*, Fichte writes: 'There is therefore absolutely no external ground nor external criterion for the binding force of an ethical command'.[224] Like Aquinas, Fichte argues that a command is binding only on the condition that it is confirmed by our own conscience but he goes further as he asserts that it is binding 'only *because* it has been confirmed in this way'.[225]

In *The Vocation of Man*, published two years after the *System* and intended for a wider audience, Fichte's message by and large remains the same but his rhetoric becomes more ferocious. The voice of conscience tells 'in each particular situation in my life, what I definitely have to do or avoid in this situation'.[226] I am also always obliged to obey that voice: 'It is simply true, without further testing and justification [*Begründung*], it is the first truth and the ground of all other truth and certainty, that I ought to obey that voice.'[227] I am obliged to obey it regardless of all consequences, even if the results of my obedience would be catastrophic for the world.[228] The conscience is not to be obeyed because of any beneficial consequences but because it commands: 'I will obey it simply because it commands.'[229] This is not to say that such obedience cannot have good consequences, for in the supersensible world these consequences are always good,[230] but these consequences should not influence us, because morality is not based on a calculation of consequences but on an unconditional fulfilling of the duty that the voice of conscience tells us to be our duty: 'To listen to it, to obey it sincerely and unhesitatingly without fear and quibbling, this is my only vocation [*Bestimmung*], the whole purpose of my life [*Daseyn*].'[231] We must listen to it and obey it because it alone can tell us our duty which is absolutely necessary for us to know, because, contrary to what the Christians have thought, there are no indifferent (*adiaphora*) actions at all. Every act is either good or evil and every other motive of

---

[221] Ibid., p. 148. Italics omitted.
[222] Ibid., p. 165.
[223] Ibid.
[224] Ibid., p. 168.
[225] Ibid., Italics original.
[226] Fichte, *The Vocation of Man*, p. 75.
[227] Ibid., p. 76.
[228] Ibid., pp. 95–6.
[229] Ibid., p. 92.
[230] See ibid., p. 95.
[231] Ibid., p. 75.

action than the one originating in conscience is categorically evil, be it an external authority, an internal impulse, or whatever kind of reasoning: 'Anything that does not have its origin in faith, in confirmation by our own conscience, is an absolute sin.'[232]

Although such an exposition of Fichtean conscience undoubtedly brings to light the essential message, we must, however, examine a bit more closely why Fichte comes to these conclusions. To begin with, Fichte maintains that the origin of the voice of conscience lies in an ethical drive (*sittliche Trieb*) to be independent. Fichte conceives this pure drive an undeniable fact. This drive is common to all human beings as rational beings, making them conceive that nothing is more intolerable than being 'in another, for another, and through another'.[233] It is a drive to be and become something for and through oneself. Yet this drive is not the only drive of human being. Like all other natural beings, the human being is bestowed with the natural drive aiming at self-preservation and pleasure. Unlike Kant, however, Fichte does not believe that the higher and the lower nature of man are mutually exclusive, but emphasizes that man's higher nature has its origin in his lower nature. Hence, the natural drive of self-preservation and pleasure is the foundation of the drive to be independent. How, then, does the drive to be independent arise from the natural drive? According to Fichte, this happens through reflection. As a reflecting being I recognize the natural drive as *my* drive, something that I can accept or resist.[234] I recognize that I am not a machine determined by my natural drives but a being that is capable of rejecting these determinations because they are mine: 'The causality of this drive comes to an end exactly at the point where I posit a drive as my own.'[235] By recognizing this I internally intuit that I am not being driven but drive myself, free of all natural restrictions: 'Through the act of reflection, the I tears itself loose from all that is supposed to lie outside of it, brings itself under its own control, and positions [*stellt*] itself as absolutely self-sufficient.'[236] Yet such freedom is purely formal and insofar as it is directed towards a mere negation of all nature, does not appear in the consciousness at all, because it *is* nothing. To become something, it must surpass this nothingness and it accomplishes it in a singular act of willing: 'An act of willing is an absolutely free transition from indeterminacy to determinacy, accompanied by a consciousness of this transition.'[237] It is free transition because it obtains its form from the pure drive, but it is also determinate because every act of willing is an act that wills something. Yet contrary to the pure drive, I am indeed conscious of my free will. I am conscious of being able to choose freely not only between several possible ways to satisfy a drive but also *not* to satisfy any of my drives. According to Fichte, this is also the point when morality enters the stage, since now it is possible to make the distinction between *unethical* and *ethical* free will. Although both of these wills originate in the form of the pure drive which elevates human being above nature, the unethical will is unethical because it

---

[232] Fichte, *The System of Ethics*, p. 168.
[233] Fichte, *The Vocation of Man*, p. 68.
[234] Fichte, *The System of Ethics*, p. 134.
[235] Ibid., p. 203.
[236] Ibid., p. 127.
[237] Ibid., p. 149.

does not want to remain above nature but freely chooses to *return* to it, whilst the ethical will freely chooses *not* to return to nature and thereby, it remains above nature as free as it was in the first place. In other words, the unethical will obtains its determination from the natural drive, not by becoming inoperative in the sense that the will would renounce its willing but by freely choosing between alternative ways of satisfying the natural drive. Instead, the ethical will obtains its content by sacrificing all the demands of natural drives – and it is here that the conscience enters the stage. Whilst the unethical will obtains its determination from nature, the ethical drive obtains it from the voice of conscience.

What is the voice of conscience? It is, as it was for Kant, an empirical effect of the supersensible moral law. Yet unlike the Kantian moral law, which had many effects, the voice of conscience is the *only* effect of the Fichtean moral law. The experience of conscience is the sole link between the sensible and the supersensible, the finite and the infinite, being the 'spiritual bond' between these two worlds, 'the oracle from the eternal world'.[238] It is the sole guarantee that one finds, not pleasure since there is 'certainly no such thing as a "pleasure" of conscience',[239] but purpose, meaning and truth in one's life. Apart from the voice of conscience, we succumb to pure nothingness from which this voice alone can save us: 'We raise ourselves out of this nothingness and maintain ourselves above this nothingness only through our morality',[240] morality that cannot be found anywhere else than in the willing obedience to the voice of conscience – and to the extent that morality is the ground of human life, this voice is constitutive of our very existence:

> The voice of conscience, which imposes his particular duty on each, is the ray of light on which we come forth from the infinite and are established as individual and particular beings; it draws the limits of our personality; it, therefore, is our true original component [*Urbestandteil*], the ground and stuff of our whole life [*der Grund und der Stoff alles Lebens*].[241]

Let us pay attention to what Fichte says here: the ground (*der Grund*) of morality and life does not lie in the supersensible world but between the two worlds where we hear the voice of conscience to which we are obliged to subject ourselves, not only in order to become moral but more profoundly, in order to exist at all. The ground does not thus lie either in the supersensible or in the sensible, but rather in the experience of their *difference*, simultaneously connecting and separating these worlds – connecting because human being becomes conscious of this other world through the experience of conscience and separating because *there is no other world without this experience.* Every time I obey the voice of conscience, my action has an effect in the supersensible world, and 'apart from this dutiful determination of the will nothing is to have an effect there'.[242] Although the infinite will is the creator of the world of reason and morality,

---

[238] Fichte, *The Vocation of Man*, pp. 106–7.
[239] Fichte, *The System of Ethics*, p. 140.
[240] Fichte, *The Vocation of Man*, p. 79.
[241] Ibid., p. 108.
[242] Ibid., p. 104.

it can be such a creator in finite will alone.[243] If there were no finite will, there would be no infinite will either, which means, in the final analysis, that the gap between the sensible and the supersensible *is* the supersensible world.[244] Thus rather than a link between two worlds, the voice of conscience is the *origin* of the supersensible world of morality: 'Truth originates [*stammt*] in conscience alone.'[245] By obeying this voice, man obeys God, but God is nothing but the living moral order of the world itself created by conscientious action. Hence, whenever I freely obey the voice of conscience, I myself become divine. I become God: 'I am immortal, imperishable and eternal as soon as I decide to obey the law of reason', echoing in the voice of conscience.[246]

Yet not even here we have what Ratzinger calls subjective conscience. In fact, the opposite is true. By obeying the voice of conscience, Fichte argues, the very individuality of man disappears and he becomes a pure presentation of universal moral law: 'It is precisely by means of this disappearance and annihilation of one's entire individuality that everyone becomes a pure presentation of the moral law in the world of sense.'[247] Eventually, it is not even obedience that is at stake here in this disappearance. In *Characteristics of the Present Age*, published in 1806, Fichte comes to the conclusion that the Moral Man, the man of duty, must be transformed into the Religious Man, that is to say, into the Man to whom not only the external law but also the internal law of conscience as law dissolves and becomes comprehended as the eternal development of the one original Divine Life. Here there are no longer any demands but pure blessedness, immediate possession of Eternity. Certainly, the Religious Man does all the same things as the Moral Man, but not because it is his duty but because he 'has a nobler, freer inspiration' to do them.[248] Hence, although Fichte himself mentions only Pietists, he actually affirms what the German mystics and Martin Luther had already preached: the one who becomes one with Christ has no longer duties, because one does cheerfully everything the voice of conscience demands. Yet instead of vanishing from the scene, the Fichtean conscience merely ceases to be an internal judge and becomes identical with the self. Now the humiliating voice has been silenced and the gap within the subject surpassed – not by the eradication of the voice but by becoming one with it. This is the meaning of Fichte's assertion that the Religious Man is in immediate possession of Eternity, and although he also emphasizes that one must first become the Moral Man before one can become the Religious Man, there is nevertheless a decisive gap between Kant and Fichte's late philosophy in this respect. According to Kant, namely, the overcoming of the gap between the law and the self, between the voice of conscience and the addressee of its message, renders man a mere puppet of God.[249] If the gap is closed, there is no longer ethics. Without the gap, the very human being

---

[243] 'That eternal will is thus surely the creator of the world, in the only way in which it can be and in which alone a creation is required: *in finite reason.*' Ibid., p. 110.

[244] Ibid., p. 106.

[245] Ibid., p. 72. Translation modified.

[246] Ibid., p. 99.

[247] Fichte, *The System of Ethics*, p. 245.

[248] Johann Gottlieb Fichte, *Characteristics of the Present Age*, trans. W. Smith (La Vergne: Dodo Press, 2008), pp. 192–4.

[249] See Kant, *Critique of Practical Reason*, p. 258.

as *human* being has ceased to exist. No wonder, then, that the mystics conceived the union with God in terms of man's evaporation – the idea that Fichte willingly adopted and that now and then has resurfaced in late-modern Western philosophy.

II

In German philosophy, particularly in Romanticism, Idealism and even in twentieth-century existentialism, the Fichtean conscience became a standard – though the emphasis is now more on the conscience which 'draws the limits of our personality' than on the one which entails 'disappearance and annihilation of one's entire individuality'. In Romanticism, moreover, Fichtean fundamentals were usually flavoured with a good deal of Rousseauism. Like Rousseau, Friedrich von Schlegel argues that the voice of conscience is 'nothing less than a divine revelation within man'.[250] Likewise, he reiterates Rousseau's account that this voice is not a remnant of human integrity after the fall, but was born with the transgression.[251] The transgression was followed by the sense of guilt and the sense of guilt is the divine origin of conscience: 'The first man, as long as he was yet innocent [*vollkommen*], knew not conscience'.[252] As a part of the soul, Schlegel defines conscience as the intuitive branch of reason that gives an immediate perception of right and wrong. In form, it is wholly distinct from and also superior to that function of reason which infers and deduces consequences, being instead a feeling:

> It is by simple feeling and immediate perception that the conscience, in obedience
> to the inner voice [*innere Stimme*], draws between right and wrong, or good and
> evil, the greatest of all distinction.'[253]

Although the voice makes itself heard differently among people because hearing it is influenced by the ideas of age, education, custom and so on, the primary and essential message of it remains unchanged, for it is the common tongue of all nations and the untaught language of human nature. Moreover, even if we hear it within ourselves, it is not our proper self, that is, our will that speaks here, but rather another self, 'of a higher and a different nature'.[254] In opposition to this other self stands a lower self, not the proper willing self either, but a false and seducing self of evil inclinations, to the effect that the proper self stands as if between these two forces, capable of deciding freely which one to follow and to obey. In order to be good, the proper self must choose to heed the 'good voice' of the higher self, supressing the lower one representing the 'evil inclinations'.[255] This should be done, not only in order for the

---

[250] Friedrich von Schlegel, *Philosophy of Life and Philosophy of Language*, trans. A. J. W. Morrison (London: Henry G. Bohn, 1847), p. 62.
[251] Ibid., p. 52.
[252] Ibid.
[253] Ibid., p. 50.
[254] Ibid.
[255] Ibid., p. 51.

proper self to become good, but also because it halts the vacillation of the proper self, understood as the undecided will:

> This inward voice, and the immediate perception of it, is an anchor on which the vessel of man's existence rides safely on the stormy sea of life, and the ebb and the flow of the will.[256]

III

Would it be misguided to maintain that German Idealism as a whole adopts the Fichtean conscience? What about Hegel? Is he not a Hobbesian critic of conscience in general and that of the Romantic notion in particular? In a sense, he is. In *The Philosophy of History*, for instance, Hegel maintains, contrary to Kant, that conscience is not a universally given endowment but a product of the Spirit unfolding in the immanence of history. According to him, the East and even the Greeks of the early period had no conscience as they were accustomed to living up to the standards of society without further reflection. It was the tradition that bestowed the measure of conduct, not conscience:

> Of the Greeks in the first and genuine form of their freedom, we may assert, that they had no conscience [*Gewissen*]: the habit of living for their country without further reflection was the principle dominant among them.[257]

Not even Antigone, nowadays often taken as the paradigm of a conscientious heroine, represents a break in the Greek tradition. In Hegel's view it was not until the Sophists that the standpoint of conscience was invented:

> It was the Sophists, the teachers of wisdom, who first introduced subjective reflection, and the new doctrine that each man should act according to his own conviction [*Überzeugung*]. When reflection once comes into play, the inquiry is started whether the principles of Law [*das Recht*] cannot be improved. Instead of holding by the existing state of things, one's own conviction is relied upon, and thus begins a subjective independent freedom, in which the individual finds himself in a position to bring everything to the test of his own conscience [*Gewissen*], even in defiance of the existing constitution.[258]

Yet although Hegel de-universalized conscience, already the quotation above indicates that his concept of conscience is profoundly Fichtean. Conscience is not a Kantian fearful inner judge of a doubled self reasserted by the subjective idea of God but conviction (*Gewisheit*). When the standpoint of conscience is at stake, duty is no longer something that stands over against the self but now the self knows with absolute certainty its duty and acts in accordance with this duty.[259] Conscience is a

---

[256] Ibid.
[257] Hegel, *Philosophy of History*, p. 253.
[258] Ibid. Translation modified.
[259] G. W. F. Hegel, *Phenomenology of Spirit*, trans. A. V. Miller (Oxford: Oxford University Press, 1977), §635, p. 637.

consciousness that has sublated its doubleness in the unity of duty and the self – and to be more precise, conscience *is* this sublation (*Aufhebung*).[260] In this sublation the self leaves behind the Kantian general rules and principles and becomes a concrete will, looking at a concrete situation and taking upon itself the responsibility of choosing the act which it knows for certain the situation to require.[261] Moreover, like Fichte but contrary to Kant, Hegel maintains that it can be a duty to have a conscience.[262] In fact, it is an absolute duty, because conscience is the unity of the will with the absolute and thereby, absolutely holy:

> Conscience expresses the absolute claim of the subjective self-consciousness to know in itself and from itself what right and duty are, and to recognise nothing except what it thus knows to be good. It asserts also that what it so knows and wills is right and duty in very truth. Conscience, as the unity of the subject's will with the absolute, is a holy place which it would be sacrilege to assault.[263]

Hence, far from profaning conscience à la Hobbes, Hegel fully affirms the traditional Christian presumption of the holiness of conscience. Moreover, being the standpoint of the modern world in its entirety, this holy conscience marks the last stage in the unfolding of the spirit whose essence is freedom. This standpoint means that man is no longer bound by authorities except his own conscience:

> Conscience is the deepest internal solitude, from which both limit and the external have wholly disappeared. It is a thorough-going retreat into itself. Man in his conscience is no longer bound by the ends of particularity. This is a higher standpoint, the standpoint of the modern world. We have now arrived at the stage of consciousness, which involves a recoil upon itself. Earlier ages were more sensuous, and had before them something external and given, whether it was religion or law. But conscience is aware of itself as thought, and knows that my thought is for me the only thing that is binding.[264]

Unlike Fichte, however, Hegel is not entirely content with the modern standpoint of conscience. In the *Philosophy of Right*, in fact, Hegel straightforwardly acclaims that to have a conscience is 'simply to be on the verge of being transformed into evil'.[265] It is on that verge because the conscience is nothing but self-certitude – and both morality *and* evil have their common root in such certitude. Conscience as self-certitude is a purely formal and abstract principle without determinate content: 'Conscience, then, in the majesty of its elevation above specific law and every content of duty, puts whatever content it pleases into its knowing and willing.'[266] In the ethics of conscience, the subjective conviction is made the absolute foundation of good and evil, but if this

---

[260] Ibid., §654, p. 397.
[261] See ibid., §§653–4, pp. 396–7.
[262] Ibid., §654, p. 397.
[263] Hegel, *Philosophy of Right*, §137, note, p. 116.
[264] Ibid., §136, addition, p. 115.
[265] Ibid., §139, note, p. 118.
[266] Hegel, *Phenomenology of Spirit*, §655, p. 397.

ethics is taken into its logical conclusion, the very distinction between good and evil evaporates:

> There is no longer any absolute vice or crime. Instead of frank and free, hardened and untroubled transgression appears the consciousness of complete justification through intention and conviction; my good intention and my conviction that the act is good make it good.[267]

IV

Here, we must take into account that evil is not such a categorical notion for Hegel as it was for Kant. For Hegel, as we know, world history is a rational process of development towards ever more perfect forms of the Spirit and it is such a process regardless of all the evil on earth. Not only wars, irrespective of whether they are just or unjust, are the means by which the dialectic of history moves on, but, according to Hegel, also some individual criminals and evildoers, particularly such 'world-historical' evildoers as Alexander the Great, Julius Caesar and Napoleon, have been humanity's greatest benefactors. At times he alludes that it is precisely such evildoers through whom the very development occurs because adherence to the ethical life of one one's own time does not entail any development but only adherence to one's own time. Although their deeds might be morally wrong, these deeds are nevertheless good from the standpoint of rational world history, as it is through them that the Spirit breaks through the limits of its current stage and enters a new one: 'From this point of view, no claims must be raised against world-historical deeds and their perpetrators by moral circles, to which they do not belong.'[268] Certainly, Hegel also holds that conscience, comprising the responsibility and moral value of an individual, has infinite worth (*unendlichen Wert*), but this infinite worth is subordinate to the infinite worth of the world Spirit:

> World history moves on a higher plane than that on which morality properly belongs, for the sphere of morality is that of private conviction [*Privatgesinnung*], the conscience of individuals, and their particular will and mode of action.[269]

However, if the morally evil is not inevitably evil from the standpoint of world history, then it necessarily follows that conscience ('my good intention and my conviction') may also be good *even if* it slips into evil, for although it is not good from the standpoint of morality it can be good from the standpoint of world history, at least retrospectively. This is, I think, Hegel's point. Let us take the Sophists as an example. According to Hegel, as we recall, the Sophists introduced the doctrine that each man should act according to his own conviction. In Hegel's estimation this opened the door for moral laxity in the whole community, plunging the 'Greek world into ruin'.[270] Yet at the same time he praises Socrates for positing the very same individual conscience and

---

[267] Hegel, *Philosophy of Right*, §140, note, p. 125.
[268] Hegel, *Philosophy of History*, p. 83.
[269] Ibid. p. 67.
[270] Ibid., p. 253.

reflection as the foundation of morality, since it is precisely this reflection by means of which Socrates was able to establish the universal principle of Good.[271] Hence, a destructive gesture of the Sophists paved the way for the establishment of what Hegel calls abstract morality (*Moralität*). Although Hegel is by no means satisfied with this morality, it nevertheless represents a higher stage in the development of the Spirit than the unreflective ethical life (*Sittlichkeit*) of the pre-Socratic Greek *polis*. In the same vein, when Luther reintroduced the standpoint of conscience into the medieval world, it entailed the destruction of this world, and although this destruction was evil from the standpoint of the established order, it was beneficial from the viewpoint of the Spirit. In fact, it was much more beneficial than the Sophistic–Socratic turning point, because, in Hegel's estimation, Luther articulated a morality of conscience that surpassed even the morality of the abstract Good. Luther's conscientious conviction, which stemmed from the 'time-honoured and cherished sincerity of the German people',[272] became the origin of the most glorious of all the revolutions because it managed to bring together the inner truth (*Moralität*) and the outer forms of life (*Sittlichkeit*), or, because it involved the 'recognition of the secular as capable of being an embodiment of truth'.[273]

V

The ending quote above already makes us see that the Hegelian critique of conscience is not similar to the Hobbesian critique of it. When Hegel says that conscience is evil, he does not mean that it is categorically evil. He means a conscience detached from the legal and ethical life of the State (*rechtlichen und sittlichen Staatsleben*). When this very same reflective conscience is attached to this life, it becomes actuality of the living good:

> Substantive ethical reality attains its right, and this right receives its due, when the individual in his private will and conscience drops his self-assertion and antagonism to the ethical. His character, moulded by ethical principles, takes as its motive the unmoved universal (the State), which is open on all its sides to actual rationality. He recognises that his worth and the stability of his private ends are grounded upon the universal, and derive their reality from it.[274]

The State, which is no less than the incarnation of divinity within immanence,[275] is thus the fixed point of the Hegelian conscience as the Catholic truth was to the Scholastics and the Word for Luther. Therefore, the Hegelian conscience can also be erroneous, and it is erroneous whenever it is separated from the legal and ethical life of the State. The State cannot recognize such a conscience just as subjective opinion can be of no avail in science. On the other hand, the State cannot do *without*

---

[271] Ibid., pp. 288–9.
[272] Ibid., p. 414.
[273] Ibid., p. 422.
[274] Hegel, *Philosophy of Right*, §152, p. 137.
[275] 'The State is the divine idea [*göttliche Idee*] as it exists on earth.' Hegel, *Philosophy of History*, p. 39.

conscience, because the State remains a mere abstraction without the innermost shrine of conscience:

> If political principles and institutions are divorced from the realm of inwardness, from the innermost shrine of conscience [*heiligthum des Gewissens*], from the still sanctuary of religion, they lack any real centre [*wirkliche Mittelpunkt*] and remain abstract and indeterminate.[276]

Hence, unlike Hobbes, Hegel does not push the conscience into the private sphere but on the contrary makes it the very centre of the public life of the State. The State is the unmoved universal, but only if the innermost shrine of conscience animates and breathes life into it. Before the Sophists, the Greeks obeyed and served the State instinctively, but afterwards the history of the West became a mere series of alienations, because the shrine of conscience was attached to transcendent principles alien to the ethical life of the State. According to Hegel, however, Luther brought conscience back into the immanence of order, because he recognized that the secular is capable of being an embodiment of truth. Simultaneously, he lifted the spirit to a higher level of development, because now the State was no longer obeyed and served instinctively but conscientiously. In Hegel's estimation, herein lies Luther's greatness: he brought about the unity of conscience and the state.

VI

Of the German idealists (if we may call him thus), let us lastly turn to Friedrich von Schelling, but rather than going into the details of Schelling's metaphysics of nature, let us briefly examine the role of conscience in *The Essence of Human Freedom*, his best-known treatise on ethics. In this philosophical investigation, Schelling famously maintains, like Pelagius 1400 years before him,[277] that man is essentially an undecided being and that this freedom includes a capacity for both good and evil: 'The real and vital concept is that freedom is the capacity for good and evil.'[278] Moreover, like many of his predecessors, particularly the German mystics, Schelling argues that the evil pertains to a dark principle on account of which one wills to preserve and enhance oneself and one's individuality, whilst the good relates to the principle of light in which such egoism, self-assertion and self-will is put in abeyance in unity with divine love. Man embodies both of these principles, because darkness – initial anarchy – is the ground of everything, including even God, whilst the light pertains to man's nature as the image of God. Therefore, man cannot decide not to have them, but he is absolutely free to decide which one to follow, for he has, as Schelling writes, the absolute freedom to allow them to act within him.[279] Unlike the mystics, however,

---

[276] Ibid., p. 52. Translation modified.

[277] 'We do neither good nor evil without the exercise of our will and always have the freedom to do one of the two, being always able to do either.' Pelagius, 'Demetrias,' p. 43.

[278] F. J. W. Schelling, *Philosophical Investigations into the Essence of Human Freedom*, trans. J. Love and J. Schmidt (New York: State University of New York Press, 2006), p. 23.

[279] Ibid., p. 54.

Schelling maintains that man cannot attain the principle of light *without* egoism and self-assertion. This is because for Schelling good and evil are not mutually exclusive principles but presuppose each other. On the one hand, he argues, like Pelagius, that the very capacity to do evil is good: 'Whoever has neither the material nor the force in himself to do evil, is also not fit for good.'[280] On the other hand, Schelling believes that the good consists of overcoming evil. Thus, affirming the evil selfhood is necessary, for without it, there is but a falling asleep of the good: 'Good without active selfhood is itself inactive good.'[281] How, then, may an individual overcome the evil principle of darkness and what does it mean to attain the good principle of light? According to Schelling, this can happen only in the struggle against selfhood and more precisely, when an individual attunes to the 'inner voice of his own better nature',[282] whereby he with the highest resoluteness fulfils his duty. Schelling calls this resoluteness religiosity (*Religiosität*) as well as conscientiousness (*Gewissenhaftigkeit*) and it entails that one acts in accordance with what one knows and does not contradict the light of cognition in one's conduct – the light that is nothing less than God himself:

> An individual for whom this contradiction is impossible, not in a human, physical
> or psychological, but rather in a divine way, is called religious, conscientious in
> the highest sense of the word. One is not conscientious who in a given instance
> must first hold the command of duty before himself in order to decide to do right
> out of respect for that command. Already, according to the meaning of the word,
> religiosity does not permit any choice between opposites, any *aequilibrium arbitrii*
> (the plague of all morality), but rather the highest resoluteness in favour of what
> is right without any choice [*die höchste Entschiedenheit für das Rechte, ohne alle
> Wahl*].[283]

Schelling's example of such an individual is Cato, who was known, as Schelling tells us, by the severity of his disposition, even by his cruelty, but it is precisely such disposition that is the seed from which true grace and divinity first come forth to bloom.[284] This is Schelling's ethics in the *Essence of Freedom*, ethics which is not, as he emphasizes, meant for women in a gynaeceum but for men exercising in the Palaestra of the Lyceum.

---

[280] Ibid., p. 63.
[281] Ibid.
[282] Ibid., p. 54.
[283] Ibid., p. 57.
[284] Ibid., p. 57.

6

From Political Theology to Theologized Politics

I

In the *Social Contract*, Jean-Jacques Rousseau famously proclaims that nothing is more contrary to the social spirit than Christianity, for it has eradicated ancient liberty and republican freedom from the world. Christianity preaches nothing but 'servitude and submission. Its spirit is too favourable to tyranny for tyranny not to take advantage of it. True Christians are made to be slaves.'[1] In a sense, Rousseau is right. We know what the Apostle Paul says in the Romans 13:

> Let every person be subject to the governing authorities. For there is no authority [*exousia*] except from God, and those that exist have been instituted by God. Therefore he who resists the authorities resists what God has appointed, and those who resist will incur judgement. For rulers are not a terror to good conduct, but to bad. Would you have no fear of him who is in authority? Then do what is good, and you will receive his approval, for he is God's servant for your good. But if you do wrong, be afraid, for he does not bear the sword in vain; he is the servant of God to execute his wrath on the wrongdoer. Therefore one must to subject oneself [*hypotassō*], not only to avoid God's wrath but also for the sake of conscience [*dia tēn syneidēsin*].

Although the passage might be an interpolation, it has profoundly influenced subsequent Christian views and doctrines concerning secular authority. In *Summa Theologiae*, Thomas writes: 'The order of justice requires that subjects obey their superiors, else the stability of human affairs would cease. Hence faith in Christ does not excuse the faithful from the obligation of obeying secular princes.'[2] The doctrine reached its apex in Luther's writings and especially in orthodox Lutheranism. According to Luther, a good Christian always obeys secular authorities. Every Christian is also 'under obligation to serve and assist the sword by whatever means' he can.[3] The sword must be served and assisted because authorities are ordained by God.[4] And these authorities must be obeyed and served irrespective of whether they act justly or unjustly: 'Christians should not, under the pretence of Christian religion'

---

[1] Rousseau, *The Social Contract*, 4.8, p. 184.
[2] Aquinas, *Summa Theologica* IIa IIae, q. 104.
[3] See Martin Luther, *Temporal Authority: To What Extent it should be Obeyed*, in *LW*, vol. 45, p. 95.
[4] 'What powers there are have been instituted by God.' Luther, *Romans* 13.1, pp. 109–10.

refuse to obey authorities 'even if they are wicked.'[5] In subsequent orthodox Reformed circles, this unreserved obedience became gradually a dogma. William Tyndale writes: 'The powers that be are ordained by God. Whosoever resists power resists the ordinance of God. They that resist, shall receive to them self damnation.'[6] Every temporal power or authority is the minister of God, Tyndale continues, and therefore everybody is obliged to obey him, not out of fear, but for the sake of conscience – both of your own and that of your neighbour. This must be done even if the temporal power or authority in question were the 'greatest tyrant in the world' because even as a tyrant he is a 'great benefit of God and a thing wherefore thou ought to thank God highly'.[7] In Calvin's *Institutes*, we find plenty of similar passages, but one example suffices here:

> Even an individual of the worst character, one most unworthy of all honour, if invested with public authority, receives that illustrious divine power which the Lord has by his word devolved on the ministers of his justice and judgement, and that accordingly, in so far as public obedience is concerned, he is to be held in the same honour and reverence as the best of kings.[8]

II

Yet even if Christianity has preached obedience to earthly authorities, the political aspect of Christianity cannot be reduced to this doctrine. With regard to Christian politics, equally important as the Romans 13 has been the famous passage in the Acts 5.29, repeated time and again by the Christians throughout Western history. Interrogated by the high priest who charged them not to preach in the name of Christ, the Apostles replied as one voice: 'We must obey God rather than men.' What then has it meant to obey God rather than men? On the one hand, it has meant that men must obey the church and its representatives rather than civil authorities. On the other hand, it has meant that men must obey their *consciences* rather than the opinion of other men, even if they were the representatives of the church, as the church itself preached that it is God who speaks in our consciences and taught that it is sin to act against it. In point of fact, almost all significant religious revolts against the authority of the church in the late medieval world revolved around this orthodox doctrine: *contra conscientiam agere peccatum est*. In his sermons, John Wyclif appealed to his conscience in his struggle against ecclesiastical authority, asserting that the final forum of merit 'rests in my own conscience' (*in consciencia mea propria stabilitur*).[9] Similarly, when Jan Hus, in 1415, was accused at the Council of Constance of heresy for holding Wyclif's doctrine of remanence, Hus refused to recant, not because he held fast to Wyclif's doctrine contrary to the teachings of the Council, but because

---

5 Ibid., 13.1, p. 110.
6 Tyndale, *The Obedience of a Christian Man*, p. 36.
7 Ibid., pp. 41, 50–1.
8 Calvin, *Institutes*, 4.20.25, p. 671.
9 Cited in Paul Strohm, *Conscience: A Very Short Introduction* (Oxford: Oxford University Press, 2011), p. 16.

abjuring something that one has never held would have meant for him acting against his conscience – and to act against conscience is a mortal sin.[10] The most famous case is of course Luther. It was precisely the *contra conscientam* doctrine that he appealed to when accused of heresy at the Diet of Worms: 'My conscience is captive to the Word of God. I cannot and will not retract anything, since it is neither safe nor right to go against conscience. I cannot do otherwise, here I stand, may God help me, Amen.'[11] As a doctrinal source for the religious upheavals of sixteenth- and the seventeenth-century Europe, this single doctrine was perhaps more important than any of the theological doctrines introduced by Luther himself.

Second, since late antiquity, theologians had opined that all human laws must be compatible with natural law, and if this had not been the case, human law had no power of binding conscience. People have no obligation, says Aquinas, to obey any authorities whose laws are contrary to natural law.[12] Such a law has no 'power of binding conscience'[13] because 'human law cannot impose its precepts in a Divine court, such as is the court of conscience'.[14] Natural law is given by God through the creation and we must obey God rather than men:

> Laws may be unjust through being opposed to the Divine good: such are the laws of tyrants inducing to idolatry, or to anything else contrary to the Divine law: and laws of this kind must nowise be observed, because, as stated in Acts 5.29, 'we ought to obey God rather than man'.[15]

In like manner, Francisco Suárez argues that laws incompatible with natural law, which is 'truly and properly divine law',[16] are null and void. He also maintains that people have an inalienable right to resist unjust rulers who violate divine law of nature, reasserting his argument by referring to the sentence in Acts: 'One must obey God rather than men.'

Not even Reformed theologians were absolutely categorical with obedience. Luther held that people are not bound to obey a prince if he commands something that is wrong ('for it is not one's duty to do wrong'),[17] that tyrants are not to be tolerated, and that every Christian is free to use his freedom to oppose them, at least in word:

> Use your freedom constantly and consistently in the sight of and despite the tyrants and the stubborn so that they also may learn that they are impious, that their laws are of no avail for righteousness, and that they had no right to set them up.[18]

[10]　Jan Hus, *The Letters of John Hus*, trans. R. M. Pope (London: Hodder and Stoughton, 1904), p. 217.
[11]　Luther, 'The Speech of Dr. Martin Luther,' pp. 112–13.
[12]　Aquinas, *Summa Theologica*, IIa Iae, q. 94, a. 4.
[13]　Ibid., IIa Iae, q. 96, a. 4.
[14]　Ibid., IIa Iae, q. 94, a. 4.
[15]　Ibid., IIa Iae, q. 96, a. 4.
[16]　Suárez, *On Laws*, 2.6.13, p. 198.
[17]　Luther, *Temporal Authority*, p. 125.
[18]　Luther, *The Freedom of a Christian*, p. 374.

Similarly, Calvin admitted that God sometimes allows and indeed induces resistance against the fury of tyrants. Quoting Acts 5.29, Calvin proclaimed:

> If they command anything against Him let us not pay the least regard to it, nor be moved by all the dignity which they possess as magistrates – a dignity to which no injury is done when it is subordinated to the special and truly supreme power of God.[19]

Moreover, both defended their arguments by referring to natural law, which, as Calvin put it, is 'the aim, the rule and the end of all laws'.[20] The legitimacy of all human laws and institutions, Calvin continued, depends on how they agree with this law and with 'conscience which God has engraved upon the minds of men'.[21] Similarly, when Calvin's successor Theodore Beza, two years after the St Bartholomew's Massacre, published a pamphlet *De jure magistratum* against tyranny in religious matters, he not only referred to the passage in the Acts, but also used the Stoic-Catholic doctrine of natural law in order to justify his argument – the law so firmly 'established and so lasting that nothing which is openly opposed and repugnant to it should be regarded as just and valid between men'.[22] According to Beza, magistrates must not be obeyed if what they command is impious or unjust, impious referring to anything contradicting the first tablet of God's law and unjust to anything that prevents or forbids one from rendering his neighbour what is his due 'by the law of nature'.[23] Althusius in turn argues, like Calvin,[24] that it is legitimate for the ephors and popular magistrates to depose a tyrant 'as quickly as a fire must be dowsed by those who see it', if he despises that law of nature on which the written laws must be based.[25] William Perkins went as far as Aquinas, asserting that if a command of the prince contradicts the Word and the Law of God, 'then is there no bond of conscience at all, but contrariwise men are bound in conscience not to obey'.[26] In fact, he went further than Aquinas, because Thomas held that the subjects should at least occasionally obey unjust rulers in order to avoid scandal,[27] whilst Perkins maintained that God's Word and Law is to be obeyed, 'though we should offend all men, yea lose all men's favour, and suffer the greatest damage that may be, even the loss of our lives'.[28] This was also the opinion of the Puritan priest William Ames. According to him, no human command, whether ecclesiastical or political, can override the law of God: 'It is that the Law of God only

---

[19] Calvin, *Institutes*, 4.20.32, p. 675.

[20] Ibid., 4.20.16, p. 664; see Luther, *Galatians* 5.14, p. 53.

[21] Calvin, *Institutes*, 4.20.16, p. 664.

[22] Theodore Beza, *De jure magistratuum*, q. 6, ed. Patrick S. Poole, accessed 24 August 2012, http://www.constitution.org/cmt/beza/magistrates.htm

[23] Ibid., q. 3.

[24] See Calvin, *Institutes*, 4.20.32, pp. 675–6.

[25] Althusius, *Politica* 28, p. 94.

[26] Perkins, *Discourse of Conscience*, p. 34.

[27] 'Man is bound to obey secular princes in so far as this is required by order of justice. Wherefore if the prince's authority is not just but usurped, or if he command what is unjust, his subjects are not bound to obey him, except perhaps accidentally, in order to avoid scandal or danger.' Aquinas, *Summa Theologica*, IIa IIae, q. 104, a. 6.

[28] Perkins, *Discourse of Conscience*, p. 10.

doth bind the conscience of man', which means that the conscience cannot 'submit itself unto any creature without idolatry'.[29] Eventually, as we have already seen, the authority of conscience surpassed even the authority of the Word. Because of this wonderful faculty, says Samuel Ward of Ipswich, man no longer needs any external guidance, not to mention external authority. The force and power of conscience is greater than any other power on earth and even the power of angels. Therefore, we must, as the Apostle Paul allegedly suggested, follow the dictate of conscience rather than the dictates of angel, potentate or prelate, 'yes, even of the Apostle himself'.[30]

III

In fact, when Rousseau laments Christianity, it is *not* the Christian preaching of submission that annoys him the most. More disturbing is the Christian teaching that 'God cannot and will not permit anyone but himself to rule over the soul'.[31] It is this freedom of the soul and conscience that is Rousseau's main enemy. Christianity detaches the soul and conscience from the body politic and its laws and it is precisely for this reason that Rousseau considers Christianity essentially an anti-political doctrine: 'This religion, having no specific connexion with the body politics, leaves the law with only the force the law itself possesses, adding nothing to it', that is, without endowing it with such holiness that might bind the 'hearts of the citizens to the state'.[32] Here Rousseau indeed captures the essential. Christianity, at least before the rise of nationalism in the West, if we are allowed to speak at the same level of generalization as Rousseau, is not only a doctrine of political slavery but it cannot be reduced to a revolutionary political movement either. In terms of politics, it is an ideology of *profanation*. The hearts and consciences of Christians are not bound to the state but to God and this entails, as Karl Barth notes, the relativity of everything present.[33] This is not to say that there would be no Christian doctrine of obedience or that there is no idea of radical freedom in Christianity. As we have seen, they are both part and parcel of this religion, but perhaps the most unique political feature of this religion is the way how it combines the elements articulated in Romans 13 and Acts 5.29. It combines them by dividing man in two.

Rousseau is thus perfectly correct: the Christian man is not a unity, but, as Paul's theological anthropology already implies, a combination of the inner (*esō hēmōn*) and the outer man (*exō hēmōn anthrōpos*) strictly separated from and opposed to each other (2 Cor. 4.16). In the Christian tradition, it is the inner man, meaning man's soul and conscience ('renewed day by day', as Paul says), that has been free from mundane obligations and accountable to God alone, whereas the outer man, meaning the body and flesh ('wasting away', to quote Paul again), has belonged to this world and has been bound by earthly relations and obligations. In other words, it has been the body that

---

[29] Ames, *Conscience*, p. 6.
[30] Ward, *Balme*, p. 49.
[31] Luther, *Temporal Authority*, p. 105.
[32] Rousseau, *The Social Contract*, 4.8, p. 182.
[33] Barth, *Ethics*, p. 487.

has had the duty to observe Romans 13, whereas the proclamation in Acts 5.29 relates to the soul alone. This distinction is present already in the writing of the Fathers and it can be found in the Scholastics as well. Thomas Aquinas writes: 'In matters pertaining to the inward movement of the will man is not bound to obey man, but God alone. Man is, however, bound to obey man in things which are to be done outwardly by means of the body.'[34] In medieval and early modern Catholicism, this doctrine was usually restricted to the realm of secular power, whereas the church, which was not merely a human institution, had power over the soul and conscience as well. With the rise of Protestantism, however, both the authority of the church and the examination of conscience were increasingly, though not of course entirely, called into question. Now the Word of God replaced the authority of the church: 'We believe and are at peace in our conscience, we run not hither and thither for pardon, we trust not in this friar or that monk neither in anything save in the word of God only.'[35] This meant that the Protestants, notably Luther himself, extended the Pauline division between the inner and the outer man to the ecclesiastical sphere as well, arguing that neither secular nor ecclesiastical authorities are entitled to rule over the soul and conscience of man: 'Among Christians there shall and can be no authority'[36] because 'every Christian is by faith so exalted above all things that, by virtue of a spiritual power, he is lord of all things without exception'.[37] However, it is the conscience of the Christian that is exalted above all things, whereas the outward man, the body, is subjected to all laws and authorities, particularly to the secular ones: 'The conscience must be free from the law, but the body must obey the law.'[38] John Calvin went along with Luther: 'We see how the law, whilst binding the external act, leaves the conscience unbound.'[39] Perkins put it as thus:

> Magistrate indeed is an ordinance of God to which we owe subjection, but how far subjection is due, there is the question. For body and goods and outward conversation, I grant all: but a subjection of conscience to men's laws, I deny.[40]

Similarly, Bishop Sanderson writes:

> He who alone knows the inward motions of conscience, He only has a power of prescribing a law to it (for the law never determines or judges of things unknown), but God only, the Searcher of hearts, can discover the inwards motions of the Mind and Conscience; therefore He has the sole right of imposing the law, or laying an obligation upon it. Hence it is that the laws of *men* oblige only the *outward* motions of the body to an outward conformity.[41]

True, these Protestants also held that one must, as the Apostle Paul had taught in Romans 13, to subject oneself to laws and authorities, 'not only to avoid God's wrath

---

[34] Aquinas, *Summa Theologica*, IIa IIae, q. 104, a. 5.
[35] Tyndale, *Obedience of a Christian Man*, p. 147.
[36] Luther, *Temporal Authority*, p. 117.
[37] Luther, *The Freedom of a Christian*, p. 354.
[38] Luther, *Galatians* 2.13, p. 114.
[39] Calvin, *Institutes*, 3.19.16, p. 142.
[40] Perkins, *Discourse of Conscience*, p. 26.
[41] Sanderson, *Lectures on Conscience*, p. 93.

but also for the sake of conscience [*dia tēn syneidēsin*]'. Yet, for them, the dictum 'for the sake of conscience' did not mean that the law extends its power *into* conscience. This may sound paradoxical, but for the early Reformed theologians this paradox was not unresolvable. According to Calvin, one is obliged to keep the law conscientiously because it is enacted by an authority and all authority is from God, but individual laws do not reach the conscience, meaning the internal government of the soul:

> The first thing to be done here is to distinguish between the genus and the species. For though individual laws [*loy en particulier*] do not reach the conscience, yet we are bound by the general command of God, which enjoins us to submit to magistrates. And this is the point on which Paul's discussion turns: magistrates are to be honoured, because they are ordained of God (Rom. 13.1). Meanwhilst, he does not at all teach that the laws enacted by them reach to the internal government of the soul [*regime spirituel des ames*], since he everywhere proclaims that the worship of God, and the spiritual rule of living righteously, are superior to all the decrees of men.[42]

In a similar vein, Perkins argues that men are subject to magistrates 'for the sake of conscience' but not 'in conscience',[43] whereas Sanderson believes that if the obligation of conscience derives from the thing commanded, the liberty of conscience is violated, but if it derives from the sovereign's lawful authority to command, then the inward liberty of conscience remains uninjured.[44] Hence, according to Calvin, Perkins and Sanderson, there is no contradiction between the obligation that the laws and the commands of human authorities be obeyed for the sake of conscience and the idea that these laws and commands do not reach the consciences of men – consciences that are not subject to any other authority than that of God alone.

IV

It is in this perspective that we must read early modern Protestant political theory, including Thomas Hobbes' theory of the state. According to Rousseau, of all Christian authors, Hobbes has been the only one daring to propose a restoration of the unity of religion and politics, without which neither the state nor the government will ever be solidly constituted.[45] This may be true, but unlike Rousseau, Hobbes did not propose to unite the Christian man. On the contrary, like his Protestant fellows, he fully subscribed to the idea that the law obliges the outward man alone, whilst the soul and conscience must be left intact by power and the law: 'There ought to be no Power over the Consciences of men'.[46] In other words, he maintains, like Luther and his followers, that the conscience of man is free from all laws. Referring to his contemporary Aristotelian Scholastics, Hobbes writes:

[42] Calvin, *Institutes* 4.10.5, p. 417.
[43] Perkins, *Discourse of Conscience*, p. 26.
[44] Sanderson, *Lectures on Conscience*, p. 164.
[45] Rousseau, *The Social Contract*, 4.8, p. 180.
[46] Hobbes, *Leviathan*, 4.47, p. 480.

There is another error in their civil philosophy (which they never learned of Aristotle, nor Cicero, nor any other of the Heathen) to extend the power of the law, which is the rule of actions only, to the very thoughts, and consciences of men.[47]

To be sure, Hobbes also holds that the laws of nature and hence sovereign's commands are a 'matter of conscience' and one should act as the law commands, not because of the penalty attached to the law but 'for the sake of the law'.[48] Yet, not unlike his Protestant predecessors, Hobbes thought that the law obliges *in foro interno* because the law is the sovereign's authoritative command, but materially it does not extend its power in men's consciences, 'where not Man, but God raigneth'.[49] One is obliged to keep the law conscientiously because it is enacted by the sovereign, but nobody is obliged to believe in his heart or to accuse oneself if one's beliefs, thoughts and opinions do not accord with particular laws,[50] 'for mens beliefe, and interior cogitations, are not subject to the command, but only to the operation of God, ordinarily, or extraordinarily'.[51] Admittedly, for Hobbes, the power of conscience was not greater than any other power on earth, as one of the very aims of his theory of the state was to downplay such conception. Yet this does not entail that Hobbes's intention was to 'retheocratize' politics, as has been recently suggested.[52] Instead, Hobbes' intention was to depoliticize religion and expulse religious zealots and religious feelings from the sphere of politics.

V

If there is a contradiction between the Christian and the Rousseaun republican political teaching, it is not that the former preaches slavery and the latter freedom but rather that whilst the Christian and especially the Reformed political teaching leaves the conscience intact, the republican doctrine penetrates to its core. In the Rousseaun republic, the law cannot be a mere rule of action. It must bind the hearts of the citizens to the state. Man is no longer divided in two, whereby the conscience belongs to God and the body to the state, for both must now be definitely and entirely subjected to the service of the state. This is the backdrop of Rousseau's famous civil confession of faith necessary in every well-ordered state:

> There is thus a profession of faith which is purely civil and of which it is the sovereign's function to determine the articles, not strictly as religious dogmas, but as sentiments of sociability [*sentiments sociabilite*], without which it is impossible to be either a good citizen or a loyal subject. Without being able to oblige anyone to believe these articles, the sovereign can banish from the state anyone who does not

---

47 Ibid., 4.46, p. 471.
48 Hobbes, *On the Citizen*, 4.21, p. 64.
49 Hobbes, *Leviathan*, 2.30, p. 244.
50 Ibid., 4.46, p. 471.
51 Ibid., 2.26, p. 198.
52 See Ronald Beiner, *Civil Religion* (Cambridge: Cambridge University Press, 2011), p. 57.

believe them; banish him not for impiety but as an antisocial being, as one unable sincerely to love law and justice, or to sacrifice, if need be, his life to his duty. If anyone, after having publicly acknowledged these same dogmas, behaves as if he did not believe in them, then let him be put to death, for he has committed the greatest crime, that of lying before the law.[53]

We can clearly see here the difference between Luther and Hobbes on the one hand and Rousseau on the other. For both Luther and Hobbes, it was enough that the subjects obeyed the law in their conduct, but Rousseau thought that a citizen incapable of sincerely loving (*incapable d'aimer sincèrement*) the laws of the state and of sacrificing (*immoler*) himself for them is not a citizen at all but an outlaw who could be banished from the state. Here and not in Hobbes we find a conscience that is no longer free in the sense that it can be detached from state regulation. Hobbes asked what 'infidel king is so unreasonable' who puts to death a subject whose beliefs differ from the beliefs of the sovereign,[54] but Rousseau declares that every reasonable sovereign should indeed kill such a person. In the Hobbesian state subjects were bound to obey the law, but not to believe in it, whilst in the Rousseaun state precisely men's beliefs and interior cogitations are subject to the commands. Thus, it was not with Hobbes but with such a republican theorists of the state as Rousseau that the dichotomy between outer obedience and inner faith was transformed into the obedience based on inner faith.

This is not to say that Hobbes would have not called into question the authority of conscience in favour of the sovereign's command in his political theory. In this respect, he was as conservative as Robert Filmer, the author of the famous *Patriarcha*, defending the divine rights of kings. In point of fact, Hobbes' argument in *Leviathan* is precisely the same as Filmer's. In his criticism of Philip Hunton's *A Treatise of Monarchy* in which Hunton, one of the most important parliamentarian pamphleteers in the Civil War, had argued that 'resistance ought to be made, and every man must oppose or not oppose, according as in conscience he can acquit or condemn the acts of his governor',[55] Filmer writes: 'Such a conclusion fits well with anarchy', for it takes away 'all government and leaves every man to his own conscience'. It makes man 'independent in state', rendering all authority illegitimate.[56] On the other hand, if we compare Hobbes with Rousseau, it is almost impossible not to recognize a significant difference. It may be true that the Hobbesian theory of the state is the 'root of Rousseau's democratic theory', as Reinhart Koselleck claims,[57] but there is still a decisive gap between Hobbes and Rousseau. In Rousseau's *Social Contract*, we encounter a state in which the conscience is no longer an instance which opens up a transcendent dimension within the immanence of political order, as it had been in the Christian tradition, but neither is it an instance which may remain in peace in the

---

[53] Rousseau, *The Social Contract*, 4.8, p. 186.
[54] Hobbes, *Leviathan*, 3.43, p. 414.
[55] Cited in Robert Filmer, *The Anarchy of a Limited or Mixed Monarchy*, in *Patriarcha and Other Writings*, ed. J. P. Sommerville (Cambridge: Cambridge University Press, 1991), p. 154.
[56] Ibid.
[57] Reinhart Koselleck, *Critique and Crisis* (Cambridge, MA: The MIT Press, 1988), p. 34, footnote 38.

private sphere, as in early modern political theory. It is, as it was for Hegel, something that must be incorporated firmly into the immanent political order itself:

> If political principles and institutions are divorced from the realm of inwardness, from the innermost shrine of conscience [*heiligthum des Gewissens*], from the still sanctuary of religion, they lack any real centre [*wirkliche Mittelpunkt*] and remain abstract and indeterminate.[58]

According to Koselleck, this incorporation of private conscience into the political order was the beginning of a series of Western upheavals from the French Revolution onwards.[59] This is certainly true, but only partially. Already the liberation of conscience first from the authority of the church and then from that of the state during the first decades of the sixteenth century had revolutionary consequences. On the other hand, it enabled the emerging nation-state to attain its power and glory, to capture the energy of religious conscience and to put it into the service of its own.

VI

In his *System of Ethics*, Fichte had emphasized, like Rousseau, that 'it is a matter of conscience to submit unconditionally to the laws of one's state', continuing that anyone who does not want to do this is 'not to be tolerated within society'.[60] In Fichte's celebrated *Addresses to the German Nation*, however, it is no longer the state (*Staat*) but the people (*Volk*), the nation (*Nation*) and the fatherland (*Vaterland*) that becomes the object of conscientious commitment, whilst the state has become a mere means, a condition.[61] The laws of the state, Fichte explains, remain on the level of understanding without ascending on the level of faith.[62] In addition to the state and its laws, however, there exists what he calls the 'spiritual law of nature' (*geistige Naturgesetz*) of the nation and the fatherland. If the state is a mere means, it is a means of this spiritual law, which is a divine end in itself. The fatherland is the manifestation of the divine within immanence, the sacred earthly embodiment of eternity, the 'eternal in the temporal'.[63] According to Fichte, it is an absolute duty of conscience to serve this divine end, and nobody is permitted, even for the sake of life, to do anything that violates this duty. Yet Fichte laments that consciences of men are not necessarily naturally bound to it. Therefore, educating consciences becomes necessary. Contrary to the Catholic education of conscience, however, the Fichtean education aims neither at exposing the secrets of consciences nor at healing consciences of their scruples, but at strengthening the resolution of consciences by establishing 'deeply and indelibly in the hearts

---

[58] Hegel, *Philosophy of History*, p. 52. Translation modified.
[59] Koselleck, *Critique and Crisis*, pp. 158–70.
[60] Fichte, *The System of Ethics*, p. 226.
[61] Johann Gottlieb Fichte, *Addresses to the German Nation*, trans. R. Jones and G. Thurnbull (Chicago: The Open Court Publishing Company, 1922), p. 138.
[62] Ibid., p. 140.
[63] Ibid., p. 136.

of all the true and all-powerful love of fatherland'.[64] In the course of such an education a pupil, carefully separated from his parents and the normal adult environment, first becomes a moral person and eventually a free and determined man of faith who loves his people, 'respecting, trusting, and rejoicing in it, and feeling honoured by descent from it'.[65] He becomes an 'active and effective' man, ready to 'sacrifice himself for his people'.[66] He becomes a man who no longer separates the divine from the temporal, as in Christianity,[67] but discovers transcendence within immanence – a man in whose soul heaven and earth, visible and invisible meet and mingle: 'Such a man fights to the last drop of his blood to hand on the precious possession unimpaired to his posterity'.[68]

[64] Ibid., p. 151.
[65] Ibid., p. 136.
[66] Ibid.
[67] Ibid., p. 131.
[68] Ibid., p. 137.

7

Remarks on Late Modern Conscience

During the nineteenth and twentieth centuries, the idea of conscience became increasingly a target of suspicion particularly in the emerging social sciences. The same tendency can be detected in philosophy as well, including that of Arthur Schopenhauer:

> Many a man would be astonished if he saw how his conscience, which seems to him such an imposing affair, is really made up. It probably consists of one-fifth fear of men, one-fifth fear of the gods, one-fifth prejudice, one-fifth vanity, and one-fifth habit; so that he is essentially no better than the Englishman who said quite frankly, 'I cannot afford to keep a conscience.'[1]

According to Schopenhauer, the conscience of a medieval man, for instance, was constituted by what he knew about the rules and precepts of the church, added to the resolve to believe and observe them.[2] Yet this scepticism of conscience did not mean that Schopenhauer would have dispensed with it in his theory of morality. On the contrary, like Kant, he places conscience at its very core. Unlike Kant, however, Schopenhauer argues that the 'juridical dramatic' in which Kant presents conscience is inessential and 'by no means peculiar to conscience'.[3] According to Schopenhauer ethics is not about law, obligation and duty at all but about compassion (*Mitleid*), which is the sole source for actions of moral worth. Conscience in turn relates to a very special dissatisfaction we feel when thinking about our actions. This dissatisfaction arises if we recognize that we have behaved too egoistically, paid too much regard to our own affairs and too little to the welfare of others, that is, if the source of our action is either egoism or malice and not compassion which desires another's weal. Conscience is thus an advocate of altruism representing the interests of others within us.[4] Schopenhauer goes on to argue that although conscience is the advocate of altruism within us and ostensibly concerns what we have done, it ultimately concerns what we are.[5] Conscience is neither a storehouse of moral principles nor a judge of our actions but rather a *recollection* of our actions – and to the extent that a person is not distinguishable from his actions, the conscience is a 'complete picture of our

---

[1] Arthur Schopenhauer, *On the Basis of Morality*, trans. E. F. J Payne (Indianapolis: Hackett Publishing Company, 1995), p. 127.
[2] Ibid., p. 128.
[3] Ibid., p. 108.
[4] Ibid., pp. 108–9.
[5] Ibid., p. 195.

character'.[6] It is this picture that makes the conscience accuse or excuse us as it presents us to ourselves either as egoists or altruists:

> From this there arises satisfaction or dissatisfaction with ourselves, with what we are, according as we have been ruled by egoism, malice, or compassion, that is to say, according as the difference we have made between our person and others has been greater or smaller.[7]

Yet although Schopenhauer insists that the person is not to be distinguished from his actions, at the same time he maintains that the person cannot be reduced to them either. In point of fact, Schopenhauer argues that ultimately the moral character of man is inborn and unchangeable. Our actions are merely an expression of this unchangeable essence not altered by instruction or by any other means. Therefore, the conscience is not only a recollection of actions, but also and ultimately the channel through which we may acquaint ourselves 'with our own unalterable character'.[8] The conscience teaches us ourselves, our true essence, our 'inner original mechanism' which relates to the course of our life as the mechanism of the clock relates to the clock-face.[9]

Internalized coercion: Nietzsche and Freud

I

If Spinoza's or Helvetius' critique of bad conscience has sometimes remained unnoticed by modern readers, few are ignorant of Friedrich Nietzsche's critique. According to Kant, all feelings are 'pathological' from the point of view of morality except those effects evoked by the moral law, including remorse and bad conscience, but Nietzsche thinks that it is precisely these Kantian 'non-pathological' feelings that are truly pathological, now in the medical sense of the word. For Nietzsche, bad conscience is 'deep sickness',[10] the 'most fearful sickness which up until now has raged in man',[11] a 'kind of castration of the seeking and forward-striving spirit'.[12] A healthy man – and even a criminal is, Nietzsche proclaims, healthier than a Christian 'broken' by conscience – laughs at the bites of conscience, if he has any:

> One is healthy when one can laugh at the earnestness and zeal with which one has been hypnotized by any single detail of our life, when one feels that the 'bite' of conscience is like a dog biting on a stone – when one is ashamed of one's remorse.[13]

---

[6]   Ibid., p. 196.
[7]   Ibid.
[8]   Ibid., p. 197.
[9]   Ibid.
[10] Nietzsche, *Genealogy of Morals*, 2.16, p. 64.
[11] Ibid., 2.22, p. 73.
[12] Friedrich Nietzsche, *The Will to Power*, ed. W. Kaufmann (New York: Vintage Books, 1968), §141, p. 91.
[13] Ibid., §233, p. 135.

Feuerbach had stated that conscience is a wonderful capacity, namely for religious alias uneducated men,[14] but now Nietzsche asserted that even the uneducated should not be tortured by this poison, even if they may deserve it.

Like Schopenhauer, Nietzsche attacks conscience also from the sceptical point of view. In *Gay Science*, he asks why somebody would take this and specifically this truth to be right, answering himself, not unlike Bentham, in an imagined common voice: 'Because my conscience tells me so; conscience never speaks immorally, since it determines what is to count as moral!'[15] But why, Nietzsche continues, do you listen to the words of your conscience? And what gives you the right to consider such a judgement true and infallible? Has not your judgement, Nietzsche asks, a prehistory in your drives, inclinations, aversions, experiences and in what you have failed to experience? Does not the cause of the words of your conscience lie merely in your blindly having accepted what has been labelled right since your childhood or in the fact that fulfilling your duties has so far brought you bread and honours? In *Beyond Good and Evil*, Nietzsche ironizes even the experience of good conscience. Conscience rewards us with relief when having done our duties we enjoy a good conscience, but what is this 'good conscience'? It is a 'long, respectable pigtail of an idea, which our grandfathers used to hang behind their heads, and often enough also behind their understandings'.[16]

Yet it is not so much his scepticism of conscience as his conception that conscience is sickness and, especially, his endeavour to discover the genealogical *origins* of this sickness in *On the Genealogy of Morals* that is Nietzsche's lasting contribution to the Western history of conscience. In *Genealogy*, Nietzsche offers two celebrated interpretations on the origins of conscience. The first relates to the activity of the so-called white beasts who are rulers by nature. According to this interpretation, bad conscience is the result of the oppression these beasts exercise over a population by enforcing people to live within the confines of peace and society. Within society those natural drives that hitherto had turned outwards – particularly drives that relate to man's natural instinct of freedom and cruelty – are now turned against oneself, because the outward expressions of drives are hindered by the rules and regulations of society invented by the bestial rulers. This is the origin of bad conscience, the bad conscience in its initial stage:

> This instinct of freedom made latent through force – as we have already understood – this instinct of freedom, forced back, trodden down, incarcerated within and ultimately still venting and discharging itself only upon itself: such is bad conscience at its origin, that and nothing more.[17]

The second interpretation involves the relationship between creditor and debtor, referring back to the basic forms of buying, selling, bartering, trading and exchanging goods. In this scheme, Nietzsche explains, debtors who default on their repayments

---

[14] Ludwig Feuerbach, *The Essence of Religion*, trans. A. Loos (New York: Prometheus Books, 2004), §41, p. 44.

[15] Friedrich Nietzsche, *Gay Science*, ed. B. Williams (Cambridge: Cambridge University Press, 2001), §335, p. 187.

[16] Nietzsche, *Beyond Good and Evil*, §214, p. 87.

[17] Nietzsche, *Genealogy of Morals*, 2.17, p. 67.

are subjected to harsh physical punishment, intended both to gratify the creditor and to inculcate a greater sense of responsibility in the defaulter. Such punishments include branding and amputation, practices which produce the depths of the soul by inscribing and defacing the surface of the body. In the long run, such inscribing of the body transforms the economic concept of debt (*Schulden*) into a moral concept of guilt (*Schuld*):

> It is in this sphere, in legal obligations, then, that the moral conceptual world of 'guilt', 'conscience', 'duty', 'sacred duty' originates – its beginning, like the beginning of everything great on earth, has long been steeped in blood. And might one not add that the world has basically never since shaken off certain odour of blood and torture?[18]

Moreover, as soon as men form communities, the creditor–debtor relationship is applied to the relationship between the members of the community and their ancestors. Now, the members of the community understand themselves as being in debt to their ancestors. The more this debt increases, the more powerful the ancestors appear to the members of the community. In the long run, the ancestors are elevated to the sphere of divinity. Here is, Nietzsche argues, also the origin of many religious phenomena, including sacrifice. It is a repayment to the ancestor-gods, though the members of the community are aware that the debt can never be repaid, which is why they feel guilty. In addition, because the men know that there is no sufficient repayment, they think that pain itself can function as a repayment. This comes to the fore especially in Christianity, because in Christianity even partial repayment becomes impossible: 'The arrival of the Christian God, as the uttermost example of godliness so far realised on earth, has brought with it the phenomenon of the uttermost sense of guilt.'[19] This God is the ultimate opposing principle to man's actual and irredeemable animal instincts and, what is more terrifying, man interprets these animal instincts as a debt towards God. According to Nietzsche, this represents a kind of madness of the will as psychic cruelty that simply knows no equal:

> The *will* of man to find himself guilty and reprehensible to the point beyond the possibility of atonement, his *will* to think himself punished without the punishment ever being commensurate with his guilt, his *will* to infect and poison things to their very depths with the problem of punishment and guilt, in order to cut off once and for all any escape from this labyrinth of *idées fixes*, his *will* to establish an ideal – that of the 'holy God' – and to feel palpable certainty of his absolute unworthiness with respect to that ideal.[20]

Here we find bad conscience in its mature and its cruellest form. It is a profoundly sick conscience, interesting to be sure, but also, Nietzsche continues, something so

---

[18]   Ibid., 2.6, p. 46.
[19]   Ibid., 2.20, p. 71.
[20]   Ibid., 2.22, p. 73.

black and sad that one must forcibly restrain oneself from gazing into these abysses for too long.

II

This is not the whole storey of Nietzschean conscience, however. Although bad conscience is an illness, it is an illness in the same sense as pregnancy is an illness.[21] It is about to give birth to something new and perhaps even healthy. This new thing bad conscience brings about is nothing less than the sovereignty of the individual capable of responsibility:

> The proud knowledge of this privilege of *responsibility*, the consciousness of this rare freedom, this power over oneself and over fate has sunk down into his innermost depths and has become an instinct, a dominant instinct – what will he call it, this dominant instinct, assuming that he needs a name for it? About that there can be no doubt: this sovereign man calls it his *conscience* ...[22]

In other words, it is the sovereignty of the individual that is the fruit of the vivisection of conscience and animal self-torture. This fruit may be a very late one, the ripest fruit on the tree of morality, as Nietzsche says, but it is no longer confined within the walls of society and the state, because this individual has 'once again broken away from the morality of custom' and become, Nietzsche continues, the 'autonomous supramoral individual', the individual who is 'entitled to make promises'.[23]

Is Nietzsche still mocking the Christian man of bad conscience here? Or is this autonomous supramoral individual capable of promise precisely what Nietzsche was desperately looking for in attempting to *overcome* the Christian man of bad conscience? Is he not the Nietzschean overman itself? At least, this individual comes close to what Nietzsche calls a man of intellectual conscience. This conscience, lacking in the 'great majority of people',[24] is not a bad conscience, nor does it blindly accept what has been labelled right since one's childhood. It does not misconceive public praise and blame ('bread and honour') as the markers of true morality, but demands that we have to become new, unique and incomparable, to become human beings who 'give themselves laws, who create themselves'.[25] It demands, in other words, what the millennia of conscience vivisection had already bequeathed to humankind: the autonomous and responsible individual. It may be true that this individual is not yet a Nietzschean overman or even the one Nietzsche calls the 'philosopher of future', for this witness of the death of God, also capable of creating, ruling and commanding, is the 'man of the *greatest* responsibility, who has the conscience for the general development of mankind'.[26] But of essence here is that also this philosopher

---

[21] Ibid., 2.19, p. 68.
[22] Ibid., 2.2, pp. 41–2.
[23] Ibid., 2.2, p. 41.
[24] Nietzsche, *Gay Science*, §2, p. 29.
[25] Ibid., §335, p. 189.
[26] Nietzsche, *Beyond Good and Evil*, §61, p. 42.

is, as was the fruit of the Christian self-torture, a man of conscience, autonomy and responsibility.

Certainly, Nietzschean responsibility is very different from, say, Kantian responsibility. For Kant, responsibility means accountability, but Nietzsche conceives accountability as an expression of the instinct for punishing and judging: 'Whenever responsibilities are sought, it is usually the instinct for wanting to punish and judge that is doing the searching.'[27] For Nietzsche, responsibility signifies responsibility for the future of the peoples and the mankind – and true responsibility, in this respect, is responsibility to shape a people and breed a race by means of strict discipline and merciless selection. The responsible aim of the man of responsibility, the philosopher of the future, is to create obedient consciences. Nietzsche admits that the majority of consciences have been obedient ever since the birth of civilization. Yet this obedience, particularly the obedience Nietzsche sees to characterize his time, does not stem from the right motives. Subjects obey because they believe in the herd values such as kindness, deference, industry, temperance, modesty, indulgence and sympathy – and because they believe their rulers represent these herd values as well (corresponding to what Nietzsche calls democratic values and herd-morality).[28] Nowadays, even the rulers pretend to obey because they suffer inwardly from a bad conscience caused by the very act of ruling – this is 'moral hypocrisy of the commanding class'.[29] In order to rule as they should, the commanding class should instead assume its responsibility and to rule openly, harshly and conscientiously. They must, as Nietzsche writes in the *Anti-Christ*, be severe with their own hearts, scorn 'beautiful feelings' and to 'make every Yea and Nay a matter of conscience [*jedem Ja und Nein ein Gewissen macht*]!'[30]

Hence not even Nietzsche, this fiercest critic of Western conscience, can do without conscience. The conscience must not be put aside, let alone abandoned, but the 'conscience should be steeled [*gesthälen*]'.[31] It has to become hard, the conscience of the creator, the artist and the ruler. It has to become a conscience that is not afraid of pain or seeking for pleasure, but looks down upon and scorns all 'hedonism, pessimism, utilitarianism or eudaimonims'.[32] It has to become a conscience that is willing to sacrifice pleasure and happiness. It has to become a conscience that endures pain with pleasure and disdains happiness to the point of unhappiness. Unfortunately, according to Nietzsche, the voice of this conscience has 'hitherto remained unheard',[33] but, to be honest, it is not impossible and not even hard to find echoes of the long tradition of Western conscience here, the tradition which culminates in German Idealism and which, in the form of Nietzschean steeled conscience, found its home in the spiritual life of the new rulers of Europe.

---

[27] See Friedrich Nietzsche, *Twilight of the Idols*, trans. D. Large (Oxford: Oxford University Press, 1998), Four Great Errors, §7, p. 31.
[28] See Nietzsche, *Beyond Good and Evil*, §202, p. 68.
[29] Ibid., §199, p. 65.
[30] Nietzsche, *Anti-Christ*, §50, p. 72.
[31] Nietzsche, *Beyond Good and Evil*, §203, p. 70.
[32] Ibid., §225, p. 93.
[33] Nietzsche, *Anti-Christ*, preface, p. 19.

III

There are remarkable similarities between Nietzsche's and Sigmund Freud's conceptions of conscience, particularly between their accounts on its origins. For Freud, as for Nietzsche, conscience is not a natural instinct, let alone an original capacity to distinguish between good and evil. Likewise, for both, conscience is the very opposite of natural instincts, their principal suppressor. In Freud's view, moreover, what conscience dictates as good is often in contradiction to what is good to the individual, whereas what it dictates as bad may very well be beneficial to him or her. What, then, is the conscience for Freud? Generally speaking, it is a function of what Freud calls the superego (*Über-Ich*) distinguished from the ego (*Ich*) in the economy of the psyche – and this function consists 'in keeping a watch over the actions and intentions of the ego and judging them, in exercising a censorship'.[34]

Freud presents his ideas on conscience and superego in many of his writings but let us concentrate here on *Civilization and its Discontents*, as it sums up what he had previously written on conscience, particularly in *Totem and Taboo* and *Ego and the Id*. In *Civilization and its Discontents*, Freud maintains that conscience alias superego is an inner substitute for an external authority, primarily parents, but to the extent that human community and its authorities gradually takes the place of parents, ultimately the dictates of conscience 'coincide with the precepts of the prevailing cultural superego'.[35] More precisely, the superego is a continuation of the severity of external authorities internalized by an individual during psychological development. This internalization of external authority takes place not because the external authority imposes norms into the mind of the child but out of the fear of the child of losing the love of his or her parents and more broadly speaking his or her surrounding community. This fear makes the child renounce natural instincts, especially aggressive ones. It is precisely such renunciation of instinct that is the dynamic source for the formation of conscience: 'Instinctual renunciation (imposed on us from without) creates conscience'.[36] Hence, contrary the Western tradition of ethics according to which conscience provides us a means to repress natural and especially aggressive instincts, Freud believes, like Nietzsche, that conscience itself is a result of such repression. What is even more striking is that once the superego has been established, the conscience not only multiplies the demands for instinctual renunciation, because the superego can pass judgement even on the most hidden desires since nothing is hidden from the superego, but every renunciation of instinct becomes a dynamic source of conscience and every renunciation *increases* the latter's severity and intolerance. Thus, the more virtuous one seeks to be, the stricter is the conscience.

According to Freud, however, the aggressiveness of the external authority does not explain the ensuing severity of the superego. Instead, it is the aggressiveness

---

[34] Sigmund Freud, *Civilization and its Discontents*, ed. J. Strachey (New York: W. W. Norton & Company, 1961), p. 100.

[35] Ibid., p. 107.

[36] Ibid., pp. 90–91.

towards the authority that explains it: 'A considerable amount of aggressiveness must be developed in the child against the authority which prevents him from having his first, but none the less his most important, satisfactions.'[37] It is this aggressiveness the conscience assumes, but now directed against the ego. This also explains why a child who has been leniently brought up can acquire a very strict conscience, whereas in delinquent children, who have been brought up without love, the tension between ego and superego is lacking: the aggressiveness of a delinquent child can be directed outwards, whilst a child who is loved must renounce aggressiveness. Hence, a severe conscience arises from the joint operation of two factors: the frustration of instinct, which unleashes aggressiveness, and the experience of being loved, which turns the aggressiveness inwards and hands it over to the superego.[38]

What holds true with a single individual in Freud's view holds true with the phylogenesis of human race and thus with the whole civilization. In primordial times, to cut a long storey short, a horrible and narcissistic primal father possessed all the women. This meant that his sons were deprived of sexual satisfaction. Frustrated as they were, they killed their father, but since they did not merely hate their father but loved him too, they felt guilty after this horrible deed: 'After their hatred had been satisfied by their act of aggression, their love came to the fore in their remorse for the deed.'[39] This identification with the father set up the superego, and since the inclination to aggressiveness against the father was repeated in the following generation, the sense of guilt persisted and even increased. According to Freud, the process of civilization is a process in which aggressive instincts are increasingly restrained and returned to where they came from, that is, directed towards the self: 'Now, in the form of "conscience", it is ready to put into action against the ego the same harsh aggressiveness that the ego would have like to satisfy upon other, extraneous individuals.'[40] This also explains, Freud continues, why the most civilized people are the unhappiest: 'The price we pay for our advance in civilization is a loss of happiness through the heightening of the sense of guilt.'[41] No wonder, then, that Freud considers conscience, particularly the sense of guilt, as the most important problem in the development of civilization. The more we become ethical, the unhappier we become. Freud thus agrees with Nietzsche: conscience is a sort of illness. According to Nietzsche, however, the birth of conscience, the turning of the instincts inward against oneself, was also the birth of the soul and more correctly, the birth of man, marking 'a violent separation from his animal past'.[42] For Nietzsche, it also was, as it was for the majority of the authors we have dealt with here, the condition of autonomy and sovereignty. For Freud, however, it merely threatens mental health and ultimately life itself, as, in the final analysis, conscience might be in the service of what Freud calls the death instinct, 'driving the ego into death'.[43]

[37] Ibid., p. 91.
[38] Ibid., p. 93, footnote 10.
[39] Ibid., p. 95.
[40] Ibid., p. 84
[41] Ibid., p. 97.
[42] Nietzsche, *Genealogy of Morals*, 2.16, p. 65.
[43] Sigmund Freud, *The Ego and the Id*, ed. J. Strachey (New York: W. W. Norton & Company, 1960), p. 55.

Now this Christian little god, this Smithian impartial spectator, this Kantian wonderful capacity had become an internalized authority, the superego, which rather than guiding us on the sea of life, causes us trouble and prevents us not only from being happy but unconsciously even to yearn death. This also makes comprehensible Freud's stance toward the superego. Traditionally, the authors had emphasized that a wise man constantly heeds the judgement of this inner judge, whilst Freud maintains that 'we are obliged, for therapeutic purposes, to *oppose* the superego'.[44] However, it is not entirely sure whether even Freud would dispense with conscience altogether. Freud speaks everywhere about the superego's attacks on the ego, but what if there were no such attacks? Would there be an ego without conscience? Perhaps there would not, because the conscience is the heir of the Oedipus complex and, more precisely, the way how the ego masters this complex without which there is no normal human psyche.[45] Thus, although the superego is a cause of mental illness, particularly of neurosis, it seems to be a necessary illness. Without it, on the other hand, the constitutional aggressiveness of human beings would have no hindrance, and, on the other, and more profoundly, the birth of the superego guarantees that the constitution of the ego remains within the boundaries of normalcy.

The voice of the other: Levinas and Derrida

I

There are, roughly speaking, two approaches to the theme of conscience in late twentieth-century Continental philosophy. On the one hand, there is what could be called a Heideggerian approach in which the voice of conscience is conceived as a constitutive experience of ethicality. On the other hand, there are those who have embraced the Nietzschean and notably the Freudian conscience – although now the cultural superego is replaced by terms such as 'power', 'ideology' and 'symbolic order'. Among the representatives of the first approach, we may count authors such as Emmanuel Levinas and Jacques Derrida, both advocating an ethics of alterity.

Levinas' philosophy is extremely nuanced, but the basic message of his ethics is simple and resonates well with the history of Western ethics: ego, egoism, self-interest, interest *tout court*, is unethical, whilst unselfishness, other regard, altruism and alike is ethical. Moreover, as with the whole ethical tradition, Levinas' ethics is based on two fundamental oppositions. On the one hand, it is based on the opposition between ethics and politics ('politics is opposed to morality'),[46] whereby ethics represents everything good and admirable, whilst politics is a matter of Machiavellian power thirsty politicians. On the other hand, it is based on the opposition between the law of the heart and the law of the limbs, though now the law of the heart is not ontological, but more like the Eckhartian ground of the soul or the Kantian moral law, *beyond*

---

[44] Freud, *Civilization and its Discontents*, p. 108. Italics mine.
[45] Freud, *The Ego and the Id*, pp. 30–3.
[46] Levinas, *Totality and Infinity*, p. 21.

being, whilst being in its entirety is reduced to the evil law of self-preservation or to 'the egoism of perseverance in being (*conatus essendi*)'.[47] Yet the simplicity ends here, as the Levinasian other regard is quite different from how it is usually understood, because here the ethicality does not stem from the subject's attitude towards the other, but from the *otherness* of the other. Unlike for Heidegger, it is not man's finitude, but this otherness that is the condition of possibility of ethicality, and more precisely, of obedience, obligation and responsibility – as Levinas thinks that concepts such as happiness and joy do not belong to the sphere of ethics proper.

Without going into the subtleties of Levinas' ethics let us examine the role of conscience in it. As already said in the Introduction, the experience of conscience does not result in autonomy for Levinas. The Levinasian ethics begins where autonomy ends, where my autonomy and freedom is radically challenged – and it is precisely the otherness of the other (Other with a capital O) that calls my alleged autonomy into question. This otherness presents me an imperative of responsibility that precedes my autonomy and freedom, for I am responsible *before* I am free. I am always already responsible for everybody and for everything, also for others' responsibility, including even those who persecute me: 'The word *I* means *here I am*, answering for everything and for everyone.'[48] It is this answering, this absolute and infinite responsibility before the Other that creates me (*le Moi*) as an ethical subject (*le Soi*) – a subject that cannot be reduced to consciousness. How, then, am I able to become such a subject? In a sense, I am always already such a subject, but the egoism of my consciousness prevents me from acknowledging it. Yet my consciousness is not invulnerable, for the Other is already inscribed in it. The Other is inscribed in my consciousness in the form of moral conscience (*la conscience moral*) without which the Other cannot present himself as Other.[49] It is the conscience that enables me to welcome (*accueillir*) the otherness of the other and thus, to recognize my obedience, obligation, and absolute and infinite responsibility for everything and everybody. In a similar way as God-consciousness for Kierkegaard, the Levinasian conscience *is* this welcoming: 'If we call a situation where my freedom is called in question conscience, association or the welcoming of the Other is conscience.'[50]

Yet although conscience is always already a part my consciousness, this does not entail that conscience arises at the level of consciousness. Like the Freudian superego, or the medieval *synderesis* for that matter, it precedes and exceeds consciousness, the reflecting ego. Conscience is not the consciousness of the Other but precisely what cannot be reduced to consciousness and taken into possession by the conceptual apparatus of the conscious ego. It is 'an experience that is not commensurate with any a priori framework – a conceptless experience', actually the only conceptless

---

[47] Emmanuel Levinas, *Otherwise than Being*, trans. A. Lingis (Pittsburgh: Duquesne University Press, 1998), p. 128.

[48] Ibid., p. 144.

[49] Levinas, *Totality and Infinity*, p. 232.

[50] Ibid., p. 100.

experience there is.[51] More profoundly, conscience is, as it was for Coleridge, the experiential *condition* of consciousness:

> The disproportion between the Other and the self is precisely conscience [*la conscience morale*]. Conscience is not an experience of values, but an access to external being: eternal being is, par excellence, the Other. Conscience is thus not a modality of psychological consciousness, but its condition. At first glance it is even its inversion, since the freedom that lives through consciousness is inhibited before the Other when I really stare, with a straightforwardness devoid of trickery or evasion, into his unguarded, absolutely unprotected eyes. Conscience is precisely this straightforwardness.[52]

At first glance, Levinas says, conscience is the inversion of consciousness, for it calls consciousness into question, challenging 'the imperialism of the ego'.[53] It disorients the ego, expels it from its place so that the ego 'has nothing in the world upon which to rest its head'.[54] Yet at the same time it is its condition, or more exactly, conscience is the condition of consciousness *precisely* because it is its inversion. Conscience precedes consciousness in the same manner as the Other precedes the self, as it shatters the egoism of the ego but at same time enables the moral self to emerge. It does so because the emergence of the ethical self presupposes that the contours of the ego be opened to external being and this external being is the Other: 'The self-accusation of remorse gnaws away at the closed and firm core of consciousness, opening it, fissioning it.'[55] In other words, although the command of conscience radically disorients the ego, divesting, emptying and turning it inside out,[56] at the same it *reorients* it in the sense that the ego is *opened* to the Other understood as the fundamental prerequisite for all morality: 'Discovering such an orientation for the ego means identifying ego and morality.'[57] Unlike in Fichte's theory of the ego, Levinas tells us, such identification does not entail universalization of the ego, as by disorienting and uprooting the ego, the call of conscience radically *individualises* it: 'It confirms the uniqueness of the ego.'[58] We could of course add that it individualized the ego in Fichte as well, for as we recall the Fichtean voice of conscience is the ray of light which establishes us as individual and particular beings,[59] but perhaps what is more essential here is that the Levinasian individualization takes place before the ego is even aware that it is challenged by the obligation of the Other.[60] Playing with the French word *conscience*, meaning

[51] Ibid., p. 101.
[52] Emmanuel Levinas, 'Signature,' in Levinas, *Difficult Freedom: Essays on Judaism*, trans. S. Hand (Baltimore: Johns Hopkins University Press, 1997), p. 293.
[53] Levinas, *Otherwise than Being*, p. 128.
[54] Emmanuel Levinas, 'Substitution,' in Levinas, *Basic Philosophical Writings*, ed. A. T. Peperzak et al. (Bloomington: Indiana University Press, 1996), p. 93.
[55] Levinas, *Otherwise than Being*, p. 125.
[56] Ibid., p. 117.
[57] Emmanuel Levinas, *Humanism of the Other*, trans. N. Poller (Urbana: University of Illinois Press, 2006), p. 33.
[58] Ibid.
[59] Fichte, *Vocation*, p. 108.
[60] Levinas, *Humanism of the Other*, p. 33.

both moral conscience and consciousness, Levinas continues: 'This is a challenge of *conscience*, not a *conscience* of the challenge.'[61] Thus, the egoist ego is always already the moral self, irreducibly responsible for everything and everyone – and although this responsibility resists my reflection, I can at least sense it pre-consciously thanks to the conceptless experience of conscience.

However, although the experience of conscience as the experience of the Other is opposed to freedom, this does not entail that it is in contradistinction to it. Given the fact that ethics comes before being, everything that *is* is based on the ethical relation – or rather non-relation – between the Other and the self, including freedom: 'The presence of the Other, a privileged heteronomy, does not clash with freedom but invests it.'[62] Dependency maintains independence. The same can be said of the opposition between ethics and politics. To be sure, like in the case of freedom, we can depict two opposed forms of politics in Levinas. On the one hand, there is politics separated from its roots in the anarchical – that is, pre-ontological – relationship with the Other defined by absolute asymmetry and unredeemable dependency. This entails the *autonomy* of the political and it corresponds to the concept of freedom as autonomy which likewise does not recognize its roots in the primordial bondage – freedom without 'shame that freedom feels for itself'.[63] On the other hand, there is ethical politics which does recognize its ethical roots. Levinas calls such politics politics of justice. In the final instance, however, both of these forms of politics have their roots in the asymmetrical relationship – Levinas also calls it proximity – as this proximity is the root of everything, the ultimate measure of everything. Without it all social and political practices and institutions would be incomprehensible:

> Justice, society, the State and its institutions, exchanges and work are comprehensible out of proximity. This means that nothing is outside of the control of responsibility of the one for the other. It is important to recover all these forms beginning with proximity, in which being, totality, the State, politics, techniques, work are at every moment on the point of having their centre of gravitation in themselves, and weighing on their own account.[64]

Furthermore, although the experience of conscience is traumatic, there is a positive psychological side to it as well. It strikes up against me, but it also exalts and elevates me and 'in the literal sense of the term, inspires me'.[65] It inspires me because I thereby find myself committed to the Good and more precisely, because the Good *has chosen me*. The accusation of conscience is thus the best that can happen to me because without it I would have no clue about this anarchic and pre-original Good – anarchic and pre-original because it comes before, beneath, and above being. Hence, there is no angelic tendency towards the Good in my nature, but this does not mean that the Good I am enslaved by is external to me. It comes from the Other, but it is also in me,

[61] Ibid.
[62] Levinas, *Totality and Infinity*, p. 88.
[63] Ibid., p. 86.
[64] Levinas, *Otherwise than Being*, p. 159.
[65] Ibid., p. 124.

in my absolute passive sensibility called conscience, for the welcoming of the Other is conscience. It is in this welcoming-of-conscience that the Good may happen to me and to the extent that it happens to me, my slavery is cancelled:

> The enslaving character of responsibility that overflows choice – of obedience prior to the presentation or representation of the commandment that obliges to responsibility – is cancelled by the bounty of the Good that commands.[66]

Thus, exactly like in the Kantian ethics of infinite guilt, in which the 'new man', heeding the voice of conscience, willingly takes the punishment of guilt upon himself, because he knows that it is the cause and at the same time the effect of his disposition for the good, the Levinasian ethical subject, though he acknowledges that he is a mere slave of the Other, attains 'contentment and moral happiness'[67] from this very slavery, because he understands that the pre-original Good has thereby chosen him. Nietzsche thought that bad conscience is sickness, whilst Freud believed that he is obliged, for therapeutic purposes, to oppose the superego, but Levinas is assured that a bad conscience (*mauvaise conscience*), which renders the ego 'countryless and homeless',[68] is the key not only to morality but to happiness as well.

II

Jacques Derrida, beyond any doubt, can also be reckoned among the late modern advocates of the ethics of alterity. But is he, like Levinas, a proponent of conscience? At first glance, Derrida's deconstruction of the metaphysics of presence seems to constitute a severe critique of the Western ethics of conscience – a critique implicitly present already in the sixth chapter ('The Voice that Keeps Silence') of *Speech and Phenomena*, where Derrida examines Edmund Husserl's phenomenological reduction based on the exclusion of indication from the inner life of the mind in the form of a silent monologue. This inner monologue ('solitary mental life') allows Husserl to establish the possibility of expression without signs, that is to say, of pure self-presence of sense without communication. One of Husserl's examples taken up by Derrida is the moral conscience: 'You have gone wrong, you can't go on like that.' According to Husserl, Derrida explains, there is no indication in the inner monologue because there is no true communication and there is no communication as the second person that emerges in this communication is a mere fiction. Therefore, the communication itself is false.[69]

Now, Derrida's own argument is that no expression is possible without indication, without some reference to an outside other than itself, some kind of standing for something else. This means that indication is by no means absent from the inner

---

[66] Levinas, *Humanism of the Other*, p. 53.
[67] Kant, *Religion within the Boundaries*, p. 91 footnote.
[68] Emmanuel Levinas, 'Ethics as First Philosophy', in *The Levinas Reader*, ed. S. Hand (Malden: Backwell, 1989), p. 81.
[69] Jacques Derrida, *Speech and Phenomena*, trans. D. B. Allison (Evanston: Northwestern University Press, 1973), p. 70.

monologue (auto-affection). If we focus on the example of moral conscience, this implies that the sense of its silent voice ('you have gone wrong') is never immediately present but always already a representation. What presents itself in this silent voice is the representation of nonpresence, what Derrida calls otherness, difference, alterity, trace and so forth. Every self-presence is always already contaminated by this trace. In Derrida's view, Husserl's own theory of time according to which the present necessarily includes traces of past and future under the heading of retention and protention already implies that such self-presence is a contradiction in terms. In the inner dialogue, as Derrida argues, this trace is the name of that temporal gap between me and myself which differentiates me as the speaker from me as the hearer: 'Sense, being temporal in nature, as Husserl recognized, is never simply present; it is always already engaged in "movement" of the trace, that is, in the order of "signification".'[70]

Arguably, temporality is only one example of Derrida's overall argument according to which immediacy and self-presence of meaning is always contaminated by otherness, but in the prespective of this study of importance here is that Derrida does not deal with the question of conscience from an ethical point of view in *Speech*. He does not do it in *Of Grammatology* either, even though he examines this same motif there in the light of the Western tradition of natural moral law. Reflecting particularly on Jean-Jacques Rousseau's accounts of the 'pneumatological' law of conscience written in the heart, Derrida argues that in the Western tradition this metaphorical law has always occupied a privileged place in relation to writing because it is allegedly more present to consciousness than the written law which is a mere supplement to it. Moreover, like in *Speech*, Derrida continues that this metaphorical law is always contaminated by otherness, difference, alterity, trace and so on. In a sense this 'pneumatological' bias can be found even in Heidegger's philosophy, for, as Derrida explains, the call of conscience as a call of being is

> closest to the self as the absolute effacement of the signifier: pure auto-affection
> that necessarily has the form of time and which does not borrow from outside
> of itself, in the world or in 'reality,' any accessory signifier, any substance of
> expression foreign to its own spontaneity.[71]

According to Derrida, however, Heidegger also transgresses the Western tradition in the sense that Heidegger no longer finds the self-presence of meaning in the silent call of conscience but a mere silence and in the final instance 'nothing'. In Heidegger, the 'difference between signified and signifier *is nothing*,'[72] whereby this very nothing stands for the traditional ('transcendental') signified as it is allegedly separated from the web of signifiers. In Heidegger's philosophy, Derrida argues, the presence of a transcendental signified is effaced whilst still remaining legible, 'destroyed whilst making visible the very idea of the sign'.[73] Hence, the voice of conscience as the voice of

---

[70] Ibid., p. 86.
[71] Jacques Derrida, *Of Grammatology*, trans. G. Spivak (Baltimore: The Johns Hopkins University Press, 1974), p. 20.
[72] Ibid., p. 23.
[73] Ibid.

being is not merely the last representative of the tradition which establishes the origin of all meaning in this spontaneous voice as it is opposed to the signifier, but opens up a new way of thinking in which 'nothing escapes the movement of the signifier',[74] namely, otherness, difference and so on.

Now, as already said, in these texts Derrida does not give an account of conscience from the *ethical* point of view. The ethical implications of Derrida's analysis, however, have not remained unnoticed. In a colloquium devoted to the work of Derrida in 1980, Jean-Luc Nancy mentions that in his reading of Husserl Derrida had left in reserve a question about the place from whence the 'you' can arise in the monologue (*who* says that 'you have gone wrong …'). According to Nancy, this 'you' arises from an alterity and otherness of the ego in its egoity and even before the emergence of any alter ego. There is thus a radical alterity at the heart of the ego itself, an unknown and unassumable 'voice' which cannot be reduced to the self-presence of the subject. This voice is not heard, because 'it remains unheard-of in linguistic acuistics as it does in the philosophical acousmatics of sense'.[75] Yet it is not unheard either, because it is heard as a pure imperative, in the final analysis as the imperative of ethicality (*éthicité*) itself, ethicality that 'cannot ward off distress'.[76] This voice does not indicate what is right and what is wrong but merely destinates and in the case of Derrida, Nancy argues, it destinates him to the maintenance of the question, namely the question of ethicality of ethics itself.

In his late writings, on the other hand, Derrida did engage with the question of ethics. In fact, already in his response to Nancy, Derrida admits that the question is important although he emphasizes that he would perhaps no longer speak about a question but about a call.[77] What then does this call in Derrida's late writings call for? Derrida does not say it in his reply to Nancy, but if we examine his later writings, it is indeed the ethicality of ethics that it calls for, that is to say, the ethicality of such ethical phenomena as hospitality, forgiveness, charity, responsibility, justice and decision. Here we also find the concept of conscience and it is nothing less than the very condition of the ethicality of ethics – namely a *bad* conscience. According to Derrida, the one who wants to be ethical must 'avoid good conscience at all costs'.[78] In Derrida's view, to be sure, the one who wants to be ethical cannot be ethical, because every allegedly ethical act is always already an unethical act, for every act entails exclusion and sacrifice. If I give money for these poor people here, I sacrifice all the rest:

> As soon as I enter into a relation with the other, with the gaze, look, request, love, command, or call of the other, I know that I can respond only by sacrificing ethics, that is, by sacrificing whatever obliges me to also respond, in the same way, in the same instant, to all the others.[79]

---

[74] Ibid., p. 22.
[75] Jean-Luc Nancy, 'The Free Voice of Man,' in P. Lacoue-Labarthe and J. L. Nancy, *Retreating the Political*, ed. S. Sparks (London: Routledge, 1997), p. 49.
[76] Ibid., p. 50.
[77] Ibid., p. 54.
[78] Derrida, *Aporias*, p. 19.
[79] Jacques Derrida, *The Gift of Death*, trans. D. Wills (Chicago: The University of Chicago Press, 1995), p. 68.

In this sense, Derrida is a good Lutheran, for as we have seen Luther taught that we can never do any good works without sin. Yet it is precisely this *impossibility* of being and doing what is good that is, for Derrida, the very condition of possibility of all responsibility. In this respect, Derrida is not only Lutheran but also profoundly Kantian. Recognition of the impossibility and one's insufficiency before the demand of the ethical, before the moral law of absolute responsibility beyond every law, which necessarily entails a bad conscience, constitutes the very sphere of ethics. Derrida's response to John Milbank in a roundtable discussion at Villanova University in October 1999 illustrates his position well. After lengthy discussion, Milbank points out that in the Middle Ages it was fully legitimate to prefer one's relatives to other people without remorse and then he wonders whether Derrida is too moralistic, as he insists that one cannot do anything moral in the ordinary sense of the word. Derrida replies as follows:

> You might call this indifference, but if you think that the only moral duty we owe is the duty to the people – or the animals – with whom you have affinity, kinship, friendship, neighbourhood, brotherhood, then you can imagine the consequences of that … If I put as a principle that I will feed first of all my cat, my family, my nation, that would be the end of any ethical politics. So when I give a preference to my cat, which I do, that will not prevent me from having some remorse for the cat dying or starving next door, or, to change the example, for all the people on earth who are starving and dying today. So you cannot prevent me from having a bad conscience, and *that is the main motivation of my ethics and politics.*[80]

Bad conscience is thus Derrida's main motivation of ethics and politics, presumably because there is no other motivation that can – with good conscience? – be called ethical. Does this mean that Derrida has changed his mind in his late philosophy? By no means. Because there is no self-presence of meaning, because auto-affection is always already hetero-affection, a good conscience, that is to say, coincidence of the self and the good is impossible and therefore, one who claims to have a good conscience (the 'assured form of consciousness') lives in what Sartre calls bad faith: 'Good conscience as subjective certainty is incompatible with the absolute risk that every promise, every engagement, and every responsible decision – if there are such – must run.'[81] What is not impossible, however, is coincidence of the self and the bad, namely bad conscience. Hence, Derrida does not deconstruct conscience, for he deconstructs merely the possibility that the *good* conscience could be a good *conscience.* The only good conscience and, in fact, the only conscience, is the bad conscience, for although this conscience is not good in the traditional sense of the word, as a sign of blessedness for instance, it is nevertheless good because it is constitutive of ethics and ethical politics.

---

[80] John D. Caputo et al., ed., *Questioning God* (Bloomington: Indiana University Press, 2001), p. 69. Italics mine.
[81] Derrida, *Aporias*, p. 19.

Ethics of the real: Lacan

I

As to the Nietzschean–Freudian heritage in late modern reflections on conscience, Louis Althusser's theory of interpellation and Michel Foucault's theory of power are prominent examples. In them, conscience appears as a vehicle of ideology or power by means of which power takes hold of the subject and more precisely, produces subjects suitable for its purposes. In other words, it is not, as it was for instance for Fichte, the self-sufficiency of the subject but, as it were, the subjected subject that follows from this subjection. For Althusser, the subject is produced by the authoritative voice that hails the individual, as this voice is reproduced within the subject by the 'small voice of conscience',[82] whilst Foucault maintains that conscience as well as self-knowledge are forms of power 'which subjugates and makes subject to'.[83] Yet although both Althusser and Foucault acknowledge the eminent role of conscience in the operation of power, the concept of conscience itself is marginal in their theorizing. This has not remained unnoticed by their likeminded followers, such as Judith Butler. In her view, the lack of the theory of conscience in Althusser's and Foucault's theories of power radically diminish their validity, for without such a theory it is impossible to explain *how* the power becomes interiorized, or, as she puts it, 'how the subject is formed in subordination'.[84] In order to explain this, Butler argues, Althusser's and Foucault's theories must be supplemented by a proper theory of conscience, for the phenomenon of conscience is not as simple as Althusser's and Foucault's theories imply: 'Power is not mechanically reproduced when it is assumed.'[85] Butler admits that conscience is the point in which power becomes effective and by means of which it is reiterated,[86] but in her view it is unlikely that conscience mechanically reproduce external power within. According to Butler, namely, the subject, which is the product of external authority interiorized in the form of conscience, always *exceeds* the power by which it is enabled: 'No subject comes into being without power', but 'its coming into being involves the dissimulation of power, a metaleptic reversal in which the subject produced by power becomes heralded as the subject who founds power'.[87]

Hence, conscience which creates and reproduces the subject does not only subordinate but also empowers the subject and enables thus resistance. This is not so because there would be a part in the subject that cannot become available to subjectivation. Instead, it means that subjectivation has effects on the formation of the

---

[82] Louis Althusser, 'Ideology and Ideological State Apparatuses,' in *Lenin and Philosophy and Other Essays*, trans. B. Brewster (New York and London: Monthly Review Press, 1971), p. 172

[83] Michel Foucault, 'The Subject and Power,' afterword in Hubert L. Dreyfus and Paul Rabinow, *Michel Foucault: Beyond Structuralism and Hermeneutics* (Sussex: The Harvester Press, 1982), p. 212. See also Michel Foucault, *Discipline and Punish: The Birth of the Prison*, trans. A. Sheridan (New York: Vintage Books, 1995), pp. 29–30.

[84] Judith Butler, *The Psychic Life of Power* (Stanford: Stanford University Press, 1997), p. 3.

[85] Ibid., p. 21.

[86] Ibid., p. 26.

[87] Ibid., pp. 15–16.

subject that exceed its intention. This does not follow from any weakness in power, but happens rather because the subject itself cannot fully assume the power which is constitutive to it – and it cannot fully assume it, because the subject comes into being only if it at least partly represses it. The subject cannot be a mere puppet of power, because a puppet is not a subject. Therefore, conscience is not a simple instantiation of the ideological state apparatuses. On the contrary, it is the vanishing point of the state's authority and hence, a revolutionary force. At the same time Butler maintains, however, that it is precisely this *failure* to determine a subject exhaustively that makes power effective: 'Interpellation works by failing, that is, it institutes its subject as an agent precisely to the extent that it fails to determine such a subject exhaustively in time.'[88] Thus, like Althusser and Foucault, Butler believes that there is no exit from power by means of conscience, for although it is more than a mere echo of customs, even more than the mere Freudian superego, it sustains power, because it is precisely this 'more' that makes power effective.

II

Butler's theory of power is informed by her reading of Jacques Lacan. In Butler's view, Lacan is right in emphasizing that the symbolic order, though constitutive of the subject, does not exhaust the subject, but necessarily fails, as this very failure is a necessary component in the sustenance of the symbolic order itself. However, Butler also disagrees with Lacan and particularly with certain Lacanians. The criticism pertains to her understanding of the Lacanian concept of the real as a part of the subject that cannot become available to subjectivation. Butler holds this presumption as false even if this part is understood as a product of subjectivation itself. Instead of 'eternal psychic facts', the politics of resistance presupposes 'critical desubjectivation', that is to say, subject's willingness *not* to be, not at least in a self-identical sense. It is this becoming nothing of the subject that marks the 'path toward a more open, even more ethical, kind of being, one of or for the future'.[89]

What about Jacques Lacan himself? His theory of conscience as superego is basically Freudian, but from the very beginning and more explicitly than Freud Lacan emphasizes the constitutive role of the superego with regard to the ego: 'The superego as a psychological agency' has 'a generic signification in man'.[90] At one point, however, it seems that Lacan's notion of superego is fundamentally at odds with the Freudian interpretation of conscience. Whilst the traditional Freudian view holds that the pangs of conscience arise when one either has transgressed or is incapable of fulfilling the moral norms and expectations of the surrounding society, Lacan argues that guilt is a consequence of one's disavowal of unconscious *desire*. This reversal is possible, because Lacan, unlike Freud, makes a distinction between two levels of moral conscience. For Lacan, the traditional moral conscience is what Freud calls the ego ideal. It preserves

---

[88] Ibid., p. 197.
[89] Ibid., pp. 130–1.
[90] Jacques Lacan, *Écrits*, trans. B. Fink (New York: Norton, 2006), p. 111.

and sustains the commonly acknowledged moral norms and values in a given symbolic order of society. The superego, though it indeed 'serves as a support for the moral conscience',[91] is a *rupture* in the symbolic order. Like the traditional conscience, it is a terrible accuser, but if we are to believe Slavoj Žižek's interpretation of Lacan, it does not accuse man of a transgression of the commonly acknowledged moral norms and values. It exerts its unbearable pressure upon us on behalf of our betrayal of our desire.[92]

The key to this enigma lies in the well-known paradox, analysed by Freud and acknowledged already by the Apostle Paul and the Fathers: the more one attempts to meet the demands of morality and religion, the more one's conscience pricks. It is characteristic of pious souls to imagine that they are guilty of faults when they are not, as Gregory the Great noted.[93] In *The Ethics of Psychoanalysis*, which will be our focus here, Lacan puts it as follows: 'Whoever attempts to submit to the moral law sees the demands of his superego grow increasingly meticulous and increasingly cruel.'[94] What, according to Žižek, is distinctive in Lacan's account is his argument that such pious souls do not just *imagine* that they are guilty, for *they indeed are guilty*. The superego does not speak in vain. It is, as the *synderesis* was for the Scholastics or *Gewissen* to Fichte, an infallible witness. Yet contrary to the Christian conscience, the Lacanian superego is not a witness to moral law and its transgression, at least not exclusively, but to what Lacan calls the law of desire. It is the disavowal of this law that renders the terrifying superego operative. Hence, if the most pious souls, those who have done everything to meet the moral demands of the surrounding society, imagine that they are guilty, they also are guilty or at least feel guilty, not because they have not managed to meet the demands, but because by trying to meet them they have betrayed their desire:

> In the last analysis, what a subject really feels guilty about [*se sent effectivement coupable*] when he manifests guilt at bottom always has to do with … the extent to which he has given ground relative to his desire.[95]

What then is desire? To put a long storey short, desire is a metonymy for our being. We are our desire. Yet desire must be distinguished from what Freud called the pleasure principle, which aims at maximizing pleasure and minimizing displeasure. Also the Freudian reality principle is at odds with the law of desire to the extent that in Lacan's view, the reality principle, although it entails the suspension of immediate pleasure, is in service of the pleasure principle, as this suspension too aims at maximizing pleasure in the long run. In both cases, what is at stake is the calculation of goods, and desire has nothing to do with such calculation. We should not confuse desire with biological needs either. The Lacanian law of desire is not a Pauline law of the limbs inasmuch it

---

[91] Jacques Lacan, *Seminar VII: Ethics of Psychoanalysis*, ed. J-A. Miller (New York: Norton, 1992), p. 310.

[92] Slavoj Žižek, *In Defence of Lost Causes* (London: Verso, 2008), pp. 89–90.

[93] See Henry Chadwick, *Studies on Ancient Christianity* (Hampshire: Ashgate, 2005), p. 42.

[94] Lacan, *Seminar VII: Ethics*, p. 319.

[95] Ibid.

is devoid of naturalistic foundation. For Lacan, the object of desire is always already a representation – and since words and symbolic processes dominate and govern the things in the human world and since there is nothing absolutely fixed in the symbolic order, desire wanders freely in the historical universe of representations. This universe may explain *what* a man desires, for he receives the objects of his desire from the symbolic order, but it does not articulate the ultimate unconscious *source* of desire. This source – the object cause of desire – can be found in the sphere Lacan calls the real (*réel*).

Lacan's real is not a reality we experience within and around us. Unlike the real, this normal reality is always mediated by the symbolic order, or, more precisely, the symbolic order *constitutes* that reality. The real, instead, resists symbolization, even absolutely. This does not mean, however, that we cannot have any access to the real, for there is, in the real, also what Lacan calls the Thing (*la Chose*). In a sense, the Thing is nothing but the Kantian thing in itself (*Ding an sich*), a noumenal sphere unreachable by theoretical understanding, as the Thing is 'beyond-of-the-signified'.[96] At the level of representations, the Thing is nothing, but neither is it nothing at all: 'It is characterised by its absence, its strangeness'.[97] It is, as Lacan puts it a little later, 'something strange to me, although it is at the heart of me'.[98] It is present through its absence as 'excluded interior'.[99] Moreover, although the Thing is beyond good and evil,[100] it is not unrelated to them, for the Thing, like the Kantian noumenal sphere, is the *origin* of good and evil. It is from the Thing that all values arise, because the whole symbolic order, including the good and the evil, revolves around the Thing.[101] Yet contrary to the Kantian noumenal sphere, the Lacanian Thing is not unrelated to the symbolic, for the Thing is, as Lacan argues, an *effect* of the symbolic: 'The Thing is that which in the real, the primordial real, suffers from the signifier'.[102] More exactly, the signifier pierces a *hole* in the real and it is this hole that is the Thing, 'a void [*vide*] at the centre of the real'.[103] At the same time, however, this piercing brings about a break in the symbolic order itself. Indeed, it is precisely the Thing that explains the fluctuation of the symbolic order. In other words, even though all values arise from the unchangeable Thing, it does not guarantee that they remain unchangeable. Quite the contrary, the Thing, because it is nothing rather than something, makes it comprehensible why our conceptions of good and evil do change: 'The notion of the creation *ex nihilo* is coextensive with the exact situation of the Thing as such'.[104]

It is this dumb Thing in the real that human desire is structurally orientated to – and in order to remain faithful to his desire, the subject must not give up orienting towards its source in the Thing. For although the Thing of desire entails the suspension

[96] Ibid., p. 54.
[97] Ibid., p. 63.
[98] Ibid., p. 71.
[99] Ibid., p. 101.
[100] Ibid., p. 104.
[101] Ibid., pp. 57, 63.
[102] Ibid., p. 118.
[103] Ibid., p. 121. Translation modified.
[104] Ibid., p. 122.

of pleasure as well as calculation, it points towards *jouissance*, that is to say, absolute pleasure, the sovereign and extreme good. It is no wonder that Lacan aligns the Thing with Eckhart's mystical spark of the soul,[105] for we recall that this source of the sovereign good was also totally empty, incommunicable and beyond good and evil, and yet at the origin of them. In one respect, however, the Lacanian Thing is more like the Scholastic *synderesis* than the Eckhartian spark. Like the Fransiscan weight (*pondus*) of *synderesis*, or the weight of the Kantian noumenal moral law, actualized through the effects of *Gewissen*, the Thing, as the 'weight of the real', is actualized through the moral command:

> The moral law, the moral command, the presence of the moral agency in our activity, insofar as it is structured by the symbolic, is that through which the real is actualized – the real as such, the weight of the real [*le poids du reel*].[106]

'The moral law', Lacan repeats, 'is articulated with relation to the real as such.'[107] Yet contrary to the Scholastic *synderesis*, the Lacanian real is articulated in this relation since the moral law is also, as it was for the Apostle Paul, *the law of its transgression*. Particularly, the superego injunction, which sustains the law, also incites one to transgress it, being 'at one and the same time the law and its destruction'.[108] It is the law's destruction precisely because it is the transgression of the law that points, in the law itself, towards the absolute pleasure of *jouissance* beyond the law:

> Without a transgression there is no access to *jouissance*, and that is precisely the function of the Law. Transgression in the direction of *jouissance* only takes place if it is supported by the oppositional principle, by the form of the Law.[109]

Unlike the *synderesis*, furthermore, the Lacanian Thing is not external to the symbolic order but, as already said, an effect of the signifying function. It is because man is a speaking being that something like the Thing is possible in the first place: 'The fashioning of the signifier and the introduction of a gap or a hole in the real is identical.'[110] Finally, whilst the *synderesis* inclines the will toward the good and away from evil, being itself the locus of the supreme good – the Sabbath of perfect ecstasy, as Bonaventure put it – the Lacanian Thing, because beyond-the-law, is the locus of *radical evil*: 'The unspeakable field of radical desire is the field of absolute destruction.'[111] Our desire is structurally orientated toward a *forbidden* enjoyment (*jouissance*) in the Thing, but it is not forbidden only because a law forbids it. It is forbidden because *jouissance* entails the destruction of the very desiring subject: '*Jouissance* implies precisely the acceptance of death.'[112]

---

[105] Ibid., p. 63.
[106] Ibid., p. 20.
[107] Ibid., p. 76.
[108] Jacques Lacan, *Seminar I: Freud's Papers on Technique*, ed. J. A. Miller (New York: Norton, 1988), p. 102.
[109] Lacan, *Seminar VII: Ethics*, p. 177.
[110] Ibid., p. 121.
[111] Ibid., p. 216.
[112] Ibid., p. 189.

However, to the extent that this Thing is the object cause of desire and desire is constitutive of the subject, the Thing is also the source of good – not good in the sense of what Lacan calls the 'service of the goods' characteristic of eudaimonism, utilitarianism, and the morality of custom, but because it gives *consistency* to the subject as desire in the freely floating universe of the symbolic order without a proper centre.[113] The Thing is evil because it threatens to destroy the subject but it is good because it bestows him with the point of orientation. This is how I read Lacan's formula: 'There is no law of the good except in evil and through evil.'[114] Yet although Lacan argues that 'the only thing of which one can be guilty is of having given ground relative to one's desire,'[115] he does not suggest, like the medieval mystics, that we must become one with the evil Thing. This is, in fact, absolutely impossible, except in the subject's phantasy – and even such phantasmatic union entails that the subject becomes a sadistic tyrant. According to Lacan, the subject can remain faithful to his desire only if he *keeps distance* to the source of his desire in the Thing.[116] Hence, Lacan's position is structurally the same as that of Kant, as Kant, unlike Fichte, believed that to become one with the noumenal moral law entails the destruction of the moral subject. There must remain a gap between the subject and the Thing, for it is precisely this gap that *is* the subject.

This ethical double demand – the demand to acknowledge the source of desire in the Thing and to keep distance to it – is also at the heart of the ethics of psychoanalysis. The measure of ethical action is not pleasure, happiness or normalization, but desire – though this measure is not a proper measure at all but more like a Lutheran law of the heart (*lex sine lege, sine modo, sine fine, nesciens limitem*), since it is, as Lacan writes, 'an incommensurable measure, an infinite measure.'[117] In psychoanalytical practice, this means that the duty of the analyst is to assist the patient in recognizing his desire so that he can do justice to it and affirm the transgressive origin of the law, for this transgressive space called the Thing is not only the origin of desire but at the same time, since it lies beyond the law, that which prevents the subject from merging with the symbolic order. In short, it enables the subject to distance himself not only from the commonly acknowledged moral norms and values in a given symbolic order of society but also from the obscene superego injunction (even though it is precisely this injunction through which the real is actualized) – and it does so because, in the final analysis, the Thing is a mere void, a mere opening. It is this void that the analyst is obliged to lead his patient to, to make him recognize that this void (*das Ding*) is his most intimate kernel. Lacan admits that this necessarily entails distress, even 'absolute

---

[113] Thus, the Thing occupies the same place of the beyond-the-law as both Christ and Satan in Christian imagination, but now without difference. 'Christ was greater than His own life, and above all virtue, custom, ordinances and the like, and so also is the Evil Spirit above them, but with a difference', as the author of the *Theologia Germanica* put it. Anonymous, *The Theologia Germanica*, trans. S. Winkworth (New York: Cosimo, 2007), p. 30, 81.

[114] Lacan, *Seminar VII: Ethics*, p. 190.

[115] Ibid., p. 321.

[116] This is the main thesis in Marc de Kesel's very illuminative reading of Lacan's Seminar VII. Marc de Kesel, *Eros and Ethics* (New York: State University of New York Press, 2009).

[117] Lacan, *Seminar VII: Ethics*, p. 316.

disarray',[118] for to encounter *das Ding* means that the subject encounters his own death. According to Lacan, however, 'there is absolutely no reason why we should make ourselves [analysts] the guarantors of the bourgeois dream'.[119] Lacan does not specify what this dream is, but he does say that at the moment of such confrontation with the deadly Thing towards which the analysis is leading, the patient must be left alone. At that crucial ethical moment, the patient 'can expect help from no one',[120] for the ethical end of analysis is not the realization of some blissful plenitude, but quite the contrary: the moment when the subject comes to terms with his utter solitude at the edge of the deadly Thing at the heart of his being.

---

[118] Ibid., p. 304.
[119] Ibid., p. 303.
[120] Ibid., p. 304.

8

The Western Politics of Conscience

I

Now, perhaps, we have reached the ultimate point in this genealogy of the experience of conscience in the tradition of the West. In this tradition, the conscience has been the voice of God and the remnant of Paradise, the witness and the effect of divine and natural law, the condition and the experience of sin, obligation and duty, an echo of tradition and a mere firmly held opinion, the condition of freedom and autonomy, an effect of cruelty and renunciation of instincts, the voice of human groundlessness and the ground of his responsibility and resoluteness, a vehicle of interpellation and a tool of power, even a cruel and irrational sadist, the precondition of consciousness and thus of the subject's very existence. Without obedience to this alien voice, we have been told, we cannot become ethical beings and good citizens – autonomous, dutiful and responsible – but at the same time, some hold, this obedience renders us mere cogs in the machine of ideology and power. This voice empowers us and authorizes us to rebel against all laws and authorities, but at the same time these same laws and authorities maintain their power through this voice. Indeed, given this heterogeneity of accounts, is it even possible to speak about *the* experience of conscience in the tradition of the West? I think it is. As far as I can see, all the authors from Cicero to Scholastics, from Luther to Barth, from Grotius to Fichte, from Hegel to Nietzsche and Heidegger, from Levinas to Derrida and Lacan, have indeed spoken about the one and the same phenomenon. Why do then their accounts of conscience sometimes seem quite different from each other? The reason for these differences pertains to the fact that they have emphasized only one or two *aspects* of the experience of conscience. In the following, I will argue that it is not impossible to bring all these different aspects and characteristics together and to figure out the common essence of Western conscience.

II

Let us first return to the critics of conscience like Montaigne and Hobbes. Montaigne believed that conscience echoes nothing but the customs of one's country, whilst Hobbes maintained that it is only a firmly held opinion. What is characteristic to both of these conceptions is that in them the focus is on the *content* of conscience. Customs and opinions may vary and they may vary infinitely, so there is nothing universal let alone universally good in the content of conscience. In fact, even the most ardent defenders of the rights of conscience, such as Fichte, have admitted this. Yet this did not prevent Fichte from revering conscience as the sole origin of moral truth because his focus was not on the content but on the *form* of the experience of conscience. What is this form? It is the experience of obligation, duty, responsibility and more broadly speaking *the experience of normativity as such*. At the most formal and universal level, the Western conscience says nothing but that one 'ought to' something. In the tradition of the West, the experience of conscience, when deprived of all content, is the experience of this ought, the pressure of normativity as such. Referring clearly to this pressure, Cyprian wrote:

> For there is indeed, unless I am mistaken, even in the very power of conscience [*conscientia*], a marvellous fear which at once disturbs and inflames us; whose power [*potestas*], the more closely you look into, the more the dreadful sense of its obligation is gathered from its very aspect of venerable majesty.[1]

Recall Franciscans' weight (*pondus*) of *synderesis* pressing upon the subject by the force of natural law, yet without revealing what this law is really about. Recall also Crusius' drive of conscience (*Gewissenstrieb*). It does not tell us what to do and what to avoid, but it discloses our indebtedness to God and our obligation to obey his law. By virtue of the experience of conscience, when deprived of content, we do not know *what* the law prescribes but we know *that* it prescribes, that it lays an obligation upon us, as Kant had it, reaffirming thus Walter of Château-Thierry's assertion that the conscience is the 'necessary condition of the law's reaching the subject'.[2] In other words, the experience of conscience gives the law its *force* and more broadly speaking renders effective every legal norm, ethical demand and political ideal. It is, as J. S. Mill says, 'a feeling of pain connected with the pure idea of duty'.[3] Therefore, the experience of conscience, or, conscience, if you like, is also the *foundation* of every law and norm, every ethical demand and moral ideal, because it bestows laws, norms, ethical demands and moral ideals their normativity, rendering them into laws, norms, demands and ideals properly speaking. It might be true that this experience is 'mystical', as Jacques Derrida says of the source of authority, but at least it offers an explanation why the Western conscience has been both conservative and progressive. Insofar as the experience of conscience is nothing but the experience of an 'ought', it does not matter what one's ideals are as long as one conceives these ideals to be normatively binding. The experience of conscience, the experience of normativity as such, makes no difference with regard to content. It is an experience of being bound normatively by *something*. This does not mean, of course, that the Western conscience makes no difference at all. It is, as the theologians since Philo and philosophers since Cicero have insisted, the antithesis of thoughtlessness, recklessness, laziness, indifference, selfishness, cowardice, idle talk and so on. It is the antithesis, not of the morality of custom as Nietzsche thought, but of thoughtless and indifferent repetition of customs. More precisely, it is the antithesis of such repetition of customs that does not recognize

---

[1] Cyprian, *On the Glory of Martyrdom* 1.2, in *ANF*, vol. 5, p. 883.
[2] Cited in D'Arcy, *Conscience*, p. 80.
[3] Mill, *Utilitarianism*, p. 29.

those customs as normatively binding. It is the antithesis of the repetition of customs without the weight (*pondus*) of these customs on one's shoulders. Hence, it does not matter if a man is reactionary or progressive, conservative or revolutionary, liberal or socialist, for if he feels the weight of normativity on his shoulders, he is a man of conscience.

Yet the history of conscience cannot be reduced to the struggle between content and form, for although the distinction explains the simultaneous variety of consciences and the universality of conscience, it does not explain why the Western tradition of ethical thought has assumed that the experience of conscience renders man an *autonomous* and *sovereign being* among beings. What is it in conscience that makes a man 'self-sufficient and independent of other creatures, like unto those self-moving engines, which have their principle of motion within themselves'?[4] If it is conscience that binds a man to the laws, norms and customs, to ethical demands and moral ideals, being a sort of *social bond in itself*, as in early modern theories of natural law, why has it simultaneously been the experience by virtue of which he breaks away from these laws, demands and ideals, cuts all the ties to the surrounding society and transform himself into a self-sufficient creature independent of others? How can the same principle constitutive to normativity and to the social bond be a principle of their destruction? In order to address this aporia (which we must, because it is this double function of conscience that is characteristic of the West), another look at history is required, this time the very origins of Western philosophy and, more precisely, Plato's Socratic dialogues.

On the Socratic origins of the politics of conscience

I

The Western ethics of conscience originates in Plato's Socratic dialogues. There is nothing original in this statement. We have seen that Apuleius identified the Socratic *daimonion* with conscience in his *De deo Socratis*. It dwells in the most profound recesses of the mind in the place of conscience, guarding and observing us, reproving if we do evil and approving if we do well. Moreover, it has been noted long ago that Socrates introduced a novel ethics in the history of the West – the ethics of conscience. Montaigne alludes to this and Hegel confirms it. More recently, authors such as Hannah Arendt and Dana Villa have emphasized the same. They both, Arendt first and Villa in her footsteps, have argued that Socrates is the inventor of an ethics, the gravitational centre of which is 'the conscientious individual rather than tradition, convention, or public norms and opinion'.[5] In Arendt's estimation, the best description of this Socratic ethics of conscience can be found at the end of the contested Platonic dialogue *Hippias Major* (304b–e), in which Socrates complains about a fictive 'close

[4]   Ward, *Balme*, p. 21.
[5]   See Dana Villa, *Socratic Citizenship* (Princeton: Princeton University Press, 2001), p. 15.

relative' who lives in his house and who is always insulting, blaming and refuting him. For Arendt, this 'close relative' is nothing but what the subsequent Western tradition has called 'conscience'.[6] It is worth quoting Socrates' lengthy passage in its entirety:

> Hippias, my friend, you're a lucky man, because you know which activities a man should practise, and you've practised them too – successfully, as you say. But it seems to me that some divine fortune [*daimonia tis tykhē*] holds me back. I am always wandering [*planaō*] and perplexed [*aporō*]. If I make a display of how perplexed I am [*emautōu aporian*] to you wise men, I get mud-spattered by your speeches when I display it. You all say what you just said, that I am spending my time on things that are silly and small and worthless. But when I'm convinced by you and say what you say, that it's the most excellent thing to be able to present a speech well and finely, and get things done in court or any other gathering, I hear every insult [*kakos*] from that man (among others around here) who has always been disgracing [*elengkhō*] me. He happens to be a close relative of mine, and he lives in the same house. So when I go home to my own place and he hears me saying those things, he asks if I'm not ashamed [*aiskhynō*] that I dare discuss fine activities when I've been so plainly refuted about the fine and it's clear I don't even know at all what that is itself! 'Look,' he'll say. 'How will you know whose speech – or any other action – is finely presented or not, when you are ignorant of the fine? And when you're in a state like that, do you think it's any better for you to live than die?' That's what I get, as I said. Insults [*kakōs*] from you and from him, blamed [*oneidizō*] by both. But I suppose it is necessary to bear all that. It wouldn't be strange if it were good for me. I actually think, Hippias, that associating with both of you has done me good. The proverb says, 'What's fine is hard' – I think I know that.

Whilst I certainly agree with Arendt's and Villa's general characterization of Socrates' ethics as an ethics of conscience, their analyses contain some fundamental problems. For Arendt, the above quoted passage from *Hippias Major* is a good example of the 'inner dialogue' characteristic of the Socratic ethics of conscience. What really is at stake here is not, however, a dialogue but an *interrogation* carried out by the relative. The relative does not discuss with Socrates but reproves (*elengkhō*) him and calls him fundamentally into question. Villa maintains in turn that the Socratic ethics of conscience has had relatively little influence on Western political and ethical thought, admitting that John Stuart Mill and Friedrich Nietzsche may be his followers. I think, quite the contrary, that Socratic ethics of conscience is the very paradigm of Western ethics. Moreover, Villa opines that the Socratic ethics of conscience does not anticipate natural law or the voice of God in man.[7] I believe that it indeed does anticipate them. On the one hand, the Socratic precept that one should never do what one believes to be wrong, became not only one of the most fundamental precepts in Christian ethics (*contra conscientiam agere peccatum est*) but also one of the cornerstones in the

---

6   Arendt, *Life of the Mind*, vol. 1, pp. 188–91.
7   Villa, *Socratic Citizenship*, p. 41.

Western natural law. As the natural law theorists from Cicero onwards have stressed, it is against natural law to act against one's conscience, and if one does so, one is punished by nature herself, which is one of the principal proofs that natural law exists in the first place. On the other hand, it was precisely Socrates who first identified the voice of conscience with the divine (*daimonion*) and who, before the people's court in Athens, proclaimed: 'I will obey the god rather than you' (*Apology* 29d). What else is this than a precursor of the Christian ethics of conscience in which one of the most fundamental and the most often-cited proclamations is that of Acts 5:29, stating that 'we ought to obey God rather than men'?

Yet the most fundamental problem is that both Arendt and Villa fail to articulate how the Socratic ethics of conscience is possible in the first place. Like many others, they maintain that the touchstone of the Socratic ethics of conscience is individual moral integrity, the principle of non-contradiction as its test. And surely, Socrates wants to preserve his integrity:

> I think it's better to have my lyre or a chorus that I might lead out of tune and dissonant, and have the vast majority of men disagree with me and contradict me, than to be out of harmony with myself, to contradict myself, though I'm only one person. (*Gorgias* 482b–c)

Yet the integrity Socrates has in mind, the absence of an inner contradiction, does not denote integrity pure and simple. Integrity, for Socrates, is not merely the absence of the inner contradiction, for one can avoid it, like Alcibiades, who constantly escapes the disharmony of the soul by keeping himself busy in the public life of the *polis*. According to Socrates, this is absolutely lamentable. The inner contradiction should not be avoided by escaping it. Integrity is something one must earn and one can earn it only if one recognizes the *possibility* of an inner contradiction. More exactly, one must be sensitive to this contradiction, that is, to one's disharmony with oneself, for without such sensitivity, Socrates seems to maintain, the very notion of integrity is rendered superficial. Even more, one has to *know* what such a contradiction means, and this knowledge presupposes the experience of it.

One is now of course tempted to ask, what is the experience of contradiction in the sphere of morality? In the tradition of the West, this experience has been called the experience of bad conscience, guilt, shame, disgrace and so on, but perhaps more important than any of these terms, denoting usually one aspect of the wholesale phenomenon, is the *essence* of this fundamental experience – the experience the Greeks identified with *synoida emautō* ('knowing with oneself'). *Synoida emautō* is a verbal construction at the etymological root of the Greek conscience (*syneidēsis*), which in classical Greek could have a neutral meaning, signifying that one is conscious of something concerning oneself, but which could involve a moral meaning as well. Common to all these ethical uses of *synoida emautō* is that it expresses a *profound sense of disorientation* – a personal, moral, political and religious sense of loss. It is this experience of disorientation originating in the experience of conscience that constitutes the essence of Socratic ethics. Recall Socrates' words in *Hippias Major* (304c) I quoted above: 'It seems to me that some divine fortune [*daimonia tis tykhē*] holds me back. I am always wandering [*planaō*] and perplexed [*aporō*].' We also remember why he is *aporos*, meaning 'helpless', 'without passage', 'without orientation'. He is *aporos* because the 'relative' living in his place constantly accuses him and puts him into shame no matter what he has done. In other words, especially if we interpret, as Arendt has done, the 'relative' as a metaphor for conscience, the Socratic conscience is not a source of opinion, not even of normativity, but first and foremost *the source of aporia*. The conscience does not tell Socrates what to do and what to avoid but merely disturbs him up to the point of absolute confusion ('when you're in a state like that, do you think it's any better for you to live than die?'). In the same passage, however, Socrates also states that it is necessary to endure all this, because he thinks that it is good for him, and it is good to him because he believes that *absolute disorientation is the necessary condition of true morality*. Only the one who, by virtue of humiliation, 'knows with himself' that he knows nothing is capable of leading virtuous life: 'I know with myself [*synoida emautō*] that I am not wise at all' (*Apology* 21b). This was a new formula of ethics in the tradition of the West. The way to true moral knowledge goes through the absolute disorientation in terms of moral knowledge itself. All the known truths have to be relativized in the confusing experience of conscience because there is no knowledge of morality without absolute moral and political disorientation.

This is also the backdrop of Socrates' famous 'method' of elenchus. We may translate *elengkhos* as 'cross-examination', but given the fact that the word derives from the verb *elengkhō*, signifying 'to reprove', 'to disgrace', 'to shame' and 'to accuse', a more illustrative translation would be humiliation. In fact, it is precisely the verb *elengkhō* Socrates employs in *Hippias Major* (403d) when he laments that his 'relative' is always disgracing him: 'I hear every insult from that man … who has always been disgracing [*elengkhō*] me.' Hence, the 'relative' employs the same method of elenchus in the case of Socrates as Socrates, the gadfly, employs when he 'cross-examines', or more precisely reproves and disgraces, the Athenians: 'I shall', Socrates proclaims, 'question and examine and disgrace [*elengkhō*] everyone in Athens, young and old, citizens and foreigners' (*Apology* 29e–30a), continuing, 'I never cease to rouse each and every one of you, to persuade and reproach you all day long and everywhere I find myself in your company' (*Apology* 30e). And, if we are to believe Plato, he was sometimes quite successful. Even Alcibiades, the proudest of the young Athenians, felt ashamed before Socrates, their self-appointed 'conscience':

> Socrates is the only man in the world who has made me feel shame – ah, you didn't think I had it in me, did you? Yes, he makes me feel ashamed, because I know with myself [*synoida emautō*] that I can't prove he's wrong when he tells me what I should do; yet, the moment I leave his side, I go back to my old ways: I cave in to my desire to please the crowd. My whole life has become one constant effort to escape from him and keep away, but when I see him, I feel deeply ashamed, because I'm doing nothing about my way of life, though I have already agreed with him that I should. Sometimes, believe me, I think I would be happier if he were dead. (*Symposium*, 216b–c)

It is sometimes complained that Plato's Socratic dialogues are aporetic and do not lead to any conclusion, but, in truth, the only aim of such a 'method' *is* aporia. In other words, the aim of the 'method' of elenchus based on the accusations Socrates makes on his interlocutors is not to figure out what virtue means but on the contrary to reveal that all our conceptions of virtue are worth nothing and ultimately to elicit absolute disorientation in terms of morality and politics. The Socratic 'method' of elenchus does not lead anywhere, or better still, it leads to *nowhere*. This is not a sign of the method's failure, because it is the aporia that was sought for in the first place. It was sought for, because Socrates believes that true moral and political knowledge can emanate from such an aporia alone. Only the one who, by virtue of disgrace and humiliation, knows with himself (*synoida emautō*) that he knows nothing, to whom the world as a whole has become impenetrable, is capable of virtue. As Socrates proclaims in *Philebus* (16b): 'There certainly is no better road [*hodos*], nor can there ever be, than that which I have always loved, though it has often deserted me, leaving me lonely and forlorn [*erēmon kai aporon*].'

II

Although Socrates outlined the tenets of the Western ethics of conscience, he was not without a model. This model can be found in Greek tragedies. Let us consider the most famous of them, Sophocles' *Antigone*. Hegel may be wrong in claiming that Antigone is not a subject of conscience, but he is certainly wrong when he asserts that there is no such a subject at all in *Antigone*. There is indeed, although this subject is revealed only at the end of the play. This subject is Creon, who acknowledges his *hamartia* (1306–10): 'Ah, no! I tremble with fear. Why does no one strike me full on my chest with a two-edged sword? I am miserable – ah – and bathed in miserable anguish!' A little later (1343–5) he continues: 'I do not know which way I should look, or where I should seek support. All is amiss [*lekhrios*] that is in my hands.' This is the moment when the conscience enters the play. It is the moment when all the landmarks of moral and political orientation vanish, the moment when one finds oneself thrown into the 'wilderness' (*agrios*) (1274). It is the moment when the known ways of the world, its authorities, laws, norms, traditions and values, are called into question, including Creon's own authority. They have become relative, superfluous, turning eventually into nothing, at least for the subject that goes through this terrible experience that 'no sacrifice can bring to an end' (1285).

Such a turning point can of course be found in almost all classical tragedies. The hero acknowledges his *hamartia*, resulting in the turmoil of his soul. To be sure, it is not always a 'conscience' but also the Furies (*erinyes*), Dike's loyal maidens of vengeance, who are understood as the cause of this terrible experience. This holds true particularly for Aeschylus. In Sophocles' plays, however, the role of the Furies is already diminished. In *Antigone*, for instance, they are mentioned only once, and even here (603) Sophocles speaks about the Furies in the mind (*phrenōn erinys*). Most clearly, however, this new attitude appears in Euripides' plays, particularly in *Orestes*. In a decisive passage (392–7) where Orestes complains about his inner sufferings, he does not mention the Erinyes at all but speaks about *synesis*:

Orestes: Here I am, the murderer of my wretched mother.

Menelaus: I have heard, spare your words; evils should be seldom spoken.

Orestes: I will be sparing; but the deity is lavish of woe to me.

Menelaus: What ails you? What is your deadly sickness?

Orestes: My conscience [*synesis*]; I know [*synoida*] that I am guilty of a dreadful crime.

Menelaus: What do you mean? Wisdom is shown in clarity, not in obscurity.[8]

This passage has given scholars the reason to attribute to Euripides the very discovery of conscience, for he demythologized, as Bruno Snell says, the Furies by rendering their objective punishments into a purely subjective experience.[9] Here, however, more essential than to speculate who discovered conscience is to focus on the *consequences* of this experience. For I contend that it is precisely these consequences, both internal and external, that are decisive regarding the Socratic ethics of conscience. What then are these consequences? First of all, the experience of conscience entails the collapse of all the familiar coordinates of the world whereby the hero finds himself, like Creon, thrown into the wilderness (*agrios*). He finds himself utterly alone and forlorn (*erēmos kai aporōs*), as Socrates describes the effects of his method in *Gorgias*. True, the exact expression *erēmos aporos*, that is, desolated, isolated and abandoned (*erēmos*), helpless or without a way (*aporos*), occurs quite rarely in tragedies. We find it in *Oedipus at Colonus* (1735) where Ismene moans: 'Unhappy me! Abandoned and helpless [*erēmos aporos*], where am I now to live my wretched life?' Yet tragedies are full of corresponding expressions, the most frequent of which is *erēmos apolis*, signifying abandoned (*erēmos*), without a city (*apolis*). We find it in Sophocles, in *Philoctetes* (1018) for instance, where Philoctetes accuses Odysseus of mistreating him: 'You bind me and intend to take me from this shore where once you left me, a friendless, lonely without a city [*erēmos apolis*], living corpse.' But it is again Euripides who employs it most frequently. We come across the expression in *Medea* (255) as well as in *Hecuba* (811) in both of which the heroine complains of being *erēmos apolis*: 'Now I am your slave,' says Hecuba to Agamemnon, 'a happy mother once, but now childless and old alike, bereft of city, utterly abandoned [*apolis erēmos*], the most wretched woman living.' We find the same motif in Euripide's *Hippolytus* (846) and *Suppliants* (1132) as well, but now it is the whole *oikos* that is desolated: 'I am destroyed: my house is desolated [*erēmos oikos*], my children are orphaned', Theseus bemoans.

III

Let us return to Socrates. Whilst the Greeks felt pity for a man who had gone through the tragic experience of *synoida emautō*, leading to the condition of *erēmos apolis*, Socrates saw in him the model for the ethical subject. Accordingly, the aim of his ethical 'method' (*elengkhos*) was to create such abandoned, cityless subjects, like him

---

[8]   Euripides does not use the reflexive pronoun *emautō* here, but this may be due to reasons of metre.

[9]   Bruno Snell, *The Discovery of the Mind: The Greek Origins of European Thought* (New York: Harper & Row, 1960), pp. 124–33.

knowing not which way to look or where to seek support: 'It is', Socrates says in *Meno* (80c), 'not from any sureness in myself that I plunge others to aporia [*poiō aporein*]: it is from myself being more in aporia [*autos aporōn*] than anyone else that I plunge others to aporia [*poiō aporein*].' Yet we must be precise here. Socrates never says that he is an *apolis* – if we do not take into account his 'exodus' (*exodos*) outside the *polis* in the beginning of *Phaedrus*. He is not an *apolis* but abandoned and helpless (*erēmos aporos*), *atopos* (displaced, out of place), as Callicles says of him in *Gorgias* (494d). As a matter of fact, it is not until the Cynics and especially the rise of Christianity that the condition of *apolis* as the true condition of wise and pious man is fully affirmed. A little before the passage in *Discourses* where Epictetus proclaims that conscience (*to syneidos*) gives a Cynic the same power as guards and arms give to kings and tyrants, he asserts that such a person is, like himself, *aoikos* and *apolis*, without a house and a city.[10] Diogenes Laertius likewise reports that Diogenes the Cynic used to say that all the curses of tragedy had lighted upon him: 'At all events he was', Laertius continues by citing some lost tragedy, '*apolis, aoikos, patridos esterēmenos*', without a city and home, deprived of a fatherland.[11] In early Christianity, this citylessness and homelessness became a paradigm. Those who live in Christ are but 'aliens [*paroikos*] and exiles [*parepidemos*]', without home (*oikos*) and without land (*demos*), as we read in 1 Peter 2:11. And although the theme is the most visibly present in the writings of early Fathers, it never disappears entirely. The true Christian is but a *peregrinus*, a 'foreigner in the world [*peregrinus in saeculo*]', as Augustine repeats throughout *The City of God*.[12]

In contrast to this Cynico-early Christian paradigm, Socrates categorically refuses to leave the *polis*, because, as he says in *Phaedrus* (230d), he is a friend of learning – and 'the country places and the trees won't teach me anything, and the people in the city [*astu*] do'. Hence, Socrates is not a Diogenes, let alone an early Christian. But we must take into account what kind of a city dweller Socrates is. For he is not a proper citizen of the *polis* either: 'I am not the politician [*ouk eimi ton politikōn*]', as he says in *Gorgias* (473e). To the Greeks, a proper citizen was one who took part in the political life of the *polis*, but Socrates discredits 'all the business commonly called politics' (*Euthydemus* 292e). Hence, Socrates does not fit in either of well-known categories in *Politics* (1253a) by means of which Aristotle distinguishes men from animals and gods. Socrates is neither a *zōon politikon*, nor is he an *apolis*, that is to say 'a lower animal [*therion*] or a god [*theos*]', but rather stands at the *threshold* of the *polis* and the *agrios*. Or, better still, he is an animal-god *within* the walls of the *polis*. Even the fundamental Socratic principle, the principle that one ought to know oneself, or, if you wish, know *with* oneself (*synoida emautō*), is articulated in terms of the animal-god, rather than in terms of a good citizen. In *Phaedrus* (230a), Socrates announces:

> I investigate not these things [things outside the *polis*], but myself, to know whether I am a monster [*therion*] more complicated and more furious than

[10] Epictetus, *Discourses* 3.22.47, pp. 146–7.
[11] Diogenes Laertius, *Lives of Eminent Philosophers* 6.38, p. 38.
[12] Citation from Augustine, *City of God* 15.1, in *NPNF1*, vol. 2, p. 284.

Typhon or a gentler and simpler creature, to whom a divine and quiet lot is given
by nature.

In other words, even though Socrates does not dwell outside the *polis* abandoned by
his fellow citizens, he is not a citizen among others but a citizen abandoned *in* the
polis, a refugee in his own city. He is *erēmos apolis* not outside the *polis* but at the heart
of it, as the new figure of the citizen – as the one who takes up the *true* political craft:

> I believe that I'm one of a few Athenians – so as not to say I'm not the only one, but the
> only one among our contemporaries – to take up the true political craft [*epikherein tē*
> *hōs alēthōs politikē tekhnē*] and practise politics [*prattein ta politika*]. (*Gorgias* 521d)

It is not the Aristotelian *zōon politikon* but this Socratic citizen (*erēmos aporos*) that is
the paradigmatic figure of the Western ethico-political subject and, by the same token,
of the Western citizen.

IV

We must ask, however, why Socrates conceived such a displaced *erēmos apolis*
withdrawn from the normal social and political relations of the *polis* as the true ethico-
political subject. The most obvious, yet all-too-simple, answer is that by withdrawing
from the public affairs of the *polis* Socrates is able to avoid injustice, for it is, as he says
in the *Apology* (31d–e), impossible to avoid injustice if taking part in politics. The
true key to this paradox lies rather in Socrates' understanding of the allegedly *positive*
consequences of the aporia incurred by the experience of *synoida emautō*. As already
said, the negative consequence of the experience of *synoida emautō* is an absolute
disorientation in terms of morality and politics, because it tears the subject from the
social bond and, by the same token, from itself. Such a subject stands abandoned and
helpless (*erēmos aporos*) – or, as Callicles says of Socrates in *Gorgias* (486c), he 'lives
in his city as an absolute outcast' (*atekhnōs de atimon zēn en tē polei*). However, to
live in the city as an absolute outcast also signifies that the subject is no longer *consti-*
tuted by this bond but by the very painful division within the subject itself, the same
division that cut him out of the social bond in the first place. Hence, the experience
of conscience is also a *liberating* experience. The subject stands abandoned and
perplexed, but this entails that the subject is free from the principles, norms, values
and opinions of the community. In other words, the subject is no longer dependent on
others but stands apart as a *sovereign individual*. He is like the Cyclops in Euripides'
Cyclops, for the Cyclops are, as Silenius explains to Odysseus, 'abandoned' (*erēmoi*)
and 'solitaires' (*monades*) (116), but precisely for this reason 'none of them is subject to
anyone' (*akouei d' ouden oudeis oudenos*) (120).[13] This is why Socrates commends his
'relative', who carries on ceaselessly relativizing him and his world, for he has realized

---

[13] As we can also read in Homer's *Odyssey* (9.105–15), Cyclopes are 'insolent giants without
law [*athemistos*]', but at the same time, and because of this, each of them 'makes his own law
[*themisteuō*]'. *The Odyssey with an English Translation in Two Volumes*, vol. 1, trans. A. T. Murray
(Cambridge, MA: Harvard University Press, 1919), pp. 310–13. Translation modified.

that the absolute disorientation incurred by the experience of *synoida emautō* entails a fracture in the web of immanent social relations and thereby the birth of a sovereign individual subjected to no one. Socrates is no longer dependent on the opinions of others, not even on the constitution (*politeia*) of the *polis* (*Gorgias* 513a), that is, its truths, virtues, customs and laws. The constitution of the *polis* and by the same token the constitution of the entire visible world has lost its meaning to him. It has become null and void, absolutely nothing, but it is precisely from this nothingness that the sovereign individual is born.

Thus, it is not his capacity to think that enables Socrates to distance himself from the 'routines of everyday life', as Villa maintains,[14] but the disorienting experience of being rendered *erēmos aporos* by the accusing voice of conscience. In what sense, however, is such an *erēmos aporos* qua sovereign individual *morally* superior to a normal Athenian citizen? He is superior, according to the logic of Socratic ethical politics, because a normal citizen takes care of the affairs of the *polis* in his own limited and partial perspective, measuring his action and responsibility according to the given norms and values. The displaced *erēmos aporos*, instead, measures his action according to the measureless measure of the nothing of conscience. This entails that he also takes care (*epimeleomai*) of the affairs of the *polis* (of its justice, piety and so on) (*Apology* 36c) in the same modality, that is to say, in the *modality of unlimited responsibility*. Indeed, it is precisely for this reason that he reproaches and disgraces everyone in Athens, that is, in order for the Athenians, too, to become *erēmoi aporoi* capable of taking care of the affairs of the *polis* as well as their own souls:

> I tried to persuade each of you that to care for himself [*heautou epimelēthein*] and for the perfection of his goodness and wisdom is more important than anything else, and that to care for the *polis* itself is more important than other public affairs. (*Apology* 36c)

In fact, this turn from the condition of *erēmos aporos* qua sovereign individual to the responsible political subject also has its model in the Greek tragedies. Whilst the Homeric hero blamed his misdeeds on delusions of the gods, the tragic hero acknowledges his responsibility. In *Antigone* (1317–22), Creon confesses:

> Ah this responsibility [*aitios*] can never be fastened on to any other mortal so as to remove my own! It was I, yes, I, who killed you, I the wretch [*meleos* = useless]. I admit the truth. Lead me away, my servants, lead me from here with all haste, who am no more than a dead man [*mēdeis* = nobody]!

In other words, to become *erēmos aporos* and to become a subject of responsibility are not two separates moments but *one and the same moment seen from two perspectives*: becoming *erēmos aporos* through the accusing conscience means that one acknowledges one's responsibility and vice versa, acknowledging one's responsibility through the accusing conscience means that one becomes *erēmos aporos*. Yet Socrates elevated this tragic scheme to a new level, for what is at stake for him in this responsibility is

---

[14] Villa, *Socratic Citizenship*, p. 29.

not one's guilt with regard to one's evil deeds in the past, but more profoundly one's very existence among the fellow citizens. Whilst the experience of *synoida emautō*, the condition of *erēmos aporos* and responsibility defined the life of the tragic hero at a critical juncture when he became conscious of his evil deed, in Socrates' ethics of conscience these elements are put at the heart of everyday life. In Socratic ethical politics, one is no longer an *erēmos aporos* if one finds oneself responsible for a crime. One has to *make* oneself an abandoned outcast, to commit a sort of symbolic *suicide* ('to live in a state as close to death as possible', as Socrates says of himself in *Phaedo* 67d) by means of continuous self-accusation. Due to these self-accusations, the condition of *erēmos aporos* becomes permanent and responsibility ineradicable.

In the formation of the Socratic ethico-political subject, in short, at stake is the dialectical move from the normal situation characterized by the morality of custom to the state of exception (*erēmos aporos*) through the annihilating experience of conscience (*synoida emautō*) and, finally, back to the normal situation again as seen from the altered perspective of absolute responsibility enabled and, in the last resort, necessitated by the traumatic and disorienting experience of conscience. This dialectics is also the key to the enigma scholars have been wrestling with when trying to combine the rebellious Socrates with the law-abiding Socrates loyal to the fundamental traditional principles of the *polis*, that is, the Socrates who shamelessly refuses to assimilate himself to the order of the *polis* (*politeia*) and the Socrates who in *Crito* (51b–c) proclaims that one must always 'obey the commands of one's city and country'. From the perspective of the Socratic ethics of conscience, there is no enigma here, for these two attitudes represent two moments in this ethics. It is precisely his refusal to assimilate himself to the principles of the *polis* made possible by the disorienting experience of conscience that enables Socrates to truly adhere to them in a conscientious way, namely in the modality of unlimited responsibility.

Perhaps this is even the key to Plato's famous cave allegory in the *Republic* (514a–20e), for as we recall, in the formation of the philosopher–politician, there are also three interwoven yet analytically separate moments. First the philosopher leaves behind the cave of shadows, meaning the visible world of customs and opinions. Then he with great pain and resistance (515e) ascends to the sunlight of truth, but instead of revealing anything to him the sun of truth reveals the Nothing, as the sunlight makes him absolutely blind: 'His eyes would be blinded so that he would not be able to see even one of the things that we call real' (516a). Finally, ushered by the sense of responsibility that the blinding vision of the nothing has awakened – Plato also calls it being and the supreme good – this philosopher, despite detesting political power, descends back to the cave as a changed man in order 'to take charge [*epimeleomai*] of the other citizens and to keep watch [*phylassō*] over them' (520a). True, Plato says that the philosopher must be *forced* back to the cave, but we may ask *who* it is that forces him. Definitely, he is not forced by the people in the cave, because they do not want anything from him. Furthermore, inasmuch as the philosopher is alone in the sun, it must be the philosopher himself who forces himself back to the cave and, more precisely, it is his awakened conscience that carries out the task. In short, the same experience of conscience that leads to *no-where* (the blinding non-world of the sunlight) forces the subject to take a responsible stance *now-here* (the shadowy but real world of the cave), but instead of these representing two opposed moments, there is but a single experience – the experience constitutive of the Western ethico-political subject proper, dwelling constantly in the place of no/w/here.

V

Although I agree with Arendt that Socrates might be the inventor of the ethics of conscience, her assertion that Socrates 'discovered' conscience is far from convincing.[15] Socrates did not discover conscience. As a phenomenon, it may be perennial, a kind of *Ur-phänomen*. Socrates was not even the first to articulate the experience of conscience, since the experience of *synoida emautō* was known to the Greeks of the fifth century BC. What was unique in Socrates is his attitude towards this experience. Whilst the other Greeks thought that it should be avoided at all costs, Socrates believed that one must be continuously conscious of its possibility and welcome it whenever it is about to take place. Indeed, the Greeks also had a very good reason to avoid this experience. In ancient Greece, as the scholars have stressed, existence was always existence among other men, existence in a community of reciprocity of seeing and being seen. It was not the state of one's soul but one's public reputation that deter-mined one's self-respect and worth.[16] As Philip Bosman in his study on the *synoida* word group has shown, however, the one who 'knew with himself' started to act like a coward, not looking people in the eye and avoiding contact with them.[17] Particularly, it prevented *parrhēsia*, speaking one's mind, which had become a duty of an honourable citizen in the *polis*, and hence the precondition for taking part in the political life of the Athenian democracy.[18] Therefore, it is not a surprise that the Greeks did not welcome the experience of *synoida emautō* whenever it was about to take place. The one who 'knew with himself' became an outcast, more like a slave than an honourable citizen:

> My friends, it is this very purpose that is bringing about my death that I may not be detected bringing shame [*aiskhynas*] to my husband or to the children I gave birth to but rather that they may live in glorious Athens as free men, free of speech [*parrhēsiai*] and flourishing, enjoying good repute where their mother is concerned. For it enslaves a man, even if he is bold of heart, when he is conscious [*xyneidei*] of sins [*kaka*] committed by his mother or father. (Euripides, *Hippolytos* 419–29)

Also, Socrates thought that the experience of *synoida emautō* renders a man an outcast in the city. Yet, as already said, his attitude towards it was entirely different – and

---

[15] Arendt, *Promise of Politics*, p. 22.

[16] 'One was "what the others saw in one," and hence, it was by looking, not within one's soul, but outside it, at another being related to it, that one learned to know one's worth.' Jean-Pierre Vernant, introduction to *The Greeks*, ed. Jean-Pierre Vernant (Chicago: University of Chicago Press, 1995), p. 18.

[17] Bosman, *Conscience in Philo and Paul*, pp. 77–105.

[18] See Michel Foucault, *The Government of the Self and Others*, trans. G. Burchell (New York: Palgrave MacMillan, 2010).

it was different because his self-respect had nothing to do with what others saw in him. He knew with himself, but he did not therefore start to act like a coward, not looking people in the eye or avoiding contact with them. His bad conscience did not even prevent him from using *parrhēsia*. On the contrary, he stated that no power in this world could prevent him from speaking his mind. Even death was preferable to silence: 'I shall not change my conduct even if I am to die many times over' (*Apology* 30b–c). Socrates did not give a toss about public opinion ('we must not consider at all what the many will say of us', he says in *Crito* 48a), being the most shameless man in the Athenian *polis* – if we accept Aristotle's definition of shame (*aiskhynē*) as the fear of dishonour (*adoxia*) (*Rhetoric* 1383b15) and shamelessness as contempt for public opinion (1368b20–5). Yet Socrates' shamelessness did not signify, at least not in his own opinion, that he was a bad citizen. In his own estimation, he was not shameless at all. On the contrary, he believed himself to be the only citizen capable of *true* shame. True shame, although it, too, tears a man from the social bond, leaving him alone and forlorn, is not dependent on public opinion, for true shame is not shame before others but *before oneself*. The Greeks had no word for such an uncanny experience. Even the expression *synoida emautō* fails to grasp it fully inasmuch as in the Greek context the experience of *synoida emautō* presupposed the presence or the image of others in order to become effective as a moral experience. There is no definition for it even in Aristotle's *Rhetoric* dedicated to the analysis of all imaginable moral experiences. Nonetheless, it was this as-yet nameless experience, which was to become the most fundamental ethical and political experience in the West, that Socrates took as the foundation for his new morality, oscillating between shamelessness and responsibility, between nihilism and commitment, between the universality of the nothing and the particularity of action.

Conclusion

I

Such is the Socratic backdrop of the Western ethical tradition. Contrary to Arendt's and Villa's estimation, we do not have to wait until Immanuel Kant, let alone J. S. Mill, in order to witness the resurgence of the Socratic ethics. We find it everywhere, in the Cynics, in Stoicism, in Christianity, in the early modern tradition of natural law, in the philosophy of the Enlightenment, in German idealism, as well as in twentieth-century existentialism. At first glance it might appear that the Western tradition of natural law is diametrically opposed to the logic of Socratic ethics inasmuch as natural law, instead of being a measureless measure, is immutable and eternal. However, a closer look at the history of this law reveals that there is only one thing that truly is immutable in it. It is not the content of that law, for the content has varied depending on epoch and author. It is the presumption that the universal moral law of nature is recognized by the effect of its alleged *transgression*. We learn the law of nature when it executes itself in the mode of the punishment of a guilty conscience. This punishment is the most universal and firmly established empirical ally of the universal moral law in the history of this law, its most scrupulous witness. Virtually all authors from Cicero to Kant abide by this truth: it is the guilty conscience that testifies to the existence of natural law. In the Lutheran tradition, the very function of natural law is reduced to this experience. Natural moral law punishes and humiliates the subject, revealing to him his 'blindness, misery, wickedness, ignorance, hate and contempt of God'.[19] It uproots him from the solid ground of written laws and unwritten conventions, leaving him bereft in the Nothing without moral coordinates whatsoever – except the very universality of the Nothing itself: 'The moral law', Kant writes, 'unavoidably humiliates every human being',[20] though this law is no longer known by its momentary transgression but rather by the very impossibility of its fulfilment.

We naturally find the same punishment and disorienting nothingness at the heart of the various Western descriptions of conscience itself, given its function as the witness of natural law: it accuses and reproaches, torments and terrifies, gnaws and punishes, insults and humiliates us, being a source of utmost distress, angst, anxiety, and so on. Yet conscience remains the source of such humiliation, distress and anxiety even for those to whom the era of natural law came to an end. In fact, it is precisely now that the voice of conscience *always* disturbs and disorients the subject, for as we have seen the death of God and the end of natural law signified also the end of good conscience as an ethical option. Instead of testifying to a law, the modern voice of conscience 'discourses solely and constantly in the mode of keeping silent',[21] but now it is this silence, this anarchical nothingness at the heart of the subject, that is the cause of anxiety and disorientation. On the other hand, we have also seen that the operation of conscience was articulated in such empty and silent terms from the very beginning: conscience 'intercedes for us with ineffable groanings',[22] it operates 'without discourse',[23] 'no one is able to express it in words to another',[24] and so on and so forth. Not only is the voice of conscience heard in solitude and silence, but even as a voice of God it expresses itself in silence which 'passes all understanding'.[25] In other words, it seems that conscience has always both humiliated the subject and abandoned him in empty silence: 'In conscience we have abode in the desert, where no man enters', as Augustine had it.[26] Indeed, even the subject of conscience himself is unable to enter this desert, for although the experience of conscience tears him from his safe abode in the world, the same experience entails a desubjectivization of the subject, his becoming nothing.

This nothingness at the heart of the Western ethico-political subject, it must be noted, has nothing to do with the Aristotelian–Lockean notion of the soul as an empty sheet. In the tradition of the Western ethics of conscience, the soul does not

[19] Luther, *Galatians* 3.19, p. 309.
[20] Kant, *Critique of Practical Reason*, p. 200.
[21] Heidegger, *Being and Time*, p. 318.
[22] Jerome, *In Ezekh.* 1.1.7, in *PL*, vol. 25, p. 22a–b.
[23] Aquinas, *De veritate*, q. 16, a. 1.
[24] Luther, 'Handbemerkungen zu Taulers Predigten', p. 103.
[25] Coleridge, *Aids to Reflection*, p. 374.
[26] Augustine, *Book of Psalms* 55.8, in *NPNF1*, vol. 8, p. 212.

emerge first as an empty sheet filled later on with impressions and ideas. On the contrary, the soul is always already filled with a variety of impressions and ideas, but it is precisely these impressions and ideas, that is, the interiorized norms, values and opinions, that are the most *problematic* in terms of ethics. In order to become truly ethical, the Western tradition of ethical wisdom teaches us, one must free oneself of these impressions and ideas. One has to empty one's soul by listening to the voice of conscience and to make room for the Nothing, because it is out of this nothingness that the proper – free and autonomous – ethico-political subject is born. The disorienting experience of conscience desubjectivizes and isolates the subject from the rest of society, but at the same time it reveals the futility of all authorities, principles, laws and customs. By opening the empty space of absolute silence, the conscience calls them into question, relativizing thereby everything in the immanent order of the world – and it is precisely this relativization that renders the subject free, independent, self-sufficient, autonomous, even a godlike automaton, as the authors from Cicero to Kant have maintained. We find the same uncanny dialectics in Nietzsche, for as we recall, the Nietzschean intellectual conscience revaluates the prevailing values, leaving the individual lonely and forlorn, but at the same time, by virtue of this nullification, it demands, and *can* demand, that we become new, unique and incomparable human beings who 'give themselves laws, who create themselves'.[27] We detect it in Kierkegaard, Barth, Heidegger, and Levinas as well, for although they rejected the idea of autonomy, they all believed that by desolating the subject the voice of conscience not only relativizes the prevailing norms of society but also confirms the uniqueness of the subject, so that he may become able to become who he truly is – that is to say, an authentic ethical being.

Perhaps this dialectics of conscience remained mainly implicit in pre-Kantian thought, given the prevailing assumption that the voice of conscience reveals something more substantial than a mere void at the heart of being. However, it is precisely in pre-Kantian thought and more specifically in German mystical theology that we find the best articulation of it. People must, as Eckhart and Tauler stressed, be dead to all things, lose everything and become like nothing, because they thereby become 'the lofty pillars of the universe',[28] as free and independent as God himself. When I lose myself completely in the standstill (*gelassenhait*) of the soul and heed the inner word of conscience, God is in me, including his omnipotence, righteousness and mercy.[29] In other words, it is the nullifying effect of the voice of conscience, this unfathomable abyss of the soul where one is naked (*nuda*) before God,[30] that empowers the subject – and if my interpretation is correct, it empowers the subject because the subject is no longer dependent on the web of immanent social relations but constituted by the abyssal division within. The same conscience that nullifies everything, including the subject of conscience, renders the subject sovereign, no longer bound by any existing laws, values and ideals, and yet, and precisely for this reason, capable of *creating* laws

---

[27] Nietzsche, *Gay Science*, §335, p. 336.
[28] Tauler, *Sermons*, sermon 5, p. 48.
[29] Denck, 'Whether God is the cause of Evil,' pp. 93–4.
[30] Ambrose, *Concerning Repentance* 2.11.103, in *NPNF2*, vol. 10, p. 358.

and ideals, as God creates laws and ideals *ex nihilo*. The sovereign decision emanates from a 'normative nothingness [*einem normative Nichts*] and concrete disorder', as Carl Schmitt wrote centuries later.[31]

Furthermore, to the extent that the voice of conscience nullifies the socio-political order whereby the subject is deprived of any 'law given from the outside be it the law of God or the laws of men',[32] he is rendered absolutely inexcusable. In fact, this is the fundamental function of the *law itself*, namely of that supreme law of nature to which the humiliating voice of conscience testifies and on which the written laws of God and the positive laws of men are and must be based: 'The end of natural law is to render man inexcusable', according to Calvin.[33] The same holds true with the modern conscience, even though it does not know anything about the immutable laws of nature: 'It makes each individual responsible as such', as Barth contended.[34] Without the nullifying voice of conscience, Western wisdom teaches us, accountability and responsibility remain inevitably imperfect, because there is neither accountability nor responsibility without proper individuation – and no proper individuation without the voice of conscience, for it is this humiliating voice that establishes us 'as individual and particular beings'.[35] Without the voice of conscience, which renders the subject *erēmos aporos* ('countryless and homeless' in the words of Levinas),[36] one cannot do without direction from another, as Kant required, for as long as one does not heed the call of conscience one remains embedded in the immanent web of social relations. The absence of the call of conscience evades responsibility as much as its presence evokes it. The call of conscience constitutes a freely floating subject devoid of law and identity, but it is exactly for this reason – for the reason that it 'has nothing in the world upon which to rest its head'[37] – that it becomes the subject of responsibility.

By the same token, the disorienting call of conscience enables genuine obedience, conviction and faith. Only the one whose conscience has first proclaimed the relativity of everything present, including the law of God and the laws of men, may see the truth and become faithful to it: 'The end of the law [*nomos*] is sound faith [*pistis*]', as the Apostle Paul said (1 Tim. 1:5). Sound faith arises only if the law of tradition and the tradition as law are nullified, if the *nomos*-bound identity counts for nothing: 'I count everything as loss', as Paul states in Philippians (3.9) whilst reflecting his *nomos*-bound identity, since this loss not only empowers man ('when I am weak, then I am strong', 2 Cor. 12.10), but also enables his genuine faith in Christ. I am enslaved, poor, humble, a fool, eventually 'nothing' (*egō … ouden eimi*) (2 Cor. 12.11), as the whole world (*kosmos*) is 'withering away for me' (1 Cor. 7.31), but this does not harm me, since it is the nothingness of the self and the world that gives me power and courage to believe, hope and love. The same holds true with the Christian tradition as a whole,

---

[31] Carl Schmitt, *Über die drei Arten des rechtswissenschaftlichen Denkens* (Berlin: Duncker & Humblot 1993), p. 24.
[32] Arendt, *Responsibility*, p. 68.
[33] '*Finis legis naturalis est, ut redattur homo inexcusabilis.*' Calvin, *Institutes*, 2.2.22, p. 241.
[34] Barth, *Ethics*, p. 494.
[35] Fichte, *Vocation*, p. 108.
[36] Levinas, 'Ethics as First Philosophy', p. 81.
[37] Levinas, 'Substitution', p. 93.

though it has often meant obedience to and faith in the law itself, definitely among the Catholics but also among the Protestants. We may recall the message of the *Formula of Concord*, which declares that Christians, even if regenerated, are obliged to observe the law constantly and diligently – and that it is precisely these regenerated who are *capable* of observing it because of faith.

Also recall Fichte's words, 'there is absolutely neither external ground nor external criterion for the binding force of an ethical command'.[38] Fichte does not only mean that every ethical command must be confirmed by conscience, but also that as long as an ethical command is grounded only externally, there can be no true commitment and no genuine faith in the given command, namely in the 'laws of one's state'.[39] In the same way, Hegel ostensibly criticizes the standpoint of conscience at first in asserting that it is 'the deepest internal solitude, from which both limit and the external have wholly disappeared',[40] but in the end holds that it is from this deepest internal solitude that faith in the external emanates and must emanate: it is in the innermost shrine (*heiligthum*) of conscience that the political principles and institutions are endowed with sanctity.[41] We find this same logic in Schelling's ethics, too, though it is no longer a divine law or the state that is the object of faith but the principle of faith itself. In Schelling's ethics, as we recall, the most fundamental principle is 'the highest resoluteness for the right without choice',[42] but inasmuch as the base of reality, that is, the ground of the soul, is incomprehensible anarchy, this resoluteness for the right (*Recht*) cannot rely on any other foundation than the firm faith and highest resoluteness themselves. Yet this lack of foundation in the anarchy of the ground is not a defect here, since anarchy is the very condition of possibility of firm faith and highest resoluteness. The same dialectics can be grasped in Heidegger whose silent call of conscience tears *Dasein* from the social bond and leaves it abandoned in the nullity of the limit situation (*Grenzsituation*) of being-towards-death, but it is, quite unsurprisingly, precisely this condition that renders *Dasein* capable of responsibility and resoluteness – and so on and so forth.

It may be true that this nullification of one's identity and thereby of the whole social world take place, as Arendt says, in limit situations. We have already encountered the complaint many times that people do not usually heed the voice of conscience. They obey the rules but not conscientiously. Even when they transgress the rules, they most often do it recklessly, without conscientious commitment to transgression. We have even heard the claim that it is impossible for a human being to heed the call all the time, because, as Heidegger has told us, *das Man* 'belongs to *Dasein's* positive constitution'.[43] The very plot we took as an example of the event of the call, Creon's experience of disorientation, implies the rarity of the call. Yet its rarity has not prevented philosophers and theologians from conceiving this event as the

---

[38] Fichte, *System of Ethics*, p. 168.
[39] Ibid., p. 226.
[40] Hegel, *Philosophy of Right*, §136, addition, p. 115.
[41] Hegel, *Philosophy of History*, p. 52.
[42] Schelling, *Philosophical Investigations*, p. 57.
[43] Heidegger, *Being and Time*, p. 167.

constitutive event of ethics and the ethico-political subject. Indeed, what else are the 'methods' of ethics from the Socratic *elengkhos* and the Christian *katagnōsis-metanoia* to the Kantian maxim and the Levinasian Other, even to Lacanian psychoanalysis, but efforts to incur the disorienting experience of conscience in order to uproot the subject from the solid ground and to tear him from the social bond, so that he may become an independent being capable of obligation, duty and responsibility? I believe they are precisely such means and methods. Their sole aim is to render the subject what Socrates called *erēmos aporos*. This is the condition on which Western ethics and ethical politics has established its wavering abode and that still carries on today, continuing its uncanny oscillation between humiliation and sovereignty, nihilism and faith, shamelessness and responsibility.

I a

In his *Homo Sacer: Bare Life and Sovereign Power*, Giorgio Agamben presents the famous argument that sovereignty is based on the production of bare life (*homo sacer*) understood as life that it is licit to kill but that cannot be sacrificed – life that is neither natural (*zoē*) nor political (*bios*) in the traditional Aristotelian sense, but that articulates the threshold of their separation. *Homo sacer*, the figure of bare life, is devoid of a form of life (*bios*), because he is abandoned outside the law by the sovereign power. Yet *homo sacer* is not without a relationship to the power that abandons him, for the act of abandonment does not restore his life in the natural condition (*zoē*), but exposes him to an unconditioned threat of death, and therefore his life becomes entirely dependent on sovereign power. He is, like the bandit, caught 'in the sovereign ban and must reckon with it at every moment'.[44] Without going into the details of Agamben's well-known analysis, it may be fruitful to compare *homo sacer* understood as the originary figure of life under sovereign power with *erēmos aporos* understood as the paradigmatic figure of the Western ethical subject, as there seem to be certain similarities between these two figures.

Like *homo sacer*, the *erēmos aporos* occupies the threshold between *zoē* and *bios*, between the wilderness (*agrios*) and the city (*polis*), or, to use a famous distinction in Aristotle's *Politics* (1253a, 10–18), between animal sound (*phōnē*) and human speech (*logos*). Moreover, like *homo sacer*, the ethical *erēmos aporos* articulates the very separation *zoē* and *bios*, for the voice of conscience constitutive to this subject emanates from nowhere else than from the split between *zoē–phōnē* and *bios–logos*. This voice is neither an animal *instinctus* nor a human *ratio*, but, as Teutonicus said, the instinct *of* reason, that is, the very *difference* between natural instinct (*zoē–phōnē*) and human speech (*bios–logos*), a mere crack in the ontological edifice of the universe, to use Slavoj Žižek's formulation.[45] Thus,

---

[44] Giorgio Agamben, *Homo Sacer: Bare Life and Sovereign Power*, trans. D. Heller-Roazen (Stanford: Stanford University Press, 1998), p. 183.

[45] 'There is ethics in so far as there is a crack in the ontological edifice of the universe: at its most elementary, ethics designates fidelity to this crack', the crack that for Žižek is nothing else than the very constitutive principle of the subject. Slavoj Žižek, *The Plague of Fantasies* (London: Verso, 1997), p. 214.

instead of living in two distinct spheres (*phōnē* and *logos*) at the same time, as an animal with the additional capacity to speak, the Western ethical subject (*erēmos aporos*) dwells, like the Agambenian *homo sacer*, in the groundless void of separation.

Unlike *homo sacer*, however, the Socratic political subject is not abandoned by the sovereign but *by himself* through his own traumatic self-accusation. Furthermore, like *homo sacer*, the *erēmos aporos* is, as Sophocles describes the tragic hero in *Philoctetes* (1018), a 'living corpse' (*en zōsin nekron*), or lives, as Socrates says of himself, 'as close to death as possible' (*Phaedo* 67d), but unlike *homo sacer*, *erēmos aporos* is not thereby at mercy of the sovereign. On the contrary, it is *he* who has become sovereign, not because he has somehow managed to sublate his condition as abandoned and forlorn subject, but because this condition *is* the condition of sovereign freedom. In other words, it is neither his biological life in the order of nature (*zoē*) nor his form of life in the symbolic order of the *polis* (*bios*), not even his exposure to the threat of imminent death (*homo sacer*), but his *symbolic suicide* that renders him a sovereign individual subjected to no one. This is not to say that the *erēmos aporos* would be an Agambenian sovereign, for although this sovereign occupies the same terrain of ban as *homo sacer* ('the sovereign and *homo sacer* present two symmetrical figures that have the same structure and are correlative'),[46] they are nevertheless separate figures opposed to each other. Instead, the *erēmos aporos* occupies the *zone of indistinction* of *homo sacer* and the sovereign. He is *homo sacer* as sovereign and sovereign as *homo sacer*, or rather, he is the sovereign continuously exposed to the condition of *homo sacer* through which he must in any case pass in order to become sovereign. In other words, whilst the Agambenian sovereign and *homo sacer* are separate figures opposed to each other, they converge without a remainder in the Western subject of ethics and ethical politics.

One of the most clear-cut articulations of this sovereign ethico-political subject can be found in Jean-Jacques Rousseau's *Social Contract*, though here the Vicar's voice of conscience is transformed into the voice of people.[47] In the initial situation of the contract, Rousseau tells us, the individual is pushed outside every community, law and tradition, separated and isolated from his family, relatives, friends, eventually from every human being. Yet although he is now like a bandit, he is not left outside the body politic, but rather finds himself at the heart of it, for by the contract the individual not only alienates himself *from* every existing community but also with respect *to* the new body politic constituted by the contract:

> These articles of association, rightly understood, are reducible to a single one, namely the total alienation by each associate of himself and all his rights to the whole community [*l'aliénation totale de chaque associé avec tous ses droits à toute la communauté*].[48]

---

[46] Agamben, *Homo Sacer*, p. 84.

[47] This voice, understood as the general will, is exactly like the Vicar's divine instinct, or the Scholastic *synderesis* for that matter: it radically detaches man from the social bond, it can be neither represented nor discussed, and it is 'always constant, unalterable and pure'. Rousseau, *The Social Contract*, 4.1, p. 150.

[48] Ibid., 1.6, p. 60.

This is how the individual becomes what Rousseau calls a *Sujet*, totally at the mercy of the body politic that may compel him as it wishes, even kill him. Yet Rousseau argues that the contract also renders the individual a *Citoyen* who by participating in the sovereign authority (*l'autorité souveraine*) of this new body politic obeys himself alone. On what account is the individual a sovereign *Citoyen* if he is an absolute outcast at the mercy of the community? He is the *Citoyen* because he is an alienated, abandoned and helpless *Sujet*, for it is such a subject alone that is capable of attuning to 'the voice of duty' (*la voix du devoir*) which is the true mark of the *Citoyen*.[49] To become a sovereign citizen presupposes that one becomes an abandoned outcast deprived of every community, law and tradition. The individual is a citizen capable of giving himself a law only on the condition that he is a subject exposed to the condition of *erēmos aporos*. In this lies the key to the 'working of the political machine (*le jeu de la machine politique*)'.[50]

---

[49] Ibid., 1.8, p. 64.
[50] Ibid., 1.7, p. 64.

Bibliography

Adams, John. 'On Self-Delusion.' In *The Works of John Adams*, edited by S. F. Adams. Vol. 3. Boston: Little, Brown, and Co., 1851.

Agamben, Giorgio. *Homo Sacer: Bare Life and Sovereign Power*, translated by D. Heller-Roazen. Stanford: Stanford University Press, 1998.

—*State of Exception*, translated by Kevin Attell. Chicago: Chicago University Press, 2005.

—*Language and Death: The Place of Negativity*, translated by Karen Pinkus and Michael Hardt. Minneapolis: University of Minnesota Press, 2006.

Althusius, Johannes. *Politica: Politics Methodically Set Forth and Illustrated with Sacred and Profane Examples*, translated by F. Carney. Indianapolis: Liberty Fund, 1995.

Althusser, Louis. 'Ideology and Ideological State Apparatuses.' In *Lenin and Philosophy and Other Essays*, translated by B. Brewster. New York and London: Monthly Review Press, 1971.

Ambrose. *De Abraham Libri Duo*. In *Patrologia cursus completus: Series Latina*, edited by J. P. Migne. Vol. 14. Paris: 1844–55.

—*Enarrationes in XII Psalmos Davidicos De Abraham Libri*. In *Patrologia cursus completus: Series Latina*, edited by J. P. Migne. Vol. 14. Paris: 1844–55.

—*Epistolae Prima Classis*. In *Patrologia cursus completus: Series Latina*, edited by J. P. Migne. Vol. 16. Paris: 1844–55.

—*Epistolae Secunda Classis*. In *Patrologia cursus completus: Series Latina*, edited by J. P. Migne. Vol. 16. Paris: 1844–55.

—*Concerning Repentance*. In *Nicene and Post-Nicene Fathers*, edited by Philip Schaff. Series 2, vol. 10. Peabody, MA: Hendrickson Publishers, 1995.

—*On the Duties of the Clergy*. In *Nicene and Post-Nicene Fathers*, edited by Philip Schaff. Series 2, vol. 10. Peabody, MA: Hendrickson Publishers, 1995.

Ames, William. *Conscience with the Power and Cases Thereof*. Leyden: W. Christiaens, E. Griffin and J. Dawson, 1639.

Andrew, Edward G. *Conscience and its Critics: Protestant Conscience, Enlightenment Reason, and Modern Subjectivity*. Toronto: University of Toronto Press, 2001.

Anonymous. *Quaestiones in N.T.* In *Patrologia cursus completus: Series Graeca*, edited by J. P. Migne. Vol. 28. Paris: 1857–66.

—*Rhetorica ad Herennium*, translated by Harry Kaplan. Cambridge, MA: Harvard University Press, 1954.

—*The Theologia Germanica*, translated by S. Winkworth. New York: Cosimo, 2007.

Apuleius. *On the God of Socrates*. In *The Works of Apuleius*. London: George Bell and Sons, 1878.

Arendt, Hannah. *Eichmann in Jerusalem: A Report on the Banality of Evil*. New York: Penguin Books, 1994.

—*Love and Saint Augustine*, edited by J. V. Scott and J. C. Stark. Chicago: University of Chicago Press, 1996.

—*Responsibility and Judgement*. New York: Harvest Books, 1978.

—*The Human Condition*. Chicago: The University of Chicago Press, 1958.

—*The Life of the Mind*. New York: Harvest Books, 1978.

—*The Promise of Politics*. New York: Schocken Books, 2005.

Aristophanes. *Thesmophoriazusae*. In *Aristophanes with English Translation in Three Volumes*, translated by B. B. Rogers. Vol. 3. London: William Heinemann, 1963.

Aristotle. *Rhetoric*. In *Aristotle in 23 Volumes*, translated by J. H. Freese. Vol. 22. Cambridge, MA: Harvard University Press, 1926.

—*Nicomachean Ethics*. In *Aristotle in 23 Volumes*, translated by H. Rackham. Vol. 19. Cambridge, MA: Harvard University Press, 1934.

—*Politics*. In *Aristotle in 23 Volumes*, translated by H. Rackham. Vol. 21. Cambridge, MA: Harvard University Press, 1944.

Arndt, Johann. *True Christianity*, edited by Peter C. Erb. New York: Paulist Press, 1978.

Arnold, Gottfried. *The Mystery of the Divine Sophia*. In *Pietists: Selected Writings*, edited by Peter C. Erb. Mahwah, NJ: Paulist Press, 1983.

Athanasius. *Life of Antony*. In *Nicene and Post-Nicene Fathers*, edited by Philip Schaff. Series 2, vol. 4. Peabody, MA: Hendrickson Publishers, 1995.

Augustine. *Confessions*. In *Nicene and Post-Nicene Fathers*, edited by Philip Schaff. Series 1, vol. 1. Peabody, MA: Hendrickson Publishers, 1995.

—*The City of God*. In *Nicene and Post-Nicene Fathers*, edited by Philip Schaff. Series 1, vol. 2. Peabody, MA: Hendrickson Publishers, 1995.

—*On the Holy Trinity*. In *Nicene and Post-Nicene Fathers*, edited by Philip Schaff. Series 1, vol. 3. Peabody, MA: Hendrickson Publishers, 1995.

—*A Treatise on Nature and Grace*. In *Nicene and Post-Nicene Fathers*, edited by Philip Schaff. Series 1, vol. 5. Peabody, MA: Hendrickson Publishers, 1995.

—*A Treatise on the Spirit and the Letter*. In *Nicene and Post-Nicene Fathers*, edited by Philip Schaff. Series 1, vol. 5. Peabody, MA: Hendrickson Publishers, 1995.

—*Our Lord's Sermon on the Mount*. In *Nicene and Post-Nicene Fathers*, edited by Philip Schaff. Series 1, vol. 6. Peabody, MA: Hendrickson Publishers, 1995.

—*Lectures or Tractates on the Gospel According to St John*. In *Nicene and Post-Nicene Fathers*, edited by Philip Schaff. Series 1, vol. 7. Peabody, MA: Hendrickson Publishers, 1995.

—*Expositions on the Book of Psalms*. In *Nicene and Post-Nicene Fathers*, edited by Philip Schaff. Series 1, vol. 8. Peabody MA: Hendrickson Publishers, 1995.

—*Against Julian*. Translated by M. Schumacher. Washington: The Catholic University of America Press, 2004.

Bacon, Francis. *Advancement of Learning*. Oxford: Clarendon Press, 1869.

Bainton, Roland H. *Here I Stand: A Life of Martin Luther*. New York: Meridian, 1995.

Barth, Karl. *Ethics*, translated by G. Bromiley. New York: The Seabury Press, 1981.

Bayle, Pierre. *A General Dictionary, Historical and Critical*. Vol. 6. London: James Bettenham, 1734–41.

—*A Philosophical Commentary on These Words of the Gospel, Luke 14:23, 'Compel Them to Come In, That My House May Be Full'*, edited by John Kilcullen and Chandran Kukathas. Indianapolis: Liberty Fund, 2005.

Baylor, Michael G. *Action and Person: Conscience in Late Scholasticism and the Young Luther*. Leiden: E. J. Brill, 1977.

Beiner, Ronald. *Civil Religion*. Cambridge: Cambridge University Press, 2011.

Bell, David N. 'The Tripartite Soul and the Image of God in the Latin Tradition.' *Rescherches de Théologie ancienne et médiévale* 47 (1980): 16–52.

Bentham, Jeremy. *Deontology*. Vol. 1. London: Longman, 1834.

—*Principles of Legislation*. In Jeremy Bentham, *Theory of Legislation*, edited by C. M. Atkinson. Vol. 1. London: Oxford University Press, 1914.

Bernard of Clairvaux. *On Conversion*. In Bernard of Clairvaux, *Selected Writings*, translated by G. R. Evans. New York: Paulist Press, 1987.

Beza, Theodore. *De jure magistratuum*, edited by Patrick S. Poole. Accessed 22 August 2012: http://www.constitution.org/cmt/beza/magistrates.htm

Bible: The Revised Standard Version.

Bodin, Jean. *On Sovereignty: Four Chapters from the Six Books of the Commonwealth*, edited by J. H. Franklin. Cambridge: Cambridge University Press, 1992.

Boepple, Ernst, ed. *Adolf Hitlers Reden*. München: Deutscher Volksverlag, 1933.

Boethius. *The Consolation of Philosophy*, translated by V. Watts. London: Penguin Books, 1999.

Bonaventure. *The Soul's Journey into God – The Tree of Life – The Life of St. Francis*, translated by E. Cousins. New Jersey: Paulist Press, 1978.

—'Conscience and Synderesis.' In *The Cambridge Translations of Medieval Philosophical Texts, vol. 2: Ethics and Political Philosophy*, edited by A. S. Mcgrade, J. Kilcullen and M. Kempshall. Cambridge: Cambridge University Press, 2001.

Bosman, Philip. *Conscience in Philo and Paul*. Tübingen: J. C. B. Mohr, 2003.

Breward, Ian. Introduction to *The Work of William Perkins*, edited by Ian Breward. Appleford: The Sutton Courtenay Press, 1970.

Burlamaqui, Jean-Jacques. *The Principles of Natural and Politic Law*, edited by Peter Korkman. Indianapolis: Liberty Fund, 2006.

Bush, George W. 'The Farewell Address.' Accessed 24 August 2012: http://www.presidentialrhetoric.com/speeches/01.15.09.html

Butler, Joseph. *Fifteen Sermons Preaches at the Rolls Chapel*. Cambridge: Hillard and Brown, 1827.

Butler, Judith. *The Psychic Life of Power*. Stanford: Stanford University Press, 1997.

Calvin, John. *Institutes of the Christian Religion*, translated by H. Beveridge. Grand Rapids: Eerdmans Publishing Company, 1989.

—*Commentary on the Romans*. In *Calvin's Bible Commentaries: Romans*, translated by John King. Forgotten Books, 2007.

Canrcini, Antonia. *Syneidesis: Il tema semantico della 'con-scientia' nella Grecia antica*. Roma: Edizioni dell'Ateneo, 1970.

Caputo, John D., Mark Dooley and Michael J. Scanlon (ed.) *Questioning God*. Bloomington: Indiana University Press, 2001.

Cassirer, Ernst. *The Myth of the State*. New Haven: Yale University Press, 1946.

Catechism of the Catholic Church. Accessed 24 August 2012: http://www.vatican.va/archive/ENG0015/_INDEX.HTM

Chadwick, Henry. *Studies on Ancient Christianity*. Hampshire: Ashgate, 2005.

Cicero, Marcus Tullius. *Ad Atticum*. In *Cicero's Letters to Atticus in Three Volumes*, translated by E. O. Winstedt. Vol. 3. Cambridge, MA: Harvard University Press, 1918.

—*De legibus*. In Cicero, *De re publica, De legibus*, translated by C. W. Keyes. Cambridge, MA: Harvard University Press, 1928.

—*De natura Deorum*. In Cicero, *De Natura Deorum and Academica with an English Translation*, translated by H. Rackham. London: William Heinemann, 1961.

—*Pro Cluentio*. In *Cicero, the Speeches*, translated by H. G. Hodge. Cambridge, MA: Harvard University Press, 1927.

—*De inventione*. In Cicero, *De invetione, De optimo genere oratorum, Topica with an English Translation*, translated by H. H. Hubbell. London: William Heinemann, 1960.

Clarke, Samuel. *A Discourse concerning the Unalterable Obligations of Natural Religion*. Glasgow: Griffin, 1823.

Clement of Alexandria. *Stromata, or Miscellanies*. In *Ante-Nicene Fathers*, edited by Philip Schaff. Vol. 2. Peabody, MA: Hendrickson Publishers, 1994.

Coleridge, Samuel Taylor. *Aids to Reflection*. Burlington: Chauncey Goodrich, 1829.

—*Essay on Faith*. In *The Literary Remains of Samuel Taylor Coleridge*, edited by Henry N. Coleridge. Vol. 4. London: Pickering, 1839.

Comenius, John. *The Labyrinth of the World and the Paradise of the Heart*, translated by H. Louthan and A. Sterk. Mahwah: Paulist Press, 1997.

Crusius, Christian August. *Anweisung vernünftig zu Leben*. Leipzig: J. F. Gleditsch, 1767.

Cudworth, Ralph. *A Treatise of Free Will*, edited by J. Allen. London: Parker, 1838.

Culverwel, Nathanael. *An Elegant and Learned Discourse of the Light of Nature*. Oxford: Williams, 1669.

Cumberland, Richard. *A Treatise of the Laws of Nature*, translated by J. Maxwell. Indianapolis: Liberty Fund, 2005.

Cyprian. *On the Glory of Martyrdom*. In *Ante-Nicene Fathers*, edited by Philip Schaff. Vol. 5. Peabody, MA: Hendrickson Publishers, 1994.

Cyril of Alexandria, *Contra Julianum*. In *Patrologia cursus completus: series Graeca*, edited by J. P. Migne. Vol. 76. Paris: 1857–66.

D'Alembert, Jean le Rond. 'Discours Preliminaire.' In *Encyclopédie*, edited by Denis Diderot and Jean le Rond d'Alembert. Paris, 1775–92. Accessed 24 August 2012: http://encyclopedie.uchicago.edu/

D'Arcy, Eric. *Conscience and Its Right to Freedom*. London: Sheed & Ward, 1961.

Delhaye, Philippe. *The Christian Conscience*. New York: Desclee Company, 1968.

Demosthenes. *De corona and De falsa legatione*, translated by C. A. and J. H. Vince. London: Heinemann, 1926.

Denck, Hans. 'Whether God is the cause of Evil.' In *Spiritual and Anabaptist Writers*, edited by G. H. Williams. Philadelphia: The Westminister Press, 1957.

Derrida, Jacques. *Speech and Phenomena*, translated by D. B. Allison. Evanston: Northwestern University Press, 1973.

—*Of Grammatology*, translated by G. Spivak. Baltimore: The Johns Hopkins University Press, 1974.

—*Aporias: Dying – Awaiting (on another at) the Limits of Truth*, translated by D. Tutoit. Stanford: Stanford University Press, 1993.

—*The Gift of Death*, translated by D. Willis. Chicago: The University of Chicago Press, 1995.

Descartes, René. *Passions of the Soul*, translated by S. H. Voss. Indianapolis: Hackett Publishing Company, 1989.

—*The Correspondence between Princess Elisabeth of Bohemia and René Descartes*, translated by L. Shapiro. Chicago: University of Chicago Press, 2007.

D'Holbach, Baron. *Universal Morality: or, The Duties of Man, Founded on Nature*. In *Moral Philosophy from Montaigne to Kant: An Anthology*, edited by J. B. Schneewind. Vol. 2. Cambridge: Cambridge University Press, 1990.

Diogenes Laertius. *Lives of Eminent Philosophers in Two Volumes*, translated by R. D. Hicks. Vol. 2. London: William Heinemann, 1925.

Dolar, Mladen. *A Voice and Nothing More*. Cambridge, MA: The MIT Press, 2006.

Domarus, Max, ed. *Hitler: Reden und Proklamationen 1932–1945. Band I Triumph. Erster Halbband 1932–1934*. München: Süddeutscher Verlag, 1962/3.

Duns Scotus. *On the Will and Morality*, selected and translated by Allan B. Wolter. Washington, DC: The Catholic University of America Press, 1986.

Ebeling, Heinrich. *Meister Ekharts Mystik*. Stuttgart: W. Kohlhammer Verlag, 1941.

Elden, Stuart. *Speaking against Number: Heidegger, Language and the Politics of Calculation*. Edinburgh: Edinburgh University Press, 2006.

Epictetus. *The Discourses in Two Volumes*. Vol. 2. Translated by W. A. Oldfather. London: William Heinemann, 1928.

Epitome of the Formula of Concord. Accessed 24 August 2012. http://bookofconcord.org/fc-ep.php

Erasmus. *The Epicurean*. In *The Colloquies of Erasmus*, edited by E. Johnson. Vol. 2. London: Reeves & Turner, 1878.

Euripides. *Suppliants*. In *The Complete Greek Drama*, edited by Whitney J. Oates and Eugene O'Neill, Jr. New York: Random House, 1938.

—*Orestes*. In *The Complete Greek Drama*, edited by Whitney J. Oates and Eugene O'Neill, Jr. New York: Random House, 1938.

—*Cyclops, Alcestis, Medea*, edited by D. Kovacs. Cambridge, MA: Harvard University Press, 1994.

—*Children of Heracles, Hippolytus, Andromache, Hecuba*, edited by D. Kovacs. Cambridge, MA: Harvard University Press, 1995.

Fest, Joachim C. *Das Gesicht des Dritten Reiches: Profile einer totalitären Herrschaft*. München: Piper, 2002.

Feuerbach, Ludwig. *The Essence of Religion*, translated by A. Loos. New York: Prometheus Books, 2004.

Fichte, Johann Gottlieb. *Addresses to the German Nation*, translated by R. Jones and G. Thurnbull. Chicago: The Open Court Publishing Company, 1922.

—*The Vocation of Man*, translated by P. Preuss. Indianapolis: Hackett Publishing Company, 1987.

—*The System of Ethics*, edited by T. Breatzeale and G. Zöller. Cambridge: Cambridge University Press, 2005.

—*Characteristics of the Present Age*, translated by W. Smith. La Vergne: Dodo Press, 2008.

Filmer, Robert. *The Anarchy of a Limited or Mixed Monarchy*. In *Patriarcha and Other Writings*, edited by J. P. Sommerville. Cambridge: Cambridge University Press, 1991.

Foucault, Michel. 'The Subject and Power.' Afterword in Hubert L. Dreyfus and Paul Rabinow, *Michel Foucault: Beyond Structuralism and Hermeneutics*. Sussex: The Harvester Press, 1982.

—*Discipline and Punish: The Birth of the Prison*, translated by A. Sheridan. New York: Vintage Books, 1995.

—*The Hermeneutics of the Subject*, translated by G. Burchell. New York: Picador, 2006.

—*The Government of the Self and Others*, translated by G. Burchell. New York: Palgrave MacMillan, 2010.

Franck, Sebastian. 'A Letter to John Campanus.' In *Spiritual and Anabaptist Writers*, edited by G. H. Williams. Philadelphia: The Westminster Press, 1957.

Freud, Sigmund. *The Ego and the Id*, edited by J. Strachey. New York: W. W. Norton & Company, 1960.

—*Civilization and its Discontents*, edited by. J. Strachey. New York: W. W. Norton & Company, 1961.

Gerson, Jean. *Early Works*, translated by B. P. McGuire. New York: Paulist Press, 1988.

Gillespie, Michael Allen. 'The Theological Origins of Modernity.' *Critical Review* 13:1–2 (1999): 1–30.

Grabill, Stephen J. *Rediscovering the Natural Law in Reformed Theological Ethics*. Grand Rapids: Eerdmans, 2006.

Gratian. *The Treatise on Laws with the Ordinary Gloss* (Decretum DD. 1–20), translated by J. Gordley. Washington, DC: Catholic University of America Press, 1994.

—*Decretum magistri Gratiani*. Accessed 24 August 2012: http://geschichte.digitale-sammlungen.de/decretum-gratiani/online/angebot

Greene, Robert A. 'Natural Law, Synderesis, and the Moral Sense.' *Journal of the History of Ideas* 58:2 (1997): 173–98.

—'Synderesis, the Spark of Conscience, in the English Renaissance.' *Journal of the History of Ideas* 52:2 (1991): 195–219.

—'Whichcote, the Candle of the Lord, and Synderesis.' *Journal of the History of Ideas* 52:4 (1991): 617–44.

Greene, T. M. ed. *Kant Selections*. New York: Scribner, 1929.

Gregory Nazianzen. *Select Orations*. In *Nicene and Post-Nicene Fathers*, edited by Philip Schaff. Series 2, vol. 7. Peabody, MA: Hendrickson Publishers 1995.

Gregory of Rimini. *Super primum et secundum sententiarum*. St Bonaventure, NY: Franciscan Institute, 1955.

Gregory the Great. *Moralium Libri sive expositio in librum B. Job*. In *Patrologia cursus completus: series Latina*, edited by J. P. Migne. Vol. 75. Paris: 1844–55.

Grotius, Hugo. *On the Law of War and Peace*, translated by A. C. Campbell. Kitchener: Batoche Books, 2001.

Habermas, Jürgen. *Structural Transformation of the Public Sphere*, translated by Thomas Burger. Cambridge, MA: The MIT Press, 1991.

Haffner, Sebastian. *Defying Hitler*, translated by O. Pretzel. New York: Picador, 2002.

Hegel, G. W. F. *Phenomenology of Spirit*, translated by A. V. Miller. Oxford: Oxford University Press, 1977.

—*Philosophy of Right*, translated by S. W. Dyde. Kitchener: Batoche Books, 2001.

—*The Philosophy of History*, translated by J. Sibree. Kitchener: Batoche Books, 2001.

Heidegger, Martin. *Being and Time*, translated by J. Macquarrie. Oxford: Basil Blackwell, 1962.

—'German Students.' In *The Heidegger Controversy: A Critical Reader*, edited by Richard Wolin. Cambridge, MA: The MIT Press, 1998.

—'The Self-Assertion of the German University.' In *Heidegger Controversy: A Critical Reader*, edited by Richard Wolin. Cambridge, MA: The MIT Press, 1998.

—'National Socialist Education.' In *Heidegger Controversy: A Critical Reader*, edited by Richard Wolin. Cambridge, MA: The MIT Press, 1998.

Henry of Bracton. *De Legibus et Consuetudinibus Angliae*, edited by G. Woodbine. New Haven: Yale University Press, 1922.

Herbert von Cherbury. *De Veritate*. Stuttgart: Friedrich Frommann Verlage, 1966.

Hess, Rudolf. *Reden*. München: Zentralverlag der NSDAP, 1938.

Hilary of Poitiers. *Tractatus super Psalmos*. In *Patrologia cursus completus: series Latina*, edited by J. P. Migne. Vol. 9. Paris: 1844–55.

Himmler, Heinrich. 'Rede des Reichsführer-SS bei der SS-Gruppenführertagung in Posen Am 4. Oktober 1943.' Accessed 24 August 2012: http://www.nationalsozialismus.de/dokumente/texte/page/4

Hitler, Adolf. *Mein Kampf*, translated by J. Murphy. London: Hurst & Blackett, 1939. Accessed 24 August 2012. http://archive.org/details/MeinKampf_483

Hobbes, Thomas. *Leviathan*. Cambridge: Cambridge University Press, 1991.

—*On the Citizen*, edited by E. Tuck. Cambridge: Cambridge University Press, 1998.

—*The Elements of Law Natural and Politic*, edited by J. C. A. Gaskin. Oxford: Oxford University Press, 2008.

Home, Henry. *Essays on the Principle of Morality and Natural Religion*. Hildesheim: Georg Olms Verlag, 1976.

Homer. *The Odyssey with an English Translation in Two Volumes*, translated by A. T. Murray. Vol. 1. Cambridge, MA: Harvard University Press, 1919.

Horowitz, Maryanne Cline. *Seeds of Virtue and Knowledge*. Princeton: Princeton University Press, 1988.

Howard, Jason J. 'Kant and Moral Imputation: Conscience and the Riddle of the Given.' *American Catholic Philosophical Quarterly* 78:4 (2004): 609–24.

Hume, David. *A Treatise on Human Nature*, edited by L. A. Selby-Bigge. Oxford: Clarendon Press, 1896.

—*An Enquiry Concerning the Principles of Morals*, edited by E. L. Beauchamp. Oxford: Clarendon Press, 1988.

Hus, John. *The Letters of John Hus*, translated by R. M. Rope. London: Hodder and Stoughton, 1904.

Hutcheson, Francis. *A Short Introduction to Moral Philosophy*. Hildesheim: Georg Olms Verlag, 1990.

—*A System of Moral Philosophy*. London: Poulis, 1755.

—*On Human Nature*, edited by T. Mautner. Cambridge: Cambridge University Press, 1993.

Isaeus. *Isaeus with an English translation*, translated by Edward Seymour Forster. Cambridge, MA: Harvard University Press, 1962.

Isidore of Seville. *The Etymologies of Isidore of Seville*, translated by Stephen A. Barney, W. J. Lewis, J. A. Beach and Oliver Berghof. Cambridge: Cambridge University Press, 2006.

Isocrates. *Isocrates with an English Translation in three volumes*, translated by George Norlin. Vol. 1. Cambridge, MA: Harvard University Press, 1980

Jäckel, Eberhard. *Hitler's Worldview: A Blueprint for Power*. Cambridge, MA: Harvard University Press, 1972.

Jaspers, Karl. *Man in the Modern Age*, translated by C. Paul. London: Routledge & Kegan Paul, 1933.

—*The Way to Wisdom*, translated by R. Manheim. New Haven: Yale University Press, 2003.

Jefferson, Thomas. 'A Letter to George Washington (May 10, 1789).' In *The Works of Thomas Jefferson*, edited by P. L. Ford. Vol. 5. New York: G. P. Putnam's Sons, 1904–5.

Jerome. *Commentariorum in Ezekhielem Prophetam Libri Quatuordecim*. In *Patrologia cursus completus: series Latina*, edited by J. P. Migne. Vol. 25. Paris: 1844–55.

Jesse, Eckhard. 'Hermann Rauschning – Der fragwürdige Kronzeuge.' In *Die braune Elite II: 21 weitere biographische Skizzen*, edited by Ronald Smelser, Enrico Syring and Reiner Zitelmann. Darmstadt: Wissenschaftliche Buchgesellschaft, 1993.

Jobs, Steve. 'Speech at Stanford University, June 12, 2005.' Stanford University News, Stanford Report, 14 June 2005. Accessed 24 August 2012: http://news.stanford.edu/news/2005/june15/jobs-061505.html

John Chrysostom. *Sermones V de Anna*. In *Patrologia cursus completus: series Graeca*,
    edited by J. P. Migne. Vol. 54. Paris: 1857–66.
—*Homiliarum in Genesim continuatio*. In *Patrologia cursus completus: series Graeca*,
    edited by J. P. Migne. Vol. 54. Paris: 1857–66.
—*Expositio in Psalmos*. In *Patrologia cursus completus: series Graeca*, edited by J. P. Migne.
    Vol. 55. Paris: 1857–66.
—*On Wealth and Poverty*, translated by C. Roth. Crestwood: St Vladimir's Seminary
    Press, 1984.
—*Homilies on the Statutes*. In *Nicene and Post-Nicene Fathers*, edited by Philip Schaff.
    Series 1, vol. 9. Peabody, MA: Hendrickson Publishers, 1995.
—*Homilies on the Epistle of St Paul the Apostle to the Romans*. In *Nicene and Post-Nicene
    Fathers*, edited by Philip Schaff. Series 1, vol. 11. Peabody, MA: Hendrickson
    Publishers, 1995.
John Climacus. *The Ladder of Divine Ascent*, translated by C. Luibheid and N. Russell.
    New York: Paulist Press, 1982.
John of Damascus. *Exposition of the Orthodox Faith*. In *Nicene and Post-Nicene Fathers*,
    edited by Philip Schaff. Series 2, vol. 9. Peabody, MA: Hendrickson Publishers, 1995.
Kant, Immanuel. *Thoughts on Education*, translated by A. Churton. Boston: D. C. Heath
    & Co, 1906.
—*The Metaphysics of Morals*. In Immanuel Kant, *Practical Philosophy*, edited by M. J.
    Gregor. Cambridge: Cambridge University Press, 1996.
—*Critique of Practical Reason*. In Immanuel Kant, *Practical Philosophy*, edited by M. J.
    Gregor. Cambridge: Cambridge University Press, 1996.
—'An Answer to the Question: What is Enlightenment.' In Immanuel Kant, *Practical
    Philosophy*, edited by M. J. Gregor. Cambridge: Cambridge University Press, 1996.
—*Groundwork for the Metaphysics of Morals*. In Immanuel Kant, *Practical Philosophy*,
    edited by M. J. Gregor. Cambridge: Cambridge University Press, 1996.
—*Lectures on Ethics*, edited by P. Heath and J. B. Schneewind. Cambridge: Cambridge
    University Press, 1997.
—*Religion within the Boundaries of Mere Reason*, edited by A. Wood and G. di Giovanni.
    Cambridge: Cambridge University Press, 1998.
—*Critique of Pure Reason*, edited by M. Weighelt. London: Penguin Books, 2007.
Keen, Ralph. 'Defending the Pious: Melanchthon and the Reformation in Albertine
    Saxony, 1539.' *Church History* 60:2 (1991): 180–96.
Kesel, Marc de. *Eros and Ethics*. New York: State University of New York Press, 2009.
Kierkegaard, Søren. *Works of Love*, translated by H. and E. Hong. New York: Harper &
    Row, 1962.
—*Søren Kierkegaard's Journals and Papers*, edited by H. and E. Hong. Bloomington:
    Indiana University Press, 1967.
—*Either/Or*, translated by H. and E. Hong. Princeton: Princeton University Press, 1971.
—*The Concept of Anxiety*, edited by H. and E. Hong. Princeton: Princeton University
    Press, 1980.
—*Upbuilding Discourses in Various Spirits*, edited by H. and E. Hong. Princeton:
    Princeton University Press, 1993.
—*Three Discourses on Imagined Occasions*, edited by H. and E. Hong. Princeton:
    Princeton University Press, 1993.
Kittsteiner, Heinz D. *Die Entstehung des Modernen Gewissens*. Frankfurt am Main:
    Suhrkamp, 1995.

Knutzen (Cnuzen), Matthias. 'Amicus Amicis Amica!' Reprinted in Veyssière La Croze, *Entretiens sur divers sujets d'histoire et de religion, entre My Lord Bolingbroke, et Isaac D'Orobio, rabin des Juifs portugais à Amsterdam*. London, 1770.

Kosch, Michelle. *Freedom and Reason in Kant, Schelling, and Kierkegaard*. Oxford: Oxford University Press, 2006.

Koselleck, Reinhart. *Critique and Crisis*. Cambridge: The MIT Press, 1988.

La Mettrie, Julien Offray de. 'Anti-Seneca or the Sovereign Good.' In *Machine Man and Other Writings*, edited by A. Thomson. Cambridge: Cambridge University Press, 1996.

Lacan, Jacques. *Écrits*, translated by E. Fink. New York: Norton, 2006.

—*Seminar I: Freud's Papers on Technique*, edited by J-A. Miller. New York: W. W. Norton & Company, 1988.

—*Seminar VII: Ethics of Psychoanalysis*, edited by J-A. Miller. New York: W. W. Norton & Company, 1992.

Lactantius. *The Divine Institutes*. In *Ante-Nicene Fathers*, edited by Philip Schaff. Vol. 7. Peabody, MA: Hendrickson Publishers, 1994.

Laurie, S. S. *John Amos Comenius: Bishop of the Moravians, His Life and Educational Works*. New York: Lennox Hill, 1972.

Leibniz, G. W. *New Essays on Human Understanding*, edited by B. Remnant and J. Bennet. Cambridge: Cambridge University Press, 1996.

—*Opinion on the Principles of Pufendorf*. In *Leibniz: Political Writings*, edited by E. Riley. Cambridge: Cambridge University Press, 1998.

Levinas, Emmanuel. 'Ethics as First Philosophy.' In *The Levinas Reader*, edited by Seán Hand. Malden: Backwell, 1989.

—*Totality and Infinity: An Essay on Exteriority*, translated by Alphonso Lingis. Pittsburgh: Duquesne University Press, 1969.

—*Basic Philosophical Writings*, edited by Adriaan T. Peperzak, Simon Critchley and Robert Bernasconi. Bloomington: Indiana University Press, 1996.

—*Difficult Freedom: Essays on Judaism*, translated by Seán Hand. Baltimore: Johns Hopkins University Press, 1997.

—*Otherwise than Being*, translated by Alphonso Lingis. Pittsburgh: Duquesne University Press, 1998.

—*Humanism of the Other*, translated by N. Poller. Urbana: University of Illinois Press, 2006.

Ley, Robert. *Wir alle helfen dem Führer*. München: Zentralverlag der NSDAP, 1939.

Lipsius, Justus. *Politica: Six Books of Politics or Political Instructions*, translated by J. Waszink. Assen: Uitgeverij Van Gorcum, 2004.

Locke, John. *Some Thoughts Concerning Education*. Dublin: J. Kiernan, 1712.

—*Essays on the Law of Nature*, edited by A. J. Allan. Oxford: The Clarendon Press, 1954.

—*An Essay Concerning Human Understanding*. Oxford: The Clarendon Press, 1975.

—*Second Tract on Government*. In John Locke, *Political Writings*, edited by John Wootton. Indianapolis: Hackett Publishing Company, 2003.

—*Two Treatises of Civil Government*, edited by P. Laslett. Cambridge: Cambridge University Press, 2003.

Lottin, D. Odin. *Psychologie et morale aux XII et XIII siècles*. Vol. 2. Gembloux: J. Duculot, 1948.

Luther, Martin. *Sermone aus den Jahren 1514–1517*. In *D. Martin Luthers Werke: Kritische Gesamtausgabe*. Vol. 1. Weimar: Herman Böhlau, 1883–1966.

—*Operationes in Psalmos*. In *D. Martin Luther's Werke: Kritische Gesamtausgabe*. Vol. 5. Weimar: Herman Böhlau, 1883–1966.

—'Handbemerkungen zu Taulers Predigten.' In *D. Martin Luther's Werke: Kritische Gesamtausgabe*. Vol. 9. Weimar: Herman Böhlau, 1883–1966.

—*Predigten über des zweite Buch Mose 1524–1527*. In *D. Martin Luther's Werke: Kritische Gesamtausgabe*. Vol. 16. Weimar: Herman Böhlau, 1883–1966.

—*Sermons on the Gospel of John 6–8*. In *Luther's Works in 55 Volumes*, general editor Helmut T. Lehmann. Vol. 23. St Louis, MN: Concordia Publishing House, Fortress Press, 1957–86.

—*Lectures on Romans*. In *Luther's Works in 55 Volumes*, general editor Helmut T. Lehmann. Vol. 25. St Louis, MN: Concordia Publishing House, Fortress Press, 1957–86.

—*Lectures on Galatians*. In *Luther's Works in 55 Volumes*, general editor Helmut T. Lehmann. Vols. 26–7. St Louis, MN: Concordia Publishing House, Fortress Press, 1957–86.

—*Disputation against Scholastic Theology*. In *Luther's Works in 55 Volumes*, general editor Helmut T. Lehmann. Vol. 31. St Louis, MN: Concordia Publishing House, Fortress Press, 1957–86.

—*The Freedom of a Christian*. In *Luther's Works in 55 Volumes*, general editor Helmut T. Lehmann. Vol. 31. St Louis, MN: Concordia Publishing House, Fortress Press, 1957–86.

—'The Speech of Dr. Martin Luther before the Emperor Charles and Princes at Worms.' In *Luther's Works in 55 Volumes*, general editor Helmut T. Lehmann. Vol. 32. St Louis, MN: Concordia Publishing House, Fortress Press, 1957–86.

—'Preface to the Complete Edition of A German Theology.' In *Luther's Works in 55 Volumes*, general editor Helmut T. Lehmann. Vol. 35. St Louis, MN: Concordia Publishing House, Fortress Press, 1957–86.

—'Answer to the Hyperchristian, Hyperspiritual and Hyperlearned Book by Goat Emser in Leipzig.' In *Luther's Works in 55 Volumes*, general editor Helmut T. Lehmann. Vol. 39. St Louis, MN: Concordia Publishing House, Fortress Press, 1957–86.

—*Temporal Authority: To What Extent it should be Obeyed*. In *Luther's Works in 55 Volumes*, general editor Helmut T. Lehmann. Vol. 45. St Louis, MN: Concordia Publishing House, Fortress Press, 1957–86.

—*On the Jews and their Lies*. In *Luther's Works in 55 Volumes*, general editor Helmut T. Lehmann. Vol. 47. St Louis, MN: Concordia Publishing House, Fortress Press, 1957–86.

Mahoney, John. *The Making of Moral Theology*. Oxford: Clarendon Press, 1987.

Mann, Thomas. *Reden und Aufsätze*. Vol. 1. Frankfurt: Fischer, 1965.

Marietta, Don. E. 'Conscience in Greek Stoicism.' *Numen: International Review for the History of Religions* 17:3 (1970): 176–87.

Meister Eckhart. *Teacher and Preacher*, edited by Bernard McGinn. New York: Paulist Press, 1986.

—*The Essential Sermons, Commentaries, Treatises, and Defence*, translated by E. Colledge and B. McGinn. New York: Paulist Press, 1981.

Mill, J. S. *Bentham*. In J. S. Mill and Jeremy Bentham, *Utilitarianism and Other Essays*, edited by A. Ryan. London: Penguin Books, 1987.

—*Utilitarianism*. Indianapolis: Hacket Publishing Company, 2001.

Milton, John. *Complete Prose Works*, edited by M. Kelley. Vol. 6. New Haven: Yale University Press, 1973.

Mirari Vos (15 August 1832). Accessed 24 October 2012: http://www.papalencyclicals.net/Greg16/g16mirar.htm

Molenaar, G. 'Seneca's Use of the Term Conscientia.' *Mnemosyne* 22:2 (1969): 170–80.

Montaigne, Michel de. *The Complete Essays of Montaigne*, translated by D. Frame. Stanford: Stanford University Press, 1958.

More, Henry. *An Account of Virtue*. London: Benj. Tooke, 1701.

—*An Antidote against Atheism*. In *The Cambridge Platonists*, edited by C. A. Patrides. Cambridge, MA: Harvard University Press, 1970.

Müntzer, Thomas. *Revelation and Revolution: Basic Writings of Thomas Müntzer*, edited by Michael Baylor. Bethlehem: Lehigh University Press, 1993.

Nancy, Jean-Luc. 'The Free Voice of Man.' In P. Lacoue-Labarthe and J.-L. Nancy. *Retreating the Political*, edited by S. Sparks. London: Routledge, 1997.

Newman, John Henry. 'A Letter Addressed to His Grace the Duke of Norfolk on Occasion of Mr. Gladstone's Recent Expostulation, Dec. 27, 1874.' In *Conscience, Consensus and the Development of Doctrine: Revolutionary Texts by John Henry Cardinal Newman*, edited by J. Gaffney. New York: Doubleday, 1992.

Nietzsche, Friedrich. *The Will to Power*, edited by W. Kaufmann. New York: Vintage Books, 1968.

—*On the Genealogy of Morals*, translated by D. Smith. Oxford: Oxford University Press, 1996.

—*Beyond Good and Evil*, translated by W. Kaufmann. New York: Dover Publications, 1997.

—*Twilight of the Idols*, translated by D. Large. Oxford: Oxford University Press, 1998.

—*The Anti-Christ*, translated by H. L. Mencken. Tucson: See Sharp Press, 1999.

—*Gay Science*, edited by B. Williams. Cambridge: Cambridge University Press, 2001.

Obama, Barack. 'A Politics of Conscience.' Accessed 24 August 2012: http://www.ucc.org/news/significant-speeches/a-politics-of-conscience.html

Origen. *Homiliae in Ezechielem*. In *Patrologia cursus completus: series Graeca*, edited by J. P. Migne. Vol. 13. Paris: 1857–66.

—*De Principiis*. In *Ante-Nicene Fathers*, edited by Philip Schaff. Vol. 4. Peabody, MA: Hendrickson Publishers, 1994.

—*Against Celsus*. In *Ante-Nicene Fathers*, edited by Philip Schaff. Vol. 4. Peabody, MA: Hendrickson Publishers, 1994.

—*Commentary on the Epistle to the Romans*, translated by T. P. Scheck. Washington: The Catholic University of America Press, 2001.

Ozment, Steven E. *Homo Spiritualis: A Comparative Study of the Anthropology of Johannes Tauler, Jean Gerson and Martin Luther (1509–1916) in the Context of Their Theological Thought*. Leiden: E. J. Brill, 1969.

—*Mysticism and Dissent: Religious Ideology and Social Protest in the Sixteenth Century*. New Haven: Yale University Press, 1973.

Paine, Thomas. *Common Sense*. New York: Dover Publications, 1997.

Pelagius. *The Letters of Pelagius and his Followers*, edited by B. R. Rees. Woodbridge: The Boydell Press, 1991.

Perkins, William. *A Discourse of Conscience*. In *William Perkins: His Pioneer Works on Casuistry*, edited by T. F. Merrill. Nieuwkoop: B. De Graaf, 1966.

—*The Work of William Perkins*, edited by I. Breward. Appleford: The Sutton Courtenay Press, 1970.

—*The Whole Treatise of the Cases of Conscience*. In *William Perkins 1558–1602*, edited by Thomas F. Merrill. Nieuwkoop: B. De Graaf, 1966.

Peter Lombard. *Sententiae in IV libris distinctae*. Grottaferrata: Collegium S. Bonaventurae ad Claras Aquas, 1971.

Philo of Alexandria. *The Works of Philo*, translated by C. D. Yonge. Peabody, MA: Hendrickson Publishers, 1993.

Pierce, C. A. *Conscience in the New Testament*. London: SCM Press, 1955.

Plato. *Plato in Twelve Volumes*, translated by Harold North Fowler, W. R. M. Lamb and Paul Shorey. Cambridge, MA: Harvard University Press, 1925–69.

—*Complete Works*, edited by John M. Cooper. Indianapolis: Hackett Publishing Company, 1997.

Poewe, Karla. *New Religions and the Nazis*. Abingdon: Routledge, 2006.

Potts, Timothy C. *Conscience in Medieval Philosophy*. Cambridge: Cambridge University Press, 1980.

Price, Richard. *A Review of the Principal Questions in Morals*. Strand: T. Cadell, 1787.

Pufendorf, Samuel. *Of the Law of Nature and of Nations*, translated by B. Kennett. London: J. Walthoe, 1729.

—*On the Duty of Man and Citizen*, edited by J. Tully. Cambridge: Cambridge University Press, 1991.

—*Two Books of the Elements of Universal Jurisprudence*, edited by T. Behme. Indianapolis: Library Fund, 2009.

Ratzinger, Joseph. *The Church, Ecumenism, and Politics: New Essays in Ecclesiology*, translated by Michael J. Miller. New York: Crossroads, 1987.

—*On Conscience*. San Francisco: Ignatius, 2007.

Rauschning, Hermann. *Hitler Speaks: A Series of Political Conversations with Adolf Hitler on His Real Aims*. London: Thornton Butterworth, 1939.

Reid, Thomas. *Essays on the Active Powers of Man*. Edinburgh: John Bell, 1788.

Rosenberg, Alfred. *Der Mythus des 20. Jahrhunderts*. München: Hoheneichen-Verlag, 1933.

Rousseau, Jean-Jacques. *A Discourse on the Arts and Science*, translated by G. D. H. Cole. London: J. M. Dent & Sons, 1923.

—*The Social Contract*, translated by M. Cranston. London: Penguin, 1968.

—*The Reveries of the Solitary Walker*, translated by C. E. Butterworth. Indianapolis: Hackett Publishing Company, 1992.

—*Émile*, translated by B. Foxley. London: Orion Publishing Group, 2004.

Rudolph, Kurt. *Gnosis: The Nature and History of Gnosticism*. San Francisco: Harper Collins, 1987.

Räisänen, Heikki. *Paul and the Law*. Tübingen: J. C. B. Mohr, 1983.

Sanderson, Robert. *Ad clerum*. In *XXXVI Sermons viz XVI ad aulam, VI ad clerum, VI ad magistratum, VIII ad populum*, edited by Isaac Walton. London: Tooke, Passenger & Sawbridge, 1686.

—*Lectures on Conscience and Human Law*, edited by C. H. R. Wordsworth. London: Rivingtons, 1877.

Sarasohn, Lisa T. *Gassendi's Ethics: Freedom in a Mechanistic Universe*. Ithaca: Cornell University Press, 1996.

Sartre, Jean-Paul. *Being and Nothingness*, translated by H. E. Barnes. London: Routledge, 2003.

Schelling, F. J. W. *Philosophical Investigations into the Essence of Human Freedom*, translated by J. Love and J. Schmidt. New York: State University of New York Press, 2006.

Schlegel, Friedrich von. *Philosophy of Life and Philosophy of Language*, translated by A. J. W. Morrison. London: Henry G. Bohn, 1847.

Schmitt, Carl. *Political Theology*, translated by G. Schwab. Cambridge: The MIT Press, 1985.

—*Über die drei Arten des rechtswissenschaftlichen Denkens*. Berlin: Duncker & Humblot, 1993.

Schneewind, J. B. ed. *Moral Philosophy from Montaigne to Kant: An Anthology*. Vol. 1. Cambridge: Cambridge University Press, 1990.

—Introduction to *Lectures on Ethics*, by Immanuel Kant. Edited by P. Heath and J. B. Schneewind. Cambridge: Cambridge University Press, 1997.

—*The Invention of Autonomy: A History of Modern Moral Philosophy*. Cambridge: Cambridge University Press, 1998.

Scholem, Gershom. *Major Trends in Jewish Mysticism*. New York: Schocken Books, 1961.

Schopenhauer, Arthur. *On the Basis of Morality*, translated by E. F. J. Payne. Indianapolis: Hackett Publishing Company, 1995.

Schüssler, Rudolf. 'Jean Gerson, Moral Certainty and the Renaissance of Ancient Scepticism.' *Renaissance Studies* 23:4 (2009): 445–54.

Seneca. *Epistulae Morales with an English Translation in Three Volumes*, translated by R. M. Gummere. Vol. 3. London: William Heinemann, 1962.

Seneca, the Elder. *Controversiae*, books 7–10. In *Declamations in Two Volumes*, translated by M. Winterbottom. Vol. 2. Cambridge, MA: Harvard University Press, 1974.

Shaftesbury, Anthony Ashley-Cooper, Third Earl of. *Characteristics of Men, Manners, Opinions, Times*, edited L. E. Klein. Cambridge: Cambridge University Press, 1999.

—*Soliloquy*. London: John Morphew, 1710.

Sibbes, Richard. *Bowels Opened*. London: G. M. for George Edwards, 1639.

Sikka, Sonya. *Forms of Transcendence: Heidegger and Medieval Mystical Theology*. New York: State University of New York Press, 1997.

Smith, Adam. *Theory of Moral Sentiments*. Milton Keynes: Filiquarian Publishing, 2009.

Snell, Bruno. *The Discovery of the Mind: The Greek Origins of European Thought*. New York: Harper & Row, 1960.

Sophocles, *The Plays and Fragments*, edited by Richard Jebbs. Cambridge: Cambridge University Press, 1908.

Spinoza, Benedict de. *The Tractatus Theologico-Politicus*. In Benedict de Spinoza, *The Political Works*, edited by A. G. Wernham. Oxford: The Clarendon Press, 1958.

—*Ethics*, translated by A. Boyle. London: Everyman's Library, 1989.

Steigmann-Gall, Richard. *The Holy Reich: Nazi Conceptions of Christianity, 1919–1945*. Cambridge: Cambridge University Press, 2003.

Stelzenberger, Johannes. *Syneidesis, conscientia, Gewissen*. Paderborn: Ferdinand Schöningh, 1963.

Stoker, H. G. *Das Gewissen*. Bonn: Verlag von Friedrich Cohen, 1925.

Strohm, Paul. *Conscience: A Very Short Introduction*. Oxford: Oxford University Press, 2011.

Suárez, Francisco. *A Treatise on Laws and God the Lawgiver*. In Francisco Suárez, *Selections from Three Works*, edited by Gwladys L. Williams, Ammi Brown, John Waldron and Henry Davis. Vol. 2. Oxford: The Clarendon Press, 1944.

Tatian. *Addresses to the Greeks*. In *Ante-Nicene Fathers*, edited by Philip Schaff. Vol. 2. Peabody, MA: Hendrickson Publishers, 1994.

Tauler, Johannes. *Sermons*, translated by Maria Shrady. New York: Paulist Press, 1985.

Taylor, Jeremy. *The Rule of Conscience: Bishop's Taylor's Ductor Dubitantium Abridged in Two Volumes*. Vol. 1. London: Bollingsley, 1725.

Tertullian. *An Answer to the Jews*. In *Ante-Nicene Fathers*, edited by Philip Schaff. Vol. 3. Peabody, MA: Hendrickson Publishers, 1994.

The Digest of Justinian, edited by A. Watson, T. Mommsen and P. Krueger. Philadelphia: University of Pennsylvania Press, 1985.

The Solid Declaration of the Formula of Concord. Accessed 24 August 2012: http://bookofconcord.org/sd-preface.php

Thomas Aquinas. 'On Conscience.' In Thomas Aquinas, *Selected Writings*, edited by R. McInerny. London: Penguin Books, 1998.

—*Commentary on Aristotle's Nicomachean Ethics*, translated by C. J. Litzinger. Notre Dame: Dumb Ox Books, 1964.

—*Quaestiones disputatae de veritate*. In S. Thomae de Aquino, *Opera Omnia*. Accessed 24 August 2012: http://www.corpusthomisticum.org/iopera.html

—*Summa contra Gentiles*. New York: Hanover House, 1955–7. Accessed 24 August 2012: http://dhspriory.org/thomas/ContraGentiles.htm

—*The Summa Theologica of St. Thomas Aquinas*, edited by Joseph Kenny. London: Burns Oates and Washbourne, 1920. Accessed 24 August 2012: http://www.newadvent.org/summa/

Tierney, Brian. 'Natura id est Deus: A Case of Juristic Pantheism.' *Journal of the History of Ideas* 24:3 (1963): 307–22.

Tindal, Mathew. *Christianity as Old as Creation*. London, 1730.

Trevor-Roper, H. R. ed. *Hitler's Table Talk 1941–1944*. New York: Enigma Books, 2008.

Turretin, Francis. *Institutes of Elenctic Theology in 3 Vols*, edited by J. Dennison. New Jersey: Presbyterian and Reformed Publishing Company, 1992–7.

Tyndale, William. *The Obedience of a Christian Man*, edited by D. S. Daniel. London: Penguin Books, 2000.

Vernant, Jean-Pierre. Introduction to *The Greeks*, edited by Jean-Pierre Vernant. Chicago: University of Chicago Press, 1995.

Villa, Dana. *Socratic Citizenship*. Princeton: Princeton University Press, 2001.

Vitoria, Francisco. *On the American Indians*. In *Vitoria: Political Writings*, edited by A. Pagden and J. Lawrence. Cambridge: Cambridge University Press, 1991.

Voltaire. 'Conscience.' In *Oeuvres complètes de Voltaire*. Vol. 7. Paris: Furne, 1835.

Ward, Samuel. *Balme from Gilead to Recouer Conscience*. London: Roger Jackson, 1616.

Whichcote, Benjamin. *Moral and Religious Aphorisms*. In *The Cambridge Platonists*, edited by C. A. Patrides. Cambridge, MA: Harvard University Press, 1970.

—*The Use of Reason in Matters of Religion*. In *The Cambridge Platonists*, edited by C. A. Patrides. Cambridge, MA: Harvard University Press, 1970.

Wilks, John S. *The Idea of Conscience in Renaissance Tragedy*. London: Routledge, 1990.

William of Ockham. *Quaestiones in quattuor libros sententiarum*. In *Opera philosophica et theologica*. Vol. 1. St. Bonaventure, NY: The Franciscan Institute, 1967–88.

—*Quodlibetal Questions*, translated by A. Freddoso and E. Kelley. Vol. 1. New Haven: Yale University Press, 1991.

—*A Short Discourse on Tyrannical Government*, edited by A. S. McGrade. Cambridge: Cambridge University Press, 1992.

—*On the Virtues*, edited by Rega Wood. West Lafayette: Purdue University Press, 1997.

Wolff, Christian. *Vernüfftige Gedancken von der Menschen Thun und Lassen zu Beförderung ihrer Glückseeligkeit*. Frankfurt, 1736.

Wolin, Richard, ed. *The Heidegger Controversy: A Critical Reader*. Cambridge MA: The MIT Press, 1998.

Xenophon. *Anabasis*. In Xenophon, *Hellenica (6–12)* and *Anabasis (1–3)*, translated by C. L. Brownson. Cambridge, MA: Harvard University Press, 1961.

Zachman, Randall C. *The Assurance of Faith: Conscience in the Theology of Martin Luther and John Calvin*. Minneapolis: Fortress Press, 1993.

Zanchi, Hieronymus. 'On the Law in General,' translated by J. Veenstra. *Journal of Markets & Morality* 6:1 (Spring 2003): 305–98.

Žižek, Slavoj. *The Plague of Fantasies*. London: Verso, 1997.

—*In Defence of Lost Causes*. London: Verso, 2008.

Index

9924864R00147

Printed in Great Britain
by Amazon.co.uk, Ltd.,
Marston Gate.